ECONOMIC DEVELOPMENT AND RESILIENCE BY EU MEMBER STATES

CONTEMPORARY STUDIES IN ECONOMIC AND FINANCIAL ANALYSIS

Series Editor: Simon Grima

Volume 108A:	Managing Risk and Decision Making in Times of Economic Distress *Edited by Simon Grima, Ercan Özen and Inna Romānova*
Volume 108B:	Managing Risk and Decision Making in Times of Economic Distress *Edited by Simon Grima, Ercan Özen, and Inna Romānova*
Volume 109A:	The New Digital Era: Digitalisation and Emerging Risks and Opportunities *Edited by Simon Grima, Ercan Ozen, and Hakan Boz*
Volume 109B:	The New Digital Era: Digitalisation and Emerging Risks and Opportunities *Edited by Simon Grima, Ercan Ozen, and Hakan Boz*
Volume 110A:	Smart Analytics, Artificial Intelligence and Sustainable Performance Management in a Global Digitalised Economy *Edited by Pallavi Tyagi, Simon Grima, Kiran Sood, B. Balamurugan, Ercan Ozen, and Thalassinos Eleftherios*
Volume 110B:	Smart Analytics, Artificial Intelligence and Sustainable Performance Management in a Global Digitalised Economy *Edited by Pallavi Tyagi, Simon Grima, Kiran Sood, B. Balamurugan, Ercan Ozen, and Thalassinos Eleftherios*
Volume 111A:	Smart Analytics, Artificial Intelligence and Sustainable Performance Management in a Global Digitalised Economy *Edited by Pallavi Tyagi, Simon Grima, Kiran Sood, B. Balamurugan, Ercan Ozen and Thalassinos Eleftherios*
Volume 111B:	Digital Transformation, Strategic Resilience, Cyber Security and Risk Management *Edited by Simon Grima, Eleftherios Thalassinos, Gratiela Georgiana Noja, Theodore V. Stamataopoulos, Tatjana Vasiljeva, Tatjana Volkova*
Volume 111C:	Digital Transformation, Strategic Resilience, Cyber Security and Risk Management *Edited by Kiran Sood, B. Balamurugan and Simon Grima*
Volume 112A:	Contemporary Challenges in Social Science Management: Skills Gaps and Shortages in the Labour Market, Part A *Edited by Anne Marie Thake, Kiran Sood, Ercan Özen, and Simon Grima*
Volume 112B:	Contemporary Challenges in Social Science Management: Skills Gaps and Shortages in the Labour Market, Part B *Edited by Anne Marie Thake, Simon Grima, Ercan Özen and Kiran Sood*
Volume 113A:	Sustainable Development Goals: The Impact of Sustainability Measures on Wellbeing, Part A *Edited by Ridhima Sharma, Indira Bhardwaj, Simon Grima, Timcy Sachdeva, Kiran Sood and Ercan Özen*
Volume 113B:	Sustainable Development Goals: The Impact of Sustainability Measures on Wellbeing, Part B *Edited by Ridhima Sharma, Indira Bhardwaj, Simon Grima, Timcy Sachdeva, Kiran Sood and Ercan Özen*
Volume 114:	Sustainability Development Through Green Economics *Edited by Sanjay Taneja, Pawan Kumar, Reepu, Balamurugan Balusamy, Kiran Sood and Simon Grima.*

CONTEMPORARY STUDIES IN ECONOMIC AND
FINANCIAL ANALYSIS   VOLUME 115

ECONOMIC DEVELOPMENT AND RESILIENCE BY EU MEMBER STATES

EDITED BY

SIMON GRIMA
University of Malta, Malta

INNA ROMĀNOVA
University of Latvia, Latvia

GRAȚIELA GEORGIANA NOJA
West University of Timisoara, Romania

AND

TOMASZ DOROŻYŃSKI
University of Lodz, Poland

United Kingdom – North America – Japan
India – Malaysia – China

Emerald Publishing Limited
Emerald Publishing, Floor 5, Northspring, 21-23 Wellington Street, Leeds LS1 4DL.

First edition 2025

Editorial matter and selection © 2025 Simon Grima, Inna Romānova,
Grațiela Georgiana Noja and Tomasz Dorożyński.
Individual chapters © 2025 The authors.
Published under exclusive licence by Emerald Publishing Limited.

Reprints and permissions service
Contact: www.copyright.com

No part of this book may be reproduced, stored in a retrieval system, transmitted in any form or by any means electronic, mechanical, photocopying, recording or otherwise without either the prior written permission of the publisher or a licence permitting restricted copying issued in the UK by The Copyright Licensing Agency and in the USA by The Copyright Clearance Center. Any opinions expressed in the chapters are those of the authors. Whilst Emerald makes every effort to ensure the quality and accuracy of its content, Emerald makes no representation implied or otherwise, as to the chapters' suitability and application and disclaims any warranties, express or implied, to their use.

British Library Cataloguing in Publication Data
A catalogue record for this book is available from the British Library

ISBN: 978-1-83797-998-1 (Print)
ISBN: 978-1-83797-997-4 (Online)
ISBN: 978-1-83797-999-8 (Epub)

ISSN: 1569-3759 (Series)

INVESTOR IN PEOPLE

CONTENTS

About the Editors   *vii*

About the Contributors   *ix*

Acknowledgement   *xix*

Chapter 1 Introduction – Navigating Economic Waters: Development and Resilience in EU Member States
Eleftherios Thalassinos   *1*

Chapter 2 Globalisation, Economic Integration, and Labour Market Dynamics within the European Union
Alina Ionaşcu and Graţiela Georgiana Noja   *5*

Chapter 3 Does the Quality of Governance Have the Power to Attract Foreign Investors? Evidence from the EU-13 Member States
Tomasz Dorożyński, Anetta Kuna-Marszałek and Bogusława Dobrowolska   *23*

Chapter 4 Regional Economic, Social, and Healthcare Disparities Among the European Union Member States
Małgorzata Stefania Lewandowska, Arkadiusz Michał Kowalski, Dawid Majcherek and Scott William Hegerty   *47*

Chapter 5 An Empirical Assessment of the Impact of EU Digital Policies on Economic Growth
Maria Magdalena Doroiman and Nicoleta Sîrghi   *67*

Chapter 6 Productivity and Competitiveness: Future Challenges
Inna Šteinbuka, Oļegs Barānovs, Jānis Salmiņš and Irina Skribāne   *83*

Chapter 7 International Trade: Single European Market
Margarita Dunska and Krišs Jānis Dombrovskis   *99*

Chapter 8   Financial Sector Development in New EU Member States
Marina Kudinska, Irina Solovjova and Inna Romānova   *119*

Chapter 9   The Leading Industries in the New EU Member States and Their Contribution to Increasing the EU's Export Potential
Ileana Tache   *141*

Chapter 10   Managing Climate Change Risks and Environmental Challenges Towards Sustainable Development within the European Union
Marilen-Gabriel Pirtea, Graţiela Georgiana Noja, Nicoleta-Claudia Moldovan, Irina-Maria Grecu and Alexandra-Mădălina Ţăran   *159*

Chapter 11   Quality of Life in the European Union
Kesra Nermend and Simon Grima   *177*

Chapter 12   Digitalisation and Productivity Improvement
Vida Davidaviciene and Alma Maciulyte-Sniukiene   *201*

Chapter 13   The Labour Market, Human Capital and Migration: Ageing and Stratification of Society
Biruta Sloka, Ilze Buligina, Ginta Tora, Juris Dzelme, Ilze Brante, Anna Angena and Kristīne Liepiņa   *231*

Chapter 14   Future Challenges on the Way to the Full Convergence
Andrea Imperia and Loredana Mirra   *249*

Chapter 15   Higher Education Institutions' Responses to Digital Transformation within the European Union: Skills Development and Smart Specialisation
Graţiela Georgiana Noja, Ciprian Pânzaru, Mirela Cristea and Eleftherios Thalassinos   *273*

Chapter 16   Conclusions
Simon Grima, Inna Romānova, Graţiela Georgiana Noja and Tomasz Dorożyński   *289*

Index   *293*

ABOUT THE EDITORS

Simon Grima is the Deputy Dean of the Faculty of Economics, Management, and Accountancy and the Head of the Department of Insurance and Risk Management. He is also a Professor at the University of Latvia, Faculty of Business, Management and Economics, and a Visiting Professor at UNICATT Milan. He has over 30 years of experience in various fields, including financial services, academia, and public entities. He has served as President of the Malta Association of Risk Management and Compliance Officers and is the Chairman of the Scientific Education Committee of the Public Risk Management Organisation and the Federation of European Risk Managers. [ORCID: https://orcid.org/0000-0003-1523-5120]

Inna Romānova is a Professor of Finance at the University of Latvia, the Director of the Scientific Institute of Economics and Management, and the Director of the professional master's degree programme in Financial Economics. She is an expert in Economics and Management Sciences at the Latvian Academy of Sciences. Her academic interests are in Corporate Finance and Analysis. She has more than 15 years of pedagogic experience both in Latvia and abroad, and she is a Visiting Professor in several universities in Europe. She also has professional experience in banking and finance, both in Latvia and Germany. Her research focuses on Financial Technologies and Financial Management. She is on the editorial board of several scientific journals as well as has co-edited several volumes of Emerald book series Contemporary Studies in Economic and Financial Analysis. She has participated in several research projects, including the State Research Programme project. She is the Chair of the International Scientific Conference 'New Challenges in Economic and Business Development' as well as a member of the programme committees of several conferences.

Graţiela Georgiana Noja is the Vice-Dean of the Faculty of Economics and Business Administration, West University of Timisoara, Romania, in charge of academic and student affairs, and a Professor, PhD Habil., at the same faculty, Department of Marketing and International Economic Relations. She is also a Doctoral Advisor in the field of Economics within the Doctoral School of Economics and Business Administration. She completed her studies with the highest honours at the West University of Timisoara and developed throughout the years over 15 national and international projects as a manager, project assistant, expert, researcher, task responsible, and trainer. She has around 40 publications indexed in the Web of Science Core Collection and a couple dozen other publications in relevant international journals/books/collective volumes. She is an active member of the International Strategic Management Association and has a wide membership in various educational organisations, research networks, scientific and review committees of top-tier journals, and international conferences. Her main research and teaching activities are developed within the framework of the Economics and International Business area, with a keen focus on European economic integration, international migration, digital transformation, and sustainable economic development. [ORCID: https://orcid.org/0000-0002-9201-3057]

Tomasz Dorożyński, PhD, works in the Department of International Trade, University of Lodz. He is a member of several organisations of researchers in international economics and International Business (IB), such as Academy of International Business (AIB), European International Business Academy (EIBA), Euro-Asia Management Studies Association (EAMSA; Board and Advisory Committee Member), and Academy of International Business Central and Eastern Europe (AIB-CEE). His research achievements include more than 120 peer-reviewed publications. So far, he has been involved in 17 research projects, also as project manager. His research work focuses, inter alia, on internationalisation, foreign direct investment, investment attractiveness, entrepreneurship, special economic zones, and regional development. Results of his studies have been presented on numerous occasions at international conferences, for example, in the United Kingdom, the United States, Japan, South Korea, Norway, Sweden, Denmark, and Brazil. He is a member of the Management Geography Research Group (Japan) and a Visiting Scholar at the Vilnius Tech (Lithuania). He has lectured in various countries including Italy, France, Portugal, Germany, Lithuania, Hungary, Estonia, Romania, Latvia, and Slovakia. [ORCID: https://orcid.org/0000-0003-3625-0354]

ABOUT THE CONTRIBUTORS

Anna Angena, Mag.sc.admin., Mag.oec., is a doctoral student, University of Latvia, and participated in several research projects related to supervision and involvement of students at risk in vocational education.

Oļegs Barānovs, Dr.oec., is Lead Researcher of the European Policy Research Institute of the Latvian Academy of Sciences, Senior Economic Analyst of the Ministry of Economics of the Republic of Latvia. He is a member of the Economic Policy Committee of the European Council of Ministers. His main research interests include analysis of the economic development of Latvia and the European Union, productivity development and its promotion policy, as well as issues of the European Semester. He is author of more than 20 scientific papers.

Ilze Brante, Mag.ped., is a doctoral student, University of Latvia, and participated in several research projects related to quality of vocational education in several aspects, work-based learning, and involvement of students at risk in vocational education.

Ilze Buligina, Dr.sc.admin., Leading Researcher at the University of Latvia, has participated in several research projects and is conducting research on various aspects of vocational education and training, including work-based learning and involvement of students at risk in vocational education, and has participated in research related to several aspects of silver economy, cooperation with social partners and their role in the development of qualified specialists, knowledge triangle, and innovations in education.

Mirela Cristea is a Professor, PhD, at the University of Craiova (Romania), Faculty of Economics and Business Administration, Department of Finance, Banking, and Economic Analysis, Center for Economic, Banking, and Financial Research (CEBAFI). Her main research directions and teaching activities are insurance and private pension funds, banking administration, and interdisciplinary research in economics. She obtained the scientific title of PhD in Economics at the University of Craiova, and graduated the Post-Doctoral School in Economics and Applied Sciences in Economics at the Romanian Academy from Bucharest, on the subject of the private pension system in Romania. She received two awards from the Faculties on Economics Association from Romania, in 2007 and 2013, for two books on life insurance and pension system subjects. In addition, she is a reviewer and member of the scientific and organisational committees for numerous journals and conferences. [ORCID: https://orcid.org/0000-0002-6670-9798]

ABOUT THE CONTRIBUTORS

Vida Davidavičienė has 20 years of academic and scientific experience. Her research interests are information and communication technology development's influence on society, business, and economics. She is an author of more than 100 scientific publications, 7 textbooks, and 8 books (monograph) parts. She is a member of the management science and communication science boards at Vilnius Tech. She is a member of the scientific committees of several scientific journals and international scientific conferences. She is an expert at the Research Council of Lithuania and member of the Lithuanian Standards Board Technical Committee LST TK 90 Human Resources and Knowledge Management. [ORCID: https://orcid.org/0000-0002-0931-0967]

Bogusława Dobrowolska, PhD, is Assistant Professor at the Department of Economic and Social Statistics, Faculty of Economics and Sociology, University of Lodz. Her scientific interests include the application of statistical and econometric methods in economic and social research. She is the author of several dozen journal papers and chapters. Since 2013, she has given classes accredited by Predictive Solutions (previously IBM SPSS Poland). The classes deal with statistics using the application of PS IMAGO software. Since 2021, she has been the statistical editor of the journal *Studies in Law and Economics*. [ORCID: https://orcid.org/0000-0003-3497-6223]

Krišs Jānis Dombrovskis is a third-year Business Administration bachelor's student with a specialisation in International Business at the University of Latvia, Faculty of Business, Management and Economics. His academic interests are in economics, finance, and management. He is currently focussing his academic endeavours on tax-related topics, specifically, transfer pricing. During the time of his studies, he has gathered extensive knowledge in data analysis.

Maria Magdalena Doroiman is a PhD student, at the Doctoral School of Economics and Business Administration, at the Faculty of Economics and Business Administration, West University of Timisoara (Romania). She is a PhD student in her second year, in the field of Economics. Her research interests are in digital transformation and economic growth. Her doctoral thesis is a project that studies aspects of the role of digitisation in increasing market competitiveness. She holds a master's degree in European studies and the economics of integration from the West University of Timisoara (Romania). She is currently a teacher of Economics and Business Studies, at 'Grigore Moisil' Theoretical High School and 'Francesco Saverio Nitti' Economic College from Timisoara (Romania).

Margarita Dunska, Dr.oec., is a Professor at the University of Latvia, Faculty of Business, Management, and Economics, Department of Global Economics Interdisciplinary Studies, Vice-Dean for Academic Affairs. Her academic interests are in economics, international economics, and finance. For many years, she is one of the leading experts in these topics. She is also an expert in the Academic Information Center, has participated in the accreditation of several programmes

About the Contributors

at other universities. She also has many years of experience in administrative work in higher education. In recent years, she has been the director of biggest study programmes at the faculty.

Juris Dzelme, Dr.chem., Leading Researcher at the University of Latvia, has participated in several research projects related to quality of higher education in several aspects; involvement of students at risk in vocational education; and knowledge triangle and innovations in education, quantum chemistry, artificial intelligence, and nanotechnologies.

Irina-Maria Grecu is a PhD candidate in Economics at the West University of Timisoara (Romania), Faculty of Economics and Business Administration. She holds a master's in Management and European Integration and a BA in Economics and International Business at the West University of Timisoara, where she graduated with highest honours. Her main research activities are centred on international migration and labour market outcomes.

Scott William Hegerty, PhD, is Professor of Economics and Chair of the Department of Anthropology, Economics, Geography and Environmental Studies, Global Studies, and Philosophy at Northeastern Illinois University in Chicago. He specialises in International Macroeconomics, Urban Geography, and Applied Statistical Methods. He received his PhD and MA in Economics from the University of Wisconsin-Milwaukee, and his Bachelor of Science in History from UW-Eau Claire. His research focuses on Central and Eastern Europe, as well as on large US cities, and he has published widely in these areas.

Andrea Imperia is Assistant Professor in Economics at the Department of Social and Economic Sciences at Sapienza University of Rome. He received his Master in Quantitative Methods for Economics at Tor Vergata University of Rome and his doctorate in Economics at Sapienza. He has written on labour economics, the 2001 Argentinean crisis, the US economic and financial crisis of 2007–2008, Walras's theory of capital, and Gustav Cassel's general equilibrium analysis.

Alina Ionaşcu is a Doctoral Candidate at the West University of Timisoara. Her research delves into the nexus of globalisation and European economic integration. Her academic journey, enriched by a master's in European studies and an ongoing master's in business law, equips her with diverse perspectives on these themes. Her experience extends to an Erasmus exchange in Lille, France, and a Student Evaluator in an Economic Studies role at the Romanian Agency for Quality Assurance in Higher Education. This blend of education and experience underpins her commitment to exploring the theoretical underpinnings of globalisation and integration, as evidenced in her systematic and bibliometric analysis of relevant scientific literature. [ORCID: https://orcid.org/0009-0008-5893-2261]

ABOUT THE CONTRIBUTORS

Arkadiusz Michał Kowalski is Associate Professor, Head of the Department of East Asian Economic Studies, and Deputy Director of the World Economy Research Institute at the SGH Warsaw School of Economics. He graduated with a Master of Science in Economics from the University of Southampton, winning the Taught Postgraduate Student competition organised by the Regional Science Association International British and Irish Section. He has been involved as a manager or researcher in different European or domestic research projects in these fields, which resulted in more than 100 publications, including books, chapters, articles in scientific journals, and expert's reports.

Marina Kudinska is a Professor of Finance at the Faculty of Business, Management, and Economics of the University of Latvia. Her academic interests are in banking, risk analysis and digital finance. She has participated in several research projects. She is a member of the programme and scientific committees of several international scientific conferences, as well as member of the editorial board of two scientific journals of accounting, finance, and auditing studies. She has 35 years of pedagogic experience in higher education institutions. She has written seven study books on banking and finance and over 50 scientific publications. She has many years of experience in advising on banking issues.

Anetta Kuna-Marszałek, PhD, is Head of Department of International Trade, Deputy Head of Institute of Economics, Faculty of Economics and Sociology, University of Lodz. Her primary research interests focus on the various aspects of contemporary economics, including research on the world trading system, the interlinks between trade liberalisation and environmental policies, and green economy. She is currently working on the internationalisation of business activities, foreign direct investment, investment attractiveness, and institutional quality. Her research achievements include more than 100 peer-reviewed publications. [ORCID: https://orcid.org/0000-0001-5687-7272]

Małgorzata Stefania Lewandowska is Associate Professor of SGH Warsaw School of Economics, Collegium of World Economy, Department of International Management. She holds a Habilitation in Management, a PhD in Economics, and a Master of Business Administration from the Université du Québec à Montréal, Canada. She is author and co-author of books, papers, and chapters on management in international business, international cooperation of enterprises, business models of firms, and innovation policy. Her primary areas of research are innovation determinants and strategies, open innovation, innovation policy, and eco-innovation. She is a member of international associations: Academy of International Business and European International Business Academy.

Kristīne Liepiņa, Mag.oec., University of Latvia, has participated in several research projects related to adult education in several aspects, involvement of inhabitants in education and employment, and analysing several aspects of *silver economy* as well as the interaction between higher education and quality of life.

About the Contributors xiii

Alma Maciulyte-Sniukiene is an Associate Professor at the Vilnius Gediminas Technical University. She has 20 years of professional experience in the telecommunication field and 14 years of academic experience. She holds a bachelor degree in Telecommunication and Economics, master's degree in Economics, and PhD in Economics. In 2015, she defended her dissertation in the field of Economics. Since this period, she has participated in research projects financed by EU structural funds. She is a member of European Regional Science Association and Eurasia Business and Economics Society. Her research areas are regional economic development, productivity, information and communication technology, and core infrastructure. [ORCID: https://orcid.org/0000-0001-6661-7407]

Dawid Majcherek, PhD, is Assistant Professor at the SGH Warsaw School of Economics, Collegium of World Economy, Department of International Management. He specialises in health economics, sports economics, econometrics, machine learning, clustering, and spatial analysis. He received his PhD in Economics and MA in Quantitative Methods in Economics and Information Systems from the Warsaw School of Economics. He has been working in the pharmaceutical industry since 2013 on various topics related to marketing, sales, management, salesforce effectiveness, finance, market access including pricing, and pharmacoeconomics.

Loredana Mirra is an Assistant Professor in Economics at the Department of Economics and Finance of the Tor Vergata University of Rome. She is the Deputy Coordinator of CREG (Interdepartmental Centre for Economics and Law Research) at Tor Vergata University of Rome. She holds a doctorate in 'Theory and Quantitative Methods for the Analysis of Development' at the University of Molise, a Master of Science in Economics and Econometrics at the University of Southampton, and a Master of Science in Economics and Institutions at Tor Vergata University of Rome. Her research interests are applied economics, spatial econometrics, economic growth, regional economics, and sustainable development. She serves as a referee for several international journals.

Nicoleta-Claudia Moldovan, PhD Habil., is Professor at the Finance Department from the Faculty of Economics and Business Administration (FEBA), West University of Timisoara. She is PhD Advisor in Economics, finance specialisation, and also holds a postdoctoral degree in Economics. She has 30 years of experience in research and teaching in higher education. Her research mainly addresses entrepreneurship, public policies, good governance, fiscal policies, and economic competitiveness. She is the Director of the Accreditation Department within the Romanian Agency for Quality Assurance in Higher Education and an Evaluator in the Finance domain. She was a Project Manager for projects financed through the Romanian Operational Programme 'Human Capital' and a member of different research projects. [ORCID: https://orcid.org/0000-0002-1916-2638]

Kesra Nermend is a Professor at the University of Szczecin and is a Leading Researcher in Decision Support Methods and Cognitive Neuroscience. He is the Head of the Department of Decision Support Methods and Cognitive Neuroscience, Director of the Institute of Management, Director of the Center for Transfer and Technology, and President of the Center for Research and Development. Her research focuses on the application of quantitative methods and information technology tools in analysing socioeconomic processes, with a particular emphasis on multicriteria methods, multidimensional data analysis, and cognitive neuroscience techniques in studying social behaviour and consumer preferences in business decision-making processes. Her research is carried out within the Cognitive Neuroscience Laboratory and the Virtual Reality Laboratory, housed in the Institute of Management.

Ciprian Pânzaru is a Professor at the West University of Timisoara (Romania), Sociology Department. He coordinates disciplines such as the Sociology of Migration, Labour Economics, Social Mobility, and Economic Sociology. His areas of interest include agent-based modelling, computational sociology, international migration, labour market issues, and population forecasting. He attended the postdoctoral programme in Economics, financed from the European Social Fund, studying the effect of demographic changes on the social security system. He was a Visiting Researcher at the Department of Applied Economics of the Free University of Brussels. Currently, he is a PhD Supervisor and leads at the West University of Timisoara a Research Group on Social and Economic Complexity. [ORCID: https://orcid.org/0000-0001-7652-4159]

Marilen-Gabriel Pirtea has been the Rector of the West University of Timisoara since 2012 (after being Chancellor, Vice-Dean, and Dean of the Faculty of Economics and Business Administration in Timisoara). Since 2016, he has been a member of the Romanian Parliament, in the Budget and Finance Commission, and in 2022–2023, he's been appointed as Honorary Advisor of the Romanian Prime Minister, in charge of the integration of Romanian universities into the European education and research area. Since August 2023, he has been an Honorary Advisor to the Vice-Prime Minister of Romania. He is a Professor and Doctoral Advisor in the field of finance, his main interests being in company financial management, direct investment and business financing, international finance, and corporate governance. He is the main author of 4 books and co-author of 13 books, as well as author or co-author of more than 150 scientific articles and studies, and manager or part of the teams of more than 35 research projects. He has often offered lectures on the topics of corporate governance or finance and financing of different entities and has been invited as a guest lecturer in universities from Italy, the United States, Spain, Serbia, Slovenia, Great Britain, etc. For his activity, he has been awarded numerous distinctions, including that of Doctor Honoris Causa of two different Romanian universities and Professor Emeritus of another university. [ORCID: https://orcid.org/0000-0002-3956-4394]

About the Contributors

Jānis Salmiņš, Mg.oec., University of Latvia, Faculty of Economics and Management, holds master's degree of Economic Sciences. The author is Deputy Head of Analytical Service in Ministry of Economics, from 2016 to 2019, Advisor to the Prime Minister on Macroeconomic Policy, and since 2016 member of Statistics Council. The author's main themes of action include analysis of current economic situation and future trends, proposals for economic policy development, development of strategic planning documents and impact assessment of political initiatives, and proposals for necessary changes in economic policy for sustainable economic development.

Nicoleta Sîrghi, PhD Habil., is Professor of Economics, at the West University of Timisoara (Romania), Faculty of Economics and Business Administration. Her current research field is related to the study of the microeconomics and game theory with applications in economics. She has published in the *International Journal of Bifurcation and Chaos, Sustainability, Transformations in Business and Economics, Journal of Economic Computation and Economic Cybernetics Studies and Research*, etc. She is a member of the editorial board of *Timisoara Journal of Economics and Business* and a reviewer for many international journals and conferences. She is a member of the scientific council of the European Real Estate Economics and Finance – Public Goods and Values (ERECO-PGV) network and a member of professional economics associations: Regional Science Association International, International Association of French-Speaking Economists, and ERECO-PGV network. [ORCID: https://orcid.org/0000-0001-6345-0373]

Irina Skribāne, Mg.oec., is Researcher of the Productivity Research Institute of the Faculty of Business, Management, and Economics of the University of Latvia 'UL Think tank LV PEAK', Lecturer of the University of Latvia's Faculty of Business, Management, and Economics, and Analyst of the Ministry of Economics of the Republic of Latvia. The author's areas of research work are economic growth and structural transformation, productivity and competitiveness analysis, and investment and investment policy. The author has contributed to more than 20 scientific papers.

Biruta Sloka, Dr.oec., is Professor and Leading Researcher at the University of Latvia and has participated in several research projects and delivered study courses at several levels: doctoral, master, and bachelor. The author has experience in participating in Council of Statistics of Republic of Latvia and is a member of European Statistics Advisory Committee. The author has participated in the work of Association of Statisticians of Latvia, Association of Econometrists of Latvia, and Association of Professors of Latvia. The author has experience in participating in several scientific boards of international scientific conferences; has participated as reviewer of international scientific papers; and has participated as supervisor of doctoral theses and reviewer of doctoral dissertations.

xvi ABOUT THE CONTRIBUTORS

Irina Solovjova is a Professor of Finance at the Faculty of Business, Management, and Economics of the University of Latvia. Her academic interests are related to economics and finance. The main research areas are assessment of the stability of the banking system, reliability of the commercial banks, and risks of companies and banks. She has more than 20 years of teaching experience in teaching various study courses at the Faculty of Business, Management, and Economics. She is the author of 2 scientific monographs and more than 30 articles in scientific journals and conference proceedings. She is an expert in Economics and Management Sciences at the Latvian Academy of Sciences. She has participated in more than 10 research projects, including the European Science Foundation (ESF) and Latin American Studies (LAS) projects.

Inna Šteinbuka, Dr.oec., is Chair of Latvian Fiscal Discipline Council, Professor at the University of Latvia (UL), Deputy Chair of the UL Board, Director of the UL Productivity Research Institute, full member of the Latvian Academy of Sciences, and Governor of Latvia in Asia-Europe Foundation (ASEF, Singapore). Since September 2011, she has been serving at the European Commission as Head of the EC Representation in Rīga. She has been working at the European Commission since 2005. Prior to joining the European Commission, she was Chair of the Public Utilities Commission of Latvia and Senior Advisor to the Executive Director of Nordic–Baltic constituency at the International Monetary Fund in Washington, DC. She has previously held various positions at the Ministry of Finance. Her areas of research work include macroeconomics, fiscal policy, productivity, and competitiveness. She is author of more than 35 scientific papers and co-author of 4 monographs.

Ileana Tache, PhD, is Professor at Transilvania University of Brasov, Department of Marketing, Tourism-Services, and International Business. Her teaching and research activity focuses on Economics, European Economic Policies, History of Economic Thought, and History of European Construction. Her teaching stays at Trier University, Pescara University, University of the Aegean, Piri Reis University, and Piraeus University. She has published papers in *SAGE Open*, *Sustainability*, *International Advances in Economic Research*, *International Journal of Social Economics*, and *Rivista di Studi Politici Internazionali*. She is Editor of a book published by Cambridge Scholars Publishing. She is Coordinator of Jean Monnet projects: Ad Personam Jean Monnet Chair, Jean Monnet Center of Excellence. [ORCID: https://orcid.org/0000-0003-4559-3367]

Alexandra-Mădălina Țăran is a Teaching Assistant and PhD student in the finance field, studying different aspects related to the relationship between public sector governance and health systems. Her research mainly addresses the public economic field, namely public policies, welfare, and good governance, with interdisciplinary research directions that focus on health economics, digitalisation, well-being, sustainability, and economic growth. She has already presented part of his research results at international conferences and published articles in

About the Contributors

journals indexed by Web of Science and other international databases. [ORCID: https://orcid.org/0000-0002-7721-423X]

Eleftherios Thalassinos, PhD (UIC, Chicago, USA, 1983), DHC degrees in Economics (Danubius University of Galati, Romania, 2013; University of Craiova, Romania, 2015; and Rostov State University of Economics, Russia, 2018), MBA (De-Paul University, Chicago, USA, 1979), BA (University of Athens, Greece, 1976), is a Jean Monnet Chair Professor experienced in European Economic Integration and International Finance. He is the Editor-in-Chief of *ERSJ, IJEBA,* and *IJFIRM* and Chair of ICABE. He is Guest Editor in the Book Series Contemporary Studies in Economic and Financial Analysis published by Emerald; *Contributions to Management Sciences* by Springer; *Business, Technology and Finance* by Nova; *JRFM, Resources, Risks and Sustainability* by MDPI. He is a member of the editorial boards of several journals. His professional experience includes quantitative analysis, technical and financial analysis, banking, business consulting, project evaluations, international business, international finance, and maritime economics. He has a long track of publications in several journals, collective volumes, and chapter books. Among them a publication as a chapter book in the *World Scientific Handbook in Financial Economics Series,* Vol. 5, dedicated to the memory of Late Milton Miller, Nobel Prize winner in Economics in 1990. Parallel to his academic career, he has performed as Bank Director for 12 years, Ministerial Advisor for 6 years, Public Servant for 4 years, and independent consultant for a long time. [ORCID: https://orcid.org/0000-0003-3526-4930]

Ginta Tora, Mag.hist., Mag.sc.admin., University of Latvia, has participated in several research projects and conducting research related to quality of higher education in several aspects, involvement of students at risk in vocational education, the impact of education on social processes, aspects of social inclusion, several aspects of silver economy, cooperation with social partners and their role in the development of qualified specialists, and has participated in research related to knowledge triangle and innovations in education.

ACKNOWLEDGEMENT

Part of this work was supported by a grant from the Romanian Ministry of Research, Innovation, and Digitalization, the project with the title "Economics and Policy Options for Climate Change Risk and Global Environmental Governance" (CF 193/28.11.2022, Funding Contract no. 760078/23.05.2023), within Romania's National Recovery and Resilience Plan (PNRR) - Pillar III, Component C9, Investment I8 (PNRR/2022/C9/MCID/I8) - Development of a program to attract highly specialized human resources from abroad in research, development and innovation activities

CHAPTER 1

INTRODUCTION – NAVIGATING ECONOMIC WATERS: DEVELOPMENT AND RESILIENCE IN EU MEMBER STATES

Eleftherios Thalassinos

University of Piraeus, Greece

In the intricate tapestry of the European Union (EU), the accession of 13 nations – Bulgaria, Croatia, Cyprus, Czechia, Estonia, Hungary, Latvia, Lithuania, Malta, Poland, Romania, Slovakia, and Slovenia – marked a pivotal juncture in the collective narrative of economic development and resilience. As these nations transitioned into full-fledged EU membership, a spectrum of experiences, challenges, and triumphs unfolded, shaping the contours of their economic trajectories.

Our special issue, titled 'Economic Development and Resilience by EU Member States', aspires to illuminate the nuanced journey undertaken by these nations, delving into the determinants of imbalances that have marked their economic landscapes. The volume stands as a beacon, spotlighting the diverse challenges faced by each country, spanning the intricate realms of the financial market, foreign direct investment, export-oriented industries, and the complex terrain of energy markets, with a resolute focus on achieving sustainability goals and fostering energy independence.

The narrative unfolds as a comprehensive examination of the evolving economic narratives of the 13 member states, culminating in a meticulous analysis of their unique paths. By scrutinising the intricacies of financial dynamics, foreign investments, and the pivotal role of leading industries with export potential, we aim to dissect the factors that have both propelled and impeded the economic development of these nations.

Economic Development and Resilience by EU Member States
Contemporary Studies in Economic and Financial Analysis, Volume 115, 1–4
Copyright © 2025 by Eleftherios Thalassinos
Published under exclusive licence by Emerald Publishing Limited
ISSN: 1569-3759/doi:10.1108/S1569-375920240000115001

Crucially, this volume does not merely scrutinise challenges; it endeavours to provide pragmatic policy measures, serving as a reservoir of actionable insights for policymakers and stakeholders alike. The proposed solutions are designed to catalyse the resolution of these topical issues, ensuring a harmonious convergence of these nations within the larger European economic framework. In essence, the success of these endeavours will not only fortify the economic foundations of the individual nations but will also contribute significantly to enhancing the overall competitiveness of the EU.

As we navigate through the intricacies of each nation's economic narrative, this special issue serves as a vital repository, addressing a critical gap in the existing literature. By offering a unique synthesis of achievements and challenges, it aims to foster a deeper understanding of the economic dynamics of the new EU members. In doing so, we hope to contribute to the ongoing discourse surrounding European economic integration, resilience, and the quest for sustainable development.

Join us on this intellectual journey as we unravel the economic odyssey of these nations, exploring the tapestry of challenges and triumphs that define their path towards resilience and development within the EU.

Beyond the economic intricacies, this special issue casts its gaze upon the profound social impacts woven into the economic fabric of these 13 member states. The narratives unfold against the backdrop of societal transformations, demographic shifts, and the ebb and flow of cultural dynamics that have shaped the lived experiences of their citizens. The exploration of economic development is, therefore, inseparable from the broader tapestry of social evolution.

In the pursuit of economic resilience, these nations have witnessed transformative shifts in education, employment, and standards of living. Examining the socioeconomic landscape, our volume seeks to unravel the threads connecting economic growth to improvements in education and skill development. It delves into the evolving nature of employment opportunities, dissecting the impacts on income distribution and social mobility. By doing so, we aim to capture the holistic essence of these nations' development stories, acknowledging the interplay between economic prosperity and societal well-being.

Moreover, as these countries navigated the complex web of EU regulations, policies, and frameworks, the impact on governance structures and societal trust became a focal point of investigation. The intricacies of legal harmonisation, administrative reforms, and the quest for a unified European identity provide additional layers to the narrative, shaping the contours of political and social landscapes.

The economic and social impacts extend far beyond national borders, resonating collectively within the broader context of Eastern Europe. The experiences of these 13 nations contribute significantly to the ongoing discourse surrounding regional integration, fostering collaboration and cohesiveness. The volume thus becomes a vital lens through which we can scrutinise the broader implications for the Eastern European region as a whole, offering insights into the dynamics of regional cooperation, cross-border investments, and the potential for shared prosperity.

In the grand tapestry of European economic integration, the experiences of Bulgaria, Croatia, Cyprus, Czechia, Estonia, Hungary, Latvia, Lithuania, Malta, Poland, Romania, Slovakia, and Slovenia stand as both individual brushstrokes and integral

Introduction 3

components of a collective masterpiece. This special issue is an invitation to explore, analyse, and understand the multifaceted impacts – both economic and social – that have shaped the destinies of these nations and, by extension, the broader Eastern European landscape. Together, we embark on a journey to unravel the complexities, celebrate the achievements, and confront the challenges that define the economic and social odyssey of these EU member states and the Eastern European region at large.

The accession of 13 nations – Bulgaria, Croatia, Cyprus, Czechia, Estonia, Hungary, Latvia, Lithuania, Malta, Poland, Romania, Slovakia, and Slovenia – into the EU marked a transformative juncture in their economic and social trajectories. This special issue, Economic Development and Resilience by EU Member States, offers a comprehensive exploration of the distinct economic and social landscapes that have unfolded since their integration.

ECONOMIC DYNAMICS

As we embark on this analytical journey, the determinants of economic imbalances take centre stage. Each nation's financial market, foreign direct investment strategies, and export-oriented industries shape their economic trajectories uniquely. For example:

Bulgaria and Romania showcase resilience in absorbing foreign investments, while grappling with challenges tied to income inequality and structural reforms.

Poland stands out with its robust industrial sector, navigating the delicate balance between growth and environmental sustainability.

Baltic nations (Estonia, Latvia, and Lithuania), known for their dynamic economies, exemplify the potential of innovation and digitalisation in fostering economic development.

SOCIAL IMPLICATIONS

The economic odyssey of these nations is inseparable from its societal impacts, reflecting in education, employment, and cultural dynamics:

Czechia presents a unique story, where economic prosperity intertwines with a burgeoning tech sector and shifts in educational paradigms.

Hungary grapples with the dual challenge of economic growth and societal changes, particularly in the context of immigration patterns and cultural identity.

Cyprus and Malta showcase the symbiosis between economic development, tourism, and evolving societal norms.

REGIONAL DYNAMICS

Beyond individual narratives, the collective impact of these countries extends to the broader Eastern European region:

The Visegrád Group (Czechia, Hungary, Poland, Slovakia) exemplifies regional collaboration, influencing economic policies and fostering shared prosperity.

The Baltic states and the Balkans (Croatia, Slovenia) offer a glimpse into the regional dynamics, shaping cooperative frameworks and cross-border investments.

In this volume, we aim not only to dissect challenges and achievements but also to provide actionable policy measures. As these nations navigate economic waters, the impact on governance structures, societal trust, and regional collaboration becomes pivotal. Join us in unravelling the complex economic and social tapestry of these EU member states, contributing to a deeper understanding of Eastern Europe's journey towards development, resilience, and shared prosperity.

CHAPTER 2

GLOBALISATION, ECONOMIC INTEGRATION, AND LABOUR MARKET DYNAMICS WITHIN THE EUROPEAN UNION*

Alina Ionaşcu[a] and Graţiela Georgiana Noja[b]

[a]*West University of Timisoara, Faculty of Economics and Business Administration, East-European Center for Research in Economics and Business, Doctoral School of Economics and Business Administration, Timisoara, Romania*
[b]*West University of Timisoara, Faculty of Economics and Business Administration, East-European Center for Research in Economics and Business, Timisoara, Romania*

ABSTRACT

Purpose: *This research delves into the nuanced interrelations between economic globalisation, European integration, and labour market dynamics, specifically focussing on understanding how trade and financial globalisation impact economic growth and the stability of the European Union (EU) labour markets. The aim is to emphasise the multidimensional effects of globalisation and European integration within this context.*

Need for study: *This research responds to the critical need for an in-depth analysis of these dynamics of globalisation, providing essential insights for*

---

*This work was supported by a grant from the Romanian Ministry of Research, Innovation, and Digitalization, the project with the title "Economics and Policy Options for Climate Change Risk and Global Environmental Governance" (CF 193/28.11.2022, Funding Contract no. 760078/23.05.2023), within Romania's National Recovery and Resilience Plan (PNRR) – Pillar III, Component C9, Investment I8 (PNRR/2022/C9/MCID/I8) – Development of a program to attract highly specialised human resources from abroad in research, development and innovation activities.

Economic Development and Resilience by EU Member States
Contemporary Studies in Economic and Financial Analysis, Volume 115, 5–22
Copyright © 2025 by Alina Ionaşcu and Graţiela Georgiana Noja
Published under exclusive licence by Emerald Publishing Limited
ISSN: 1569-3759/doi:10.1108/S1569-375920240000115002

informed economic and policy decision-making at the level of the EU in a globalised landscape.

Methodology: *This research employs a systematic review and bibliometric analysis to examine a broad range of literature from 1990 to 2023. Analysing over 1,000 academic articles to identify trends in discussions on European integration and globalisation using the VOSviewer tool assesses the relationship between globalisation, European integration, and labour market performance in EU countries using statistical data provided by Eurostat.*

Findings: *European integration and globalisation continue to open avenues for economic growth while concurrently exposing economies to various risks, including economic instability and wage disparities. Financial globalisation emerges as a dual-edged credential, amplifying global financial risks and influencing income redistribution patterns.*

Practical implications: *The study emphasises the need for well-crafted policies to address labour market challenges in EU-13 countries. Policymakers should prioritise investment in education, skills training, entrepreneurship, innovation ecosystems, and workforce adaptability. Regional cooperation is also advised to leverage collective strengths, share best practices, and foster solidarity among EU-13 member states.*

Keywords: Globalisation; regional integration; labour market; economic growth; European Union

JEL classifications: F62; J21; J31; F65; O11

1. INTRODUCTION TO GLOBALISATION AND EUROPEAN ECONOMIC INTEGRATION

At the onset of the 21st century, globalisation has emerged as a transformative force, redefining the world's economic, societal, and political fabric. Characterised by enhanced interconnectedness and interdependence among nations, this era has been distinguished by the seamless flow of goods, services, capital, and labour across international borders. Such dynamics have paved the way for a global economy where geographical distances are increasingly inconsequential, promoting an environment of shared prosperity and presenting challenges related to economic disparity, cultural erosion, and sovereignty.

Parallel to the global narrative, European economic integration, primarily through the EU, offers a nuanced lens to observe globalisation's multifaceted impacts. The EU's foundation, motivated by the desire for peace and economic stability post-World War II, has evolved into an ambitious integration project encompassing diverse nations. This union has effectively facilitated the free exchange of resources and labour among its member states, enhancing economic efficiency and fostering a sense of European identity (Ahir et al., 2022). However, this integration is not without its complexities, as it navigates the delicate balance between deepening economic ties and respecting the unique cultural and political sovereignties of its member countries.

This backdrop sets the stage for a detailed examination of globalisation's dynamics and European economic integration's unique position within this global process. The analysis seeks not only to understand these phenomena in isolation but also to unravel the intricate web of relationships that link them to broader economic, social, and political outcomes. In doing so, it aims to contribute to the discourse on how globalisation can be harnessed for collective benefit while mitigating its adverse effects, leveraging the European experience as a case study for broader global application. This exploration is particularly pertinent in an era where the forces of globalisation are increasingly under scrutiny, and the quest for sustainable and inclusive growth remains a paramount challenge for the international community.

Globalisation, fuelled by technological progress, the easing of trade barriers, and financial market liberalisation, has significantly integrated the global economy. This integration has made national borders less relevant to economic activities, with the advancement of information technology further enhancing global connectivity and financial exchanges. However, this process has its drawbacks, as it has been associated with increased income inequality, environmental concerns, and the potential erosion of national sovereignty. These issues have ignited a global debate on the overall effects of globalisation on worldwide welfare, highlighting the complex balance between its benefits and challenges (Ahir et al., 2022).

The EU stands as a profound example of economic integration achievable among sovereign states, conceived in the shadow of World War II to foster economic collaboration to avert future conflicts within Europe. This vision has blossomed over decades, transitioning from a mere common market into a sophisticated economic and political union that now includes 27 member nations. A pivotal moment in this journey was adopting a single currency, the euro, by 19 countries, symbolising a significant milestone in economic convergence (Mosley, 2000). This integration has enabled unprecedented freedom in the movement of goods, services, capital, and labour across member states, profoundly influencing Europe's economic fabric. The EU's evolution showcases the potential for diverse nations to forge deep economic ties while maintaining their sovereignty, setting a precedent for regional cooperation worldwide.

This inquiry is predicated on the imperative to decipher the complex symbiosis between global economic fluxes and efforts towards regional consolidation (Psycharis et al., 2020). As the globe contends with the multifaceted challenges engendered by globalisation, such as pronounced economic disparities and escalating geopolitical tensions, the paradigm established by the EU furnishes pivotal insights. These insights are instrumental in strategising the effective navigation of these challenges, thereby optimising the merits of economic symbiosis while judiciously mitigating its inherent adversities (Carey & Geddes, 2010).

In doing so, this chapter seeks to contribute to the ongoing dialogue on how nations can navigate the waters of globalisation, leveraging the lessons learned from European integration to foster economic growth, social cohesion, and political stability in an increasingly interconnected world.

The research encompasses a multidisciplinary perspective, incorporating insights from economics, political science, sociology, and international relations to elucidate the multifaceted dynamics of globalisation, economic integration, and labour market phenomena within the EU, with a keen focus on the new EU member states.

The period under scrutiny witnessed an intensification of globalisation processes within the EU context, with notable events such as the COVID-19 pandemic and the armed conflict in Ukraine exerting significant influence on economic and social dynamics. The pandemic, which emerged in 2019 and persisted into subsequent years, introduced unprecedented challenges to global connectivity, disrupting supply chains, trade flows, and labour mobility within the EU. Scholarly literature documents the pandemic's impact on economic activity, employment patterns, and policy responses, underscoring the imperative of resilience-building and cooperation in the face of systemic shocks.

Concurrently, the armed conflict in Ukraine, which escalated in 2014 and persisted throughout the period under review, introduced geopolitical tensions that reverberated across the EU. Scholars have examined the conflict's implications for regional stability, energy security, and diplomatic relations within the EU, shedding light on the complex interplay between political dynamics and economic integration efforts. Moreover, analyses have explored the EU's response to the conflict, including diplomatic initiatives, economic sanctions, and efforts to support conflict resolution and humanitarian assistance in Ukraine.

Amidst these geopolitical and public health challenges, economic integration remained a central focus of scholarly inquiry. The establishment of the single market in 1993 stands as a landmark achievement, epitomising the EU's commitment to dismantling barriers to the free movement of goods, services, capital, and labour. Subsequent developments, including adopting the euro currency and accessing new member states, have further propelled economic integration efforts. Academic discourse delves into the implications of these initiatives, exploring their impact on trade patterns, investment flows, and macroeconomic stability within the EU.

Furthermore, the study cautiously evaluates the effectiveness of the EU's cohesion policy, particularly concerning utilising structural and cohesion funds. While these funds are intended to mitigate regional disparities and alleviate unemployment, empirical evidence suggests their impact has been mixed.

The findings aim to provide policymakers, scholars, and the global community with a deeper understanding of the opportunities and obstacles presented by globalisation and regional economic integration, offering a roadmap for future collaboration and development. Moreover, policymakers should focus on optimising growth potential by investing in digital infrastructure, promoting research and development activities, and facilitating financing access for small- and medium-sized enterprises (SMEs) to enhance their participation in global value chains.

This comprehensive analysis draws upon various scholarly articles, empirical studies, and theoretical frameworks to explore the multifaceted nature of globalisation and European economic integration. By examining the successes and setbacks of the EU's integration process, the study sheds light on the broader implications of globalisation for economies and societies worldwide, underscoring the importance of strategic cooperation and governance in navigating the challenges of the 21st century.

2. SYSTEMATIC LITERATURE REVIEW ON GLOBALISATION AND REGIONAL ECONOMIC INTEGRATION

The issue of globalisation is highly complex and offers a wide range of global interactions, such as the expansion of cultural influences and the broadening of international economic and business relations worldwide, leading to an increasing degree of integration and interdependence between national economies. The term 'globalisation' has different connotations for various specialists and the public, but it is perceived as a multidisciplinary phenomenon that profoundly influences human existence (Walter, 2021).

The term 'globalisation' was popularised and more pronounced by Levitt (1983) in his article, 'Globalization of Markets', which emphasised the growing degree of integration and interdependence between national economies. Integration is hereby captured as a multifaceted process that describes the interconnectivity of national economies in the global marketplace. It involves trade in goods, services, ideas, and technology, as well as the movement of factors of production, such as labour, capital, and knowledge, across international borders. Integration also involves the coordination of public policies between countries to facilitate the smooth functioning of the global economy.

Globalisation has been studied across various academic disciplines, each with a unique perspective on the phenomenon. Economists view globalisation as an outcome of market forces, where the emergence of a global market has enabled countries to specialise in their comparative advantages, leading to increased efficiency and prosperity. Historians view globalisation as an era dominated by international capitalism, where multinational corporations have become the driving force of the global economy, shaping the world in their image. Sociologists see globalisation as a convergence of social preferences regarding lifestyles and values, with cultures and identities blending to create a more interconnected world. Political scientists view globalisation as a gradual erosion of national or state sovereignty, where countries have ceded power to international organisations and multinational corporations, leading to a loss of control over their domestic policies.

The rise of globalisation is attributed to several factors, focussing on the growth-generating facets of globalisation, such as international trade, foreign direct investment (FDI), finance, international migration, telecommunications, and transport. It is vital to approach globalisation cautiously, as it can positively and negatively affect societies and economies. Therefore, it is essential to continue a comprehensive and collaborative dialogue to ensure that the benefits of globalisation are widely shared and its negative impacts are minimised.

Financial globalisation, in particular, emerges as a double-edged phenomenon, exacerbating global financial vulnerabilities while influencing income redistribution within and across countries. However, it is imperative to acknowledge the nuanced complexities inherent in these phenomena. While European integration and globalisation present opportunities for economic advancement, they also coincide with rising protectionist sentiments and a discernible trend towards economic retrenchment, even within the EU. This emerging pattern of reduced economic openness poses significant challenges to EU member states' continued integration and prosperity.

Regional economic integration is a complex and multifaceted process that gradually eliminates trade and investment barriers between nations. This process can take various forms, such as free trade agreements, customs unions, and common markets, each with its own rules and regulations. Economic integration aims to create more comprehensive and unified economic systems that benefit all participating countries. This can result in increased trade and investment flows, greater efficiency and productivity, and improved competitiveness (Pirtea et al., 2015). However, economic integration also poses challenges, such as the need to harmonise regulations and standards, address disparities in economic development, and ensure that the benefits are shared fairly among all participants. Overall, regional economic integration is a dynamic process that requires ongoing cooperation and negotiation among participating countries. Economic integration may be perceived as the culmination of the historical progression of technical, economic, and social frameworks or as a conscious endeavour by human society to enhance its economic status, viewed as a political choice (Amzad, 2008). The former perspective implies that economic integration is a natural process that arises due to the evolution of various societal structures. The latter viewpoint, however, suggests that economic integration is a deliberate move taken by society to improve its economic standing. Both perspectives are valid and offer different insights into the driving forces behind economic integration. Ultimately, the decision to pursue economic integration is complex, involving many factors, including political, social, and economic considerations.

Bourenane and Mwanycky (1997) argue that regional economic integration is a fundamental step towards achieving unification, signifying the existence of consistent norms and principles that guide behaviour in a particular region. In this approach, the integration process involves creating a common market, eliminating trade barriers, and promoting economic cooperation among member countries. Additionally, it aims to align the region's policies and regulations, including administrative and legal frameworks, to facilitate the smooth functioning of the integrated market. Haile (2000) defines regional integration as a gradual process that involves merging member countries' economic and industrial structures. This process aims to create a synergy that can enhance national economic welfare more effectively than individual country-level policies. It involves the harmonisation of regulations, the coordination of macroeconomic policies, and the integration of infrastructure and transport networks. The goal is to establish a common economic space to boost trade and investment, create jobs, and improve living standards for the region's inhabitants.

Economic integration brings together two or more countries to form a more robust economic alliance. This leads to economic growth through the coordination of fiscal policies, efficient allocation of resources, and expansion of regional borders. Integration also improves cost efficiency and global trade. The World Trade Organisation's (WTO) efforts towards globalisation admit customs unions and free trade agreements as specific elements of regional integration, as they are seen as free trade actions, which is one of the fundamental objectives of the WTO.

Economic integration can only be achieved by implementing appropriate microeconomic and macroeconomic policies, government policies, trade liberalisation, foreign investment rules, and enterprise-level strategies. Achieving economic integration involves a multifaceted approach that requires the regulation of financial markets, promoting competition, identifying appropriate stages of development, and advancing infrastructure, particularly in transport and communications. These factors are essential in creating an environment conducive to economic integration, which allows countries to collaborate and work together towards mutually beneficial goals.

Several key indicators need to be considered to measure the effectiveness of economic integration. These include intra- and extra-EU trade, FDI flows, joint activities, and technology diffusion (Contractor et al., 2020). The Organisation for Economic Co-operation and Development (OECD) has also identified international trade, FDI, the activity of multinational firms, and the international diffusion of technology as critical indicators of regional integration and economic globalisation (OECD, 2010). These indicators provide a comprehensive framework for assessing the effectiveness of economic integration and provide valuable insights into the progress made in achieving economic cooperation and growth.

Overall, the integration process is a complex and challenging undertaking that requires the commitment and cooperation of member countries. It requires a shared vision, long-term planning, and careful implementation to realise the full benefits of economic integration.

Both regional integration and globalisation have brought about significant changes to the world economy, impacting different countries and individuals in various ways. Understanding these complex and dynamic processes is crucial for policymakers, researchers, and citizens alike as they navigate the challenges and opportunities of a globalised world. However, each of these disciplines explains only part of the phenomenon, and a multidisciplinary comprehensive approach is necessary to understand globalisation fully. The EU integration process represents a multifaceted and arduous endeavour that demands member states' unwavering commitment and cooperative efforts. For instance, establishing the EU single market has facilitated the free movement of goods, services, capital, and labour across borders, leading to increased trade and economic integration among member states. Additionally, adopting a common currency, the euro has further deepened economic ties within the eurozone, promoting financial stability and reducing business transaction costs.

Both regional integrations, exemplified by the EU, and globalisation have engendered profound transformations within the global economy. Furthermore, technological advancements in information technology and telecommunications have accelerated globalisation, enabling firms to reach new markets and consumers worldwide through digital platforms and e-commerce. However, it is paramount to recognise the nuanced complexities that accompany globalisation and integration. For example, a burgeoning tide of protectionist sentiments exists alongside the perceived benefits of globalisation, such as increased trade and investment flows. The trade tensions between the United States and China, characterised by tariffs and retaliatory measures, illustrate protectionism's challenges to liberalising trade and investment.

Moreover, within the EU, there is a discernible trend towards economic retrenchment, exemplified by growing scepticism towards further integration and calls for reasserting national sovereignty. The Brexit referendum, resulting in the United Kingdom's decision to leave the EU, exemplifies this trend and underscores the challenges faced in maintaining cohesion and solidarity among member states.

3. BIBLIOMETRIC ANALYSIS OF THE RELEVANT SCIENTIFIC LITERATURE

We conducted a comprehensive scientific investigation into globalisation and European economic integration, focussing on the EU. We employed a refined bibliometric analysis methodology to dissect the complex trends and dynamics observed over the past 30 years.

This analysis utilises the advanced capabilities of the VOSviewer tool, enabling us to map the intricate interconnections between crucial themes and concepts in this field. We specifically focus on the critical roles played by economic, financial, and trade globalisation, examining their implications for international trade, financial markets, and labour market dynamics within the EU context.

Through this rigorous analytical framework, we aim to elucidate the multifaceted impacts of globalisation on EU economic growth and labour market stability. By doing so, we seek to provide an in-depth understanding of the complex interdependencies that characterise the relationship between globalisation processes and the European integration project, shedding light on the nuanced ways in which commercial activities and financial globalisation contribute to the EU's economic and labour market landscape.

Through applying the VOSviewer analysis tool, we developed a focussed methodology to uncover connections within the themes of economic globalisation, European integration, and labour market dynamics from over a thousand academic articles. This method allows for examining keyword co-occurrence, highlighting terms that prominently feature, such as economic globalisation, European integration, and labour market dynamics.

We explored the debates around globalisation's impacts, analysing the intricate relationships among international trade, financial markets, and the interconnections between economic growth, globalisation, and labour market conditions, thereby identifying vital thematic nodes relevant to these subjects.

The bibliometric analysis depicted in Fig. 2.1 illustrates the interconnected nature of various research themes within the context of globalisation. The dominant cluster, centred on 'globalisation' and 'international trade', suggests a strong focus within the literature on the economic aspects of globalisation. Tightly linked

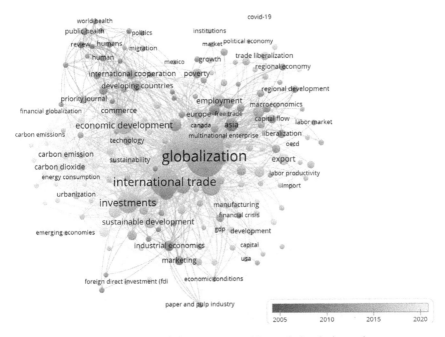

Fig. 2.1. Keyword Co-occurrence Network Analysis on the Theme of Globalisation. *Source*: Own research in VOSviewer.

to this are concepts like 'Economic development', 'Investments', and 'Financial globalisation', indicating substantial attention on how globalisation impacts economic growth and financial systems.

Notably, the 'Labour market' appears connected to 'Employment' and 'Labour productivity', signifying an analytical thread that examines the implications of globalisation on labour dynamics within economies. The temporal axis, indicated by the colour gradient, shows how these themes have possibly evolved or remained consistent over time from 2005 to 2020. From 2005 to 2020, the EU underwent profound economic transformations characterised by deepening integration into the global economy, expansion of the single market, and engagement in trade agreements. This era witnessed significant milestones, including the accession of Central and Eastern European countries in 2004, which expanded the single market and fostered greater economic cohesion. Additionally, adopting the euro currency by new member states such as Estonia and Latvia further facilitated cross-border transactions and promoted economic stability within the eurozone. Furthermore, the EU actively pursued trade agreements with various regions and countries worldwide to strengthen its position in the global trading system. Examples include the Comprehensive Economic and Trade Agreement (CETA) with Canada and negotiations for the Transatlantic Trade and Investment Partnership (TTIP) with the United States. However, amidst these integration efforts, challenges emerged, notably the 2008 financial crisis, which led to rising protectionist sentiments and concerns over trade imbalances within the eurozone.

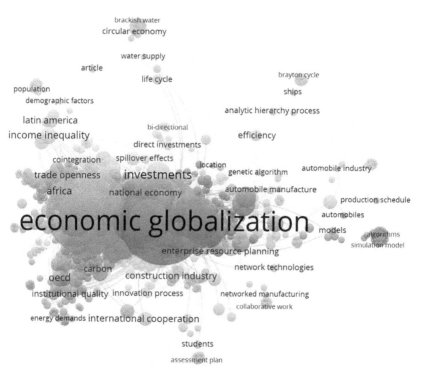

Fig. 2.2. Co-occurrence of Keywords Specific to the Topic of Economic Globalisation. *Source*: Own research in VOSviewer.

The figure also subtly connects these economic discussions with broader social and environmental issues, as evidenced by nodes like 'Sustainability' and 'Carbon emissions', suggesting an awareness in the literature of the wider implications of globalisation. Overall, the figure underscores globalisation research's complex and multidimensional nature, encompassing economic, social, and environmental perspectives.

The bibliometric network displayed in VOSviewer visualisation captures the intricate relationships among key terms related to economic globalisation, European integration, and labour market dynamics (Fig. 2.2). The predominant node, 'Economic globalisation', is intricately linked with 'Investments' and 'National economy', indicating a significant focus on capital flows and their macroeconomic implications. The cluster around 'Cointegration' and 'Trade openness', especially concerning 'Africa' and 'Latin America', suggests an examination of globalisation's effects on different regions and their economic ties with the European market.

Interconnections with 'Institutional quality' and 'International cooperation' underscore the significance of governance and collaborative efforts in smoothing globalisation. Notably, the linkages to 'Labour market' dynamics and the 'Construction industry' point to sector-specific labour responses to economic globalisation. The visualisation hints at an academic discourse considering how trade policies and

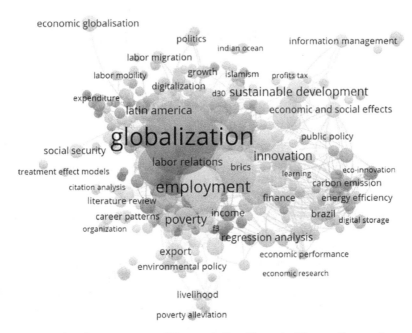

Fig. 2.3. Co-occurrence of Keywords Specific to the Themes Economic Growth – Economic Globalisation – Labour Market. *Source*: Own research in VOSviewer.

financial globalisation intricacies affect EU economic growth and labour stability (Dreher, 2006). The nuanced interplay of these elements reflects the complex tapestry of globalisation's impact on various facets of economies and societies.

The bibliometric visualisation captured in Fig. 2.3 provides a granular view into the intersection of European integration and labour market dynamics within the broader context of economic globalisation. The proximity of 'Labour mobility' to 'Economic globalisation' likely denotes the free movement of workers within the EU – a fundamental principle of the internal market and a driver for economic growth and employment. The presence of 'Public policy' and 'Environmental policy' concerning 'Economic performance' suggests an analysis of the EU's regulatory framework, which aims to balance economic growth with social and environmental sustainability. This visualisation could indicate the ongoing scholarly discourse on how EU policies shape labour markets, addressing issues such as job creation, skill matching, and the impact of financial globalisation on employment stability. It encapsulates the complex interactions between policy, market dynamics, and economic forces that are at play in the evolving European single market.

Fig. 2.4. Co-occurrence of Keywords Specific to the Topic of Financial Globalisation. *Source*: Own research in VOSviewer.

The bibliometric visualisation under discussion provides a complex representation of how financial globalisation and trade issues relate to economic growth and labour market stability in the EU (Fig. 2.4). Financial globalisation encompasses the liberalisation of capital accounts, the proliferation of multinational corporations, and the increase of cross-border financial services. These factors can lead to economic growth through enhanced capital allocation and increased competition, but they also pose systemic risks, as evidenced by the node of the financial crises. For example, removing capital controls can lead to volatile capital flows, affecting the EU's financial system and labour market stability. Trade issues such as tariff negotiations, anti-dumping measures, and trade liberalisation directly affect the EU's internal market. For instance, trade liberalisation can not only promote efficiency and consumer welfare but can also lead to industry restructuring and job displacement. The EU's standard commercial policy and the role of the European Central Bank in managing monetary policy and financial stability are concrete examples of EU-wide responses to these challenges.

The visualisation suggests a scholarly focus on dissecting these phenomena to understand their nuanced impacts on the EU's economic health and labour dynamics. The interconnections between these nodes reflect the importance of coherent policies to mitigate the adverse effects of financial globalisation and trade issues on the EU's economy and workforce.

4. GLOBALISATION, REGIONAL INTEGRATION, AND LABOUR MARKET INFERENCES AT THE LEVEL OF EU COUNTRIES

To grasp a comprehensive view of the pivotal role of globalisation and European economic integration, we aim to uncover the multifaceted effects of this complex phenomenon. We have therefore scrutinised globalisation's dual effects, investigating how it fosters economic growth while potentially introducing elements of

Globalisation, Economic Integration, and Labour Market Dynamics 17

instability into economies. We shall explore financial globalisation's influence on income distribution, questioning whether it perpetuates inequality or enhances economic parity. Further, we will analyse labour market dynamics within the EU, examining how global economic integration influences employment patterns, job security, and workforce mobility. Through this analysis, we aim to provide a comprehensive picture of globalisation's diverse impacts on European economic landscapes.

In the forthcoming, we will delve deeply into Eurostat's labour market flow statistics, covering the transition from the second quarter to the third quarter of 2023 (Fig. 2.5) to unearth the empirical effects of globalisation on EU economies. This exploration is designed to illuminate the complex dynamics within the EU labour market, including the steadfastness of employment, the pathways through which individuals gain employment, and the factors leading to exits from the labour force. This detailed analysis will extend beyond mere statistical interpretation, aiming to uncover the more profound economic implications of these labour market movements within global economic integration and its influence on the European labour market's stability and adaptability.

By doing so, we anticipate contributing a nuanced understanding to the scholarly discourse on how global economic trends, policy decisions, and labour market characteristics interconnect and shape the labour landscape in the EU amidst the challenges and opportunities globalisation presents (Eurostat, 2023).

In the second to third quarter of 2023, a significant portion of the EU's unemployed remained so, while a smaller fraction found employment or exited the workforce. Similarly, most employed individuals retained their jobs, with few becoming unemployed or leaving the workforce. Those outside the labour force largely stayed in that status, with some gaining employment or becoming unemployed. These data, indicating labour market fluidity and the resilience

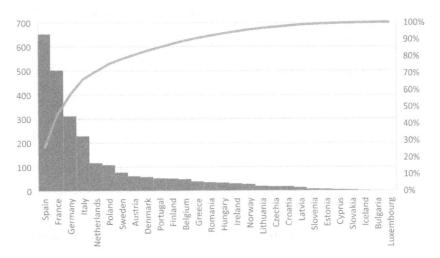

Fig. 2.5. Labour Market Flows in Q2 2023 in European Countries. *Source*: Eurostat (2023).

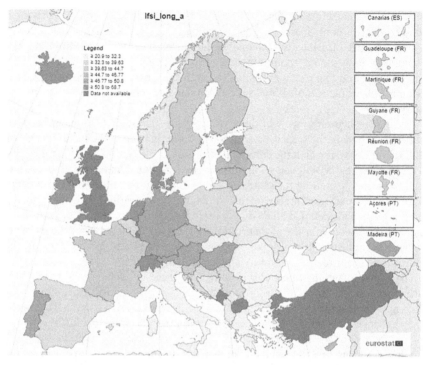

Fig. 2.6. Transitions in Labour Market Status in the EU, 2021–2022 (in % of Initial Status-Population Aged 15–74 Years). *Source*: Eurostat (2023), https://ec.europa.eu/eurostat/databrowser/view/lfsi_long_q/default/map?lang=en

or vulnerability of employment statuses, underscore the dynamic nature of the labour market in response to economic conditions and policy measures within the EU. Analysing these transitions provides insight into the labour market's adaptability and the challenges those seeking employment face (Eurostat, 2023).

Fig. 2.6 indicates that in 2021, within the EU, 37.0% of those unemployed remained so in 2022, while 38.5% found employment, and 24.5% exited the labour force. Among those employed in 2021, 94.0% retained their jobs into 2022, 1.7% transitioned to unemployment, and 4.3% left the labour force. These data, presented as percentages based on the initial labour market status, highlight the fluidity and transitions within the EU labour market, reflecting the dynamic nature of employment and unemployment trends.

5. CONCLUSIONS

Through exhaustive data analysis and specialised literature, the study brings to light the intricacy of challenges and opportunities, accentuating the imperative for adaptive policies adept at efficaciously responding to global and European dynamics. This intro establishes the groundwork for subsequent in-depth discussions geared towards profoundly interpreting the outcomes and delineating future research avenues.

A thorough examination of the globalisation phenomenon reveals a substantial reconfiguration of national economies, highlighted by the amplification of economic and financial interdependence on a global scale. This dynamic is emblematically exemplified by the integration of international financial markets, which facilitates the cross-border flow of capital with unprecedented freedom and speed. Within the EU, the adoption of the single currency, the euro, marked a decisive stage in the economic integration process, promoting the fluidity of trade and investments between member states and strengthening the single market. This transformation illustrates how globalisation and integration policies have reshaped economic paradigms, generating opportunities for growth and competitiveness. Simultaneously, it has necessitated meticulous coordination of economic policies at the supra-national level to ensure the alignment of national interests with the continuously evolving global dynamics.

European integration serves as a catalyst for economic and political stability through a suite of sophisticated structural and financial mechanisms. The EU's Structural and Cohesion Funds, designed to mitigate regional disparities, exemplify the EU's commitment to fostering harmonious and equitable development among its member states. Concurrently, the European Stability Mechanism (ESM) represents a proactive approach to preventing and managing economic crises, offering targeted financial support to member states in distress. By promoting economic and political cohesion, these initiatives play a crucial role in fortifying a stable and resilient framework within the EU, underscoring the significance of synergy among member states for the efficient management of macroeconomic challenges.

The document analysis underscores how globalisation and integration within the EU have fundamentally reshaped the labour market, highlighting a complex interplay between economic growth and emerging inequalities. The study details the diversified impact of these processes on employment rates, labour force structure, and wage dynamics, raising the acute need for adaptive economic and social policies. By emphasising the necessity of a multidimensional approach, the research underscores the strategic importance of striking a balance between economic benefits and social imperatives, aiming to ensure an equitable distribution of prosperity and strengthen social cohesion in globalisation. This perspective broadens the understanding of the consequences of European integration on the labour market, highlighting the complexity and interdependence of economic phenomena at a transnational level. As globalisation continues to shape European economies, its impact on the labour market remains a critical and profound subject of analysis. The study explores how global economic integration influences employment patterns, job security, and labour mobility within the EU, revealing various multifaceted effects.

First, globalisation has heightened labour mobility within the EU, facilitating the free movement of workers between member states. This mobility, while contributing to economic growth and aligning workforce skills with market demands, raises issues related to job security and wage disparities, potentially exacerbating regional and national inequalities.

Second, the analysis of labour market flows, based on Eurostat data for the transition from the second to the third quarter of 2023, offers a perspective on the fluidity of the labour market and the resilience or vulnerability of employment statuses. The data indicate that a significant portion of the unemployed remain in this state, while only a fraction manage to find employment or exit the labour force. This dynamism underscores the reactive nature of the labour market concerning economic conditions and internal policy measures.

The study emphasises the need for cohesive policies within the EU that effectively balance the benefits of economic growth stemming from globalisation with job security and inequality challenges. Concrete examples of such policies include initiatives promoting flexible and inclusive work environments, such as telecommuting and flexible hours, which enhance workforce adaptability and mobility. For instance, the EU's directive on work–life balance, adopted in 2019, seeks to improve access to flexible working arrangements and parental leave, thereby fostering more excellent work–life balance for employees.

Additionally, policies ensuring social protection and equal opportunities for all workers are indispensable for mitigating the adverse effects of globalisation on job security and inequality – robust social safety nets, including unemployment benefits and healthcare coverage, support workers during economic uncertainty. Moreover, measures promoting lifelong learning and skills development, such as vocational training programmes and adult education initiatives, empower workers to adapt to changing economic demands and technological advancements, reducing the risk of job displacement and enhancing employment prospects.

By implementing such policies, the EU can effectively address the dual challenges of fostering economic growth while ensuring social inclusion and equality in the labour market. Furthermore, the insights gleaned from the study contribute significantly to the academic and political discourse on how globalisation and European economic integration influence labour market dynamics. These findings provide a solid foundation for developing more effective and equitable economic and social policy strategies, guiding policymakers in navigating the complexities of a globalised economy while promoting inclusive and sustainable growth within the EU. In response to the detrimental impacts of war, the pandemic, and distortions in global value chains on employment dynamics, EU-13 member states must strategically allocate resources towards investment in reskilling and upskilling initiatives. Furthermore, recognising the heightened susceptibility of workers to economic disruptions, EU-13 member states must fortify social protection mechanisms. This entails augmenting unemployment benefits, facilitating access to job training and placement services, and ensuring affordable healthcare and social services for affected individuals and families.

Moreover, fostering entrepreneurship and bolstering support for SMEs are pivotal for nurturing economic resilience and job creation within EU-13 member states. Policymakers should devise incentives and support structures to enable SMEs to innovate, access financing, and seamlessly integrate into global value chains, diversifying the economic landscape and reducing dependence on vulnerable sectors. EU-13 member states should also prioritise regional cooperation and solidarity initiatives to lessen the adverse repercussions of external shocks on the labour market. Collaborative endeavours, including the exchange of best practices, pooling resources for joint ventures, and synergy in infrastructure development, research, and innovation, can effectively mitigate the impact of economic disruptions.

Subsequently, in the aftermath of conflicts and economic upheavals, EU-13 member states must facilitate the smooth integration of displaced workers into the labour market. This necessitates providing comprehensive vocational training, language proficiency programmes, and targeted job placement assistance to expedite their transition into new employment avenues. In recognition of the intertwined nature of economic, social, and environmental domains, EU-13 member states should prioritise investment in sustainable development initiatives. This encompasses the promotion of green jobs, renewable energy adoption, and sustainable agricultural practices, yielding employment opportunities and contributing to long-term economic robustness and environmental sustainability.

Given the complexity of globalisation and European integration phenomena, an extensive array of future research directions is warranted to deepen the understanding of the interactions between these processes and their effects on economic and social structures. This endeavour should include a detailed exploration of the impact of digitalisation and automation on the labour market, highlighting how these technologies are reshaping skill requirements and employment models (Noja & Panzaru, 2021). Concurrently, it is crucial to analyse how sustainability initiatives can be aligned with economic growth objectives to reconcile economic development with ecological imperatives. Moreover, labour mobility within the EU presents a fertile ground for studying the influence of migration on social and economic cohesion, both in host member states and countries of origin, with a particular focus on addressing regional inequalities.

Special attention should also be given to economic and social resilience in the face of global shocks, analysing the capacity of national systems and the community bloc to respond to crises effectively. Additionally, exploring the role of emerging technologies in shaping the future of work presents a promising area with the potential to inform public policies to facilitate the transition to a knowledge economy. By addressing these themes within a rigorous academic framework, future research can offer valuable insights for developing innovative and sustainable policies capable of navigating the complexity of the economic and social realities of the 21st century.

REFERENCES

Ahir, H., Bloom, N., & Furceri, D. (2022). *The world uncertainty index*. [Working Paper No. 29763]. NBER. http://www.nber.org/papers/w29763

Amzad, H. K. N. (2008). Trade and regional integration: Analysis of the effectiveness in the GCC. *International Journal of Islamic and Middle Eastern Finance and Management, 1*(2), 95–112. htpps://doi.org/10.1108/17538390810880964

Bourenane, N., & Mwanycky, S. (1997). *Economic cooperation and regional integration in Africa: First experiences and prospects* (pp. 1–274). Academy Science Publishers.

Carey, S., & Geddes, A. (2010). Less is more: Immigration and European integration at the 2010 general election. *Parliamentary Affairs, 63*(4), 849–865.

Contractor, F. J., Dangol, R., Nuruzzaman, N., & Raghunath, S. (2020). How do country regulations and business environment impact foreign direct investment (FDI) inflows? *International Business Review, 29*(2), 101640.

Dreher, A. (2006). Does globalisation affect growth? Evidence from a new index of globalization. *Applied Economics, 38*(10), 1091–1110. https://doi.org/10.1080/00036840500392078

Haile, K. (2000). *Regional integration in Africa: A review of the outstanding issues and mechanisms to monitor future progress* [Paper presentation]. African Knowledge Networks Forum Preparatory Workshop, ECA, Addis Ababa.

Levitt, T. (1983). Globalization of markets. *Harvard Business Review.* https://hbr.org/1983/05/the-globalization-of-markets

Mosley, L. (2000). Room to move: International financial markets and national welfare states. *International Organization, 54*(4), 737–773.

Noja, G., & Panzaru, C. (2021). Five possible impacts of digitalisation in Romania. *European Review of Applied Sociology, 14*(22), 1–10. https://doi.org/10.1515/eras-2021-0001

Organisation for Economic Co-operation and Development. (2010). *Measuring globalization – OECD economic globalisation indicators.* https://www.oecd-ilibrary.org/industry-and-services/measuring-globalisation-oecd-economic-globalisation-indicators-2010_9789264084360-en

Pirtea, M., Nicolescu, C., Botoc, C., & Lobont, O. (2015). Board gender and firm value: an empirical analysis. *Economic Computation and Economic Cybernetics Studies and Research, 49*(4), 21–32.

Psycharis, Y., Tselios, V., & Pantazis, P. (2020). The contribution of cohesion funds and nationally funded public investment to regional growth: Evidence from Greece. *Regional Studies, 54*(1), 95–105.

Walter, S. (2021). The backlash against globalization. *Annual Review of Political Science, 24*, 421–442.

Węgrzyn, G. (2023). Influence of the COVID-19 pandemic on the transition of people on the Polish labor market – Hidden threats. *International Journal of Management and Economics, 59*(2), 168–179. https://doi.org/10.2478/ijme-2023-0012

CHAPTER 3

DOES THE QUALITY OF GOVERNANCE HAVE THE POWER TO ATTRACT FOREIGN INVESTORS? EVIDENCE FROM THE EU-13 MEMBER STATES[*]

Tomasz Dorożyński[a], Anetta Kuna-Marszałek[a] and Bogusława Dobrowolska[b]

[a]Department of International Trade, Faculty of Economics and Sociology, University of Lodz, Poland
[b]Department of Economic and Social Statistics, Faculty of Economics and Sociology, University of Lodz, Poland

ABSTRACT

Purpose: *This chapter aims to assess the governance quality (GQ) in the EU-13 member states (MS) over the 2004–2022 period, examining the relationship between GQ and investment attractiveness, measured by foreign direct investment (FDI) inward stock as a % of gross domestic product (GDP). Studies on the relationship of institutions and governance on FDI inflow conducted for the EU-13 MS are relatively rare.*

Methodology: *First, countries of the EU-13 exhibiting similar levels of GQ (hierarchical cluster analysis) are identified using the Worldwide Governance*

---

[*] This chapter presents the next stage of the research project using the authorship synthetic index of governance quality. Previous ones based on a similar methodology included the EU and CEE countries (see Dobrowolska et al., 2021, 2023; Dorożyński et al., 2020).

Economic Development and Resilience by EU Member States
Contemporary Studies in Economic and Financial Analysis, Volume 115, 23–45
Copyright © 2025 by Tomasz Dorożyński, Anetta Kuna-Marszałek and Bogusława Dobrowolska
Published under exclusive licence by Emerald Publishing Limited
ISSN: 1569-3759/doi:10.1108/S1569-375920240000115003

Index (WGI). We use the values obtained from the authors' original synthetic index of governance quality *(SIGQ) to compare levels of GQ among the EU-13 MS between 2004 and 2022. Third, FDI inflows to the EU-13 MS. Finally, a correlation matrix and contingency coefficients are used to examine the relationship between FDI inflows and groups of countries with similar SIGQ and the relevance of six individual GQ dimensions for FDI inflows in the EU-13 MS.*

Findings: *The EU-13 MS differ significantly in the overall GQ measured by the WGI. Statistical analysis results are used to validate the hypothesis about a positive relationship between GQ and the inflow of FDI. The approach adopted for this chapter and its value-added lie in dividing the EU-13 MS into groups based on their similar performance concerning GQ (measured by six governance dimensions) and proving that GQ matters for FDI inflows.*

Practical implications: *High-quality governance can contribute to the investment attractiveness of countries and influence FDI flows, with implications for practice.*

Keywords: Governance quality; institutional quality; investment attractiveness; foreign direct investment; EU-13 member states; hierarchical cluster analysis

JEL classifications: F21; F23

1. INTRODUCTION

Today, capital flows, particularly FDI, determine how fast modern economies and regions grow. From the perspective of the host countries, the most beneficial is the inflow of FDI, accompanied by the transfer of technology, management methods, and skills, all of which significantly impact the country's competitiveness. Overall, the benefits of FDI inflows for economies are well documented in the literature. Most studies show that FDI drives technology transfers, supports the development of human capital, enhances international trade, helps create a competitive environment for business, and accelerates the growth of domestic enterprises, ultimately having a positive impact on economic growth (Baiashvili & Gattini, 2020; Bajo-Rubio, 2021; Beugelsdijk et al., 2008; Blomström et al., 1992, 1997; Labidi et al., 2024; OECD, 2002; Pegkas, 2015; Singhal & Singh, 2023; Yao & Wei, 2007). Thus, attracting FDI is particularly interesting to economies in order to accelerate their growth and get them more integrated into the global economy.

Realising the critical role of FDI, most governments attempt to attract it. They start by providing a business environment that guarantees high absorption capacity for investment and technology, that is, an environment conducive to generating business opportunities and open to foreign investment. The country should focus on improving the investment climate to attract foreign investors. There are traditional advantages, such as location, availability of raw materials, low-cost inputs, cheap and skilled labour, which are always important; nevertheless, the willingness of foreign investors to invest also depends on the credibility of the host country. The latter, in turn, is dictated by the level of economic development, economic and political stability, economic policy (e.g. taxation), regulatory framework, and institutional development of bodies supporting entrepreneurship. All of these elements make up what is known as good governance, a process that ensures transparency of operations and accountability of institutions, enhances institutional efficiency, helps to support a country's economic competitiveness, and builds trust in the business community. Therefore, countries must improve GQ (Alam & Shah, 2013), which will help them attract more FDI (Younsi & Bechtini, 2019).

Many studies have demonstrated that better quality of governance in host countries translates into more FDI (Dobrowolska et al., 2021, 2023; Dorożyński et al., 2020; Hayat, 2019; Sabir et al., 2019). By contrast, weak and inefficient government operations discourage FDI due to political instability, weak rule of law, lack of accountability and transparency, and inactive mechanisms for the reduction of corruption (Hossain & Rahman, 2017); in addition, poor governance leads to increased costs and uncertainty (Globerman & Shapiro, 2003). Governance can also have an indirect effect on FDI inflows as it has an impact on factors that attract investment. Determinants of FDI inflows also include human capital or the quality of public infrastructure, factors that are also influenced by good governance.

Although researchers have recently been paying more attention to the impact of institutions on FDI, studies devoted to this relationship for Central and Eastern European (CEE) countries remain relatively scarce. In investors' eyes, the CEE region is often perceived as a single entity, even though the countries differ substantially concerning their ability to attract FDI. What they have in common, however, is a spectacular increase in investment attractiveness following European Union (EU) accession (10 countries in 2004, Romania and Bulgaria in 2007, and Croatia in 2013). There are many factors behind this. In our view, institutional factors may play an important role, as they differ between these countries contemplated as potential investment locations.

In this regard, our chapter attempts to answer the following questions: Is there a relationship between GQ and FDI inflows? How does governance influence FDI inflows into the EU-13? Which of the six individual characteristics of GQ has the most significant impact on FDI in the new EU MS? Therefore, this chapter's primary goal is to conduct empirical research on the role of GQ in attracting FDI to the new EU-13 member states (MS) in the post-accession period (2004–2022). The main hypothesis proposed for the study argues that the relationship between GQ and the value of FDI inward stock seen about the country's GDP is positive in EU-13. We used various statistical methods to validate it, that is, hierarchical cluster analysis, contingency analysis, synthetic index values, and simple descriptive statistics. We used the WGI to assess the quality of governance. The indicators that make up the WGI examine the GQ in six dimensions: (1) voice and accountability, (2) political stability and absence of violence, (3) government effectiveness, (4) regulatory quality, (5) the rule of law, and (6) control of corruption and are widely used by academics (Dobrowolska et al., 2023; Misi Lopes et al., 2023).

2. LITERATURE REVIEW

Recent years have witnessed a growing interest in concepts such as 'governance', 'quality of governance', and 'institutional quality', described in terms of good or poor quality, which has contributed, among other things, to the development of various indicators that measure the relevance of these concepts (Agnafors, 2013; Baland et al., 2010; Dobrowolska et al., 2021, 2023; Dorożyński et al., 2020; Kaufmann, 2021; Rotberg, 2018; Rothstein & Teorell, 2008). Researchers emphasise the importance of being a capable state which is accountable vis-á-vis its citizens and observes the rule of law (Kaufmann & Kraay, 2007; Rothstein & Teorell, 2008). According to the World Bank, good governance can be described by the following characteristics: open and development-oriented policymaking, professional administration, working in the public interest, rule of law, transparent processes, and a robust civil society. In this context, it is 'central to creating and maintaining an enabling environment for development' (*Governance and Development*, 1992, p. 47) and is synonymous with sound development management. Good governance is not only related to the government (Wolfowitz, 2006); it mostly relates to the exercise of political and administrative authority at all levels to manage the affairs of a country, which was underlined in subsequent World Bank publications (Lateef, 2016; *The World Bank Group*, 1994; *World Development Report 1997*, 1997; *World Development Report 2002*, 2002). Strong institutions serve as the backdrop against which governments ensure stable economic conditions (Samarasinghe, 2018), and their governance capacity determines the effectiveness of public policies and strategies. Birdsall (2016) sees good governance as 'fair competition', and Fukuyama adds the aspect of 'execution', saying that how a regime administers itself is critical and links governance with 'government's ability to make and enforce rules, and to deliver services, regardless of whether that governance is democratic or not' (Fukuyama, 2013, p. 3).

Kaufmann et al. (1999) proposed the definition among the most frequently quoted ones. It defines governance as

> the traditions and institutions by which authority in a country is exercised. This includes (1) the process by which governments are selected, monitored and replaced, (2) the capacity of the government to formulate and implement sound policies effectively, and (3) the respect of citizens and the state for the institutions that govern economic and social interactions amongst them. (Kaufmann et al., 1999, p. 1)

Many authors equate governance with institutional quality (Kaufmann et al., 1999, 2003; Zhuang et al., 2010) and use the terms 'governance', 'institutions', and 'institutional quality' interchangeably throughout their papers. On the other hand, some believe that this is the correct way to approach them (Alonso & Garcimartín, 2018; Dobrowolska et al., 2021, 2023) or that we can say that 'governance indicators can be based on criteria related to institutional quality, adapting them to the different functions of the state' (Alonso & Garcimartín, 2018).

Institutions and their quality can be understood very broadly and at many levels of analysis; hence, we can distinguish between economic, political, legislative, or social institutions. The division is based on core aspects on which these institutions focus, such as property rights, their enforcement and contract theory, the form of government, existing constraints, the distribution of power, or the decisions and actions taken by authorities. When comparing the institutional settings of different countries, one can see significant differences between economic and political institutions. The differences concern how property rights are enforced, the legislative framework, the level of corruption, democracy versus dictatorship, constraints imposed on politicians and political elites, or electoral rules (Pęciak, 2010).

Increased interest in good governance and institutions has triggered attempts to measure the phenomenon. However, due to the multidisciplinary nature of the concept that references other non-economic and hardly measurable disciplines, such as law, sociology, or political science, it escapes quantification. Magnusson and Tarverdi (2020) claim that governance is an unobservable variable, and caution should be exercised when comparing the level of governance among countries, even if the comparison relies on the same measure. Alonso and Garcimartín (2018) provide a long list of reasons why we should take a critical approach to available governance indicators: (1) most of them are subjective; (2) some indicators are based on highly questionable assumptions (ideological bias); (3) there is a confusion between outcomes and criteria; (4) aggregation (governance/ institutional quality represent a multifaceted reality, and therefore it is not possible to capture the entire reality of governance using one single indicator); (5) low quality of information; (6) lack of a theoretical model. Although they admit that the indicators created over the last two decades are 'still far from satisfactory' (Alonso & Garcimartín, 2018), they appreciate the efforts to build new databases and sets of indicators to measure institutional quality and good governance.

The World Bank, whose WGI is widely used, is the leading institution in the construction of governance indicators (Beschel, 2018; Dobrowolska et al., 2023; Hartley & Zhang, 2018; Misi Lopes et al., 2023; Rotberg, 2018). WGI measures the quality of national governance by aggregating various indicators (essentially normative) of government effectiveness, quality of law, and control of corruption. All attributes can be estimated by crowdsourcing (surveys among experts) but are more difficult to calibrate with nationally generated statistics (Rotberg, 2018). WGI is not a perfect measure; as an indicator showing good governance, it has also been criticised, principally for its poorly defined conceptual constructs or its being based on invalid assumptions (Alonso & Garcimartín, 2018; Erkkilä, 2016; Hartley & Zhang, 2018; Thomas, 2010). Nevertheless, the WGI is widely used by academics and practitioners because it provides a globally comparative context for assessing broad measures of governance (Erkkilä, 2016).

As mentioned, the concept of governance covers the management of the development process that affects both the public and private sectors. It encompasses the principles and institutions that provide the framework for public and private activities, including accountability for economic and financial performance and the regulatory framework for business. Researchers have observed several dependencies occurring between governance and, among others, economic growth (Cooray, 2009; Fawaz et al., 2021; Khyareh, 2023; Mahran, 2022; Misi Lopes et al., 2023; Raza et al., 2021; Saidi et al., 2023; Zhuo et al., 2021), sustainable development (Dhaoui, 2019; Magoni et al., 2021; Omri & Ben Mabrouk, 2020), or entrepreneurship (Abegaz et al., 2023; Khyareh, 2023). The latter relationship seems particularly obvious – we intuitively sense that the quality of a country's institutional environment must impact the external environment of firms (Gugler et al., 2013). In this context, the importance of good governance can also be considered part of a country's investment attractiveness. Dunning (2002) already stated that institutional factors, such as good governance and economic freedom, are becoming increasingly essential and popular determinants of FDI because multinational firms' goals shift from market-seeking and resource-seeking to efficiency-seeking. Thus, better performance in aspects of institutional quality means a more active and efficient consumer market in a country with consumer demand high enough to guarantee that investment projects carried out in this country are profitable (Aibai et al., 2019).

Numerous empirical studies have demonstrated that countries with strong institutions attract more FDI (Anghel, 2005; Bénassy-Quéré et al., 2007; Buchanan et al., 2012; Dobrowolska et al., 2021, 2023; Gani, 2007; Globerman & Shapiro, 2002; Hayat, 2019; Khan et al., 2022; Mengistu & Adhikary, 2011; Peres et al., 2018; Sabir et al., 2019; Shah & Afridi, 2015). For instance, Gani (2007), who investigated the relationship between governance indicators and FDI in a group of Asian and Latin American countries, found that the rule of law, government efficiency, regulatory quality, corruption control, and political stability are positively correlated with FDI. Mengistu and Adhikary (2011) showed that political stability and absence of violence, government effectiveness, rule of law, and control of corruption were the critical determinants of FDI inflows in 15 Asian economies over the period 1996–2007, as they exhibited consistent results under different models. However, they found no significant evidence for voice and accountability and regulatory quality in FDI inflows. Shah and Afridi (2015) studied the importance of good governance for FDI inflows in South Asian Association for Regional Cooperation (SAARC) MS from 2006 to 2014. The results showed that political stability and regulatory quality significantly and positively affect inward FDI. In contrast, corruption was a factor that discouraged multinational corporations from investing in the region. On the other hand, using a panel dataset of 110 countries (developed and developing) over the period 2002–2012, Peres et al. (2018) found that institutions have an insignificant impact on FDI in developing countries because institutional structures are usually weak in these countries, while in developed countries institutional quality has a positive and significant effect on FDI. Authors used corruption and the rule of law as measures of institutional quality. They infer that the relevance of governance indicators tends to be a critical point in attracting FDI inflows.

Subject-matter literature also offers analyses whose results suggest that the quality of governance does not affect FDI or economic growth. Examples of such studies providing evidence for a negative and insignificant relationship between GQ and inflows of FDIs include, for example, Saidi et al. (2023) and Nondo et al. (2016). The first of these studies covered 102 developing countries from 1996 to 2014, while the second was carried out for 45 sub-Saharan African countries from 1996 to 2007. The countries examined scored very low on all dimensions of institutional quality. As stressed by the authors, the main findings need to be considered with great caution as they do not discount the importance of institutional quality in the development process of these countries. It seems likely that 'institutional quality may affect FDI indirectly by stimulating other variables, including human capital, infrastructure, and health of workers – which in turn directly affect FDI' (Nondo et al., 2016, p. 1). Saidi et al. (2023) also presented similar conclusions and comments.

In general, unsatisfactory institutional quality may become an obstacle to the inflow of FDI, as it poses certain investment risks and leads to the overall higher cost of doing business (Aziz, 2018). Asiedu (2005) showed that corruption, lack of the rule of law, and political instability discourage FDI inflows, Daude and Stein (2007) came to the same conclusions concerning unpredictable policies and lack of government involvement. It is often highlighted that foreign investors appreciate having no problems with the regulatory framework, bureaucracy, judiciary, property rights, contract execution, or performance and content requirements. Weak institutions are like a tax because they increase the investment cost, thus impeding the inflow of FDI (Buchanan et al., 2012). Therefore, governments should be ready to 'adjust policies and institutions', as otherwise, they may experience smaller FDI streams that may hinder economic growth (Van Bon, 2019).

The region of CEE, particularly countries that joined the EU in 2004 and later, has attracted many foreign investors over the last two decades. During this time, these countries have seen several changes that affected their governance and institutional quality. These changes have been driven by various factors, such as privatisation, globalisation, and marketisation, and have focussed primarily on improving the existing body of law, ensuring high-quality legislation and law-making procedures, improving law enforcement by the judiciary and administration to improve business certainty and protect the interests of entrepreneurs, improving the institutional capacity of government departments to perform services that are crucial for entrepreneurs, or improving the performance of tax administration. New EU MS (EU-13 MS) are relatively rarely investigated regarding the relationship between good governance and FDI inflow. Broader studies (covering not just this group of countries but the entire region of CEE) revealing the impact of institutional quality on investment attractiveness can be found in, for example, Dobrowolska et al. (2021, 2023), Dorożyński et al. (2020), Doytch and Eren (2012), or Owczarczuk (2020). The studies demonstrate that CEE countries differ significantly regarding the overall quality of governance (Dobrowolska et al., 2023).

3. FDI INFLOW TO THE EU-13 MS

Multinational enterprises (MNEs) are looking for optimal locations in almost all countries and regions around the world that are politically and economically safe. A foreign investor is primarily interested in finding a specific location where he could bring his project to a successful conclusion. However, in the last few years, we have experienced several shocks that have affected business investment decisions. These have been felt in many parts of the world, including CEE.

The first shock that brought about a substantial drop in global FDI was the COVID-19 pandemic, which hit in 2020, bringing FDI flows back to the level reported in 2005 (in 2020, FDIs fell by 33% to USD 1 trillion). The crisis was the most painful in potentially productive types of FDI, that is, greenfield investment in industry and infrastructural projects. After a strong rebound in 2021, global FDI fell again by 12% in 2022 to USD 1.3 trillion, mainly due to overlapping global crises – the war in Ukraine, high energy prices, and soaring public debt in many countries. The decline was primarily felt in developed economies, where FDI fell 37% to USD 378 billion, mainly in Europe and North America (World Investment Report, 2021, 2023).

Subsequently, the war in Ukraine has produced numerous turbulences and risks relating to security but also political and economic issues, which are still ongoing. Nevertheless, investors continue to see the EU-13 as an attractive, relatively low-cost location with a skilled workforce for their projects. Investing in one of the new EU member state gives unrestricted access to the entire EU market. Although the EU-13 MS vary considerably in their ability to attract FDI, they are attractive for potential investors as a region.

At the end of 2022, the total value of the FDI inward stock in three leading countries of the EU-13 (Poland, Malta, and the Czech Republic) was more significant than the value of FDI in all other new EU countries combined (ca. USD 698 billion compared to USD 534 billion) (see Fig. 3.1). Poland is the unquestionable leader in this ranking. However, it should be considered that its population potential is close to 64% of the EU-13.

Yet, the same values reveal a different picture when we look at the FDI inward stock in relation to GDP (see Fig. 3.2). In this perspective, Malta is an undisputed leader, followed by Cyprus, Estonia, and the Czech Republic (respectively, 1,281%, 205%, 77%, and 70% of their GDP). At the bottom of the ranking are Poland, Lithuania, Romania, and Slovenia, whose share of FDI stock in GDP is lower than 40%. These data point to the need to examine the institutional factors that may be partly responsible for these disparities.

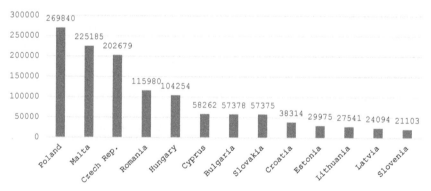

Fig. 3.1. FDI Inward Stock in Millions of USD (as of the End of 2022, Current Prices). *Source*: Own elaboration based on United Nations Conference on Trade and Development (UNCTAD) statistical database.

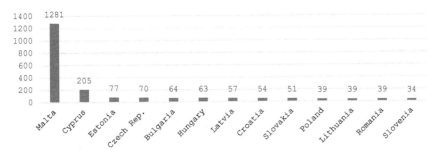

Fig. 3.2. FDI Inward Stock as a % of GDP (as at the End of 2022). *Source*: Own elaboration based on United Nations Conference on Trade and Development (UNCTAD) statistical database.

4. THE QUALITY OF GOVERNANCE BASED ON THE WORLDWIDE GOVERNANCE INDICATORS

The question of GQ has for many years been examined by diverse institutions and international organisations that have assessed it for individual countries or regions of the world. As a result, annual reports with rankings of countries have started to be produced based on selected assessment criteria. Foreign investors often check these rankings seeking data that would help them make informed location decisions and by authorities responsible for economic policy, including national, regional, or local investment incentives schemes.

Several comparative studies are based on aggregate data related to GQ and rankings published by the World Bank, the European Central Bank, the International Institute for Management Development, and the World Economic Forum. The problem with institutional quality indicators is that they are usually highly correlated (Buchanan et al., 2012; Globerman & Shapiro, 2002). To avoid the problem, we used the six aggregate governance measures, such as the Worldwide Governance Indicators, which are presented with their definitions in Table 3.1.

Table 3.1. Definitions of GQ Indicators in the WGI.

Indicator	Definition
Voice and accountability	Measures perceptions of the extent to which a country's citizens can participate in selecting their government, as well as freedom of expression, freedom of association, and free media
Political stability and absence of violence	Measures perceptions of the likelihood of political instability and politically motivated violence, including terrorism
Government effectiveness	Measures perceptions of the quality of public services, the quality of the civil service and the degree of its independence from political pressures, the quality of policy formulation and implementation, and the credibility of the government's commitment to such policies
Regulatory quality	Measures perceptions of the ability of the government to formulate and implement sound policies and regulations that permit and promote private sector development

(Continued)

Table 3.1. (*Continued*)

Indicator	Definition
Rule of law	Measures perceptions of the extent to which agents have confidence in and abide by the rules of society, particularly the quality of contract enforcement, property rights, the police, and the courts, as well as the likelihood of crime and violence
Corruption control	Measures perceptions of the extent to which public power is exercised for private gain, including forms of corruption, whether insignificant or significant, as well as the capture of the state by elites and personal interests

Source: GQ indicators are adapted from the World Bank. Metadata Glossary (2024).

These aggregate indicators are combinations of the opinions expressed by entrepreneurs, citizens, and experts who participated in surveys in developed and developing countries. They are based on more than 30 individual data sources supplied by various survey institutes, experts, non-governmental organisations (NGOs), international organisations, and companies. These data sources are then processed and combined to create the six aggregate indicators mentioned above using a statistical methodology commonly called an unobserved components model. This methodology is known for generating margins of error for each governance estimate. These margins of error need to be considered when comparing countries in different periods.

5. GQ AND FDI INFLOW INTO THE EU-13 MS – STATISTICAL ANALYSIS

We employed hierarchical cluster analysis methodology in the first step to preselect countries representing similar GQ. This type of analysis is typically used to identify homogeneous groups of elements based on selected characteristics in a given set of data (James et al., 2014; Lasek, 2002). Using Ward's method, one of the agglomerative methods of hierarchical cluster analysis, we obtained a dendrogram showing a hierarchical structure arranged in order of decreasing similarity of the components in our set (see Fig. 3.3).

The analysis allowed us to divide all of the EU-13 MS into three groups that represent similar levels of GQ:

(a) Group 1_{gov}: The Czech Republic, Slovenia, Malta, Cyprus, and Estonia.
(b) Group 2_{gov}: Latvia, Lithuania, Poland, Slovak Republic, and Hungary.
(c) Group 3_{gov}: Bulgaria, Romania, and Croatia.

Hierarchical cluster analysis was successfully deployed to distinguish groups of countries with similar GQ, yet it failed to tell us which group performs better. Therefore, in the second step, we compared the GQ among the three groups. We constructed an authors' original *synthetic index of governance quality* (SIGQ) for each EU-13 member state based on the data from 2004 to 2022. This measure is a sum of percentile ranks for the countries published by the WGI for six dimensions of governance over the investigated period. The ranking of the EU-13 MS based on the SIGQ is presented in Fig. 3.4.

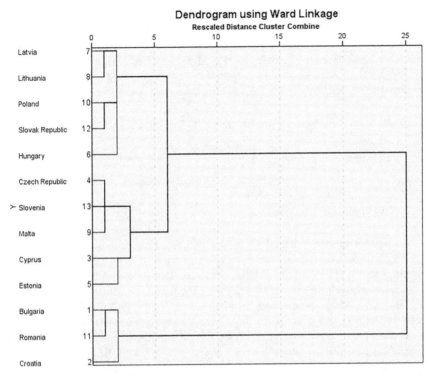

Fig. 3.3. Dendrogram for the EU-13 MS Obtained Using Ward's Linkage Method. *Source*: Own compilation using PS IMAGO.

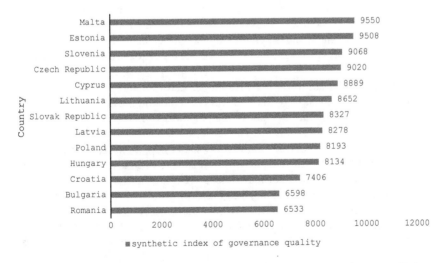

Fig. 3.4. Ranking by the SIGQ in the EU-13 MS, 2004–2022. *Source*: Own compilation using PS IMAGO.

Using the SIGQ, we calculated the mean value of the index for the three groups of countries. The ranking revealed that the highest GQ was reported by countries from Group 1_{gov}: the Czech Republic, Slovenia, Malta, Cyprus, and Estonia. On the other hand, Group 3_{gov}, Bulgaria, Romania, and Croatia, are where investors can expect the lowest quality of governance. The mean values of the SIGQ for group 3 are significantly lower than for the other two (see Table 3.2).

Table 3.2. The Mean Value of the SIGQ for the EU-13 MS, 2004–2022.

Group	Country	Mean of SIGQ
Group 1_{gov}	Czech Republic, Slovenia, Malta, Cyprus, Estonia	9,206.86
Group 2_{gov}	Latvia, Lithuania, Poland, Slovak Republic, Hungary	8,316.79
Group 3_{gov}	Bulgaria, Romania, Croatia	6,845.77

Source: Own compilation using PS IMAGO.

Then, we extended our analysis to include partial rankings showing index values for six dimensions of GQ (see Fig. 3.5). Estonia leads in three of the six partial rankings and is second in two. Malta, the Czech Republic, and Slovenia also perform relatively well. In almost all categories, the weakest performers are Romania and Bulgaria, which joined the EU in 2007, and Croatia in 2013. The differences between the best and worst performing countries in each sub-ranking reach 70%.

In the third stage, we analysed the descriptive statistics of the FDI inward stock in relation to GDP for the EU-13 at the end of 2022. It is clear from Table 3.3 that we are dealing with very diverse data, highly skewed, and with high kurtosis. The 5% trimmed mean and *M*-estimators differ significantly from the mean, indicating the absence of homogeneity in the examined population.

Given the circumstances, we divided the countries into three groups arranged in ascending order of FDI inward stock as a % of GDP based on measures of position such as percentiles (33 and 66). We transformed the FDI inward stock as a % of GDP variable measured on a numerical scale into a variable measured on an ordinal scale. As a result, we obtained the following groups of countries:

(a) Group 1_{fdi}: Cyprus, the Czech Republic, Estonia, and Malta.
(b) Group 2_{fdi}: Bulgaria, Croatia, Hungary, Latvia, and Slovak Republic.
(c) Group 3_{fdi}: Lithuania, Poland, Romania, and Slovenia.

Based on the above analyses, in the study's next step, we looked at the relationship between the GQ in the EU-13 MS from 2004 to 2022 and FDI inward stock as a share of GDP at the end of 2022. The correlation analysis started with drafting the scatterplot for the variables (see Fig. 3.6).

The scatterplot confirms previous conclusions, which revealed a considerable differentiation of the FDI inward stock as a share of GDP among the EU-13 mainly due to the value of this variable for Malta. Therefore, we decided to assess how much the SIGQ differs across the three distinguished groups of the EU-13 arranged in the ascending order of FDI as a % of GDP based on the measures of position such as percentiles (see Fig. 3.7).

Quality of Governance Attracts Foreign Investors 35

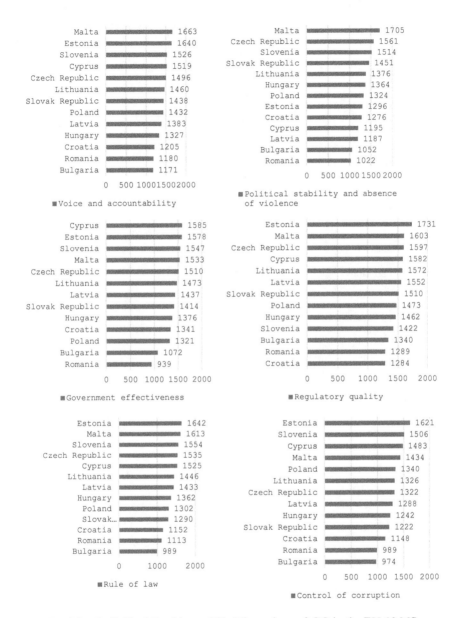

Fig. 3.5. Individual Rankings of Six Dimensions of GQ in the EU-13 MS, 2004–2022. *Source*: Own compilation using PS IMAGO.

It turned out that the highest median of the SIGQ among the EU-13 MS was found for Group 1_{fdi}, meaning that the most significant inflows of FDI as a share of GDP are typical of countries with the highest GQ. The median values are lower in Group $2_{fdi,}$ which comprises countries with moderate FDI

Table 3.3. FDI Inward Stock in Relation to GDP in the EU-13 (as at the End of 2022).

Descriptives	Statistic	Standard Error
Mean	159.43	94.23
5% Trimmed mean	104.12	
Standard deviation	339.77	
Minimum	33.77	
Maximum	1,280.69	
Range	1,246.92	
Interquartile range	34.41	
Skewness	3.51	0.62
Kurtosis	12.44	1.19
Percentiles 33	46.24	
Percentiles 50	56.91	
Percentiles 66	65.69	
M-Estimators		
Huber's *M*-estimator[a]	57.63	
Tukey's biweight[b]	53.20	
Hampel's *M*-estimator[c]	53.31	
Andrews' wave[d]	53.20	

Source: Own compilation using PS IMAGO.
[a]The weighting constant is 1.339.
[b]The weighting constant is 4.685.
[c]The weighting constants are 1.700, 3.400, and 8.500.
[d]The weighting constant is 1.340*pi.

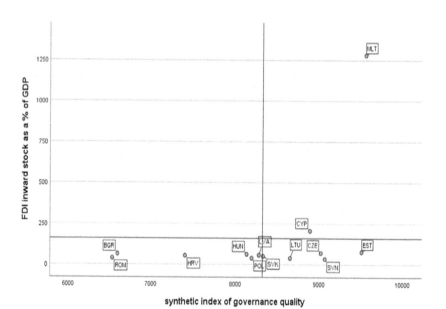

Fig. 3.6. Scatterplot for the SIGQ and FDI Inward Stock as a Share of GDP.
Source: Own compilation using PS IMAGO.

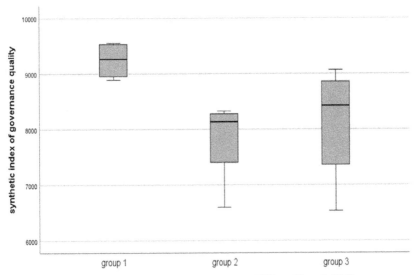

Fig. 3.7. Boxplot for the SIGQ in Three Groups of Countries Based on the FDI Inward Stock as a % of GDP in the EU-13 MS as at the End of 2022. *Source*: Own compilation using PS IMAGO.

inward stock as a share of GDP. In addition, we investigated the relevance of individual dimensions of GQ for FDI inflows. The results of our considerations are presented in Figs. 3.8(a)–(f). The distribution of median values in all areas covered by the study is analogous to the distribution in the synthetic index. The most significant differences between the groups can be found in the following dimensions: *voice and accountability*, *government effectiveness*, *regulatory quality*, and the *rule of law*.

The contingency table (Table 3.4) was created as a result of first grouping countries in the ascending order of FDI as a share of GDP based on percentiles and then dividing them into groups representing a similar quality of governance. By examining the data from Table 3.4, one may assume that countries with higher GQ usually report higher FDI inward stock as a % of GDP (e.g. the Czech Republic, Malta, Cyprus, and Estonia). The country that is an exception to this rule is Slovenia.

To assess the power of the correlation between the dimensions of GQ and FDI inward stock as a share of GDP, we used the contingency coefficient (see Table 3.5). The value of the latter for the six dimensions of GQ for the EU-13 was 0.657, indicating a moderate positive correlation between the QG and FDI inward stock as a % of GDP. The values of the contingency coefficients between the six dimensions of GQ and FDI as a % of GDP suggest that five of the six dimensions matter for investment inflows. A significantly lower contingency coefficient value was obtained only for one variable, that is, political stability and absence of violence.

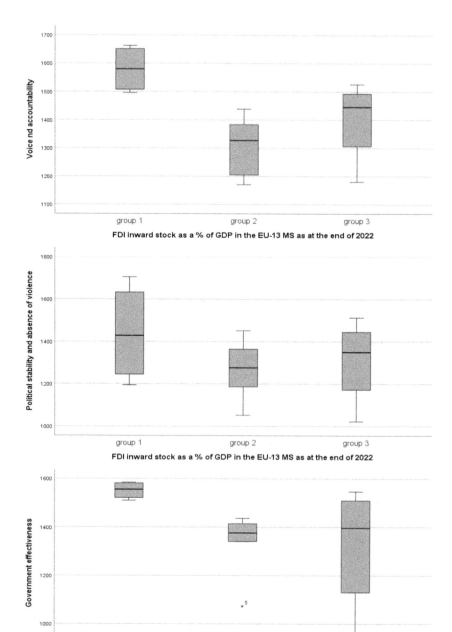

Quality of Governance Attracts Foreign Investors 39

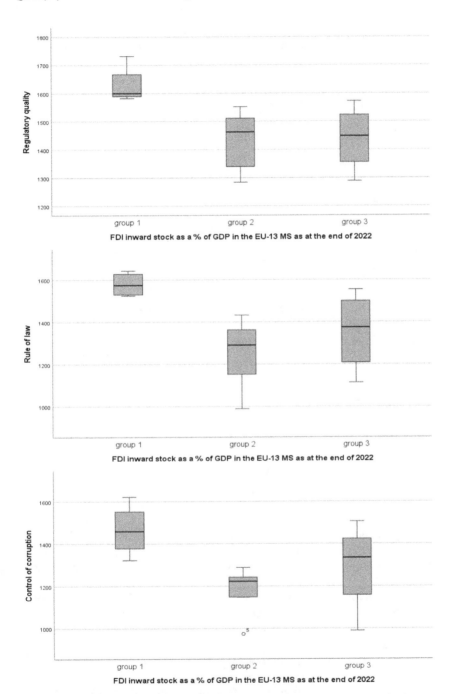

Fig. 3.8 (a–f). Boxplot for the SIGQ of Six Dimensions of Governance in Groups of Countries Based on FDI Inward Stock as a % of GDP. *Source*: Own compilation using PS IMAGO. *Note*: Number 5 – Bulgaria.

Table 3.4. Correlation Matrix for Groups of the EU-13 MS for the GQ and FDI Inward Stock as a % of GDP.

Groups of Countries with Similar Levels of FDI Inward Stock as a % of GDP	Groups of Countries with Similar GQ			Total
	Group 1_{gov} Czech Republic, Slovenia, Malta, Cyprus, Estonia	Group 2_{gov} Latvia, Lithuania, Poland, Slovak Republic, Hungary	Group 3_{gov} Bulgaria, Romania, Croatia	
Group 1_{fdi} Cyprus, Czech Republic, Estonia, Malta	4	0	0	4
Group 2_{fdi} Bulgaria, Croatia, Hungary, Latvia, Slovak Republic	0	3	2	5
Group 3_{fdi} Lithuania, Poland, Romania, Slovenia	1	2	1	4

Source: Own compilation using PS IMAGO.

Table 3.5. Contingency Coefficients Between the Six Dimensions of Governance and FDI Inward Stock as a % of GDP in the EU-13 MS.

Dimensions of Governance	Contingency Coefficient
(1) Voice and accountability	0.595
(2) Political stability and absence of violence	0.298
(3) Government effectiveness	0.590
(4) Regulatory quality	0.709
(5) Rule of law	0.595
(6) Control of corruption	0.595
Six dimensions of governance	0.657

Source: Own compilation using PS IMAGO.

6. CONCLUSIONS

The principal goal of this chapter was to assess the GQ in the EU-13 MS after the EU accession and to examine the relationship between the GQ and FDI inward stock as a % of GDP, reflecting the investment attractiveness of countries. The literature review and our statistical analysis led us to the following conclusions:

(a) There is a long list of location determinants for MNEs. Still, most economists and international business (IB) researchers agree that institutional quality is one of the main determinants of the investment attractiveness of countries.

(b) Numerous studies have confirmed that better GQ in host countries helps to attract more FDI projects. In contrast, weak and ineffective business environments discourage foreign investors due to political and legal instability, bureaucracy, lack of accountability and transparency, inactive mechanisms to reduce corruption, and other institutional constraints.

(c) The EU-13 MS, despite their many internal problems (e.g. public debt, inflation, unstable government) and external issues (e.g. war in Ukraine, limited access to resources), are still one of the most attractive investment locations in the world. This is also due to their membership in the EU and access to the single internal market.

(d) The EU-13 differs significantly in terms of the overall GQ, as measured by the WGI, and its six main dimensions. At the same time, we found that the countries covered by the study can be divided into groups representing similar quality of governance. Using hierarchical cluster analysis, we selected three groups. The countries in these groups show similar characteristics, for example, political stability, rule of law, and control of corruption.

(e) Statistical analysis showed a moderate yet positive correlation between GQ and the inflow of FDI, which confirms our hypothesis. The most important of the partial variables is the quality of the regulatory framework, which measures the perceptions of the government's ability to formulate and successfully put in place sound policies and regulations that permit and promote private sector development.

(f) It is, therefore, undeniable that institutional quality is one of the statistically significant factors differentiating the investment attractiveness of the new EU MS. At the same time, the study's results confirm that improving the quality of governance in all its dimensions can effectively boost the competitiveness of CEE in relation to other areas in the world. It is all the more critical as the region's comparative advantage based on cheap and abundant labour and low production costs is insufficient in the long run.

REFERENCES

Abegaz, M. B., Debela, K. L., & Hundie, R. M. (2023). The effect of governance on entrepreneurship: From all income economies perspective. *Journal of Innovation and Entrepreneurship, 12*(1), 1. https://doi.org/10.1186/s13731-022-00264-x

Agnafors, M. (2013). Quality of government: Toward a more complex definition. *American Political Science Review, 107*(3), 433–445. https://doi.org/10.1017/S0003055413000191

Aibai, A., Huang, X., Luo, Y., & Peng, Y. (2019). Foreign direct investment, institutional quality, and financial development along the belt and road: An empirical investigation. *Emerging Markets Finance and Trade, 55*(14), 3275–3294. https://doi.org/10.1080/1540496X.2018.1559139

Alam, A., & Shah, S. Z. A. (2013). Determinants of foreign direct investment in OECD member countries. *Journal of Economic Studies, 40*(4), 515–527.

Alonso, J. A., & Garcimartín, C. (2018). Measuring governance as if institutions matter: A proposal. In D. V. Malito, G. Umbach, & N. Bhuta (Eds.), *The Palgrave handbook of indicators in global governance* (pp. 69–95). Springer International Publishing. https://doi.org/10.1007/978-3-319-62707-6_4

Anghel, B. (2005). *Do institutions affect foreign direct investment?* [Mimeo, Universidad Autónoma de Barcelona].

Asiedu, E. (2005). *Foreign direct investment in Africa: The role of natural resources, market size, government policy, institutions and political instability* [WIDER Working Paper Series, 2005/24, Article RP2005-24].

Aziz, O. G. (2018). Institutional quality and FDI inflows in Arab economies. *Finance Research Letters, 25*, 111–123. https://doi.org/10.1016/j.frl.2017.10.026

Baiashvili, T., & Gattini, L. (2020). *Impact of FDI on economic growth: The role of country income levels and institutional strength* [EIB Working Papers, 2020/02]. https://ideas.repec.org//p/zbw/eibwps/202002.html

Bajo-Rubio, O. (2021). The role of foreign direct investment in growth: Spain, 1964–2013. *Applied Economic Analysis, 30*(90), 263–276. https://doi.org/10.1108/AEA-07-2021-0157

Baland, J.-M., Moene, K. O., & Robinson, J. A. (2010). Chapter 69-governance and development. In D. Rodrik & M. Rosenzweig (Eds.), *Handbook of development economics* (pp. 4597–4656). Elsevier. https://doi.org/10.1016/B978-0-444-52944-2.00007-0

Bénassy-Quéré, A., Coupet, M., & Mayer, T. (2007). Institutional determinants of foreign direct investment. *The World Economy, 30*(5), 764–782. https://doi.org/10.1111/j.1467-9701.2007.01022.x

Beschel, R. P. (2018). Measuring governance: Revisiting the uses of corruption and transparency indicators. In D. V. Malito, G. Umbach, & N. Bhuta (Eds.), *The Palgrave handbook of indicators in global governance* (pp. 161–179). Springer International Publishing. https://doi.org/10.1007/978-3-319-62707-6_7

Beugelsdijk, S., Smeets, R., & Zwinkels, R. (2008). The impact of horizontal and vertical FDI on host country economic growth. *International Business Review, 17*(4), 452–472. https://doi.org/10.1016/j.ibusrev.2008.02.004

Birdsall, N. (2016). Middle-class heroes: The best guarantee of good governance. *Foreign Affairs, 95*(2), 25–32.

Blomström, M., Fors, G., & Lipsey, R. E. (1997). Foreign direct investment and employment: Home country experience in the United States and Sweden. *The Economic Journal, 107*(445), 1787–1797. https://doi.org/10.1111/j.1468-0297.1997.tb00082.x

Blomström, M., Lipsey, R. E., & Zejan, M. (1992). *What explains developing country growth?* [NBER Working Paper, 4132, pp. 1–31]. https://doi.org/10.3386/w4132

Buchanan, B. G., Le, Q. V., & Rishi, M. (2012). Foreign direct investment and institutional quality: Some empirical evidence. *International Review of Financial Analysis, 21*, 81–89. https://doi.org/10.1016/j.irfa.2011.10.001

Cooray, A. (2009). Government expenditure, governance and economic growth. *Comparative Economic Studies, 51*(3), 401–418.

Daude, C., & Stein, E. (2007). The quality of institutions and foreign direct investment. *Economics and Politics, 19*(3), 317–344.

Dhaoui, I. (2019). Good governance for sustainable development. *Munich Personal RePEc Archive, 92544*, 1–9.

Dobrowolska, B., Dorożyński, T., & Kuna-Marszałek, A. (2021). Institutional quality and its impact on FDI inflow: Evidence from the EU member states. *Comparative Economic Research. Central and Eastern Europe, 24*(4), 23–44.

Dobrowolska, B., Dorożyński, T., & Kuna-Marszałek, A. (2023). The quality of governance and its impact on FDI inflows. A comparative study of EU member states. *Comparative Economic Research. Central and Eastern Europe, 26*(3), 7–30. https://doi.org/10.18778/1508-2008.26.19

Dorożyński, T., Dobrowolska, B., & Kuna-Marszałek, A. (2020). Institutional quality in Central and East European countries and its impact on FDI inflow. *Entrepreneurial Business and Economics Review, 8*(1), 91–110. https://doi.org/10.15678/EBER.2020.080105

Doytch, N., & Eren, M. (2012). Institutional determinants of sectoral FDI in Eastern European and Central Asian countries: The role of investment climate and democracy. *Emerging Markets Finance & Trade, 48*, 14–32.

Dunning, J. (2002). Determinants of foreign direct investment: Globalization induced changes and the role of FDI policies. In *Annual World Bank conference on development economics, Europe 2002–2003: Toward pro-poor policies-aid.* World Bank Publications.

Erkkilä, T. (2016). Global governance indices as policy instruments: Actionability, transparency and comparative policy analysis. *Journal of Comparative Policy Analysis: Research and Practice, 18*(4), 382–402. https://doi.org/10.1080/13876988.2015.1023052

Fawaz, F., Mnif, A., & Popiashvili, A. (2021). Impact of governance on economic growth in developing countries: A case of HIDC vs. LIDC. *Journal of Social and Economic Development, 23*(1), 44–58. https://doi.org/10.1007/s40847-021-00149-x

Fukuyama, F. (2013). What is governance? *Center for Global Development, 314*, 1–18.

Gani, A. (2007). Governance and foreign direct investment links: Evidence from panel data estimations. *Applied Economics Letters, 14*(10), 753–756. https://doi.org/10.1080/13504850600592598

Globerman, S., & Shapiro, D. (2002). Global foreign direct investment flows: The role of governance infrastructure. *World Development, 30*(11), 1899–1919. https://doi.org/10.1016/S0305-750X(02)00110-9

Globerman, S., & Shapiro, D. (2003). Governance infrastructure and US foreign direct investment. *Journal of International Business Studies, 34*(1), 19–39. https://doi.org/10.1057/palgrave.jibs.8400001

Governance and development. (1992). The World Bank. https://doi.org/10.1596/0-8213-2094-7

Gugler, K., Mueller, D. C., Peev, E., & Segalla, E. (2013). Institutional determinants of domestic and foreign subsidiaries' performance. *International Review of Law and Economics, 34*, 88–96. https://doi.org/10.1016/j.irle.2013.01.003

Hartley, K., & Zhang, J. (2018). Measuring policy capacity through governance indices. In X. Wu, M. Howlett, & M. Ramesh (Eds.), *Policy capacity and governance: Assessing governmental competences and capabilities in theory and practice* (pp. 67–97). Springer International Publishing. https://doi.org/10.1007/978-3-319-54675-9_4

Hayat, A. (2019). Foreign direct investments, institutional quality, and economic growth. *The Journal of International Trade & Economic Development, 28*(5), 561–579. https://doi.org/10.1080/0963 8199.2018.1564064

Hossain, M. S., & Rahman, M. Z. (2017). Does governance facilitate foreign direct investment in developing countries? *International Journal of Economics and Financial Issues, 7*(1), 164–177.

James, G., Witten, D., Hastie, T., & Tibshirani, R. (2014). *An introduction to statistical learning with applications in R*. Springer. https://doi.org/10.1007/978-1-4614-7138-7_2

Kaufmann, D. (2021). *It's complicated: Lessons from 25 years of measuring governance*. Brookings. https://www.brookings.edu/articles/its-complicated-lessons-from-25-years-of-measuring-governance/

Kaufmann, D., & Kraay, A. (2007). *Governance indicators: Where are we, where should we be going?* The World Bank. https://doi.org/10.1596/1813-9450-4370

Kaufmann, D., Kraay, A., & Mastruzzi, M. (2003). *Governance matters III: Governance indicators for 1996–2002* [Policy Research Working Paper 3106]. https://elibrary.worldbank.org/doi/abs/10.1596/1813-9450-3106

Kaufmann, D., Kraay, A., & Zoido-Lobatón, P. (1999). *Governance matters. The World Bank* [Policy Research Working Paper 2196, pp. 1–61].

Khan, H., Weili, L., & Khan, I. (2022). The role of institutional quality in FDI inflows and carbon emission reduction: Evidence from the global developing and belt road initiative countries. *Environmental Science and Pollution Research, 29*(20), 30594–30621. https://doi.org/10.1007/s11356-021-17958-6

Khyareh, M. M. (2023). Entrepreneurship and economic growth: The moderating role of governance quality. *FIIB Business Review*, 1–10. https://doi.org/10.1177/23197145231154767

Labidi, M. A., Ochi, A., & Saidi, Y. (2024). Relationship analysis between FDI and economic growth in African countries: Does governance quality matter? *Journal of the Knowledge Economy*, 1–30. https://doi.org/10.1007/s13132-023-01710-1

Lasek, M. (2002). *Data mining. Zastosowania w analizach i ocenach klientów bankowych*. Biblioteka Menedżera i Bankowca.

Lateef, K. S. (2016). *Evolution of the World Bank's thinking on governance. Background paper: Governance and the law* (pp. 1–36). World Bank. https://doi.org/10.1596/26197

Magnusson, L. M., & Tarverdi, Y. (2020). Measuring governance: Why do errors matter? *World Development, 136*, 105061. https://doi.org/10.1016/j.worlddev.2020.105061

Magoni, M., Adami, R., & Radaelli, R. (2021). Governance for sustainable development. In W. Leal Filho, A. Marisa Azul, L. Brandli, A. Lange Salvia, & T. Wall (Eds.), Partnerships for the goals (pp. 547–561). Springer International Publishing. https://doi.org/10.1007/978-3-319-95963-4_79

Mahran, H. A. (2022). The impact of governance on economic growth: Spatial econometric approach. *Review of Economics and Political Science, 8*(1), 37–53. https://doi.org/10.1108/REPS-06-2021-0058

Mengistu, A. A., & Adhikary, B. K. (2011). Does good governance matter for FDI inflows? Evidence from Asian economies. *Asia Pacific Business Review, 17*(3), 281–299. https://doi.org/10.1080/13602381003755765

Metadata Glossary. (2024). World Bank. https://databank.worldbank.org.

Misi Lopes, L. E., Packham, N., & Walther, U. (2023). The effect of governance quality on future economic growth: An analysis and comparison of emerging market and developed economies. *SN Business & Economics, 3*(6), 108. https://doi.org/10.1007/s43546-023-00488-3

Nondo, C., Kahsai, M. S., & Hailu, Y. G. (2016). Does institutional quality matter in foreign direct investment? Evidence from sub-Saharan African countries. *African Journal of Economic and Sustainable Development, 5*(1), 12–30. https://doi.org/10.1504/AJESD.2016.074441

OECD. (2002). *Foreign direct investment for development: Maximising benefits, minimising costs.* Organisation for Economic Co-operation and Development. https://www.oecd-ilibrary.org/finance-and-investment/foreign-direct-investment-for-development_9789264199286-en

Omri, A., & Ben Mabrouk, N. (2020). Good governance for sustainable development goals: Getting ahead of the pack or falling behind? *Environmental Impact Assessment Review, 83*, 106388. https://doi.org/10.1016/j.eiar.2020.106388

Owczarczuk, M. (2020). Institutional competitiveness of Central and Eastern European countries and the inflow of foreign direct investments. *Catallaxy, 5*(2), 87–96. https://doi.org/10.24136/cxy.2020.008

Pęciak, R. (2010). Niektóre wskaźniki pomiaru jakości instytucji. *Prace Naukowe Uniwersytetu Ekonomicznego we Wrocławiu. Ekonomia, 10*(139), 27–38.

Pegkas, P. (2015). The impact of FDI on economic growth in Eurozone countries. *The Journal of Economic Asymmetries, 12*(2), 124–132. https://doi.org/10.1016/j.jeca.2015.05.001

Peres, M., Ameer, W., & Xu, H. (2018). The impact of institutional quality on foreign direct investment inflows: Evidence for developed and developing countries. *Economic Research-Ekonomska Istraživanja, 31*(1), 626–644. https://doi.org/10.1080/1331677X.2018.1438906

Raza, S. A., Shah, N., & Arif, I. (2021). Relationship between FDI and economic growth in the presence of good governance system: Evidence from OECD countries. *Global Business Review, 22*(6), 1471–1489. https://doi.org/10.1177/0972150919833484

Rotberg, R. I. (2018). Good governance: Measuring the performance of governments. In D. V. Malito, G. Umbach, & N. Bhuta (Eds.), *The Palgrave handbook of indicators in global governance* (pp. 33–48). Springer International Publishing. https://doi.org/10.1007/978-3-319-62707-6_2

Rothstein, B., & Teorell, J. (2008). What is quality of government? A theory of impartial government institutions. *Governance, 21*(2), 165–190. https://doi.org/10.1111/j.1468-0491.2008.00391.x

Sabir, S., Rafique, A., & Abbas, K. (2019). Institutions and FDI: Evidence from developed and developing countries. *Financial Innovation, 5*(1), 1–20. https://doi.org/10.1186/s40854-019-0123-7

Saidi, Y., Ochi, A., & Maktouf, S. (2023). FDI inflows, economic growth, and governance quality trilogy in developing countries: A panel VAR analysis. *Bulletin of Economic Research, 75*(2), 426–449. https://doi.org/10.1111/boer.12364

Samarasinghe, T. (2018). *Impact of governance on economic growth* [MPRA Paper]. https://mpra.ub.uni-muenchen.de/89834/

Shah, M. H., & Afridi, A. G. (2015). Significance of good governance for FDI inflows in SAARC countries. *Business & Economic Review, 7*(2), 31–52.

Singhal, P. B., & Singh, P. (2023). Role of FDI in economic growth and development: An empirical study. *European Economic Letters, 13*(3), 17–22. https://doi.org/10.52783/eel.v13i3.200

The World Bank Group: Learning from the past, embracing the future. (1994). World Bank. https://documents.worldbank.org/en/publication/documents-reports/documentdetail/904351469672188027/The-World-Bank-Group-learning-from-the-pa

Thomas, M. A. (2010). What do the worldwide governance indicators measure? *The European Journal of Development Research, 22*(1), 31–54. https://doi.org/10.1057/ejdr.2009.32

Van Bon, N. (2019). The role of institutional quality in the relationship between FDI and economic growth in Vietnam: Empirical evidence from provincial data. *The Singapore Economic Review, 64*(3), 601–623. https://doi.org/10.1142/S0217590816500223

Wolfowitz, P. (2006). *Coordinating for good governance, development committee, annual meetings 2006.* World Bank. https://documents.worldbank.org

World development report 1997: The state in a changing world. (1997). Oxford University Press. https://doi.org/10.1596/978-0-1952-1114-6

World development report 2002: Building institutions for markets – Overview. (2002). World Bank. https://documentos.bancomundial.org/es/publication/documents-reports/documentdetail/832301468330010493/World-development-report-2002-building-institutions-for-markets-overview

World Investment Report. (2021). *Investing in sustainable recovery.* UNCTAD.

World Investment Report. (2023). *Investing in sustainable energy for all*. UNCTAD.

Yao, S., & Wei, K. (2007). Economic growth in the presence of FDI: The perspective of newly industrialising economies. *Journal of Comparative Economics, 35*(1), 211–234. https://doi.org/10.1016/j.jce.2006.10.007

Younsi, M., & Bechtini, M. (2019). Does good governance matter for FDI? New evidence from emerging countries using a static and dynamic panel gravity model approach. *Economics of Transition and Institutional Change, 27*(3), 841–860. https://doi.org/10.1111/ecot.12224

Zhuang, J., de Dios, E., & Martin, A. L. (2010). *Governance and institutional quality and the links with economic growth and income inequality: With special reference to developing Asia* [SSRN Scholarly Paper 1619116]. https://doi.org/10.2139/ssrn.1619116

Zhuo, Z., Muhammad, B., & Khan, S. (2021). Underlying the relationship between governance and economic growth in developed countries. *Journal of the Knowledge Economy, 12*(3), 1314–1330. https://doi.org/10.1007/s13132-020-00658-w

CHAPTER 4

REGIONAL ECONOMIC, SOCIAL, AND HEALTHCARE DISPARITIES AMONG THE EUROPEAN UNION MEMBER STATES*

Małgorzata Stefania Lewandowska[a],
Arkadiusz Michał Kowalski[a], Dawid Majcherek
and Scott William Hegerty[b]

[a]*Warsaw School of Economics, Poland*
[b]*Northeastern Illinois University, USA*

ABSTRACT

Purpose: *The objective of this chapter is to provide an international comparative analysis of the economic, social and healthcare inequalities in the European Union (EU) from the perspective of 13 EU member states (EU-13) that have joined the union in 2004, 2007, and 2013.*

Need for study: *Significant disparities exist in the development levels among various regions and countries in the EU.*

---

*This chapter has been supported by the Polish National Agency for Academic Exchange under the Strategic Partnerships Programme, Grant Number BPI/PST/2021/1/00069/U/00001. The publication was supported by the Dean of the Collegium of World Economy of SGH Warsaw School of Economics under 'Deans Grant 2024'.

Economic Development and Resilience by EU Member States
Contemporary Studies in Economic and Financial Analysis, Volume 115, 47–66
Copyright © 2025 by Małgorzata Stefania Lewandowska, Arkadiusz Michał Kowalski,
Dawid Majcherek and Scott William Hegerty
Published under exclusive licence by Emerald Publishing Limited
ISSN: 1569-3759/doi:10.1108/S1569-375920240000115004

Methodology: *The study compares EU-13, PIGS countries (Portugal, Italy, Greece, and Spain), and EU-10 over the last 20 years, focussing on income competitiveness, unemployment rates, employment structures in services, industry, and agriculture, and social and healthcare disparities. Data on gross domestic product (GDP) per capita, internet access, and unmet medical needs are also analysed. The Summary Innovation Index (SII) is dynamically analysed to determine the key factors of international competitiveness, including innovation.*

Findings: *Employment in agriculture in EU-13 countries is five times higher than in EU-10 countries, and income gaps persist between the two regions. However, EU-13 is closing these gaps with PIGS countries. Digitalisation has improved, and there are no visible disparities in internet access. The Human Development Index and unmet healthcare needs are diminishing. Performance groups, such as Innovation Leaders and Strong Innovators, are dispersed across Europe.*

Practical implications: *This study offers a new research agenda for critically investigating economic, social, and healthcare inequality topics, which are of crucial importance. The findings may serve as the foundation for future cohesion policy development in order to maximise its effectiveness in achieving the EU's integrity.*

Keywords: EU-13; PIGS; EU-10; economic disparity; social disparity; healthcare; convergence

JEL classifications: F15; F63; I14; I15; J00

1. INTRODUCTION

As an outcome of the economic and financial crisis of 2008, the pandemic, and subsequent political instability, the issue of inequities has become increasingly prominent on the public and political agenda (OECD, 2020). Not only can inequality be associated with financial resources, but it can be related to a wide range of other elements, including access to fundamental services, such as healthcare, education, and infrastructure (Brandily, 2020). Thus, when discussing disparities among regions, this term is used to refer to varying degrees of socioeconomic development (Widuto, 2019).

In social justice theories, inequality (disparity, unfairness) refers to a lack of equality, particularly in terms of status, rights, and opportunities (Alkire et al., 2015, chapter 9). Economic inequality refers to the distribution of economic factors within a group, population, or country. The debate revolves around two perspectives: the first focuses on unequal resources (inequality of opportunities), such as access to employment or education, and the second focuses on inequality in material dimensions of human well-being (inequality of outcomes), such as income, educational attainment, and health status (UN, 2015).

In this vein, the primary objective of the EU's cohesion policy is to strengthen social, economic, and territorial cohesion while simultaneously minimising regional imbalances. The EU's cohesion policy is a fundamental principle of the EU's establishment and originates from the Treaty of Rome in 1957 (Treaty of Rome, EEC).

It enhances economic, social, and territorial cohesion within the EU. Its goal is to correct disparities among countries and regions. Cohesion policy aims to provide support to all regions and cities within the EU in employment generation, business competitiveness, economic expansion, and sustainable development enhancements to the quality of life of citizens (EC. Europa.eu, 2024). A total of €392 billion, which represents about one-third of the total EU budget, has been allocated for cohesion policy from 2021 to 2027 to achieve various development targets across all EU regions. Despite this immense spending, the disparities among EU countries and regions are still visible.

In the larger context of the EU's cohesion policy, this chapter examines the evolution of disparities in the EU regions in terms of economic, social, healthcare, and innovative performance to assess the past and current situation and its evolution within the period of 20 years. When analysing selected variables related to socioeconomic performance of different countries, we compile databases on frequently used statistical indicators. So-called σ-convergence is also examined, which occurs when the observed variable differential between countries, measured usually as the standard deviation, decreases over time.

Our research sample covers the EU as a whole (all 27 countries), the EU-13 (Bulgaria, Croatia, Cyprus, Czechia, Estonia, Hungary, Latvia, Lithuania, Malta, Poland, Romania, Slovakia, and Slovenia), the PIGS countries (Portugal, Italy, Greece, and Spain), and the EU-10 (Austria, Belgium, Denmark, Finland, France, Germany, Ireland, Luxembourg, the Netherlands, and Sweden). The analyses were conducted for years 2005–2022, beginning just after new member states joined the EU on 1 May 2004. The calculation of average includes weights based on population of each country in the selected regions.

In order to compare economic, social, and healthcare disparities among the EU countries, the following country-level data sources were used: GDP per capita in Euros, including purchasing power standard (PPS) from the EU statistics on income and living conditions (EU-SILC) and the European community household panel (ECHP) surveys (Eurostat, 2024a), unemployment as a percentage of population in the labour force (Eurostat, 2024b), tertiary sector employment based on Nomenclature statistique des Activités économiques dans la Communauté Européenne (NACE) (Eurostat, 2024c, 2024d, 2024e), the Human Development Index (HDI) (UN, 2024), internet access in households (Eurostat, 2024f), self-reported unmet needs for medical examination due to financial or distance or long waiting list (Eurostat, 2024g), and the SII (European Commission, 2024).

The remainder of this chapter is structured as follows: in the first part, we look at economic disparities among above-described groups of countries. In the next step, we look at social and healthcare disparities, and lastly, we focus on innovation performance. Discussion and conclusions make up the last part of this chapter.

2. ECONOMIC DISPARITIES

The primary features of international competitiveness include income competitiveness, which focuses on an economy's potential to ensure a set income level for its population in order to improve their quality of life. The fundamental measure of income competitiveness of an economy is the value of GDP per capita. Despite its limitations, this remains the most extensive measure of economic performance and is commonly utilised in macroeconomic assessments. This indicator has traditionally been used to categorise countries into developed and developing categories, illustrating the disparity in the socioeconomic progress of different nations (Kowalski, 2021). Using GDP per capita eliminates the impact of a country's absolute size, allowing for comparisons between countries of varying populations. To facilitate cross-country comparisons, values are converted into PPSs to adjust for variations in price levels.

Fig. 4.1, which presents the data on GDP per capita adjusted by PPSs in Euros for the period 2000–2022, shows that there are persistent but diminishing income differences between the EU-13 and the EU-10. The EU-13 converges especially quickly towards the PIGS countries, which face their own set of economic challenges. EU-13 countries have undergone considerable structural adjustments, modernising their industrial sectors and embracing service-oriented economies. These changes have improved efficiency and productivity, contributing to higher growth rates. The PIGS countries, by contrast, have struggled with structural rigidities, including labour market inflexibility and lower levels of competitiveness in some sectors.

Despite the fact that GDP per capita is commonly used in studies on global competitiveness, it has several drawbacks. For instance, it fails to accurately represent the current state of the economy, factors related to competitiveness, and various crucial aspects of the population's quality of life – such as income disparities among various social groups and the situation in the labour market. Concerning the latter, the unemployment rate is an indicator commonly used for analysing regional economic and social disparities between countries and regions (Floerkemeier et al., 2021). It directly reflects the level of economic activity and health within a region, with low unemployment rates typically associated with economic growth and stability. It is also sensitive to economic changes, making it a timely indicator of economic shifts, including those due to technological advancements, market demand fluctuations, and policy changes. Beyond economic health, the unemployment rate provides insights into social well-being and disparities. High unemployment can lead to increased poverty, reduced access to healthcare and education, and heightened social tensions (Austin et al., 2018). It has a huge impact on quality of life, as unemployment affects not just the individuals who are jobless but also their families and communities, leading to broader social issues such as increased crime rates, mental health problems, and reduced social cohesion.

Fig. 4.2, based on data on unemployment rate as a percentage of the population in the labour force, demonstrates that the unemployment rate in the EU had increased during financial crises, but it has been decreasing after 2013. It has been at a similar level in the EU-13 and the EU-10 (4.1% and 5.0% in 2022, respectively). However, the analysis demonstrates a much higher unemployment rate in the PIGS countries (10.1% in 2022) compared to other parts of Europe. The economic base in the PIGS countries, which is heavily reliant on tourism, agriculture, and services, was more vulnerable to downturns. In contrast, countries in

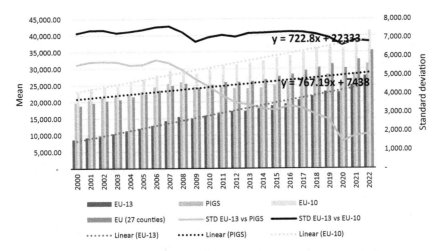

Fig. 4.1. GDP Per Capita Adjusted by Purchasing Power (PPS) in Euros.
Source: Author's elaboration based on Eurostat data (Eurostat, 2024a).

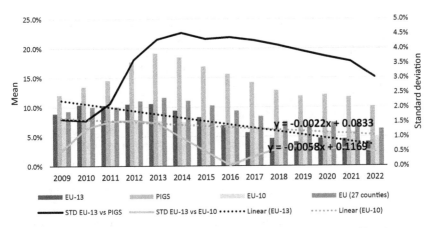

Fig. 4.2. Unemployment Rate (% of Population in the Labour Force).
Source: Author's elaboration based on Eurostat data (Eurostat, 2024b).

the EU-13 and some parts of the EU-10 benefitted from a more diversified economic base, including industrial and technological sectors, which have seen faster growth in recent years. The PIGS countries have particularly high rates of youth unemployment. Young people often face difficulties entering the job market due to a lack of experience, skill mismatches, and the economic focus on sectors that might not offer long-term career prospects. The disparity in unemployment rates across Europe underscores the importance of tailored economic and labour market policies to address specific regional challenges, promote sustainable growth, and ensure a more balanced economic recovery across the EU.

The unemployment rate provides a standardised metric for the comparison of economic and social conditions across different regions and countries. Comparing unemployment rates can also shed light on structural differences between economies, such as the reliance on certain industries, labour market flexibility, and the role of the informal sector. While the unemployment rate is a powerful tool for analysing regional economic and social disparities, it is important to use it alongside other indicators for a fuller understanding of a region's economic health and social conditions. One of the key dimensions of economic development is related to the structure of the economy, that is, employment in services, industry, and agriculture. This structure evolves as economies grow and develop, typically shifting from agriculture to industry and then to services. This transition reflects changes in productivity, technological advancements, and shifts in domestic and international demand (Herrendorf et al., 2014). Currently, we are observing the phenomenon of servitisation, characterised by an increasing presence of the service sector in the economy, as well as the broadening of service functions within industry and agriculture. Management practice changes are evident through the merging of production and services. Traditional distinctions between services and the manufacturing sector are increasingly blurred. Industrialisation of services is advancing while there is an increasing focus on the service aspect in manufacturing, often associated with the adoption of new technologies. Services are becoming more industrialised, leading to changes in traditional craft processes that resemble those seen in manufacturing (Kowalski & Weresa, 2020). These observations indicate the increasing significance of the service sector in terms of socioeconomic development. Data on employment in the tertiary sector, industry, and agriculture are presented in Figs. 4.3–4.5.

Fig. 4.3, with data on tertiary sector employment, demonstrates the long-term increase in the level of employment in the service sector within the EU. This is part of a broader structural transformation seen in advanced economies worldwide, where the service sector becomes increasingly dominant over manufacturing (Fig. 4.4) and agriculture (Fig. 4.5). This transition is driven by productivity improvements, technological advancements, and changing consumer preferences. Technological advancements have increased productivity in agriculture and manufacturing, reducing the number of workers needed in these sectors and pushing the workforce towards the service sector. The highest level of employment in the service sector is in EU-10 countries, which reflects broader economic trends and the region's ability to adapt to and capitalise on the opportunities presented by technological advancements, globalisation, and changing societal needs. As the most advanced economies, they were the first to enter a structural transformation where the share of agriculture and manufacturing in the economy declines, while services became the dominant sector. The employment structure in EU-13 has been changing in favour of the service sector; however, its share in the economy is still much lower than in the EU-10 and PIGS countries. It is a result of historical and economic background as EU-13 countries transitioned from centrally planned to market economies after the fall of communism in the late 20th century. This transition required restructuring their economies, which historically relied heavily on manufacturing and agriculture. Many EU-13 countries have

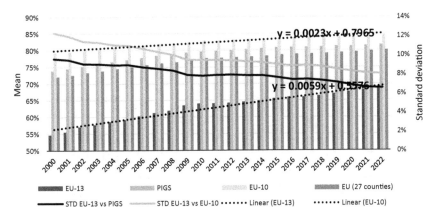

Fig. 4.3. Tertiary Sector Employment (% of Working Population). *Source*: Author's elaboration based on Eurostat data (Eurostat, 2024c).

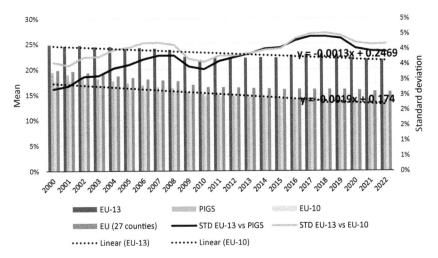

Fig. 4.4. Industry Sector Employment (% of Working Population, Except Construction). *Source: Author's elaboration based on Eurostat data (Eurostat, 2024d). Note: NACE B-E (except construction).*

maintained a strong industrial base. Fig. 4.4 shows that the decline in employment in industry (NACE B-except construction) is higher in EU-10 in comparison to EU-13 countries. Manufacturing, particularly in sectors such as automotive, electronics, and machinery, plays a significant role in their economies, attracting foreign investment and supporting exports. While the service sector is growing, it is still in a phase of development and expansion. The EU-10 and PIGS countries have historically attracted more FDI into the service sector, including financial services, retail, and telecommunications, partly due to their larger markets and

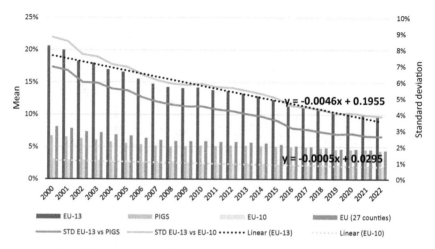

Fig. 4.5. Agriculture, Forestry, and Fishing Sector Employment (% of Working Population). *Source: Author's elaboration based on Eurostat data (Eurostat, 2024e). Note: NACE A.*

established regulatory frameworks. Fig. 4.5 shows that employment in agriculture is almost five times higher in EU-13 in comparison to the EU-10 (10% and 2%, respectively).

3. SOCIAL AND HEALTHCARE DISPARITIES

Social and healthcare disparities are measured by three indexes: The HDI (Fig. 4.6), the level of internet access in percentage (Fig. 4.7), and self-reported unmet needs for medical examination due to long distance or financial problems or long waiting list (% of population) (Fig. 4.8).

The HDI was developed by the United Nations in 1990. Since then, it has garnered significant interest from social scientists, decision-makers, and the general public. This development indicated recognition that traditional measures of income and economic performance, like real wages or GDP per capita, are inadequate for evaluating quality of life and welfare (Holubec & Tomka, 2023). The HDI is an aggregate measure of average fulfilment in three fundamental elements of human development: longevity and health, knowledge, and a reasonable quality of living. Health is assessed through 'life expectancy at birth', while education is evaluated by the 'average years of schooling for persons aged 25 and older', and the 'projected years of schooling for school-age children'. The standard of living is evaluated by 'gross national income per capita' (Human Development Report, 2021). The scores from the three HDI dimension indices are then integrated into a composite index that ranges from 0 to 1.0 (UNDP, 2022).

Fig. 4.6 presents data for the HDI from 2000 till 2021. It is visible that starting from 2000, the index is rising for all EU countries, indicating the steady growth in the quality of life in the three dimensions that the HDI index measures.

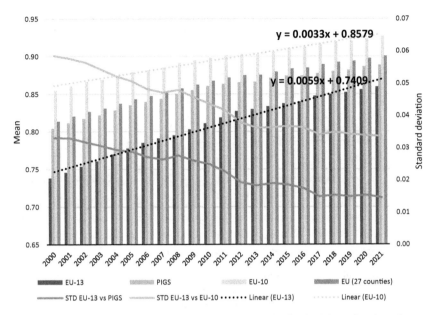

Fig. 4.6. Human Development Index. *Source*: Author's elaboration based on United Nations data (UN, 2024). https://hdr.undp.org/data-center/documentation-and-downloads

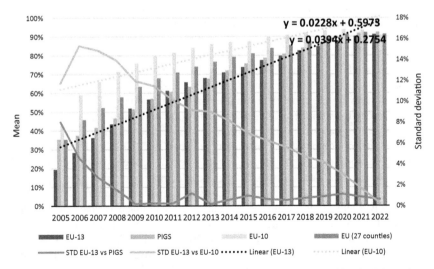

Fig. 4.7. Level of Internet Access in Households (%). *Source*: Author's elaboration based on Eurostat data (Eurostat, 2024f).

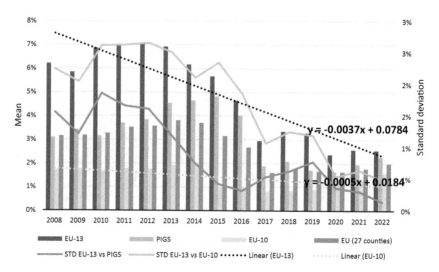

Fig. 4.8. Self-reported Unmet Needs for Medical Examination Due to Long Distance or Financial Problems or Long Waiting List (% of Population). *Source*: Author's elaboration based on Eurostat (Eurostat, 2024g).

If we look at regression parameter x for both groups of countries: EU-13 and EU-10, we can observe that the dynamics of the HDI index are almost twice as fast for the EU-13 than for the EU-10 ($0.0033x$ parameter in linear regression for EU-10 vs $0.0059x$ parameter in linear regression for EU-13). It is also worth mentioning that the HDI for EU-13 in 2000 accounted for 0.74 (where the maximum is 1.0), whereas in 2021, it attained 0.86. In the same period of time, HDI for EU-10 raised from 0.86 in 2000 to 0.93 in 2021. The trend of the convergence of EU-13 countries can be observed by the line of standard deviation for EU-13 versus EU-10, which dropped from the level of 6% in 2000 to 3% in 2022. Accordingly, the gap also decreased between EU-13 and PIGS (standard deviation line) showing the drop of that data from 3% in 2000 to 1% in 2021.

It is crucial to guarantee sufficient access to communication infrastructures in all geographical regions to address connectivity disparities caused by factors such as country size, topography, and population density (OECD. Going Digital Toolkit). In this vein, another measure that we use in order to picture the social disparities is the level of internet access in households. The information in this section is gathered yearly by the National Statistical Institutes using Eurostat's annual model 'questionnaires on ICT (Information and Communication Technologies) usage among households and individuals'. The questionnaire is revised each year. The household survey contains questions at both the household and individual levels (Statista, 2024).

Fig. 4.7 presents such data for the period from 2005 to 2022 for the EU countries.

In 2005, access to the internet in the group of EU-13 was only 19%, but for the PIGS, it attained 36% and for EU-10 43%. Over the last 17 years, a large increase in the access was reported. More than 91% of all EU-13 households have already an internet connection, as well as 92% of PIGS and 91% of EU-10 households.

Regional Economic, Social, and Healthcare Disparities

If we look at regression parameter x for both groups of countries: EU-13 and EU-10, we can observe that for EU-13, it is 3.9375, whereas for EU-10, $x = 0.2798$, showing that the dynamics of internet access percentage among EU-13 is raising much faster than for EU-10.

The trend of the convergence of EU-13 countries can be observed by the blue line of standard deviation for EU-13 versus EU-10 that dropped from the level of 11.73% in 2005 to 0.22% in 2022. Accordingly, the gap also decreased between EU-13 and PIGS (the light red standard deviation line), showing the drop of that data from 8.04% in 2000 to 0.61% in 2021. The EU is close to full convergence in terms of access to the internet among EU member states.

In order to have more comprehensive picture of the regional disparities within EU, we decided to analyse the Eurostat data on 'self-reported unmet needs for medical examination due to long distance or financial problems or long waiting list, as a percentage of the population' (Eurostat, 2024h).

As equitable availability of healthcare is one of the social determinants of citizens' health (Modranka & Suchecka 2014), health policies in both individual countries and the EU aim to provide equal access to modern and effective medical care for all Europeans (EU, 2019). Having access to medical care encompasses the supply of services that are on time, suitable, easily accessible, and responsive to user preferences and expectations. Unequal access can lead to certain groups receiving inadequate treatment compared to their demands or receiving more undesirable or less effective care than others, resulting in negative experiences, outcomes, and health status (TheKingsFund, 2022).

The EU defines unmet health requirements as the 'percentage of people who needed healthcare but did not receive it within a year before an incident'. The EU identifies three factors that contribute to unmet health needs: high treatment costs, geographic remoteness and transportation challenges, and slow system responsiveness and queues for treatment (Eurostat, 2024h).

Fig. 4.8 presents the data from 2008 till 2022 on self-reported unmet needs for medical examination due to long distance or financial problems or long waiting lists. The goal of the EU-SILC questionnaire, which is developed from the EU statistics on income and living conditions (EU-SILC), is to gather timely, comparable cross-sectional and longitudinal data on living circumstances, social exclusion, income, and poverty.

At the beginning of the surveyed period in 2008, self-reported unmet needs in the EU-13 were claimed by 6% of the population and declined in 2022 to around 2.5%. At the same period of time, this declaration for PIGS was 3.1% and 2.27% and for EU-10 countries 1.2% and 1.58%, respectively.

If we look at the regression parameter x for both groups of countries, we can observe that for EU-13, it is -0.3685, whereas for EU-10, it was $x = 0.0534$, showing that the dynamics of decline in the reported unmet needs for healthcare among EU-13 was much faster than for EU-10.

The trend of the convergence of EU-13 versus EU-10 countries can be observed by the blue line of standard deviation, which dropped from the level of 2.24% in 2008 to 0.48% in 2022. Accordingly, the gap also decreased between EU-13 and PIGS (light red standard deviation line), showing the drop of those data from 1.56% in 2008 to 0.14% in 2021. However, we should bear in mind that data are declarative, which impose limitations to interpretation to this result.

4. LEVEL OF INNOVATIVENESS

Various economic theories, such as the new theory of growth, the new economic geography, and the notion of knowledge-based economy, regard innovation as a critical determinant for international competitiveness. It drives the development of new products, services, and processes that can significantly enhance efficiency and productivity. It enables firms and economies to adapt to changing market demands and technological advancements, fostering sustainable growth. By investing in innovation, countries and businesses can differentiate themselves in the global market, creating a competitive edge that attracts investment and talent. Moreover, innovation contributes to solving complex challenges, opening up new opportunities for economic expansion and societal improvement. This dynamic process of continuous improvement and adaptation through innovation is essential for maintaining and enhancing international competitiveness (García-Sánchez et al., 2021).

One of the most important sources on the innovativeness of the European countries in an international comparative perspective is the European Innovation Scoreboard (EIS) report, which analyses various indicators related to innovation performance. These indicators are included in the SII, for which the values are provided in Fig. 4.9.

Fig. 4.9 demonstrates that the level of innovativeness in EU-13 lags behind the EU-10 and PIGS countries, with a slight convergence occurring between EU-13 and EU-10. PIGS countries are improving SII by 6 pp., while EU-13 countries are improving SII by 5 pp. in the years 2016–2022. This split is historically

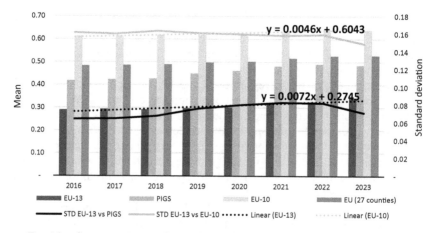

Fig. 4.9. Summary Innovation Index. *Source*: Author's elaboration based on European Commission (2024).

entrenched in the global distribution of labour, in which advancement in technology has been the realm of developed economies, which include the Triad: North America, Western Europe, and Japan (Kowalski, 2022). Western Europe benefits from well-established and supportive ecosystems for innovation, including policies, legal frameworks, and institutions that encourage research, development, and entrepreneurship. EU-13 countries are still in the process of developing these comprehensive ecosystems.

One of the main barriers to innovation in the EU-13 is a low level of collaboration between science and business, as well as between different businesses. It is associated with a lack of trust, stemming from the centrally planned economy. Another problem involves complex regulatory frameworks, which can hinder innovation by making it difficult for start-ups and established businesses to navigate legal requirements, obtain necessary permits, or comply with industry standards. Start-ups and innovative businesses in the EU-13 may find it more challenging to access venture capital and other forms of investment compared to their Western European counterparts.

This restricts their ability to scale up innovative projects. While EU-13 countries participate in EU framework programmes such as Horizon, the capacity to absorb and make the most of these opportunities is limited. Additionally, EU-13 countries have experienced the emigration of skilled and talented individuals to Western Europe and beyond, attracted by higher wages, better research facilities, and more opportunities. This brain drain challenges the development of national innovation systems as it depletes the region of the talent necessary for driving innovation. To address all barriers to innovation in the EU-13, a comprehensive approach is required, which includes increasing R&D investment, simplifying regulatory frameworks, improving educational quality with a focus on science, technology, engineering, and mathematics (STEM) fields and entrepreneurial skills, promoting collaboration between academia and industry, improving accessibility to finance, and creating a culture that values innovation and tolerates failure.

5. DISCUSSION

This chapter aimed to conduct an international comparative analysis of economic, social, and healthcare inequalities within the EU. The analysis focuses on 13 EU member states (EU-13) that have joined the union in 2004, 2007, and 2013, contrasted with the PIGS countries and the EU-10. This study looks for convergence between EU-13 and EU-10 or the PIGS countries in the above dimensions.

A considerable amount of EU financing is allocated to structural and cohesion programmes, which aim to achieve economic convergence and cohesion. It was therefore extremely important to evaluate whether convergence occurs inside the EU. There are notable differences in the levels of development among different regions and countries in the EU, particularly following its expansion in the early 21st century. This expansion brought together many Western European countries with robust market economies and most of the EU-13 countries transitioning from central economic planning systems. After the detailed analysis of economic, social, healthcare, and innovativeness indicators, we may conclude that:

- There are persistent income gaps between Western European countries (EU-10, PIGS) and EU-13 countries. However, the EU-13 countries have been steadily converging with Western Europe, with the convergence process particularly rapid in catching up with the GDP per capita of PIGS economies.
- The unemployment rate in the EU decreased after 2013, with similar levels in the EU-13 and EU-10, but significantly higher in PIGS, especially among young people.
- The long-term employment shift towards the service sector within the EU reflects a global structural transformation in advanced economies, driven by productivity gains, technological advancements, and evolving consumer preferences. While Western European countries lead in service sector employment, showcasing their adaptability to technological and societal changes, the EU-13 are also transitioning towards services, albeit at a slower pace due to their historical emphasis on manufacturing and agriculture.
- The level of HDI for EU-13 countries has grown steadily within the last 20 years, indicating the growth of quality of life in this region. Although it is still lower than the one of Western countries, the convergence of that indicator is visible.
- The level of internet access reported by individuals is on the raise, and the almost full convergence between EU-13 and EU-10 countries is clearly noticeable.
- Data on self-reported unmet needs for medical examinations due to long distance or financial problems or long waiting lists, derived from the EU-SILC, show that overall, the problem is slightly diminishing, and the drop is clearly visible among the EU-13 countries, allowing one to draw the conclusion regarding convergence with the EU-10 countries.
- Innovation levels in the EU-13 are behind those in Western and Southern Europe (EU-10 and PIGS), with only slight convergence noted with the EU-10. The EU-13 faces challenges like low collaboration between science and business and between businesses, complex regulatory frameworks, limited access to venture capital, and brain drain due to the emigration of skilled individuals.

The synthetic overview of the obtained results for all the studied dimensions is presented in Table 4.1.

Our results, especially for the data on innovativeness, are consistent with an analysis of financial data from finished and ongoing projects under Horizon 2020 (European Commission, 2020), the largest EU funding programme for research and innovation, with a budget of almost €80 billion for the years 2014 to 2020. The analysis showed a notable imbalance in the allocation of EU funds for health, demographic change, and well-being between countries in Western Europe and Central and Eastern Europe (CEE). A policy encouraging cooperation between research groups in the EU15 and the EU13 should be implemented in order to rectify this discrepancy. Participants in the EU13 should become more engaged as a result of this. If not, there will be a greater difference in the ability of EU member states to innovate (Lewandowska, 2022).

Regional Economic, Social, and Healthcare Disparities

Table 4.1. Synthetic overview of the results

Dimension	Indicator	Period	Cohesion with	
			PIGS countries	EU10 countries
Economic	GDP per capita	2000–2022	**	*
Economic	Unemployment	2009–2022		**
Economic	Employment in tertiary sector	2000–2022	**	**
Social	HDI	2000–2021	***	***
Social	Internet access	2005–2022	***	***
Health	Unmet need	2008–2022	***	***
Innovation	SII	2016–2023	*	

Source: own elaboration

Attention:

***if standard deviation between regions in relation to EU-13 average <5% (strong cohesion).

**if standard deviation between regions in relation to EU-13 average between 5% and 15% (medium cohesion).

*if standard deviation between regions in relation to EU-13 average between 15% and 25% (weak cohesion).

Empty: no cohesion.

More promising results were obtained by Grafström and Alm (2024), who investigated the level of technological divergence or convergence across EU member states, considering the efficacy of the EU's pronounced convergence targets and looking at six key indicators: scientific journal publications, patents, high-tech exports, gross domestic expenditure on R&D, government budget on R&D, and human resources in science and technology as a share of the active population. For the data from 2000 through 2019, they found out gradual catching up in terms of innovative skills among EU member states.

As already shown, the EU is close to full convergence in terms of access to the internet among EU member states. Also, the other data indicate that in 2022, only 2.4% of the EU population lacked the financial means to access the internet. Data for individual countries show, however, that Romania had the highest percentage of people at risk of poverty unable to afford an internet connection at 25.0%, followed by Bulgaria at 20.5%, and Hungary at 16.5%. Denmark and Finland had the lowest shares at 1.0%, followed by Cyprus and Luxembourg at 1.5% (Eurostat, 2023).

There is a positive trend of convergence in unemployment, employment in the tertiary sector, HDI, and medical access among the EU-13 and EU-10 countries. The introduction of digital innovation, especially in the healthcare, may be one of the solutions that speed up this process (Majcherek et al., 2023).

However, still more effort should be undertaken to regional disparities in GDP per capita, agriculture employment, and SII in order to achieve better convergence and reduce regional disparities in those dimensions. If locations closer to the technology frontier benefit more from lower knowledge costs, this could lead to an increasing productivity gap between more and less advanced areas, sometimes called as 'left behind'. An important concern regarding 'left behind' areas is that once a region, city, or locality loses its economic traction and falls behind faster-growing places, it becomes hard for the 'left behind' area to reverse its decline and regain its growth and activity (Fiorentino et al., 2023, Pike et al., 2023, Tomaney et al., 2023). Widening country differences inside the EU may pose a threat to its long-term stability and cohesion (Antonelli & Fusillo 2023).

6. CONCLUSIONS

We may conclude that despite the huge effort taken by the EU as a whole, regional disparities (although diminishing over time) are still present.

The COVID pandemic era showed that in order to reduce the existing inequalities, traditional market failure tools are insufficient (Bourdin & Levratto, 2023). To advance the economy, the idea of the 'Entrepreneurial State' (Mazzucato, 2013) should be implemented. In order to do this, governments must create new markets and introduce new goods and services rather than just preserving the ones that already exist (Mazzucato, 2018, 2019, 2021).

Unfortunately, in the realm of policy, there are no silver bullets or universally applicable solutions. The convergence is a long-lasting process, which requires the implementation of a wise, but at the same time realistic, approach. As a remedy, an idea to implement the '3I' policy is proposed, cantered on three pillars that overlap and reinforce one another. These are *Investment*: designed to create the qualifications that people will require in the future and at the same time design socioeconomic and environmental circumstances for human flourishing; *Insurance*: implemented to protect people from the unavoidable eventualities of uncertain times while also safeguarding their capabilities; and *Innovation*: the process of creating capabilities that do not currently exist (UNDP, 2022). Especially, innovation will be crucial for effectively overcoming the numerous unpredictable difficulties that lie ahead. The most essential reason for policymakers to have an extensive knowledge of innovation is the function that innovation plays in boosting enterprise efficiency and a country's economic growth (Crépon et al., 1998; Van Leeuwen & Klomp, 2006). The diversity of levels from which innovation policy has an impact should also be taken into account. One of the effects of globalisation is de-territorialisation, also associated with the concept of disembodying or decontextualisation of relationships. Paradoxically, the loosening of local ties does not translate into a reduced role of regional policy; on the contrary, processes of decentralisation of decisions give them new, greater importance. However, one should also remember about the role of innovation policy pursued at the supranational level, the premises of which may be different from the premises of policy pursued at the local or regional level, an example of which is the policy within EU. Coordination of policies carried out at so many levels is a major challenge. It is important that support from different levels does not overlap one with the other and, more importantly, does not have contradictory effects (Kuhlmann, 2001).

This chapter has highlighted concerns that necessitate additional investigation. The results point out that the role of cohesion policy ought to go much beyond basic investment. It is important for it to have a significant impact by prioritising organisation and capacity building, including initiatives for collaboration and support members of civil society and other stakeholders (McKay et al., 2024).

Also, it is necessary to develop policies that go beyond the EU boundaries and are specifically designed to address the unique needs and challenges of each current candidate countries: Albania, Bosnia and Herzegovina, Georgia, Moldova, Montenegro, North Macedonia, Serbia, Turkey, Ukraine, and potentially Kosovo (European Union Enlargement, 2024). These policies should promote both economic growth and integration of future member states in line with the requirements and goals set by the EU (European Commission, 2024a).

And lastly, our analysis shows that an alternative strategy is necessary, one that reinforces Europe's top-performing regions while developing novel methods to foster opportunities in regions experiencing industrial decline and underdevelopment. There is ample new theory and data to substantiate this strategy, which is called 'place-sensitive distributed development policy', possible to implement only when the quality of institutions is enhanced (Iammarino et al., 2019). This postulate goes in line with the results by Bernardelli and Próchniak (2023), showing that relatively often countries with the same model of capitalism (continental, Nordic, Mediterranean, liberal and patchwork, the latter that characterise countries from the CEE region) are highly similar to each other. This means that the institutional environment in a given country, including the model of capitalism, partially explains the similar time paths of financial and macroeconomic variables in EU countries. Unfortunately, in many European regions, insufficient institutional ability is a major obstacle to development. The state of local structures and administration, particularly in terms of increasing faith in government and its competence, affects the potential for regional prosperity and success (Di Cataldo & Rodrıguez-Pose, 2017). In poor institutional ecosystems, investing in other economic growth drivers such as infrastructure, skills, and innovation frequently yields limited returns. It calls for the necessity of surpassing conventional strategies and guiding areas towards self-transformation by venturing into interconnected sectors and engaging in more intricate initiatives, which, in certain situations, involves cultivating innovative economic initiatives (Boschma et al., 2023).

Summing up, we do believe that this comprehensive research, presenting an international comparative analysis of economic, social, and healthcare inequalities within the EU, has generated novel insights into the problem of regional inequalities, at the same time serving as a basis for policymakers implementing cohesion policy. This chapter has also highlighted anxiety that necessitates additional investigation, concerning the design of future policy, particularly in light of the new EU enlargement.

REFERENCES

Alkire, S., Foster, J. E., Seth, S., Santos, M. E., Roche, J. M., & Ballon, P. (2015). *Multidimensional poverty measurement and analysis*. Oxford University Press.

Antonelli, C., & Fusillo, F. (2023). The limited transferability of knowledge, patent costs and total factor productivity: European evidence. *The Journal of Technology Transfer*. https://doi.org/10.1007/s10961-023-10057-3

Austin, B. A., Glaeser, E. L., & Summers, L. H. (2018). *Jobs for the Heartland: Place-based policies in 21st century America* (No. w24548). National Bureau of Economic Research. https://doi.org/10.3386/w24548

Bernardelli, M., & Próchniak, M. (2023). Analiza podobieństwa państw Unii Europejskiej w zakresie stabilności systemu finansowego, ścieżek zmian cen i wzrostu gospodarczego przy wykorzystaniu metody dynamic time warping. *Ekonomia Międzynarodowa, 42*, 5–25. https://doi.org/10.18778/2082-4440.42.01

Boschma, R., Miguelez, E., Moreno, R., & Ocampo-Corrales, D. B. (2023). The role of relatedness and unrelatedness for the geography of technological breakthroughs in Europe. *Economic Geography, 99*(2), 117–139.

Bourdin, S., & Levratto, N. (2023). Regional implications of COVID-19. *International Regional Science Review, 46*(5–6), 515–522. https://doi.org/10.1177/01600176231189433

Brandily, P., Brébion, C., Briole, S., & Khoury, L. (2021). A poorly understood disease? The impact of COVID-19 on the income gradient in mortality over the course of the pandemic. *European Economic Review, 140*. https://doi.org/10.1016/j.euroecorev.2021.103923

Crépon, B., Duguet, E., & Mairesse, J. (1998). Research, innovation and productivity: An econometric analysis at the firm level. *Economics of Innovation and New Technology, 7*(2), 115–158.

Di Cataldo, M., & Rodrıguez-Pose, A. (2017). What drives employment growth and social inclusion in EU regions? *Regional Studies, 51*, 1840–1859.

EC. Europa.eu. (2024). https://ec.europa.eu/regional_policy/policy/what/investment-policy_en

European Union Enlargement. (2024). European Commission. https://commission.europa.eu/strategy-and-policy/policies/eu-enlargement_en

European Commission. (2020). *Horizon 2020*. Retrieved January 7, 2021, from https://ec.europa.eu/programmes/horizon2020/en/h2020-section/societal-challenges

European Commission. (2024a, February). *Directorate-General for regional and urban policy, forging a sustainable future together – Cohesion for a competitive and inclusive Europe* [Report of the high-level group on the future of cohesion policy]. Publications Office of the European Union. https://data.europa.eu/doi/10.2776/974536

European Commission. (2024b). https://research-and-innovation.ec.europa.eu/statistics/performance-indicators/european-innovation-scoreboard_en#documents-and-media

European Union. (2019). *The State of Health in the EU: Companion Report 2019.*

Eurostat. (2023). *How many EU people can afford an internet connection?* https://ec.europa.eu/eurostat/web/products-eurostat-news/w/edn-20230801-1

Eurostat. (2024a). https://ec.europa.eu/eurostat/databrowser/view/sdg_10_10/default/table?lang=en

Eurostat. (2024b). https://ec.europa.eu/eurostat/databrowser/view/une_rt_a__custom_9235262/default/table?lang=en

Eurostat. (2024c). https://ec.europa.eu/eurostat/databrowser/view/nama_10_a64_e__custom_9235489/default/table?lang=en

Eurostat. (2024d). https://ec.europa.eu/eurostat/databrowser/view/nama_10_a64_e__custom_9235489/default/table?lang=en

Eurostat. (2024e). https://ec.europa.eu/eurostat/databrowser/view/nama_10_a64_e__custom_9235489/default/table?lang=en

Eurostat. (2024f). https://ec.europa.eu/eurostat/databrowser/view/isoc_ci_in_h__custom_9239623/default/table?lang=en

Eurostat. (2024g). https://ec.europa.eu/eurostat/databrowser/view/hlth_silc_08__custom_9239809/default/table?lang=en

Eurostat. (2024h). *HLTH_UNM.* https://ec.europa.eu/eurostat/databrowser/explore/all/popul?lang=en&subtheme=hlth.hlth_care.hlth_unm&display=list&sort=category&extractionId=hlth_silc_08b

Fiorentino, S., Glasmeier, A. K., Lobao, L., Martin, R., & Tyler, P. (2023). 'Left behind places': What are they and why do they matter? *Cambridge Journal of Regions, Economy and Society, 17*(1), 1–16. https://doi.org/10.1093/cjres/rsad044.

Floerkemeier, M. H., Spatafora, M. N., & Venables, A. (2021). *Regional disparities, growth, and inclusiveness.* International Monetary Fund. https://doi.org/10.5089/9781513569505.001

García-Sánchez, A., Siles, D., & de Mar Vázquez-Méndez, M. (2021). Competitiveness and innovation: effects on prosperity. In A. García-Sánchez, D. Siles, and M. de Mar Vázquez-Méndez (Eds.), *Tourism research in Ibero-America* (pp. 35–48). Routledge.

Grafström, J., & Alm, C. (2024). Diverging or converging technology capabilities in the European Union? *Journal of Technology Transfer.* https://doi.org/10.1007/s10961-024-10070-0

Human Development Report. (2021). https://hdr.undp.org/data-center/human-development-index#/indicies/HDI

Herrendorf, B., Rogerson, R., & Valentinyi, A. (2014). Growth and structural transformation. In P. Aghion & S. N. Durlauf (Eds.), *Handbook of economic growth* (Vol. 2, pp. 855–941). Elsevier.

Holubec, S., & Tomka, B. (2023). Human development index: Changes in East Central Europe, 1913–2010. *Politická Ekonomie, 71*(2), 130–152. https://doi.org/10.18267/j.polek.1378

Iammarino, S., Rodriguez-Pose, A., & Storper, M. (2019). Regional inequality in Europe: evidence, theory and policy implications. *Journal of Economic Geography, 19*(2), 273–298.

Kowalski, A. M. (2021). Global south–global north differences. In W. Leal Filho, A. M. Azul, L. Brandli, A. Lange Salvia, P. G. Özuyar, & T. Wall (Eds.), *No poverty. Encyclopedia of the UN sustainable development goals* (pp. 389–400). Springer. https://doi.org/10.1007/978-3-319-95714-2_68

Kowalski, A. M. (2022). Innovation divide in the world economy: China's convergence towards the Triad. *Technological and Economic Development of Economy, 28*(5), 1350–1367. https://doi.org/10.3846/tede.2022.16865

Kowalski, A. M., & Weresa, M. A. (2020). Competitiveness of the service sector – A conceptual approach, definition and measurement methods. In A. M. Kowalski & M. A. Weresa (Eds.), Poland: Competitiveness report 2020. *The role of service sector* (pp. 13–25). Warsaw School of Economics Publishing. https://doi.org/10.33119/978-83-8030-400-0.2020

Kuhlmann, S. (2001). Future governance of innovation policy in Europe-three scenarios. *Research Policy, 30*(6), 953–976.

Lewandowska, M. S. (2022). Meeting grand challenges: Assessment of Horizon 2020 health, demographic change and wellbeing projects. In M. Weresa, C. Ciecierski, & L. Filus (Eds.), *Economics and mathematical modeling in health-related research* (pp. 121–145). Brill.

Majcherek, D., Hegerty, S. W., Kowalski, A. M., Lewandowska, M. S., & Dikova, D. (2023). Opportunities for healthcare digitalization in Europe: Comparative analysis of inequalities in access to medical services. *Health Policy, 139*(2024), 1–7. https://doi.org/10.1016/j.healthpol.2023.104950

Mazzucato, M. (2013). *The entrepreneurial state: Debunking public vs. private sector myths*. Anthem Press.

Mazzucato, M. (2018). *Mission-oriented research & innovation in the European Union* [Technical report]. Directorate-General for Research and Innovation (European Commission).

Mazzucato, M. (2019). *Governing missions in the European Union* [Technical report]. Directorate-General for Research and Innovation (European Commission).

Mazzucato, M. (2021). *Mission economy*. Allen Lane-Penguin.

McKay, L., Jennings, W., & Stoker, G. (2024). Understanding the geography of discontent: Perceptions of government's biases against left-behind places. *Journal of European Public Policy, 31*(6), 1719–1748.

Modranka, E., & Suchecka, J. (2014): The determinants of population health spatial disparities, comparative economic research. *Central and Eastern Europe, 17*(4), 173–185. https://doi.org/10.2478/cer-2014-0039

OECD. (2020, September). *OECD economic outlook* [Interim report]. OECD Publishing. https://dx.doi.org/10.1787/34ffc900-en.

OECD. *Going digital toolkit*. https://goingdigital.oecd.org/en/indicator/17

Pike, A., Béal, V., Cauchi-Duval, N., Franklin, R., Kinossian, N., Lang, T., Leibert, T., MacKinnon, D., Rousseau, M., Royer, J., Servillo, L., Tomaney, J., & Velthuis, S. (2023). 'Left behind places': A geographical etymology. *Regional Studies, 58*(6), 1167–1179.

Statista. (2024). https://www.statista.com/statistics/377753/household-internet-access-in-poland/

TheKingsFund. (2022). https://www.kingsfund.org.uk/insight-and-analysis/long-reads/what-are-health-inequalities

Tomaney, J., Blackman, M., Natarajan, L., Panayotopoulos-Tsiros, D., Sutcliffe-Braithwaite, F., & Taylor, M. (2023). Social infrastructure and 'left-behind places'. *Regional Studies, 58*(6), 1237–1250.

Treaty of Rome, EEC. European Parliament. https://www.europarl.europa.eu/about-parliament/en/in-the-past/the-parliament-and-the-treaties/treaty-of-rome

UN. (2015). *Concepts of inequality development* (Issues No. 1). (1957). United Nations, Department of Economic and Social Affairs (un.org).

UN. (2024). https://hdr.undp.org/data-center/documentation-and-downloads

UNDP (United Nations Development Programme). (2022). *Human development report 2021–22: Uncertain times, unsettled lives: shaping our future in a transforming world.* UNDP. https://report.hdr.undp.org/?_gl=1%2a1jn4pxu%2a_ga%2aODk4NzMyNzI0LjE3MDg3NzM3ODA.%2a_ga_3W7LPK0WP1%2aMTcwODc3Mzc4MC4xLjEuMTcwODc3NDM0My4zNi4wLjA

Van Leeuwen, G., & Klomp, L. (2006). On the contribution of innovation to multi-factor productivity. *Economics of Innovation and New Technologies, 15*(4/5), 367–390.

Widuto, A. (2019). *Regional inequalities in the EU, briefing.* European Parliament, European Parliamentary Research Service. www.eprs.ep.parl.union.eu

CHAPTER 5

AN EMPIRICAL ASSESSMENT OF THE IMPACT OF EU DIGITAL POLICIES ON ECONOMIC GROWTH

Maria Magdalena Doroiman[a] and Nicoleta Sîrghi[b]

[a]Doctoral School of Economics and Business Administration, West University of Timisoara, Timisoara, Romania
[b]Department of Economics and Economic Modelling, West University of Timisoara, Timisoara, Romania

ABSTRACT

Purpose: *The economies of the European Union (EU) countries are significantly affected by new developments in technology and digital transformations, requiring tailored policies to bridge gaps and boost economic development. This chapter analyses the impact of the digital economy in EU countries according to the level of economic growth.*

Need for study: *Assessing the interaction between economic growth and digitalisation, focussing on digital transformations, digital skills, and economic growth, this chapter designs advanced theoretical and empirical research by building on certain important research issues.*

Methodology: *The research framework relies on assessing the correlation between the Digital Economy and Society Index (DESI) and economic growth. Based on Eurostat data, this research employs panel econometric models to uncover causal relationships between digital policies and economic growth, incorporating macroeconomic variables and country-specific digital policies. The models are designed through the panel-corrected standard errors (PCSEs) method and robust regression with Huber iteration (RRHI) to ensure unbiased and robust estimates.*

Economic Development and Resilience by EU Member States
Contemporary Studies in Economic and Financial Analysis, Volume 115, 67–82
Copyright © 2025 by Maria Magdalena Doroiman and Nicoleta Sîrghi
Published under exclusive licence by Emerald Publishing Limited
ISSN: 1569-3759/doi:10.1108/S1569-375920240000115005

Findings: *Main findings include that digitalisation coordinates and digital skills are essential for improving economic development in the EU, with benefits for economic growth. These advances affect balance and overall performance and can support policymakers in strengthening their understanding of this scientific field.*

Practical implications: *The degree of development and the underlying technology underlying determine how the digital economy affects economic growth. Decision-makers can utilise these results to improve digital policies within the EU, favourably impacting the economic development of EU member states.*

Keywords: Digitalisation; digital skills; digital policies; digital transformation; economic growth; econometric modelling

JEL classifications: I31; J24; O10; O30

1. OVERVIEW OF THE CURRENT EUROPEAN CONTEXT AND THE POTENTIAL IMPACT OF DIGITALISATION

The EU has initiated and enforced an extensive set of policies that address important aspects of digital transformation, including innovation, data protection, digital skills development, cyber security, and the establishment of a digital single market. Their purpose is to encourage growth and address various societal and governance challenges, as these policies are important for the EU economy.

The impact of these policies on driving growth is multidimensional, highlighted by their potential to stimulate innovation, facilitate digital trade, ensure responsible handling of data management, and enhance competitiveness while remaining adaptable to changes in the digital landscape. Furthermore, at the EU level, there has been an emphasis on innovation through the implementation of programmes such as Horizon Europe and the European Innovation Council (EIC). These programmes provide funding for innovative research and projects and, in turn, can generate innovative growth opportunities that drive innovation.

The impact of digital policies on economic growth is a complex and multifaceted topic, encompassing various aspects of governance, economy, and society. EU policy evaluation should explore how strategic initiatives aimed at transformation are successfully influencing economic performance among member states.

An examination of the correlation between digital policies and their impact on the economies of EU countries can be done using methods that include the use of the DESI as an important tool to assess digital progress and explore its association with economic growth. It is essential to shift focus towards emphasising digital skills, an aspect that has been overlooked in favour of the infrastructure. This new perspective on the effectiveness of digital policies will provide policymakers with relevant information to refine and optimise their strategies for sustainable economic development in the EU.

The EU's digital policies contribute to the promotion of economic advancement through the encouragement of innovation and the facilitation of digital trade. These policies are essential for maintaining competitiveness in today's economy while effectively managing the challenges and opportunities brought about by ongoing digitalisation.

The current European context is marked by a concerted effort to embrace digitalisation as a strategic imperative for economic growth and societal progress. In recent years, the potential impact of digitalisation on Europe has become increasingly evident. The DESI not only highlights the progress made by individual countries but also draws attention to and emphasises areas that need improvement. As Europe faces the challenges of economic recovery, digital transformation plays a crucial role in fostering innovation, improving competitiveness, and overcoming societal challenges.

Our research addresses a significant gap in the literature on the specific relationship between digital skills, as measured by the DESI, and economic growth in EU member states. Studies on this topic for the EU member states are currently insufficient, let alone a classification of these nations based on economic development status. The objective of our research is to analyse the impact of the digital economy in EU countries according to the level of economic growth. The correlation between the DESI and economic growth was also evaluated.

The methodological framework consists of robust regression models to establish causal relationships between digital skills development and economic growth, factoring in both macroeconomic variables and country-specific digital policy implementations. After the overall introduction of the current context and the potential impact of digitalisation, the structure of our chapter comprises a literature review in Section 2, followed by the data, methodology, and an advanced empirical analysis in Section 3. Based on the results and discussions presented in Section 4 of our research, concluding remarks and policy implications enclose the main findings and provide a comprehensive perspective on the entire research endeavour.

2. LITERATURE REVIEW

2.1. Digital Policies in the EU

Ideational processes and institutional dynamics are considered crucial factors that shape policy development and drive policy change (Béland, 2009). The way policymakers perceive the significance of innovation and economic growth plays a crucial role in their decisions and impacts the agenda-setting process within EU institutions, ultimately determining the priority given to digital policies for driving economic growth. As new ideas arise and institutional contexts change, policymakers may need to adjust policies to align with shifting economic priorities and technological advancements. In this context, the digital policies of the EU have evolved, with a focus on the transformative impact of the new digital technologies on the economy and society.

While previous digital policies of the EU primarily concentrated on the telecommunications sector (Newman, 2020), developments in policy since 2010 have been driven by recognising the significance of harnessing data as a resource and driver of economic growth within the EU. The EU's digital policy has been examined in relation to various policies regarding artificial intelligence (Niklas & Dencik, 2021; Smuha, 2021; Unicane, 2021), privacy (Tsoukalas & Siozos, 2011), or general data protection regulation (GDPR) (Goyal et al., 2021; Laurer & Seidl, 2021). Policies like the AI-Act, the Digital Services Act (DSA), and the Digital Markets Act (DMA) represent this hybrid approach, where economic, legal, and strategic aspects are intertwined.

The dynamic digital governance in the EU is marked by the principles of digital sovereignty and digital constitutionalism. According to Pohle and Thiel (2020), the importance of developing technological capabilities to strengthen the digital autonomy of the EU is emphasised.

In Europe, the term 'digital sovereignty' is frequently used to refer to a well-structured, value-driven, and regulated digital environment, supporting individual rights and freedoms, security, and the competitive environment (Codagnone & Weigl, 2023). The concept relies on the EU's ambition to have control over its data, innovation capabilities, and authority to create and enforce laws in the digital environment, to strengthen its autonomy in the field by updating existing legal, regulatory, and financial measures while upholding European values.

Digital constitutionalism addresses the challenges generated by technology by recognising new rights and obligations in the digital domain (Gill et al., 2015; Padovani & Santaniello, 2018), to ensure that digital policies serve not only economic and strategic objectives but also uphold personal freedoms, privacy, and inclusive access to digital technologies and create a digital environment that respects both individual rights and collective European interests. These concepts emphasise the need for regulatory frameworks that safeguard rights and responsibilities and limit the influence of public and private entities in the digital world.

Beyond the big ambitions at the EU level, there are contradictory policies that do not stimulate European companies in the digital ecosystem, such as the GDPR compliance requirements, on one side, and the objective to reduce small- and medium-sized enterprises' (SMEs) administrative burden, on the other side. While aiming for digital innovation, we obtain only the governance of the digital (Florida, 2021). According to Codagnone and Weigl (2023), there is a 'positive policy bubble', an oversupply of policies and legislative acts in the EU, issued to enable fair and competitive digital markets and to safeguard the fundamental rights of the citizens.

Achieving an effective European digital policy necessitates overcoming ambiguity, multilevel governance, fragmentation, and overlapping policy arenas (Ackrill et al., 2013), which can create difficulties in decision-making and policy implementation. There is a need in digital policy-making to ensure that regulatory actions align with the intended goals and values, with a balanced, coherent, and effective approach at the European level.

Following the pandemic, the EU significantly increased its focus on digitisation and developed a series of new digital policies, with a role in increasing economic competitiveness. As the digitalisation wave presents both opportunities and challenges for economic growth across EU member states, a strategic approach is needed to harness its full potential (Almeida, 2021; Małkowska et al., 2021).

The EU has an extensive range of digital policies aimed at promoting digital transformation.

Our research investigates the role of EU digital policies in shaping this dynamic between digital transformations and economic growth. Thus, the econometric analysis in our model takes into account the relationship between economic growth and the DESI.

2.2. The Role of DESI in Analysing the Impact of Digital Policies in the EU

The DESI was created in 2014 not only to measure the effectiveness of the EU's digital policies in stimulating economic growth but also as a reference point for performing comparative analyses of the different facets of digitisation in each EU member state. Since then, DESI has served as an important tool for shaping European policies towards the goal of harmonious digital development. Currently DESI is the most important instrument for monitoring and assessment of a digital progress at the EU level (Banhidi et al., 2020; Kovács et al., 2022; Laitsou et al., 2020; Yalçın, 2021)

Beyond monitoring, it aims to ensure that digital transformation supports inclusive growth, addresses socioeconomic inequalities, and maintains sustainable and secure digital environments (Stavytskyy et al., 2019). By incorporating the DESI into policy frameworks, EU authorities can effectively connect progress with policy objectives, fostering a balanced and inclusive digital transformation within the EU and potentially in neighbouring regions (Liu, 2021).

The DESI has gone through refinements to better capture the evolving digital landscape and align with adjusted digital policies at the EU level. Currently, the DESI consists of four main dimensions that cover several policy areas, the 'Digital Compass' outlined in Article 4 of the EU Decision 2022/2481 (EU, 2022):

- Digital skills (formerly named Human Capital): this dimension of DESI focuses on aspects like basic and advanced digital skills, education, and training. By enhancing human capital in digital technologies, countries can better use digital tools and technologies to improve overall economic performance (Bejaković & Mrnjavac, 2020). Moreover, digital skills impact labour market indicators reflected as an increase in the employment rate (Başol & Yalçın, 2021; Katz, 2000).
- Digital infrastructures (formerly named Connectivity): this assesses the availability and quality of digital infrastructure, including fixed and broadband networks. Improved connectivity enables data exchange and information sharing, which are crucial for implementing smart energy systems and monitoring energy consumption (Qu, 2017; Zhang et al., 2021).
- Digital transformation of businesses (formerly called Integration of Digital Technology): this dimension evaluates how businesses and the public sector adopt technologies, with digitalisation being a key driver for entrepreneurship (Ghazy et al., 2022). Also, by integrating these technologies into energy systems, countries can optimise energy production processes, and distribution methods, enhance energy efficiency, and reduce waste (Noja et al., 2022).

- Digitalisation of public services (Digital Public Services): efficient digital public services can streamline administrative processes, facilitating rapid access to information and transparency, but attention should be paid to the digital inequality that might affect vulnerable citizens who do not have adequate access to technology and are not well informed (Ranchordás, 2020; Zhuk, 2022).

From Fig. 5.1, it can be seen the correlation between DESI and the 'Digital Compass', as the index has been modified (EU, 2022) and integrated into the Digital Decade Report, assuming its role as the main tool for monitoring progress towards the Digital Decade Targets for 2030.

2.3. Economic Growth Through Digitalisation

The relationship between economic growth and digitisation has been widely studied; thus, the Solow (1957) growth model shows that if there is no technological progress, there will be no sustained growth. Later, Romer (1990) placed even more importance on new technologies and efficient methods of production, as internal processes that enhance a nation's human capital are the key to economic expansion (Zhao, 2019).

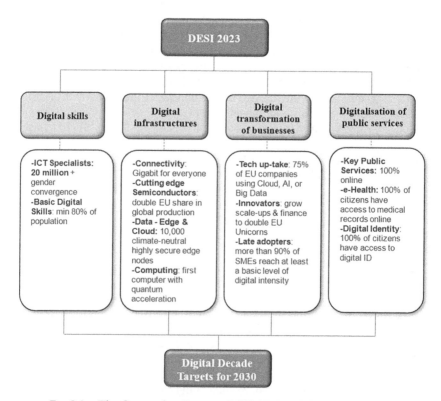

Fig. 5.1. The Connection Between DESI 2023 and the Digital Decade Targets for 2030. *Source*: Own process based on Eurostat data.

The accelerated development of digital technologies has led to the definition of new concepts to identify the components of digitalisation that could generate economic growth. In this sense, specialised studies show that in the US economy, the growth was not only due to new technological products but also due to new markets, while China's growth was initially due to the inability of the service sector to satisfy domestic demand, which led to the growth of the online markets (Danilin, 2019; Wang & Wei, 2023; Zhang et al., 2021).

Some studies strongly support the idea that digitalisation has an impact on economic growth by influencing both internal and external performance metrics. Chesbrough introduced in 2003 the concept of innovation facilitated by digital platforms as a means to accelerate innovation cycles (Durmusoglu, 2004), while Freeman and Soete (1997) argued that digital technologies have made innovation more accessible by reducing barriers to entry. This idea was also supported by Schwab (2016), who introduced the concept of the fourth industrial revolution.

Digitalisation has also significantly influenced efficiency, as digital tools have streamlined business processes and enhanced business networks (Kauffman et al., 2010). Brynjolfsson and McAfee (2014) argue that automation and data analysis have greatly improved productivity and efficiency, but on the other hand, this might cause increasing inequality in a global economy.

Dynamic capabilities have become a factor in determining a company's competitive advantage, where the effect of digitalisation enables companies to better respond to rapidly changing market conditions (Teece, 2018; Warner & Waeger, 2019).

According to Porter and Heppelmann (2014), smart connected products are reshaping competition and creating market opportunities. Digitalisation has also played an important role in integrating value chains, either through blockchain technology that could revolutionise supply chain management (Durach et al., 2021; Tapscott & Alex, 2016) or through platforms that facilitate collaboration among different economic entities, leading to more efficient and effective transactions (Beverungen et al., 2022; Loonam & O'Regan, 2022).

Furthermore, the scientific literature explores the various mechanisms through which digitalisation fosters economic growth. Through process optimisation, digital technologies reduce the workload and improve operational efficiency, resulting in increased productivity, and human resources can be redirected towards more complex activities (Ghazy et al., 2022; Sorbe et al., 2019; Zeng & Lei, 2021). Nevertheless, despite significant investments in information technology, scholars noticed a lack of corresponding increases in productivity growth, and this is called 'the productivity paradox', highlighting the complex relationship between technology investments and growth from which the human factor cannot be excluded (Murakami, 1997; van Ark, 2016). Innovative business models are other outcomes of digitalisation, enabling the development of products and services and creating opportunities for startups and established businesses to explore new markets and customer segments (Rachinger et al., 2018; Ritter & Pedersen, 2020; Tsai & Su, 2022). The adoption of digital technologies empowers businesses to enhance their competitiveness both locally and globally, and the digital tools enable companies to optimise their operations, improve customer experiences, and offer better pricing, thereby strengthening their position in the market (Dabbous et al., 2023; Porter & Heppelmann, 2014).

While digitalisation drives efficiency, and innovation, fuels market growth, and enhances competitiveness, it also brings to light concerns regarding its impact on income and social inequality, inclusivity for both individuals and businesses, and its environmental impact (Horvath & Szabo, 2019; Kwilinski et al., 2020; Xu et al., 2022). Additionally, it raises concerns about the need for comprehensive regulations addressing employment, taxation, cybersecurity, data privacy, and competition (Ackrill et al., 2013; Niklas & Dencik, 2021).

In this context, the digital policies implemented by the EU become crucial for navigating through the complexities of digitalisation to achieve the expected economic growth. The DESI holds a pivotal role within this system, serving as a comprehensive monitoring tool to evaluate the progress of the EU member states towards the digital objectives (Stavytskyy et al., 2019). By aligning digital advancements with policies, EU authorities should ensure that the digital transformation supports inclusive growth, addresses socioeconomic inequalities, and maintains sustainable and secure digital environments, thus bridging the gap between technological progress and policy objectives.

3. MODELLING THE IMPACT OF EU DIGITAL POLICIES ON ECONOMIC GROWTH

3.1. Data and Methodology

Based on the examination of the current scientific literature, we consider that our research distinguishes itself from previous studies by employing a comprehensive approach to assess the impact of current EU digital policies on economic growth. Specifically, we focus on digital skills, which are monitored at the EU level using the updated DESI components in 2023.

In our research, in order to examine the relationship between EU digital policies and economic growth, a model was built that included not only the digital skills components from DESI but also specific productivity metrics provided by Eurostat. As some of these indicators are measured at the EU level only after the pandemic period (1a2, 1a3, 1a4 – see Table 5.1), as a recognition of their relevance in a more digitalised world, the analysed period is focussed on the 2021–2022 interval for all EU-27 member states. Some of these variables are directly related to the digital goals: 1a2 'At least basic digital skills' is related to the goal of having basic digital skills for at least 80% of the population by 2030, while 1b1 'ICT specialists' is directly connected to the goal of having more than 20 million ICT specialists at the EU level by 2030, with a higher participation of women.

The indicators selected as proxies for the variables included in the empirical models are the real GDP per capita and the GDP growth rate, indicators commonly used as a proxy for economic development. It is important to note that GDP has its limitations when it comes to capturing societal well-being and long-term goals (Ward et al., 2016), and accordingly, the use of GDP per capita and the GDP growth rate are considered more relevant for economic growth in different contexts.

The digital public policies implemented in the last decade led to an increase in the number of people with basic or advanced digital skills, but still their number is

Impact of EU Digital Policies on Economic Growth

Table 5.1. Variables Used in the Empirical Analysis.

	Variables	Unit of Measure
1	1a1: Internet use	% individuals
2	1a2: At least basic digital skills	% individuals
3	1a3: Above basic digital skills	% individuals
4	1a4: At least basic digital content creation skills	% individuals
5	1a5: Enterprises providing ICT training	% enterprises
6	1b1: ICT specialists	% of total employment
7	1b2: ICT graduates	% graduates
8	Real labour productivity	% change on the previous year
9	Real gross domestic product (GDP) per capita	% change on the previous year
10	GDP growth rate	% change on the previous year

Source: Own process based on Eurostat data.

very low related to the targets: the average rate for 1a2 in 2022 is 53.92%, while 15 of the EU countries are under this level, with high polarities, as Finland (79.18%) and Netherlands (78.94%) are the top performers, while Romania (27.82%) and Bulgaria (31.18%) are far lagging. Related to the ICT specialists, in 2022, the average rate at the EU level is 4.6% of total employment, while the top performers are Sweden (8.6%) and Luxembourg (7.7%), and the lowest levels are in Greece (2.5%) and Romania (2.8%). A detailed visualisation of the relationship between basic digital skills and the prevalence of ICT specialists across EU member states is presented in Fig. 5.2.

These disparities and the significance between top and bottom performers highlight the need to prioritise digital skills in our study. In this way, the factors that contribute to the reduction of disparities can be highlighted, as well as the potential solutions to reduce the gap. This understanding will also serve as a foundation for future policy directions, emphasising the importance of tailored approaches that take into account the specific circumstances of each member state. By analysing this information, we can develop impactful strategies to improve digital literacy and skills, ensuring that all EU countries can fully participate in and reap the benefits of the digital economy.

Our analysis employs several panel econometric models to establish causal relationships between digital policy credentials and economic growth, factoring in both macroeconomic variables and country-specific digital policy implementations. The models are designed and estimated through the PCSEs method and RRHI to provide bias-free and robust estimates.

PCSE is a statistical technique used to address issues of heteroskedasticity and autocorrelation in panel data models, especially when the panel is large in terms of cross-sections (N) but not as long in the time dimension (T). PCSEs adjust the standard errors of the coefficients in regression models to provide more accurate inference, particularly in the context of time-series cross-sectional data. This method is often employed in political science and economics research to ensure the robustness of empirical findings derived from panel data analysis.

RRHI is another statistical method used to estimate regression coefficients while mitigating the influence of outliers in the data. This approach combines

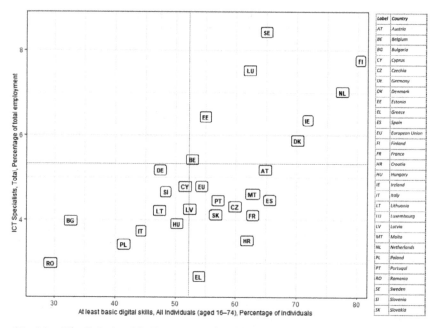

Fig. 5.2. The Relationship Between Basic Digital Skills and the Prevalence of ICT Specialists in the EU. *Source*: Own process in RStudio based on Eurostat data.

robust regression techniques with iterative procedures based on the Huber loss function to achieve more reliable parameter estimates. Observations with small residuals are given less weight, while observations with large residuals are down-weighted to reduce their influence on the parameter estimates. This iterative process helps the model adapt to the presence of outliers and improves the robustness of the regression coefficients.

3.2. Empirical Findings

Based on the descriptive statistics presented in Table 5.2, we identified a significant variation in digital engagement across different metrics; for example, while internet usage is relatively high at an average of 88.58%, the percentage of businesses providing ICT training is much lower averaging at 21.77%. We can observe a gap between basic and advanced digital skills; on average, 56.29% of the population possesses digital skills, but only 27.79% have advanced digital skills, and this suggests an opportunity for improvement in enhancing digital literacy. Regarding training, there is considerable variability among different member states as indicated by a relatively high standard deviation (7.72), and this implies that there is a wide disparity in how much training is provided across different states. Moreover, there is potential for growth in the area of digital content creation skills, since an average of 67.54% of the population already possesses basic skills in this area.

Impact of EU Digital Policies on Economic Growth

Table 5.2. Descriptive Statistics.

Variables	Observations	Mean	Standard Deviation	Minimum	Maximum
1a1: Internet use	54	88.57704	5.584165	73.93	97.97
1a2: At least basic digital skills	54	56.29407	11.98961	27.82	79.18
1a3: Above basic digital skills	54	27.79333	10.15344	7.82	51.77
1a4: At least basic digital content creation skills	54	67.54074	10.65787	41.46	83.34
1a5: Enterprises providing ICT training	54	21.7689	7.718739	5.9009	39.8
1b1: ICT specialists	54	4.874074	1.424077	2.5	8.6
1b2: ICT graduates	52	4.826923	1.854419	1.4	10.1
Real labour productivity	54	3.259259	3.219898	−4.8	11.8
Real GDP per capita % change	54	5.285185	3.232816	−0.8	15.6
GDP growth rate	54	5.264815	2.896593	−1.3	13.6

Source: Own process in Stata based on Eurostat data.

To assess the relationship between specific factors or credentials of EU digital policies and economic growth, we designed two-panel regression models. The dependent variables are two proxies of economic growth, used alternatively: the total GDP growth rate and the real GDP per capita growth rate. The explanatory variables include tailored measures of EU digital policies. The models are processed based on two advanced econometric procedures, namely PCSE and RRHI. Table 5.3 gives the benchmark regression results of digital policies related to GDP growth.

PCSEs and RRHI techniques were employed to analyse the panel data and address issues like heteroskedasticity and outliers. We found that key variables like internet use, digital skills levels, ICT training, ICT specialists, ICT graduates, and labour productivity have a notable impact on economic growth metrics.

The data processed by our model show a significant positive correlation between enterprises that provide ICT training, the number of ICT graduates, and GDP growth. This underlines the crucial role of digital education and training in driving economic growth, indicating that investment in developing digital skills is essential to improving economic performance.

However, the fact that a rise in the quantity of ICT specialists leads to reduced growth rates might suggest a complex connection between the availability of digital skills and their demand in the labour market. This could reflect a temporary mismatch or saturation in certain sectors, implying the need for policies that increase not only the quantity but also the quality and relevance of ICT specialists to meet current market requirements. As well, this is an important indicator supporting the need to enhance continuous training in this field. Specifically, higher levels of enterprises providing ICT training and more ICT graduates are associated with significantly higher GDP growth.

The robust and significant positive relationships between real labour productivity and both economic growth proxies highlight labour productivity as a pivotal factor in economic growth. This finding supports the argument that enhancing labour productivity through digital innovation is essential for ensuring sustained economic development.

Table 5.3. Regression Results

Methods:	PCSEs	RRHI	PCSEs	RRHI
Variables	GDP Growth Rate	GDP Growth Rate2	Real GDP Per Capita % Change 1	Real GDP Per Capita % Change 2
1a1: Internet use	−0.0845	−0.0709	−0.0713**	−0.0845
	(0.0653)	(0.0598)	(0.0254)	(0.0525)
1a2: At least basic digital skills	0.0149	−0.0758	0.00155	−0.0442
	(0.0919)	(0.1190)	(0.0727)	(0.1040)
1a3: Above basic digital skills	0.0878	0.111	0.0883	0.108
	(0.0615)	(0.0873)	(0.0452)	(0.0767)
1a4: At least basic digital content creation skills	−0.0283	0.0368	−0.0216	0.00634
	(0.0446)	(0.0705)	(0.0289)	(0.0619)
1a5: Enterprises providing ICT training	0.0562***	0.049	0.0252	0.0249
	(0.00885)	(0.0388)	(0.0193)	(0.0341)
1b1: ICT specialists	−0.346***	−0.292	−0.393***	−0.376
	(0.1010)	(0.2520)	(0.0658)	(0.2220)
1b2: ICT graduates	0.466***	0.300*	0.377***	0.302**
	(0.0338)	(0.1240)	(0.0356)	(0.1090)
Real labour productivity	0.671***	0.725***	0.890***	0.866***
	(0.0945)	(0.0628)	(0.0814)	(0.0551)
_cons	7.463	6.768	7.203***	8.827*
	(5.719)	(4.5110)	(1.7170)	(3.9610)
N	52	52	52	52
R^2	0.684	0.797	0.889	0.881

Source: Authors' research.
Note: Standard errors in parentheses.
$^*p < 0.05$, $^{**}p < 0.01$, $^{***}p < 0.001$.

Results are consistent in sign across different estimation procedures, thereby enhancing the reliability and stability of the estimation process.

Overall, our analysis supports existing literature by proving that digital human capital factors and productivity play an important role in driving economic growth. This study brings new shreds of evidence regarding the relationship between EU digital policies, skills development initiatives, and economic outcomes among member states.

4. CONCLUSIONS

Our research highlights the critical role that digital human capital and productivity play in driving economic growth in the EU by focussing on the development of relevant digital skills and the use of technology to enhance productivity.

Based on this analysis, we presented evidence that factors like digital skills and ICT training are vital for economic growth. This aligns with existing research indicating that a workforce equipped with digital skills is essential for harnessing technological advancements in the digital economy. These results are more relevant to the new EU member states that often face more pronounced disparities in digital skills, infrastructure, and integration of digital technology, which might impact their growth potential. Still, these challenges also provide unique opportunities for accelerated development through targeted investments in digital education, infrastructure, and innovation.

Our findings also suggest a direct relationship between the number of ICT specialists and economic growth, but only increasing their numbers without considering market demand and skill relevance may not lead to the desired outcomes. It is crucial to adopt an approach to developing ICT specialists focussing on quality, specialisation, and alignment with industry needs. As the new EU member states might have budgetary constraints and other priorities, it is critical to ensure that their education and training systems are adaptable and responsive to the evolving needs and the ICT specialists should be considered as key drivers for further innovation and competitiveness, especially in emerging industries. The study also underscores how labour productivity significantly impacts economic growth, highlighting the immense potential of digital technologies to enhance productivity. Implementing policies that foster digital innovation within businesses, particularly in sectors where substantial productivity gains can be achieved, will likely yield positive economic benefits. In order to improve labour productivity, it is crucial for the new EU member states to focus on the integration of digital technologies across all sectors, prioritising education and fostering innovation, in order to reduce the major disparities compared to other countries.

The study's results strongly support the idea that EU digital policies should prioritise digital education and training, encourage the adoption of digital technologies to enhance labour productivity, and also ensure that ICT specialist skills may remain relevant to changing market demands. It is important to develop tailored policies that address the needs and circumstances of each member state, as this may be more effective in fully harnessing the potential of digitalisation for economic growth.

In our future research, we aim to explore the long-term effects of digital policies on economic growth and explain how different sectors are influenced by digitalisation based on innovation. Also, another future research direction will be to study how digital policies can contribute to inclusive growth and reduce disparities between EU member states, which would provide more valuable information for policymakers.

REFERENCES

Ackrill, R., Kay, A., & Zahariadis, N. (2013). Ambiguity, multiple streams, and EU policy. *Journal of European Public Policy, 20*(6), 871–887. https://doi.org/10.1080/13501763.2013.781824

Almeida, F. (2021). Innovative response initiatives in the European Union to mitigate the effects of COVID-19. *Journal of Enabling Technologies, 15*(1), 40–52. https://doi.org/10.1108/JET-09-2020-0039

Banhidi, Z., Dobos, I., & Nemeslaki, A. (2020). What the overall digital economy and society index reveals: A statistical analysis of the DESI EU28 dimensions. *Regional Statistics, 10*, 42–62. https://doi.org/10.15196/RS100209

Başol, O., & Yalçın, E. C. (2021). How does the digital economy and society index (DESI) affect labor market indicators in EU countries? *Human Systems Management, 40*(4), 503–512. https://doi.org/10.3233/HSM-200904

Bejaković, P., & Mrnjavac, Ž. (2020). The importance of digital literacy on the labour market. *Employee Relations: The International Journal, 42*(4), 921–932. https://doi.org/10.1108/ER-07-2019-0274

Béland, D. (2009). Ideas, institutions, and policy change. *Journal of European Public Policy, 16*(5), 701–718. https://doi.org/10.1080/13501760902983382

Beverungen, D., Hess, T., Köster, A., & Lehrer, C. (2022). From private digital platforms to public data spaces: Implications for the digital transformation. *Electronic Markets, 32*(2), 493–501. https://doi.org/10.1007/s12525-022-00553-z

Codagnone, C., & Weigl, L. (2023). Leading the charge on digital regulation: The more, the better, or policy bubble? *Digital Society, 2*(1), 4. https://doi.org/10.1007/s44206-023-00033-7

Dabbous, A., Barakat, K. A., & Kraus, S. (2023). The impact of digitalization on entrepreneurial activity and sustainable competitiveness: A panel data analysis. *Technology in Society, 73*, 102224. https://doi.org/10.1016/j.techsoc.2023.102224

Danilin, I. V. (2019). Development of the digital economy in the USA and China: Factors and trends. *Outlines of Global Transformations: Politics, Economics, Law, 12*(6).

Durach, C. F., Blesik, T., von Düring, M., & Bick, M. (2021). Blockchain applications in supply chain transactions. *Journal of Business Logistics, 42*(1), 7–24. https://doi.org/10.1111/jbl.12238

Durmusoglu, S. S. (2004). Open innovation: The new imperative for creating and profiting from technology. *European Journal of Innovation Management, 7*(4), 325–326. https://doi.org/10.1108/14601060410565074

EU. (2022). *Decision (EU) 2022/2481 of the European Parliament and of the council of 14 December 2022 establishing the digital decade policy programme 2030.* https://eur-lex.europa.eu/legal-content/EN/TXT/PDF/?uri=CELEX:32022D2481

Freeman, L., & Soete, C. (1997). *The economics of industrial innovation.* Routledge.

Ghazy, N., Ghoneim, H., & Lang, G. (2022). Entrepreneurship, productivity and digitalization: Evidence from the EU. *Technology in Society, 70*, 102052. https://doi.org/10.1016/j.techsoc.2022.102052

Gill, L., Redeker, D., & Gasser, U. (2015). *Towards digital constitutionalism? Mapping attempts to craft an internet bill of rights* [Berkman Center Research Publication No. 2015-15]. https://ssrn.com/abstract=2687120 or http://dx.doi.org/10.2139/ssrn.2687120

Goyal, N., Howlett, M., & Taeihagh, A. (2021). Why and how does the regulation of emerging technologies occur? Explaining the adoption of the EU general data protection regulation using the multiple streams framework. *Regulation & Governance, 15*(4), 1020–1034. https://doi.org/10.1111/rego.12387

Horvath, D., & Szabo, R. Z. (2019). Driving forces and barriers of industry 4.0: Do multinational and small and medium-sized companies have equal opportunities? *Technological Forecasting and Social Change, 146*, 119–132. https://doi.org/10.1016/j.techfore.2019.05.021

Katz, L. F. (2000). Technological change, computerization, and the wage structure. In E. Brynjolfsson & B. Kahin (Eds.), *Understanding the digital economy* (pp. 217–244). The MIT Press.

Kauffman, R. J., Li, T., & van Heck, E. (2010). Business network-based value creation in electronic commerce. *International Journal of Electronic Commerce, 15*(1), 113–144. https://doi.org/10.2753/JEC1086-4415150105

Kovács, T. Z., Bittner, B., Huzsvai, L., & Nábrádi, A. (2022). Convergence and the Matthew effect in the European Union based on the DESI index. *Mathematics, 10*(4), 613. https://doi.org/10.3390/math10040613

Kwilinski, A., Vyshnevskyi, O., & Dzwigol, H. (2020). Digitalization of the EU economies and people at risk of poverty or social exclusion. *Journal of Risk and Financial Management, 13*(7), 142. https://doi.org/10.3390/jrfm13070142

Laitsou, E., Kargas, A., & Varoutas, D. (2020). Digital competitiveness in the European Union era: The Greek case. *Economies, 8*(4), 85. https://doi.org/10.3390/economies8040085

Laurer, M., & Seidl, T. (2021). Regulating the European data-driven economy: A case study on the general data protection regulation. *Policy & Internet, 13*(2), 257–277. https://doi.org/10.1002/poi3.246

Loonam, J., & O'Regan, N. (2022). Global value chains and digital platforms: Implications for strategy. *Strategic Change, 31*(1), 161–177. https://doi.org/10.1002/jsc.2485

Małkowska, A., Urbaniec, M., & Kosała, M. (2021). The impact of digital transformation on European countries: Insights from a comparative analysis. *Equilibrium, 16*(2), 325–355. https://doi.org/10.24136/eq.2021.012

Murakami, T. (1997). *The impact of ICT on economic growth and the productivity paradox.* https://www.nomurafoundation.or.jp/en/wordpress/wp-content/uploads/2014/09/19971011_Takeshi_Murakami_2.pdf

Newman, A. L. (2020). Digital policy-making in the European Union. *Policy-making in the European Union, 8,* 275–296.

Niklas, J., & Dencik, L. (2021). What rights matter? Examining the place of social rights in the EU's artificial intelligence policy debate. *Internet Policy Review, 10*(3).

Noja, G. G., Cristea, M., Panait, M., Trif, S. M., & Ponea, C. S. (2022). The impact of energy innovations and environmental performance on the sustainable development of the EU countries in a globalized digital economy. *Frontiers in Environmental Science, 10.* https://doi.org/10.3389/fenvs.2022.934404

Padovani, C., & Santaniello, M. (2018). Digital constitutionalism: Fundamental rights and power limitation in the internet eco-system. *International Communication Gazette, 80*(4), 295–301. https://doi.org/10.1177/1748048518757114

Pohle, J., & Thiel, T. (2020). Digital sovereignty. *Internet Policy Review, 9*(4).

Porter, M. E., & Heppelmann, J. E. (2014). How smart, connected products are transforming competition. *Harvard Business Review,* November 1.

Rachinger, M., Rauter, R., Müller, C., Vorraber, W., & Schirgi, E. (2018). Digitalization and its influence on business model innovation. *Journal of Manufacturing Technology Management, 30*(8), 1143–1160. https://doi.org/10.1108/JMTM-01-2018-0020

Ranchordás, S. (2020). Connected but still excluded? Digital exclusion beyond internet access. *SSRN Electronic Journal, 40,* 244–257. https://doi.org/10.2139/ssrn.3675360

Ritter, T., & Pedersen, C. L. (2020). Digitization capability and the digitalization of business models in business-to-business firms: Past, present, and future. *Industrial Marketing Management, 86,* 180–190. https://doi.org/10.1016/j.indmarman.2019.11.019

Schwab, K. (2016). *The fourth industrial revolution* (2016th ed.). World Economic Forum.

Smuha, N. A. (2021). From a 'race to AI' to a 'race to AI regulation': Regulatory competition for artificial intelligence. *Law, Innovation and Technology, 13*(1), 57–84. https://doi.org/10.1080/17579961.2021.1898300

Sorbe, S., Gal, P., Nicoletti, G., & Timiliotis, C. (2019). *Digital dividend: Policies to harness the productivity potential of digital technologies.* OECD. https://doi.org/10.1787/273176bc-en

Stavytskyy, A., Kharlamova, G., & Stoica, E. A. (2019). The analysis of the digital economy and society index in the EU. *TalTech Journal of European Studies, 9*(3), 245–261.

Tapscott, D., & Alex, T. (2016). How blockchain will change organizations. MIT Sloan Management Review. https://sloanreview.mit.edu/article/how-blockchain-will-change-organizations/.

Teece, D. J. (2018). Dynamic capabilities as (workable) management systems theory. *Journal of Management & Organization, 24*(3), 359–368. https://doi.org/10.1017/jmo.2017.75

Tsai, W.-Y., & Su, C.-J. (2022). Digital transformation of business model innovation. *Frontiers in Psychology, 13.*

Tsoukalas, I. A., & Siozos, P. D. (2011). Privacy and anonymity in the information society – Challenges for the European Union. *The Scientific World Journal, 11,* 458–462. https://doi.org/10.1100/tsw.2011.46

Unicane, I. (2021). Artificial Intelligence in the European Union: Policy, ethics and regulation. In T. Hoerber, G. Weber and I. Cabras (Eds.), *The Routledge handbook of European integrations* (pp. 254–269). Taylor & Francis.

Wang, Q., & Wei, Y. (2023). Research on the influence of digital economy on technological innovation: Evidence from manufacturing enterprises in China. *Sustainability, 15*(6), 4995. https://doi.org/10.3390/su15064995

Ward, J. D., Sutton, P. C., Werner, A. D., Costanza, R., Mohr, S. H., & Simmons, C. T. (2016). Is decoupling GDP growth from environmental impact possible? *PLOS ONE, 11*(10), e0164733. https://doi.org/10.1371/journal.pone.0164733

Warner, K. S. R., & Waeger, M. (2019). Building dynamic capabilities for digital transformation: An ongoing process of strategic renewal. *Long Range Planning, 52*(3), 326–349. https://doi.org/10.1016/j.lrp.2018.12.001

Yalçın, E. C. (2021). Efficiency measurement of digitalization on EU countries: A study based on data envelopment analysis. *International Journal of Management, Knowledge and Learning, 10* (1), 323–333. https://doi.org/10.53615/2232-5697.10.323-333

Zeng, G., & Lei, L. (2021). Digital transformation and corporate total factor productivity: Empirical evidence based on listed enterprises. *Discrete Dynamics in Nature and Society, 2021*, e9155861. https://doi.org/10.1155/2021/9155861

Zhang, W., Zhao, S., Wan, X., & Yao, Y. (2021). Study on the effect of digital economy on high-quality economic development in China. *PLOS ONE, 16*(9), e0257365. https://doi.org/10.1371/journal.pone.0257365.

Zhao, R. (2019). Technology and economic growth: from Robert Solow to Paul Romer. *Human Behavior and Emerging Technologies, 1*(1), 62–65. https://doi.org/10.1002/hbe2.116

Zhuk, I. (2022). Public administration system in the field of finance under the influence of digitalization. *Economic Affairs, 67*(3). https://doi.org/10.46852/0424-2513.3.2022.11

CHAPTER 6

PRODUCTIVITY AND COMPETITIVENESS: FUTURE CHALLENGES

Inna Šteinbuka[a], Oļegs Barānovs[b], Jānis Salmiņš[b] and Irina Skribāne[a]

[a]*University of Latvia, Latvia*
[b]*Ministry of Economics, Latvia*

ABSTRACT

Purpose: *This chapter aims to provide a comparative analysis of productivity and competitiveness in 13 new European Union member states (EU-MS).*

Need for study: *The need for this study is determined by the slow growth of productivity in the EU, the necessity of the 'productivity renaissance', and the need for considerable acceleration of productivity growth in the new EU-MS at the lower end. The authors examine the reasons for the productivity backlog in these countries. Latvia, where productivity is among the lowest in the EU, has been selected as a case study.*

Methodology: *A special methodology has been applied to assess the impact of the redistribution of labour resources on the overall productivity dynamics in the Latvian economy. The core methodological approach used in the study is the method of structural changes' impact analysis, shift-share analysis. The main sources of the statistical data used in the study are the Central Statistical Bureau of Latvia (2024), the Statistical Office of the European*

Economic Development and Resilience by EU Member States
Contemporary Studies in Economic and Financial Analysis, Volume 115, 83–97
Copyright © 2025 by Inna Šteinbuka, Oļegs Barānovs, Jānis Salmiņš and Irina Skribāne
Published under exclusive licence by Emerald Publishing Limited
ISSN: 1569-3759/doi:10.1108/S1569-375920240000115006

Union (Eurostat, 2024), and the Organization for Economic Cooperation and Development (OECD).

Findings: *The findings include the identification of the reasons for low-productivity dynamics, an impact assessment of the COVID-19 pandemic and recent geopolitical factors on productivity, a comparative analysis of productivity trends in 13 new EU-MS, especially in the Baltic states in the international context, specific conclusions on Latvia's productivity development, and future challenges.*

Practical implications: *The authors have elaborated policy recommendations for policymakers, which can be used to improve productivity and competitiveness in Latvia and other new EU-MS.*

Keywords: Productivity; competitiveness; innovation; investment; comparative analysis

JEL classifications: J30; O40

INTRODUCTION

The productivity issue has become especially relevant in the last decades when the trajectory of productivity growth in developed countries demonstrated an overall decline. The productivity growth in the European Union (EU) and the euro area remains very subdued, lagging behind the United States, other advanced economies, and emerging markets. The average productivity in the new (since 2004) EU member states (EU-MS) is significantly lower than in the 'old' EU countries. The relatively low productivity in the EU, particularly in the new EU-MS, has a negative impact on the EU's external competitiveness and requires urgent solutions. According to the OECD, many factors hold back productivity growth, including demographics, inequality, education, environment, and private and public debt. The slow productivity development is also significantly affected by the decrease in the growth of knowledge-based capital accumulation and business start-ups. The biggest problem is slowing the pace at which innovation spreads through the economy (OECD, 2015).

To achieve sound policy decisions based on impartial analysis, special institutions have been set up in most OECD countries – the Productivity Councils, which act as advisory bodies in economic policy, structural reform, and regulation. In 2015, the OECD established the Global Productivity Forum (GFP), which aims to promote international cooperation between Productivity Councils (OECD, 2022).

Likewise, the European Commission (EC) has also set up a productivity analysis dialogue platform. Based on a proposal by the EC in September 2016, the Council of the EU adopted a recommendation inviting the MS to establish National Productivity Boards (NPBs). The NPBs were envisaged as objective, neutral, and independent institutions for analysing national productivity challenges and contributing to evidence-based policymaking. At present, 19 EU-MS have an NPB. Almost half of the new EU-MS, mostly non-euro area MS (Estonia, Bulgaria, the Czech Republic, Romania, Hungary, and Poland), have not yet established an NPB. With their annual reports, NPBs contribute to evidence-based policymaking. In turn, their impact depends on the country's culture of evidence-based policymaking (i.e. whether governments are the main customers of their reports and those of other independent research institutions) (García et al., 2023).

This chapter provides a comparative analysis of productivity and competitiveness in 13 new EU-MS: Bulgaria, Croatia, Cyprus, the Czech Republic, Estonia, Hungary, Latvia, Lithuania, Malta, Poland, Romania, Slovakia, and Slovenia. The study examines the reasons for the backlog in these countries. Latvia, where productivity is among the lowest in the EU, has been selected as a case study.

The research is based on the macroeconomic approach and includes qualitative and quantitative analysis, particularly the aggregate productivity growth decomposition methods. The authors elaborated a case study of the Latvian economy to determine the impact of the redistribution of labour resources on the overall productivity dynamics. In this study, the authors used the *shift-share analysis* – a special method of impact analysis of structural changes. The case study largely reflects the results of the comprehensive Productivity Report 2023, in which the authors participated (UL Think Tank LV PEAK, 2023). The research uses statistical data from the Central Statistical Bureau of Latvia, Eurostat, OECD, and other sources.

This chapter presents productivity dynamics in 13 new EU-MS and factors contributing to productivity growth. It also describes the impact of structural changes on productivity based on Latvia's case study and focuses on the main policies for fostering productivity growth in the new EU-MS.

LITERATURE REVIEW

Productivity is considered a key engine of economic growth and competitiveness and is widely used in international comparisons and assessments of national performance. According to Nobel Laureate Paul R. Krugman (1994), 'productivity isn't everything, but in the long run, it is almost everything. A country's ability to improve its standard of living over time depends almost entirely on its ability to raise its output per worker' (p. 11).

Productivity has been very widely studied in the world scientific literature. Many monographs and articles on productivity issues can be found in scientific research collections. Theoretical research on economic growth and productivity argues that changes in physical capital, labour, and total factor productivity determine the economy's growth rate (Solow, 1956). The research makes it evident that economic development requires a structural transformation that shifts resources from less to more productive sectors of the economy (Kuznets, 1979). The differences in the ease of resource reallocation can explain why some countries are more productive than others (Parente & Prescott, 2000).

The empirical literature on economic growth and productivity supplements the fundamental research. 'This empirical research attempted to, first, test the validity of recent growth theories in contrast to (or in conjunction with) the neo-classical growth theory, and second, determine the quantitative importance of various proposed drivers of growth' (Kim & Loayza, 2019, p. 4).

Numerous working papers have been issued by international organisations, such as the OECD, the International Monetary Fund (IMF), the EC, and the World Bank (WB). The fundamental issue of these studies is seeking effective solutions for raising productivity.

The comprehensive literature analysis on Latvia's economic development allowed the authors of this chapter to elaborate on Latvia's case study (Baranovs et al., 2021), representing the evidence-based reasons for Latvia's productivity lagging.

It is increasingly recognised that productivity-enhancing policies can be a challenging task. Such a task is further complicated by the fact that when it comes to productivity, there is no 'silver bullet' solution nor a standard set of reforms that can be implemented in the same way in any country (Renda & Dougherty, 2017).

PRODUCTIVITY DYNAMICS IN 13 NEW EU-MS AND THE MOST IMPORTANT FACTORS CONTRIBUTING TO PRODUCTIVITY GROWTH

The productivity dynamics in 13 new EU-MS, except Malta and Cyprus, have been rather impressive over the past few decades, outstripping average growth rates of the EU average.

However, the new EU-MS productivity level still shows a significant lag compared to the highly developed countries. In 2022, the productivity level in the new EU-MS varies from 93% in Malta to 56% in Bulgaria of the EU average (see Fig. 6.1).

Progress in productivity convergence in the new EU-MS has been uneven over the last two decades. In the period from 2000 to 2022, among the new EU-MS, the fastest productivity convergence to the EU average was observed in Romania and the Baltic states, while there was divergence in Malta and Cyprus (see Fig. 6.2).

Some challenges to convergence have stemmed from worldwide factors – such as globalisation, digitalisation, global warming, and, more recently, pandemic and energy crises – but others are European specific, like incomplete financial integration, less effective fiscal governance, and subpar innovation performance (OECD, 2021). However, the main factor why the new EU-MS productivity level shows a significant lag is the result of low total factor productivity and significant differences in the quality of human and physical capital.

Analysis of convergence rates in the new EU-MS shows that, in general, higher productivity growth was observed after accession to the EU, which per se was a significant stimulus for foreign investment, mainly as debt-generating flows. In addition, the EU's structural funds have become an important engine that fosters productivity and growth. After the global financial crisis, a downward trend

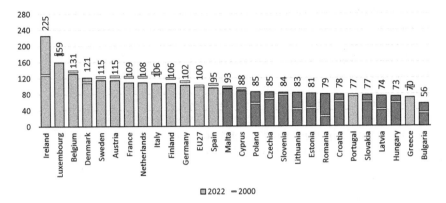

Fig. 6.1. Productivity (Gross Domestic Product (GDP) Per Employee) by Purchasing Power Standards, EU = 100. *Source*: Author compilation adapted from Eurostat database.

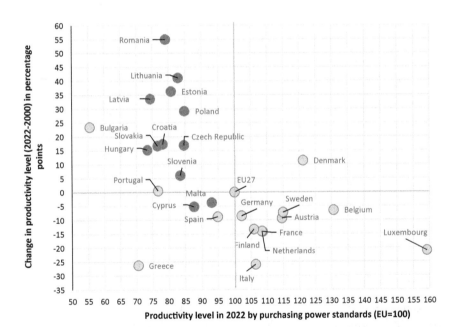

Fig. 6.2. Productivity Level in 2022 and Change in Productivity Level from 2000 to 2022 in the EU. *Source*: Author compilation adapted from Eurostat database.

of productivity growth rates can be explained by harder access to credit, hampering physical capital development, modernisation, and investment in innovation. The lack of investment remained a fundamental challenge of productivity growth after the financial crisis, particularly during the COVID-19 and energy crises. As a result, in the majority of new EU-MS, the rate of productivity convergence is slowing. Simultaneously, the risk of falling into a middle-income trap is increasing.

Productivity growth in the new EU-MS is determined by several key factors, such as:

- investments in industries and capital inflows;
- investments in human capital, improving the skills and abilities of the population, as well as increasing the amount of knowledge;
- investments in research, development, and innovation;
- deepening of integration into global value chains (GVCs) and increasing export potential;
- development of new products, services, and methods;
- the ability to use the advantages of new technologies;
- increasing the role of technical progress and digitisation; and
- skilful management of the production process, smart organisation of the concentration and territorial location of production facilities, and creation of interconnections between industries.

Productivity growth depends on price and cost competitiveness, trade and current account balances, export market shares, and a broad range of other factors affecting 'non-cost competitiveness'. These factors include the sectorial composition of trade, its quality, the capacity to keep up with product and process innovation, the attractiveness as a destination for foreign direct investment (FDI), and the capacity to exploit GVCs, which in turn depends on the quality of institutions, public administration, regulatory frameworks, human capital, digital skills, infrastructure, etc. (EC, 2023a).

After the global financial crisis, the EU in 2011 introduced a special set of regulations designed to correct risky macroeconomic developments and prevent the decrease in competitiveness within EU-MS. To this end, it was suggested that with a scoreboard of indicators such as strong growth in unit labour costs (ULCs), excessive current account deficits, unsustainable public debt, and housing bubbles, the EC identifies the countries and fundamental issues, which require in-depth economic analysis. Depending on the severity of the imbalances, the EC proposes a policy recommendation under either the 'preventive arm' or the 'corrective arm' of the macroeconomic imbalance procedure (EC, 2016).

As regards the latest macroeconomic imbalances, the '2024 European Semester: Alert Mechanism report' noted that strong nominal growth in 2022 facilitated the debt deleveraging, which should continue to be supported by inflation, easing some long-standing imbalances, while pressures from tighter financing conditions have grown. The entrenchment of deteriorations in cost competitiveness is becoming a risk, as price and cost pressures could continue to diverge, and some high inflation countries may display core inflation stickiness and high ULC growth. The current account balances broadly increased in 2023, primarily due to soaring energy prices. House price growth has eased and, in some cases, turned negative as house prices respond to higher interest rates (EC, 2023b).

Productivity and Competitiveness

Although the reasons and extent of macroeconomic imbalances in the new EU-MS are very different, external sustainability and cost competitiveness in almost all these countries are serious factors of concern. There are growing risks of weakening cost competitiveness in several new EU-MS. This is evidenced by the fact that labour costs are growing faster than productivity.

A particularly strong increase in nominal ULC can be observed in all Baltic countries. In the period from 2019 to 2022, the nominal ULC annually in Latvia grew by 16.7%, in Estonia – by 19% and in Lithuania – by 27.7%, which is much faster than the EU average (6.5%) and the average of the Eurozone countries (7.9%). The illustration of a substantial rise in labour costs and nominal ULC in the Baltic countries as compared with productivity can be clearly seen in Fig. 6.3. The significant increase in labour costs is influenced by both wage convergence processes in the integrated EU labour market and a more tense situation in the domestic labour market.

One of the most important reasons why labour costs are increasing is the shortage of labour supply (especially skilled labour), which is evidenced by the long-term low unemployment rate. In the short to medium term, measures to promote economic activities will largely determine changes in productivity and labour costs.

Productivity and competitiveness determine their export market share, which are different in all new EU-MS. For example, in all Baltic states, the export market share was increasing. However, the amplitude of growth rates is very large. In five years (2018–2022), the market share of the export of goods and services considerably increased in Lithuania (28.8%), especially impressive seems the increase of the export market share of services, which reached 51.7%. Estonia showed the second-best result compared to its closest neighbours. Despite the weakness of productivity and competitiveness factors, Latvia's export market share was also growing but much slower. It increased by 15.3% in five years, including 3.6% in

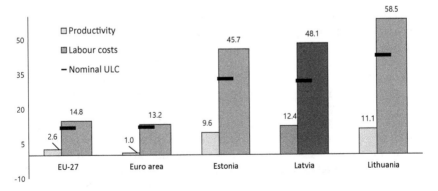

Fig. 6.3. Nominal ULC, Productivity, and Labour Costs in the Baltic States and the EU, in 2018–2022, Cumulative Changes in Percentage. *Source*: Author compilation adapted from Eurostat database.

Table 6.1. Export Market Shares – 5 Years (2018–2022) Growth in the Baltic States, % Change.

	Goods and Services	Goods	Services
Estonia	17.0	13.2	28.1
Latvia	15.3	19.9	5.5
Lithuania	28.8	21.4	51.7

Source: Eurostat database.

2022. This outcome was mainly determined by the increase in the market share of the export of goods – by 19.9% (Latvia's growth rate is slightly slower compared to Lithuania, however considerably faster compared to Estonia), while the increase in the market share of the export of services was more moderate – by 5.5% (see Table 6.1).

To overcome the risks of weakening competitiveness in the new EU-MS, it is necessary to increase the sophistication of goods exports by increasing the share of products whose competitive advantages and position in global markets are based on qualitative factors rather than low costs and price competitiveness.

STRUCTURAL CHANGES AND THE PRODUCTIVITY: CASE OF LATVIA

The choice of Latvia as a case study is determined by three reasons. First, economic growth and productivity dynamic in Latvia after EU accession are quite similar in all new EU-MS. Second, the structural factors of low productivity in Latvia are rather typical (to a different extent) for the new EU-MS. Third, since 2020, the authors of this chapter have actively participated in Latvia's productivity research and contributed to Latvia's annual productivity reports (UL Think Tank LV PEAK, 2023).

The authors conclude that fostering productivity heavily depends on knowledge-intensive activities, representing only a small share of the Latvian economy. The relatively low level of productivity in Latvia is significantly linked to structural factors. Low-tech industries strongly dominate in the structure of Latvian manufacturing. A significant share belongs to the traditional sectors such as food and wood processing, which together contribute to almost half of the total value added of manufacturing, nearly 1.5 times more than the EU average.

In 2022, only 4% of the total number of employees in manufacturing were employed in high-tech industries, which is almost twice less than the EU average. On the other hand, the employees in low and medium-low technological intensity industries accounted for nearly 84%, that is, 1.3 times more than the EU average. In 2020–2022, the productivity growth in high- and medium-high-tech industries was faster than in industries with lower technological intensity (see Fig. 6.4).

However, these sectors account for a relatively small share of the total manufacturing value added, so their contribution to overall productivity growth is

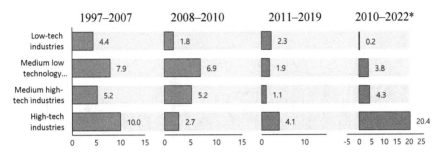

Fig. 6.4. Productivity Growth Rates in Manufacturing in Latvia by Technological Intensity, Average Per Year, in Percentage. *Source*: Author compilation adapted from Eurostat database. *Note*: *2022 – authors' assessment.

rather limited. An increase in productivity can be achieved by promoting the reallocation of resources to sectors with a higher technological and productivity level.

As Simon Kuznets (1979) argued, 'It is impossible to attain high rates of growth of per capita or worker product without commensurate substantial shifts in the shares of various sectors'. In Latvia, the impact of labour resource reallocation on productivity trajectory was assessed by applying a special methodology – a shift-share analysis described in the Economic Survey of Singapore (2018). The shift-share analysis enables to measure how the changes in overall productivity affect specific sectors, assuming no change in the number of employees. In addition, this method allows us to assess to what extent overall productivity is affected by labour force reallocation towards high-productivity sectors and sectors with more rapid productivity growth.

From 1997 to 2022, aggregate labour productivity in Latvia increased mainly due to within-sector effects. In other words, productivity increases mainly occurred in individual economic sectors, which benefitted from the substantial impact of factors such as skilled management, skilled employees, technology improvement, innovation, and favourable market conditions (see Fig. 6.5).

The shift effect (structural change) in Latvia is relatively weak – approximately 0.5 percentage points of the annual productivity growth (1997–2022). The positive structural change effect shows that during the analysed period, industries with higher productivity have attracted more employees than industries with lower productivity. However, the impact on overall productivity growth was relatively small.

It is instructive to note that during the years of rapid economic growth (1997–2007), the positive contribution of shift effect to the overall productivity growth was, on average, 0.8 percentage points per year, while in the post-crisis years (2011–2019), it was only 0.1 percentage points. During the years of economic recession (2008–2010), labour productivity in several sectors significantly decreased. However, the impact of these changes on overall productivity dynamics was partially offset by positive structural changes, that is, the greater attraction of labour resources in sectors of higher productivity. Also, during the COVID-19

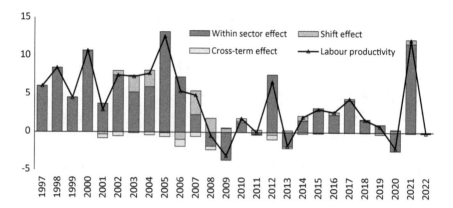

Fig. 6.5. Impact of Structural Changes on Productivity in the Private Sector in Latvia. Average per Year, in Percentage. *Source*: Author compilation adapted from Central Statistical Bureau of Latvia database.

pandemic and energy crisis (2020–2022), the shift effect was positive – labour was reallocated towards a higher productivity sector. However, its contribution to the increase in overall productivity is smaller than the within-sector effect. Significant investments in digitisation can largely explain this.

Also, in manufacturing, the increase in productivity is mainly explained by the within-sector effect. Since 1996, the contribution of the within-sector impact to the annual growth of productivity in manufacturing has been almost four percentage points. The low- and medium-low technology industries – the food industry and woodworking – significantly contributed to the increase in productivity. On the contrary, the contribution of high and medium-high technologies was almost twice as low.

Although the shift effect on the productivity dynamics in manufacturing is weak – 0.5 percentage points of the annual productivity growth (1997–2022), it is primarily related to the gradual redistribution of labour resources in favour of industries with higher technological activity. In recent years, the contribution of the high- and medium-high-tech sector to the productivity growth in manufacturing has been increasing, indicating positive structural changes in the industry.

The shift-share analysis demonstrates that between 2013 and 2022, the share of employees increased in sectors with higher productivity and decreased in industries with lower productivity. For example, employment is growing in economic sectors such as computers and electronic equipment manufacturing, with productivity above the national average. At the same time, many jobs are being created in the economic sectors with low productivity, which clearly shows inefficient use of the labour force. The productivity gap between the high-tech and low-tech manufacturing sectors remains relatively small.

The macro-level approach used in the study is not sufficient to explain why the productivity gap is so small. The explanation requires additional analysis of structural indicators of manufacturing, such as company size, export markets, innovative activities, participation in GVCs, etc. There may be a wide gap in the industry between productivity leaders and laggards, which some studies (based on firm-level data) have noted as a serious barrier to overall productivity growth. Despite its limits, the study allows us to conclude that in Latvia, the labour force reallocation to high-value-added activities is slow and unable to accelerate any substantial increase in the aggregate productivity level in the near future.

MAIN POLICIES FOR FOSTERING THE PRODUCTIVITY GROWTH

The weakest point of productivity growth is innovation. In turn, the increase in innovation depends on investment in research and development (R&D) and requires substantial knowledge and skills performance. Low investment in R&D, insufficient innovation, and average educational performance negatively affect the efforts of the new EU-MS to achieve higher productivity.

All EU countries have specific reasons for their innovation abilities. Among the new EU-MS assessed by the Global Innovation Index (GII), the best rank (25th out of the 132 countries surveyed) has been granted to Malta. Romania ranked 47th 'locates' at the lowest end compared to the other 12 new EU-MS.

Latvia ranked 37th on the GII 2023 out of the 132 countries surveyed (with Estonia in 16th and Lithuania in 34th position) (vide Fig. 6.6).

In the European Innovation Scoreboard 2023 (annual publication of the EC), the EC classified six new EU-MS (Romania, Bulgaria, Latvia, Poland, Slovakia, and Croatia) as 'emerging innovators', which in diplomatic language means the worst performance scores. None of the new EU-MS has overcome the barrier of 'innovation leaders'. Cyprus, which belongs to the 'strong innovators' group, shows the best outcome. Estonia (12th place out of 27) is the closest candidate to join the 'strong innovators' group. For now, Estonia and five other new EU-MS (Hungary, Lithuania, Malta, and the Czech Republic) belong to 'moderate innovators'.

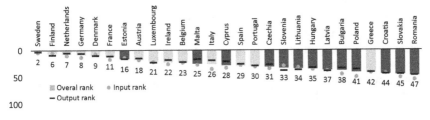

Fig. 6.6. EU Country Rank in the GII 2023. *Source*: The World Intellectual Property Organization (WIPO, 2023).

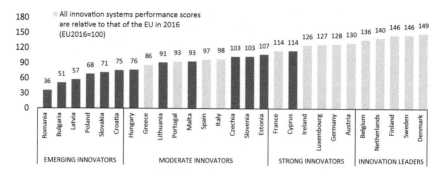

Fig. 6.7. EU Country Performance Scores in the European Innovation Scoreboard 2023. *Source*: The EC.

The authors have profoundly studied the reasons for insufficient innovation and the 'recipes' for improving for the case of Latvia, which takes 25th place among 27 EU-MS. Furthermore, the EC recently lowered Latvia's score from 'moderate' to 'emerging' innovator. Latvia lags behind the EU average in almost all indicators. There is a more significant lag in the investments of companies in R&D, in the number of innovative companies, and in the areas of environmental sustainability. The main weaknesses of Latvia's innovation system are low R&D expenses in the business sector, low government support of business R&D, and insufficient company expenses for innovation per employee. On the positive side, Latvia has a relatively better rating than other areas for the development of human resources, digitisation, and the use of information technology. However, even in these relatively successful areas, Latvia's indicators do not exceed 80% of the European average. The main strengths of Latvia's innovation system are the number of residents with higher education, joint publications of the public and private sectors, and the level of digital skills of society. The mentioned indicators exceed the EU average level (vide Fig. 6.7) (EC, 2023c).

The authors believe that achieving a breakthrough in the field of innovation in all new EU-MS is possible when society changes its attitude towards innovation. Policymakers should clearly understand that innovation is not a leisure pursuit but an indispensable precondition for the increase in prosperity and well-being. The government should considerably improve innovation stimulus, the legal framework of innovation (including the innovation procurement), and the state-aid system for creating and implementing intellectual property.

Developing research and innovation (R&I) systems requires appropriately qualified specialists and professional R&I management. The shortage of skills, relatively weak interaction between research and industry, and insufficient cooperation within the industrial sector are the key negative factors that hinder the development of the R&I system.

The crisis caused by COVID-19 has shown that the use of digital technologies helps to limit the negative impact on business models and to reduce unemployment. According to the 'Report on the State of the Digital Decade 2023', all MS

Productivity and Competitiveness 95

should attract investments and use their untapped digital potential to contribute further to the collective efforts to achieve the EU's Digital Decade connectivity targets (EC, 2023d).

For the new EU-MS, the use of digital opportunities is fundamental to the maintenance of productivity and the improvement of living standards. In some countries, a digital divide has occurred between cities and the countryside. Much of the population lacks the digital skills necessary to use the internet effectively. The integration of digital technologies in businesses in some of the new EU-MS is below the EU average. Their population is not fully prepared for a digital boom in the economy. Core policies must be to increase digital skills, with a specific focus on each target group (for instance, the aged population) to avoid the risk of future imbalances. An additional challenge is to create modern regulatory frameworks for the application of digital tools in business models, streamline key policies in the field of intellectual property rights, elaborate on new types of remote employment, and improve international cooperation, particularly as regards taxation of the digital economy, data analysis, and the measuring of processes.

The prospects for productivity growth are closely linked to companies becoming more deeply integrated into global markets by increasing the share of knowledge-intensive products and services in total exports. This depends on the ability to implement technological modernisation, innovate, and increase participation in GVCs.

The supply and quality of labour play a key role in raising productivity. The main directions for improving the availability and quality of the relevant workforce include solving the issues of demographics and migration, improving access to quality education at all levels, and stimulating reskilling and upskilling.

The ongoing structural changes require timely adaptation. The government needs to set up an inter-institutional cooperation platform based on analysis and forecasting of future technology trends. In addition, a dialogue with businesses is crucial for implementing proactive changes in the structure of the workforce both in the medium and long terms (adjustment of the education system) and in the short term (adult retraining programmes).

CONCLUSIONS

One of the new EU-MS's challenges is strengthening the long-term economic growth potential by increasing productivity levels. It faces the risks posed by the geopolitical situation, globalisation, population ageing, rapid technological progress, and the need to increase investments related to climate change.

The dynamics of productivity in the new EU-MS have been relatively rapid over the past few decades, outstripping average growth rates for the EU as a whole. However, compared to highly developed countries, the new EU-MS remains significantly behind in productivity, which is mainly explained by low total factor productivity and significant differences in the quality of production resources (human and physical capital).

The low level of productivity strongly correlates with the low level of innovation. The EC classified six new EU-MS (Romania, Bulgaria, Latvia, Poland, Slovakia, and Croatia) as 'emerging innovators'. None of the new EU-MS has overcome the barrier of 'innovation leaders'. Cyprus, which belongs to the group of 'strong innovators', shows the best outcome. Estonia, Hungary, Lithuania, Malta, and the Czech Republic belong to the group of 'moderate innovators'.

The case study of Latvia shows that a low level of productivity is determined by the low level of innovation in the business sector. In turn, serious obstacles to increasing innovation capacity are the dominant position of low-tech industries in manufacturing and the relatively small number of large companies. The shift-share analysis shows that employment is growing faster in economic sectors with high productivity, such as manufacturing computers and electronic equipment. However, many jobs are still being created in low-productivity sectors. The reallocation of the labour force to high-value-added activities is insufficient for accelerating aggregate productivity.

The fundamental factors of productivity are related primarily to investments (including investments in innovation and human capital), capital deepening, ability to integrate into GVCs, and increase in export potential. The organisation and management of the production process, specialisation and concentration of production, territorial location of production plants, and the creation of horizontal and vertical connections between industries are also of key importance for fostering productivity.

Increasing productivity and competitiveness requires a comprehensive and broader approach – strong performance in one area cannot compensate for weak performance in another.

REFERENCES

Baranovs, O., Salmins, J., & Skribane, I. (2021). Productivity factors and dynamics in Latvia. In I. Romanova (Ed.), *New challenges in economic and business development – 2021: Post-crisis economy* (pp. 54–66). University of Latvia. https://dspace.lu.lv/dspace/bitstream/handle/7/57079/Baranovs_O_Salmins_J_Skribane_I_NC_21.pdf?sequence=1&isAllowed=y

Central Statistical Bureau of Latvia. (2024, February). *Statistics database.* https://stat.gov.lv/en

Economic Survey of Singapore. (2018). *A shift-share decomposition analysis of labour productivity growth in Singapore* [Box Article 2.1]. https://www.mti.gov.sg/-/media/MTI/Legislation/Public-Consultations/2018/A-Shift-Share-Decomposition-Analysis-of-Labour-Productivity-Growth-in-Singapore/ba21_aes2017.pdf/

European Commission. (2016, November). *The macroeconomic imbalance procedure* [European Economy Institutional Paper 039]. https://economy-finance.ec.europa.eu/document/download/c2789728-1580-4a8a-bc84-be028a3bfca8_en?filename=ip039_en.pdf

European Commission. (2023a, October 30). *Euro area competitiveness: State of play, challenges and trade-offs for policy* [Technical note to the Eurogroup, Brussels]. https://www.consilium.europa.eu/media/67819/competitiveness-steering-note-for-eg-002.pdf

European Commission. (2023b, November 21). *Alert mechanism report 2024* [Commission staff working document, Strasbourg]. https://commission.europa.eu/document/download/f15332b8-c703-413b-8c98-c54eb2276052_en?filename=SWD_2023_901_1_EN_autre_document_travail_service_part1_v6.pdf

European Commission. (2023c). *European innovation scoreboard 2023.* https://research-and-innovation.ec.europa.eu/statistics/performance-indicators/european-innovation-scoreboard_en

Productivity and Competitiveness

European Commission. (2023d). *Report on the state of the digital decade 2023*. https://digital-strategy. ec.europa.eu/en/library/2023-report-state-digital-decade

García, L., Giamboni, L., & Vigani, M. (2023, June). *National productivity boards: Institutional set-up and analyses of productivity* [European Economy Discussion Paper 185]. https:// economy-finance.ec.europa.eu/publications/national-productivity-boards-institutional-set-and-analyses-productivity_en

Kim, Y. E., & Loayza, N. V. (2019). *Productivity growth patterns and determinants across the world* [Policy Research Working Paper 8852]. World Bank Group. https://documents1.worldbank.org/ curated/en/130281557504440729/pdf/Productivity-Growth-Patterns-and-Determinants-across-the-World.pdf

Krugman, P. R. (1994). *The age of diminished expectations: U.S. economic policy in the 1990s* (p. 11). MIT Press.

Kuznets, S. (1979). Growth and structural shifts. In W. Galenson (Ed.), *Economic growth and structural change in Taiwan. The postwar experience of the Republic of China* (p. 130). Cornell University Press.

OECD. (2015). *The future of productivity*. OECD Publishing.

OECD. (2021). *Enhancing regional convergence in the EU* [Economics Department Working Paper No. 1696, p. 3]. https://www.oecd.org/publications/enhancing-regional-convergence-in-the-european-union-253dd6ee-en.htm

OECD. (2022). *Global forum on productivity* [Activities report 2022]. https://www.oecd.org/global-forum-productivity/GFP-Activity-Report-2022.pdf

Parente, S. L., & Prescott, E. C. (2000). *Barriers to riches*. The MIT Press.

Renda, A., & Dougherty, S. (2017). *Pro-productivity institutions: Learning from national experience* [OECD Productivity Working Papers 2017-07, p. 197]. chrome-extension://efaidnbmnnnibp-cajpcglclefindmkaj/https://www.oecd-ilibrary.org/deliver/d1615666-en.pdf?itemId=%2Fconten t%2Fpaper%2Fd1615666-en&mimeType=pdf

Solow, R. M. (1956). A contribution to the theory of economic growth. *The Quarterly Journal of Economics, 70*(1), 65–94. https://doi.org/10.2307/1884513

Statistical Office of the European Union (Eurostat). (2024, February). *Statistics database*. https:// ec.europa.eu/eurostat/data/database

UL Think Tank LV PEAK (The Productivity Research Institute 'University of Latvia Think Tank LV PEAK'). (2023). *Latvia's 2022 productivity report*. https://www.lvpeak.lu.lv/en/productivity-council-of-latvia/latvias-productivity-report/

World Intellectual Property Organization (WIPO). (2023). *Global innovation index 2023*. https://www. wipo.int/global_innovation_index/en/2023/

CHAPTER 7

INTERNATIONAL TRADE: SINGLE EUROPEAN MARKET

Margarita Dunska and Krišs Jānis Dombrovskis

University of Latvia, Latvia

ABSTRACT

Purpose: *This chapter aims to identify the interaction of various aspects of international trade and the impact on economic integration and economic development in the European Union (EU). Foreign trade is essential for the economy of every country, especially for small, open economies, such as several EU member states. International trade characterises economic trends; it is one of the indicators of the balance of payments and reflects the macroeconomic stability in the country.*

Need for study: *Economic development analysis involves assessing the external balance of each country or the union of countries, such as the EU, with a focus on the analysis of international trade balance and trends, crucial for the stability of each economy and the operation of the single market and economic integration.*

Research methodology: *Statistical analysis of foreign trade data and the determination of mutual statistical relationships. It evaluates the trade balances of the EU member states, turnover, and international trade within the EU (intra-EU trade).*

Findings: *The EU's economic integration is based on single-market principles, ensuring free international trade and a significant impact on future economic growth. Economic openness of each member state, characterised by foreign trade turnover to gross domestic product (GDP), is essential for compliance with optimal currency zone criteria. The EU's enlargement opened the single market to Central and Eastern European countries, creating conditions for economic*

Economic Development and Resilience by EU Member States
Contemporary Studies in Economic and Financial Analysis, Volume 115, 99–118
Copyright © 2025 by Margarita Dunska and Krišs Jānis Dombrovskis
Published under exclusive licence by Emerald Publishing Limited
ISSN: 1569-3759/doi:10.1108/S1569-375920240000115007

transformation and common future development. However, the study confirms significant differences in international trade between new member states.

Practical implications: *Ensuring the development of export capacity and justify the need for export support.*

Keywords: International trade; free trade; trade balance; economic integration; single market; economic openness; export orientation

JEL classifications: F02; F15; F18

INTRODUCTION

Based on generally accepted knowledge and several scientific research results, it can be emphasised that openness to trade or the development of international trade, integration in world markets, and export competitiveness are among the basic elements of a successful growth strategy in any economy.

Trading was an ancient method to promote business by exchanging goods, and it has become the most essential and efficient business nowadays, not only on the micro-scale between individuals but also on the macro-scale of companies and countries. It is one of the most critical factors that help end global poverty (World Bank Group, 2018). Open trade helps businesses grow faster, innovate, improve productivity, and provide higher income with more opportunities for people both locally and globally. In a simple way to understand, trading is the way to exchange the lacking resources between two or more parties that are including natural resources (i.e. land and minerals), labour resources (i.e. education levels and skills levels), capital (Krugman, 1995; Ricardo, 2004) which are using to produce goods or services which create a general global balance of commodity flows. Trade is the exchange of goods and services across national borders. Free trade benefits countries and individuals by giving consumers access to the products of the world's most efficient producers, thereby increasing overall global productivity, competition and efficiency and reducing or eliminating barriers to investment (Yu, 1994).

International trade without restrictions and on the principles of mutual benefit is one of the prerequisites for improving each partner country's export capacity and competitiveness, thus for economic growth and development in the context of the international economy. The development and practical implementation of the idea of free trade between countries gave an impetus to regional integration and its expansion to the customs union and the single market, especially among European countries. The significant expansion of the EU since 2004 also showed the benefits of the new member states from operating in the single market, using free trade conditions and developing their export orientation and inclusion in the market economy. It must be considered that 11 of the 13 new EU member states are Eastern and Central European countries, whose economies underwent a complicated period of transformation from a socialist to a market economy system. The study of the international trade situation of these countries, especially their inclusion in the EU's internal trade, is essential for further understanding the development of the single market and for increasing the competitiveness of each country's exports and the entire economy. In this chapter, the authors analyse the trends in trade in the 13 new member states from 2004 to 2022, using some indicators from 2002, shortly before the significant enlargement, to see the situation even before joining.

LITERATURE REVIEW

The issue of export competitiveness is one of the most popular research questions, while the impact of exports on development and growth is a topic of debate in several scientific circles (i.e. Lages & Montgomery, 2004; Mullen et al., 2009; Navarro-García & Arenas-Gaitán, 2014; Samen, 2010). Exports can be considered an essential diagnostic tool for countries' economic conditions and for specific industries' competitiveness (Aggarwal & Huelin, 2011). It is also possible to analyse the development of regional competitiveness in the context of the regional economy (Braslina et al., 2020). According to Samen (2010), export growth can be a critically important process for every country for several micro- and macroeconomic reasons. This author emphasises that export growth is essential, given that (1) export is a significant source of foreign currency that allows financing imports; (2) exports are necessary to take advantage of economies of scale that arise from expanding production in response to foreign customer demand; and (3) export is a potential investment in employment and raising the gross national product. Thus, it can be said that exports are one of the main means for economic development, integration into global markets, learning new technologies, and increasing resource distribution efficiency, production productivity, and competitiveness.

Aware of the importance of international trade and the impact of increasing the export competitiveness and competitiveness of countries on the growth of the economy and the welfare of nations, the ideas of trade liberalisation and international (regional) economic integration have been developed in both theory and practice for several decades.

Samuelson (1948) discussed how breaking down customs barriers and promoting international trade could impact prices. He highlighted some key points: so long as different countries produce a mix of similar and different goods, free trade helps equalise the prices of resources used in production within and between countries. If the initial amounts of resources required for production do not differ from country to country, the ability to move goods can effectively replace the need to move the resources themselves. Even if there are significant differences in the initial amounts of resources between countries, and people could move around, they would only need to move a bit. Beyond a certain point, the ability to move goods globally would be enough to ensure equal prices. Samuelson also suggested that while moving goods efficiently can maximise overall productivity, the actual wages of workers in one country compared to another might be lower, not just relative to each other but even compared to when each country operates independently.

Samuelson's analysis in 1948 reveals the complex dynamics of international trade, emphasising the role of free trade in equalising resource prices and optimising global productivity. Developing these ideas, Lipsey (1957) delves into the trade-offs and gains for each party involved in free trade. The development of global trade creates the general equilibrium between countries in complementary goods (Krugman, 1995) and commodities specialised in products that make comparative advances (Ricardo, 2004; Samuelson, 1948) in support to promote economic growth and encourage the interest in economic development, special in importing and exporting. The general equilibrium approach provides a strategic framework for nations to identify their product strengths and weaknesses, facilitating more effective participation in free trade. Besides, the Kemp–Wan theorem (Kemp & Wan, 1976) adds another layer, suggesting that well-constructed customs unions within regions can enhance individual and collective welfare without negatively impacting the broader global community. It should be mentioned that Jacob Wiener made an essential contribution to the theory of customs unions in the book *Customs Union Questions* (Viner, 1950) – how customs unions can lead to changes in trade patterns that influence the direction and volume of trade which are causing trade creation and trade diversion. Together, these theories highlight the complexities of international trade relations and provide valuable insights for researchers and policymakers working in the field of economic cooperation and regional integration.

The process of international economic integration is formed and develops along with the development of trade liberalisation and the trend of opening up national economies. The purpose of international economic integration is to resolve key issues such as negotiations on the reduction of tariff barriers; negotiations on the reduction of non-tariff barriers; reduction of restrictions on the operation of services, minimising obstacles to international investment activities, minimising barriers to international labour transfer activities; and adaptation of other international trade policy instruments and rules. International economic integration is the connection, exchange, and cooperation process between a national economy and other national economies or regional and global economic organisations.

The Free Trade Agreement is the simplest possible form of integration – the participants agree to abolish mutual barriers to trade in goods, while each participating country at the same time maintains its own policy vis-á-vis non-participating third countries (Hosli & Saether, 1997). Nowadays, Free Trade Agreements can be bilateral, multilateral/regional, or territories aimed at liberalising trade in one or several groups of goods by reducing barriers between importers and exporters (Barone, 2023). The scope of 'trade' is understood broadly and can include all profitable business activities, including trade in goods, services, investment, and other related matters to trades or indirectly to trade (intellectual property, public procurement, labour, environment, etc.). The so-called static effects mainly refer to the immediate or short-term effects of trade agreements on the economy. These impacts do not relate to long-term economic changes but describe the immediate consequences of changes in trade patterns, tariffs, and economic welfare (Viner, 1950). The Kemp–Wan theorem (Kemp & Wan, 1976) shows the static effects of

International Trade 103

a customs union under the condition that it is appropriately formed with the following elements: the countries included in the regional agreement must impose a set of external tariffs so that imports from outsider countries would not change, promote the creation of trade embracing full internal free trade in the union, and provide compensation mechanisms for regional governments. Kemp and Wan have shown that, in theory, it is always possible to create a regional agreement that maintains or improves the welfare of individual members, creating a net improvement for the group and not harming the rest of the world.

Since 1961, Bela Balassa has used several forms of economic integration, including Free Trade Areas, Customs Unions, Common Markets, and Economic and Monetary Unions (EMUs) (Balassa, 1976). Balassa's classification of economic integration models, ranging from Free Trade Areas to EMUs, highlights countries' various mechanisms to promote international cooperation. It should be noted that all these forms of international integration are used in the EU, forming the basis for the successful cooperation of all member states. Historically, the existence of European communities began directly from the introduction of free trade principles. When the largest expansion of the EU took place in 2004, the common activity was already characterised by all four forms of integration, including the monetary union and the common or single market as a support for economic cooperation. On the other hand, free trade and the operation of the customs union continue to form the basis for the strengthening of economic ties between the member states and economic growth, as well as the application of the common foreign trade policy in the interests of the entire union.

The example of the EU developed in this field is not only the concept of international economic integration but also the theory of regional economic integration. The existing theory on regional economic integration provides that economic integration positively impacts the overall national economies of member states and works to stimulate the reinforcing effects of regionalisation and the strategic operations within a region (Rugman & Verbeke, 2005). In general, removing trade barriers and forming a single regional market have been associated with a positive increase in intra-regional trade among member nations (Rose, 2000; Rose & Van Wincoop, 2001). As Akpanke (2021) underlines, regional integration of various states' economies is the basis of broader regional market creation for investments and trade. It is usually expressed in written agreements, where the goals and objectives between member countries and their organisational structure are stated. Regional integration helps to increase productivity gain, efficiency, and competitiveness by reducing border barriers and impediments to investment and trade. It allows countries to overcome costly divisions integrating goods, services, and factors' markets, thus facilitating the flow of trade, capital, and labour, in case reducing the divisions between countries created by geography, poor infrastructure, and inefficient policies is an impediment to economic growth (Akpanke, 2021). On the other side, there are risks to regional integration that need to be identified and managed. Regional integration's impact on trade and investment flows, allocation of economic activity, growth, and income distribution is often difficult to assess. Countries may have different preferences on priorities for regional integration, depending on their connectivity gaps, economic geography, or preferences for sovereignty in specific areas. A lack of adequate complementary policies and institutions may lead to inefficient outcomes. Regional integration creates winners and losers, notably within countries. Policies and institutions are needed to ensure that regionalism is inclusive and social, environmental, and governance risks are managed (World Bank Group, 2023).

The process of regional integration in the EU involves several steps: economic, institutional, social, and political integration. Economic integration means reducing trade barriers and promoting the free movement of goods, services, and people between countries. This can be achieved by creating a customs union, a common market, or an EMU. The EU has achieved economic integration by creating the single market, the customs union, and the Eurozone. This fully corresponds to theoretical ideas about international economic integration and regional economic integration.

EUROPEAN SINGLE MARKET AND NEW MEMBER STATES – RESULTS OF ANALYSIS OF INTERNATIONAL TRADE, INCLUDING INTRA-EU TRADE

When evaluating international trade in the EU as a whole or in the group of so-called new member states (countries that joined the EU in 2004 and later), it is essential to note that, first of all, free trade is ensured within the EU (intra-EU trade), operating in the single or internal market. However, trade flows (extra-EU trade) outside the EU are formed in accordance with the operating principles of the customs union. In the international trade analysis, both goods and services flows can be considered, especially in the internal market – the EU single market, where services also have free movement. In this chapter, the authors analyse the trends in trade in goods in the new member states from 2002 (shortly before the major enlargement) to 2022.

The single market, sometimes called the internal market, is one of the cornerstones of the four freedoms. For statistical purposes, a common understanding of the single market is used within the EU and is seen as a market where, by removing barriers and simplifying existing rules, every EU country can benefit from direct access to all other member states (Eurostat, 2024a). The Treaty of Rome on the functioning of the EU states that the single (internal) market is a market with four free movements: goods, services, capital, and people. The free movement of goods or free trade in goods means that national trade barriers within the EU be removed. The Treaty of Rome, Articles 34, 35, and 36, prohibits quantitative restrictions on imports, exports, or goods in transit between member states. Additionally, member states have a single trade policy (European Commission, 2023).

The origins of the single market, as an example of the common market, can be found in the Treaty of Rome. According to the Single Market Programme of the Single European Act 1987, a deadline of 31 December 1992 was set for the completion of the single market. The Single Market Programme included examining how the internal barriers to free trade (such as physical, technical, and fiscal restrictions on trade in goods and services) might be removed and the consequences of these (Harris, 1999). In 1999, Neil Harris concluded that the

EU had made substantial progress in completing the internal market, mainly for economic reasons, to promote economic efficiency and thus enable European companies to compete more effectively. In 2023, the 30th anniversary of the EU single market was celebrated. One of the achievements of the operation of the single market during this time can be noted in the high level of competitiveness of European businesses and the European economy in world markets, evidenced by the EU's share in international trade. The EU-27 accounts for around 14% of the world's trade in goods. The EU, China, and the United States are the three largest global players in international trade (Annual Single Market Report, 2023). On the other hand, as emphasised in the European Parliament, established 30 years ago in 1993, the EU single market accounts for 56 million jobs and 25% of EU GDP. The EU has the world's largest single market – it is home to 447 million consumers and 23 million companies. Serious challenges require its transformation and renewed political commitment. It is concluded that a well-functioning single market is key to achieving strategic autonomy and resilience (European Parliament, 2023).

An extensive legislative programme of the single market was gradually established and is in use, which includes adopting a large number of directives and regulations. In 2008, the New Legislative Framework was adopted to improve the common market for goods and strengthen the conditions for placing a wide range of goods on the EU market, improving market surveillance and increasing the quality of conformity assessments. In 2011–2012, to show that the single market brings social achievements and can benefit consumers, employees, and small businesses, the European Commission adopted the Single Market Act, a series of measures to boost the European economy and create jobs. The Single Market Act I, presented by the Commission in April 2011, set out 12 levers to boost growth and strengthen confidence in the economy. In October 2012, the Commission proposed the Single Market Act II with actions to develop the single market further and exploit its untapped potential as an engine for growth. In October 2015, a new single market strategy was presented to deliver a more profound and fairer single market that will benefit both consumers and businesses (European Commission, 2024). The common approach to solving serious problems, for example, in the case of external shocks, also characterised the priorities set by the EU to support the single market. The Single Market Programme was adopted – an EU funding programme that helps the single market reach its full potential and ensure Europe's recovery from the COVID-19 pandemic. With €4.2 billion throughout 2021–2027, it provides an integrated package to support and strengthen the governance of the single market (European Commission, 2021).

The importance of the EU internal market is emphasised by the fact that in most EU member states, the share of intra-EU trade is higher than outside the EU. Differences in states' internal and external distribution of total goods trade depend on historical ties and geographic location (European Commission, 2023). At the same time, it should be noted that trade with external partners (non-EU) is also essential for each member state, and the use of common conditions creates favourable conditions for such relations. How did the new member states fit into this single market system? Most of these are Eastern and Central European countries, where the historical, geographical, political, and economic differences are evident compared to the Western European member states. Since 2004, the EU members are Cyprus, the Czech Republic, Estonia, Hungary, Latvia, Lithuania, Malta, Poland, Slovakia, and Slovenia. Bulgaria and Romania joined in 2007 and since 1 July 2013 Croatia. Together, it can be called the EU 13 group of member states. Only Cyprus and Malta have different historical backgrounds; others are former socialist economies and have gone through a difficult path of economic transformation.

A logical question can be asked – were the Central and Eastern European (CEE) countries ready for full participation in the single market only a little more than 10 years after the transition to market economy principles? In their paper 'The Opening of Central and Eastern European Countries to Free Trade: A Critical Assessment', Kuc-Czarnecka et al. (2021) emphasise that in the former COMECON (The Council for Mutual Economic Assistance) countries, the free trade shock of 1990 'killed' a large part of the manufacturing sector, but the introduction of the euro and the loss of the exchange rate adjustment mechanism between European countries in 1999 deepened industrial problems in peripheral countries. Also, in the context of the EU manufacturing policy with its drive towards industrial modernisation, investments in research and development and innovation, the CEE countries can be labelled as peripheral with significantly lower indicators. It is noted that deindustrialisation led to increased migration and population decline. The authors stress that the CEE countries 'would not benefit from more economic integration (other than as welfare recipients)' (Kuc-Czarnecka et al., 2021). At the same time, analysing exports, it was concluded that small CEE countries focus on exports. Since the beginning of the transformation process in 1990, they are classified as export-oriented economies (Estonia, Latvia, Hungary, Slovakia, and the Czech Republic). In addition, manufacturing is the dominant sector in the export structure. From 1993 to 2008, in almost all CEE countries, the share of manufacturing industry goods in total exports exceeded 80% (Kuc-Czarnecka et al., 2021). During the transformation period, during the preparation for EU membership, economic openness for the new conditions, including cooperation with the EU, played a significant role in the economic development of the countries of the CEE region (Šavriņa & Grundey, 2008). It gave impulses to the development of export capacity and trade.

Eurostat data on international trade show that export (see Table 7.1) and import volumes (see Table 7.2) increased in all new member states after joining the EU. The data have been analysed for all EU 13 countries, regardless of the year of accession, from 2002 to 2022. It should be noted that export and import flows also increased in the pre-accession period. However, it can be concluded that trade growth trends are unquestionable when operating in a single market. Evaluating the entire period in 2022, compared to the year of accession to the EU, the Czech Republic's exports increased almost 5 times, Estonia's exports – 3 times, Hungary's – 3 times, Latvia's – 4 times, Lithuania's – 5 times, Poland's – 6.5 times, Slovakia's – 4.5 times, Slovenia's exports increased by 14 (!) times during the same period; Bulgaria's – 3 times, Romania's – almost 3 times, and Croatia's – 2 times, but a much shorter period should be taken into account

Table 7.1. Exports from 2002 to 2022 for EU 13 Countries, Billion Euro.

	Bulgaria	Croatia	Czechia	Estonia	Hungary	Latvia	Lithuania	Poland	Romania	Slovakia	Slovenia	Cyprus	Malta
2002	2.46	1.83	7.92	0.84	7.05	0.89	2.48	10.33	4.65	1.87	2.75	0.26	1.37
2003	2.59	1.79	7.53	0.87	7.40	0.92	2.69	10.83	4.80	3.02	2.84	0.22	1.25
2004	3.18	2.28	9.38	1.12	9.48	1.14	2.85	14.94	5.90	3.50	3.36	0.42	1.25
2005	3.76	2.70	11.65	1.57	11.49	1.39	3.70	19.16	7.68	3.97	3.88	0.51	1.14
2006	4.73	3.10	14.05	2.84	14.22	1.72	4.58	23.32	8.78	5.53	4.70	0.47	1.28
2007	5.50	3.75	17.27	2.61	16.73	2.06	4.97	27.33	9.38	7.51	5.52	0.43	1.62
2008	6.28	3.97	19.36	2.76	18.37	2.40	7.12	32.03	10.93	9.11	5.96	0.46	1.58
2009	4.26	3.13	16.04	2.11	14.93	1.95	4.72	25.94	8.37	7.33	4.69	0.38	1.33
2010	6.31	3.60	20.65	2.92	19.44	2.58	6.87	32.47	11.65	9.31	5.40	0.44	1.72
2011	7.95	3.99	24.76	4.29	21.88	3.47	8.58	38.28	14.45	10.60	6.16	0.54	2.00
2012	8.93	4.18	28.70	4.52	21.54	4.32	10.56	44.08	14.94	12.48	6.72	0.66	2.14
2013	9.39	3.84	28.97	3.86	19.76	4.03	12.14	48.62	17.09	13.87	6.89	0.85	1.62
2014	8.77	3.96	30.11	3.64	20.20	3.96	11.92	47.99	17.34	13.42	7.17	1.35	1.20
2015	8.61	4.18	31.36	3.20	20.78	3.92	9.88	49.18	16.74	13.49	7.47	1.78	1.40
2016	8.68	4.48	31.75	3.39	22.42	3.91	9.85	49.61	16.80	13.93	7.90	1.70	1.76
2017	10.77	5.32	33.98	3.92	23.18	4.74	11.93	54.86	17.70	14.26	8.83	1.96	1.18
2018	9.92	4.97	34.72	4.93	23.80	5.29	12.72	57.28	18.33	15.06	9.49	3.17	1.27
2019	10.67	5.20	36.61	4.52	22.78	5.32	13.32	62.03	18.41	16.03	11.24	1.83	1.27
2020	9.64	4.91	33.97	4.83	22.78	5.44	12.62	62.14	16.00	15.86	12.81	1.78	1.22
2021	11.68	6.03	37.46	6.00	26.20	6.42	14.61	71.98	19.83	17.12	15.68	2.39	1.35
2022	16.53	7.69	42.42	6.44	31.14	7.91	16.74	83.91	25.52	20.55	24.64	3.05	1.62

SITC, The Standard International Trade Classification.

Source: Created by the authors on the basis of Eurostat (2024b). EU trade since 1999 by SITC. Database DS-018995.

Table 7.2. Imports from 2002 to 2022 for EU 13 Countries, Billion Euro.

	Bulgaria	Croatia	Czechia	Estonia	Hungary	Latvia	Lithuania	Poland	Romania	Slovakia	Slovenia	Cyprus	Malta
2002	3.77	3.41	13.11	1.70	15.04	1.06	3.70	19.96	6.72	5.15	2.46	1.99	1.19
2003	4.27	3.62	14.25	2.13	16.08	1.23	4.02	20.55	7.43	5.50	2.69	1.72	1.18
2004	5.25	4.13	12.68	1.91	16.51	1.50	3.86	20.22	9.78	5.46	2.28	1.74	1.13
2005	4.98	5.08	12.99	2.14	17.32	1.85	5.34	22.66	12.93	6.57	2.92	2.01	1.06
2006	6.30	5.94	16.46	2.95	19.92	2.33	6.15	30.25	15.88	9.30	3.70	2.21	1.35
2007	9.36	6.97	19.42	2.82	22.81	2.69	6.14	35.85	15.64	11.71	5.33	2.55	1.41
2008	11.14	7.86	24.88	2.52	24.74	2.85	9.37	43.82	18.37	14.15	6.53	2.95	1.31
2009	6.95	5.94	18.54	1.59	18.41	1.85	5.58	32.67	11.29	10.98	4.94	2.04	1.18
2010	8.26	6.27	26.51	2.07	22.51	2.27	7.94	43.18	13.90	14.78	6.51	2.44	1.50
2011	9.84	6.46	30.33	3.38	23.75	2.99	10.24	49.53	16.21	16.13	7.46	2.47	1.54
2012	10.86	6.32	29.67	3.67	23.11	3.23	11.09	53.98	15.70	16.59	7.28	2.17	1.55
2013	10.79	5.70	27.80	3.08	22.72	2.97	11.02	52.83	14.67	16.70	7.91	1.71	1.65
2014	10.45	4.30	29.20	2.95	20.98	2.98	10.00	55.66	15.76	15.18	8.20	2.51	2.30
2015	9.88	4.34	32.30	2.76	21.01	3.05	8.95	57.01	15.95	14.77	8.43	2.85	2.23
2016	9.38	4.78	31.10	2.80	20.60	2.86	7.84	54.89	16.95	14.33	8.40	2.78	2.93
2017	11.36	5.16	35.77	3.17	24.62	3.63	9.31	64.18	19.99	15.42	10.16	3.70	2.41
2018	12.17	5.63	40.25	4.22	27.78	4.66	10.49	74.26	22.71	16.91	12.17	4.49	2.11
2019	13.07	5.35	41.63	3.89	30.24	4.24	10.74	79.43	23.51	16.96	14.88	3.32	3.04
2020	11.94	5.38	40.53	3.76	29.80	3.85	8.50	73.77	21.25	14.49	15.25	3.23	1.99
2021	15.44	7.51	47.08	5.59	34.77	5.54	11.86	97.43	27.07	19.13	21.45	3.09	2.43
2022	24.70	12.93	62.98	5.53	49.62	6.16	19.30	131.13	36.74	24.77	31.94	4.58	3.38

Source: Created by the authors on the basis of Eurostat (2024b). EU trade since 1999 by SITC. Database DS-018995.

International Trade 109

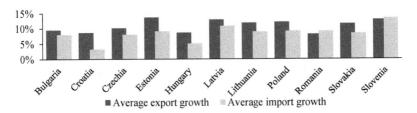

Fig. 7.1. Trade Growth from 2004 to 2022 for EU 11, Average %. *Source*: Created by the authors based on Eurostat (2024b). EU trade since 1999 by SITC. Database: DS-018995.

in the EU. This underlines the recognition that these CEE countries of the EU are export oriented and can increase the export capacity of their economy. Import flows in the considered period have similar growth trends; however, as the data in Fig. 7.1 show, annual growth rates for exports have generally been higher. The market of the new member states was fully open to the other member states within the framework of the single market.

Each country has its own situation; an in-depth analysis would be necessary, but the overall picture is visible. The situation is special in two other new member states. As mentioned above, Cyprus and Malta have a different historical background; these countries did not have to change their economic system and ideology. The trade flows of both countries are the smallest in absolute terms, with a tendency to increase, while Malta's goods exports increased by 1.3 times during this period, which is the lowest increase among the new member states. On the other hand, calculations show (Table 7.3) that the openness of Malta's economy is at the highest level (trade 318% against GDP in 2022). Landesmann and Székely (2021) recommend using the EU 11 group of new member states, excluding Cyprus and Malta, for a more complete analysis because of economic transformation from formerly communist regimes.

An analysis in 2021 from Landesmann and Székely suggests that EU 11 countries are converging towards the income levels of the EU 15[1] and are more open to trade compared to EU 15 because of increased exports and imports in the last 15 years. Data from Eurostat show that since the addition of new member states in 2004, the average trade growth year on year has been substantial: growth for exports ranges from 8% to 14%, and from 3% to 14% for imports, which, in turn, implies that these countries often are more open to trade (Landesmann & Székely, 2021).

Eurostat data on EU trade show positive growth in EU enlargement countries (see Fig. 7.1), which can be attributed to the main features of the single market that were expressed in a concentrated form by Breuss in 2002 after the end of formation of the EMU of the EU: cost savings via the abolition of trade tariffs, improved efficiency and competition, as well as the movement of foreign direct investment via the single market (Breuss, 2002).

The development of international trade in member states is of great importance in the context of the European EMU, which is the highest stage in economic integration and includes all the ideas of the common/single market. An optimum

Table 7.3. Trade Openness from 2004 to 2022 for Countries That Joined the EU Since 2004, in % Against GDP.

	Bulgaria (%)	Croatia (%)	Czechia (%)	Estonia (%)	Hungary (%)	Latvia (%)	Lithuania (%)	Poland (%)	Romania (%)	Slovakia (%)	Slovenia (%)	Cyprus (%)	Malta (%)
2004	93	82	113	130	123	93	105	71	61	140	112	114	213
2005	100	81	121	136	128	100	117	71	59	148	120	112	218
2006	111	83	127	137	149	100	124	78	62	165	130	110	254
2007	124	83	130	134	155	96	116	81	64	166	137	111	262
2008	125	82	124	137	158	91	127	81	65	162	135	113	299
2009	93	70	113	117	145	86	105	75	58	136	113	103	295
2010	103	73	128	144	157	109	130	83	70	153	127	109	302
2011	117	78	138	167	166	125	148	87	76	168	139	111	320
2012	124	79	147	171	166	128	156	89	77	176	142	113	323
2013	130	81	146	166	164	125	156	91	81	181	144	121	304
2014	130	86	158	160	168	125	143	93	83	178	146	131	288
2015	127	91	155	151	167	122	139	93	84	180	146	138	299
2016	123	92	151	150	164	119	134	98	86	184	147	140	303
2017	130	97	151	148	165	124	145	101	87	188	157	149	297
2018	129	99	148	146	163	124	149	103	86	190	161	149	303
2019	125	101	142	144	161	121	149	103	85	183	159	152	310
2020	110	90	133	138	155	120	137	100	78	168	147	163	333
2021	121	102	142	157	160	132	156	112	87	184	161	175	315
2022	138	125	152	172	187	149	176	124	93	204	186	190	318

Source: Created and calculated by the authors on the basis of World Bank Group (2024).

International Trade 111

currency area (OCA), according to Mundell's theory, is an optimal area with a single currency as the main means of payment. The word 'optimal' identifies the macroeconomic aim – to maintain balance in the economy, both internal and external. The OCA theory proposes criteria that potential members of the monetary union must meet in order to be able to abandon national monetary policy and national exchange rate adjustments (Dellas & Tavlas, 2009). The degree of economic openness and/or trade integration is one of the most important criteria for an OCA – price changes in international trade will impact domestic prices, especially in the smaller countries, which could not protect themselves against currency fluctuations. The openness of the economy is measured as the share of exports and imports in % of GDP, which indicates the integration between countries. Notably, among the new member states, eight are members of the EMU or Eurozone. In this context, as early as the late 1980s, several empirical and theoretical studies aimed to determine whether countries meet the OCA criteria – before or after joining the monetary union. As later recognised by Akiba and Iida (2014), there is a higher probability that countries meet these criteria immediately after joining the union, and it can also become an additional incentive later.

The EU enlargement provided new member states with new trade options, removed existing trade barriers, and integrated EU 11 with EU 15. Table 7.3 represents how all EU enlargement countries have progressed in trade openness, with a significant exception being in 2009 with the global economic crisis and 2020 with COVID-19. The level of openness is high in all countries, both EU 13 and EU 11 (under 100% only in Romania). The OCA criterion value is known to be 60%.

Other analyses consider a deeper insight into the topic, approving that the EU enlargement had a primary effect on market share increase – CEE economies expanded export market share faster than the world average in the period but in some cases had limited ability to exploit the increased competitiveness. Such cases are in Lithuania and Latvia, where the regions' export profiles did not align with global trade trends, and the economies faced constraints in increasing their export presence (Gilbert & Muchová, 2018).

In order to be able to assess not only the development of international trade and the increase in openness in the new member states but the development of the EU single market and the integration of member states' economies, statistics on international trade in goods between member states or intra-trade, especially on the volume and development of imports and exports, are possible. Within the framework of the European Commission, a series of online analytical publications on international trade statistics, including intra-trade analysis, are regularly created. The last such publication, 'Intra-EU Trade in Goods – Main Features', in 2023, covers 2002–2022. As emphasised, the analysis presented in this paper only looks at intra-EU goods exports because it is a more reliable indicator of total intra-EU trade in goods (European Commission, 2023). In the analysed period, the value of exports of goods to partners in the EU increased more than 10% annually on average in the following states (see Table 7.4): Latvia, Lithuania, Bulgaria, and Poland (respectively: 11.9%, 11.5%, 11.3%, and 10.8%) – all are the new member states from CEE countries group. In 13 countries from the other member states, annual average growth was between 5% and 10% and in 10

Table 7.4. Intra-EU Exports of Goods, 2002–2022, in Billion Euro and Annual Average Growth Rate, in %.

	2002	2022	Annual Average Growth Rate (%)		2002	2022	Annual Average Growth Rate (%)
Latvia	1.60	15.25	11.9	Spain	87.26	253.37	5.5
Lithuania	3.13	27.62	11.5	Portugal	19.58	55.43	5.3
Bulgaria	3.68	31.53	11.3	Belgium	152.16	412.96	5.1
Poland	33.69	259.96	10.8	Germany	363.04	863.43	4.4
Romania	10.12	66.70	9.9	Austria	59.63	140.30	4.4
Slovakia	13.56	82.59	9.5	Sweden	44.06	102.03	4.3
Czechia	33.18	187.97	9.1	Italy	147.90	329.81	4.1
Cyprus	0.20	1.09	8.9	Ireland	39.18	80.25	3.6
Estonia	2.87	14.96	8.6	Finland	24.87	46.29	3.2
Slovenia	8.28	41.91	8.4	Denmark	36.83	67.94	3.1
Croatia	3.45	16.57	8.2	Malta	0.78	1.38	2.9
Greece	6.96	30.32	7.6	France	195.57	329.75	2.6
Hungary	29.62	113.15	6.9	Luxembourg	8.72	13.30	2.1
The Netherlands	182.10	659.72	6.6				

Source: Created by the authors on the basis of Eurostat (2024b). 'Intra-EU Trade in Goods – Main Features'. Database DS-018995.

countries below 5% (in this group, only Malta is a new member state). The publication's authors conclude that 'Member States in Eastern Europe tended to have higher growth rates'.

As shown in this paper, in 2022, in most member states, the share of intra-EU exports in the total export of goods was between 50% and 75%. In some countries, this share was even above 75%: in Poland, Hungary, Slovakia, Luxembourg, and the Czech Republic (respectively: 76%, 78%, 80%, 81%, and 82%). Also, as can be observed, practically all countries are from the group of new member states. Only in three countries, Cyprus, Ireland, and Malta, was the share of intra-EU exports lower than 50% (respectively: 26%, 39%, and 45%). This means that in these countries during this period, intra-EU exports were lower than extra-EU exports (see Fig. 7.2).

As can be seen, the new EU member states are in both the first group and the second, which shows, as already mentioned, that the situation in each country is different. In addition, it can be concluded that all EU 11 or CEE countries have joined the single market to a greater extent. Considerable differences appear in the range of types of goods exported too. According to the analytical publication within the European Commission (2023), 'Intra-EU Trade in Goods – Main Features', in 2022, the share of manufactured goods in exports was higher than the share of primary goods in all member states. In Ireland, the Czech Republic, and Slovakia, the share of manufactured goods in exports was more than eight times as high as the share of primary goods (9.8, 8.7, and 8.6), while ratios below two times were in Lithuania, Latvia, Cyprus, and Greece (respectively: 2.0, 1.9, 1.6, and 1.5) (European Commission, 2023). Also, the new member states are in both groups, but the data on Lithuania and Latvia somewhat confirm Gilbert's

International Trade 113

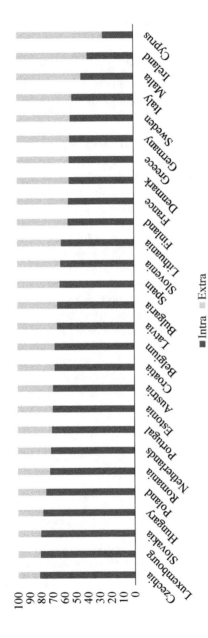

Fig. 7.2. Exports of Goods: Intra-EU and Extra-EU, 2022, in %. *Source:* Created by the authors on the basis of Eurostat (2024b). 'Intra-EU Trade in Goods – Main Features'. Database DS-018995.

and Muchová's findings (2018). It should be noted that, generally, four-fifths of the total EU goods exports in 2022 were industrially produced products.

Assuming that import flows in the EU intra-trade are challenging to evaluate statistically, the analysis can be supplemented with an insight into the participation of the new member states in the total EU imports. The data (see Fig. 7.3) show that the EU 13 countries are in different positions. The import share was small and practically unchanged for a large group of countries during the reviewed period. However, countries like Poland, the Czech Republic, Hungary, Romania, and Slovakia show higher figures and increased their share, especially Poland, from 2.7% in 2002 to 5.6% in 2022.

Another indicator used to evaluate the development of international trade and its impact on the country's economy is the trade balance, which is the difference between the country's exports and imports. The trade balance is generally considered a strong indicator and measure of broadly defined international economic competitiveness. The negative balance of trade in the manufacturing industry, for example, shows the lack of competitiveness of domestic industries, which cannot meet domestic demand and thus leads to an increase in imports. According to Kuc-Czarnecka et al. (2021) assessment, from 1992 to 2008, a negative trade balance was a constant phenomenon in the CEE countries. Starting from 2003/2004, only three countries – the Czech Republic, Slovakia, and Hungary created a positive trade balance (Kuc-Czarnecka et al., 2021). Based on Eurostat information on the volume of export and import of goods in EU 13 countries (Tables 7.1 and 7.2), it can be agreed that most of these countries have maintained a negative trade balance in the period under review. Changes took place in three Baltic countries: Estonia since 2008, Latvia since 2009, and Lithuania since 2013, export volumes of goods exceeded the import volumes. In these countries, especially in Latvia, this situation was created due to the global financial and economic crisis, when imports decreased due to the decrease in income in the economy. However, exports

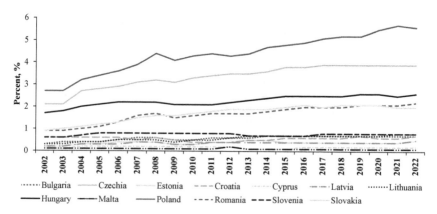

Fig. 7.3. Share of Imports by EU Member States, 2002–2022 for EU 13, Annual, in % in Total EU Import. *Source*: Created by the authors on the basis of Eurostat (2024b). EU trade since 1999 by SITC. Database: DS-018995.

International Trade 115

remained and developed due to differences in the economic cycle in trade partner countries. Calculations show that only these three countries had a positive trade balance (except Lithuania in 2022) in the last five years (and Slovakia in 2020). It is interesting that since 2012, the opposite situation has developed in Malta.

A different picture emerges when looking at the trade balance of each country for intra-EU trade. As noted in the paper 'Intra-EU Trade in Goods – Main Features' (2023), it is challenging to interpret absolute data for individual countries – their goods trade balances must be interpreted cautiously with regard to the quasi-transit phenomenon. Quasi-transit means 'operation when goods are imported by non-residents into the reporting economy from outside the EU and subsequently dispatched to another Member State as well as when the goods exported from a Member State to a non-member country are cleared for exports in another Member State' (European Commission, 2023). According to statistical analysis in 2002, considering quasi-transit, in 18 member states, there was a trade deficit for intra-EU trade in goods. In Bulgaria, Poland, Slovenia, and Spain, the trade deficit had changed to a surplus by 2022. In nine member states, there was a goods trade surplus. The trade surplus in Denmark, Finland, and Germany changed to a deficit by 2022 (European Commission, 2023). Overall, in 2022, the trade deficit was in 16 member states, including Estonia, Croatia, Cyprus, Latvia, Lithuania, Malta, and Romania; 11 countries had a positive intra-trade balance, including Bulgaria, the Czech Republic, Hungary, Poland, Slovenia, and Slovakia.

CONCLUSIONS, RECOMMENDATIONS FOR FURTHER RESEARCH

International trade is essential for the economy of every country, especially for small, open economies. Free trade benefits countries and individuals by giving consumers access to the most efficient producers, increasing competition and efficiency, and reducing or eliminating barriers to investment.

Economic integration in the EU is based on the principles of the single market, which ensures the existence and development of free international trade and common foreign trade policy within the customs union.

Taking into account the advantages of the single market in the context of integrating the goods and services market, the single market significantly impacts the level of production costs, productivity, export capacity, consumer satisfaction, and economic growth.

The development of international trade in member states is of great importance in the European EMU context and compliance with the optimal currency zone criteria – degree of economic openness and/or trade integration. The level of openness is high in all EU 13 countries (under 100% only in Romania).

The EU's enlargement opened the single market to several countries in Central and Eastern Europe, creating conditions for the completion of the transformation of these countries' economies and the common future development of the single market. The study also confirms that there are significant differences between the new member states in terms of international trade.

The development of international trade processes after joining the EU in the new member states differs, but there are common trends. From 2004 to 2022, trade flows increased in all countries, and the average annual export growth rates in practically all of these groups of EU countries exceeded the import growth rates. Evaluating the trade balance of goods in the EU 13 countries, it should be concluded that only three Baltic countries have had a positive trade balance in recent years. On the other hand, EU intra-trade analysis shows that all countries have successfully integrated into internal EU trade flows, and several countries have a positive balance. In 2022, most member states had a share of intra-EU exports, with total exports between 50% and 75%.

The EU enlargement provided new trade options for new member states, removed existing trade barriers, and integrated EU 13 with other member states.

It is important to continue studies of intra-trade between member states, with a deeper analysis of each member state's situation, in order to assess not only the development of international trade and the increase in openness in the new member states but also the development of the EU single market and the integration of member state economies.

In order to assess the whole international trade scene, it would be necessary to include in the analysis also the developments of the service market and the trends in the formation of service balances in the member states, in addition to the trade balances, by in-depth assessment of the new member states.

By studying the current account status of the balance of payments in all Member States, it would be possible to assess the general picture of international trade in goods and services, integration trends, and the equilibrium of the economy. This could be one of the directions of future research in this area.

Realising the importance of foreign trade and the importance of increasing export competitiveness both within the EU and outside the EU, it is necessary to pay attention to export support in all its manifestations, in the field of research, economic policy development, and practical decision-making in the EU as a whole and in the national member states.

NOTE

1. The EU 15 includes the older member states such as Belgium, Denmark, Germany, Finland, France, Greece, Ireland, Spain, France, Italy, Luxembourg, the Netherlands, Austria, Portugal, the United Kingdom, and Sweden.

REFERENCES

Aggarwal, R., & Huelin, A. (2011). *National trade policy for export success* (162 pp.). International Trade Centre. http://www.intracen.org/national-trade-policy-for-export-success.pdf

Akiba, H., & Iida, Y. (2014). Monetary unions and endogeneity of the OCA criteria. *Global Economic Review, 38*(1), 101–116.

Akpanke, J. (2021). Regional integration: A comparative analysis of the European Union (EU) and African Union (AU). https://www.academia.edu/50838291/

Annual Single Market Report: Single Market at 30. (2023). https://single-market-economy.ec.europa.eu/document/download/39486d20-165e-4a76-93d9-ed760c995524_en

International Trade 117

Balassa, B. (1976). Types of economic integration. In F. Machlup (Ed.), *Economic integration: Worldwide, regional, sectoral* (Chapter 1, pp. 17–40). International Economic Association Series. Palgrave Macmillan.

Barone, A. (2023). *Free trade agreement (FTA) definition: How it works, with example.* https://www.investopedia.com/terms/f/free-trade.asp

Braslina, L., Batraga, A., Legzdina, A., Salkovska, J., Kalkis, H., Skiltere, D., Braslins, G., & Bormane, S. (2020). *Barriers to the development of regional competitiveness in the context of regional economies – EU, Latvia, Region Vidzeme Case Study. Advances in human factors, business management and leadership* (Advances in Intelligent Systems and Computing, Vol. 1209, pp. 3–11). Springer.

Breuss, F. (2002). Benefits and dangers of EU enlargement. *Empirica, 29*(3), 245–274. https://doi.org/10.1023/a:1020255826824

Dellas, H., & Tavlas, G. S. (2009). An optimum-currency-area odyssey. *Journal of International Money and Finance, 28,* 1117–1137.

European Commission. (2021). *Single market programme.* https://commission.europa.eu/funding-tenders/find-funding/eu-funding-programmes/single-market programme/overview_en

European Commission. (2023). *Intra-EU trade in goods – Main features.* https://ec.europa.eu/eurostat/statistics-explained/index.php?title=Intra-EU_trade_in_goods_-_main_features# Evolution_of_intra-EU_trade_in_goods

European Commission. (2024). *Single market act.* https://single-market-economy.europa.eu/single-market/single-market-act_en

European Parliament. (2023). *30 years of the EU single market: Time to face new challenges.* https://www.europarl.europa.eu/news/en/press-room/20230113IPR66633/30-years-of-the-eu-single-market-time-to-face-new-challenges

Eurostat. (2024a). *Glossary: Single market.* https://ec.europa.eu/eurostat/statistics explained/index.php?title

Eurostat. (2024b). *Database.* https://ec.europa.eu/eurostat/

Gilbert, J., & Muchová, E. (2018). Export competitiveness of Central and Eastern Europe since the enlargement of the EU. *International Review of Economics & Finance, 55,* 78–85. https://doi.org/10.1016/j.iref.2018.01.008

Harris, N. (1999). *European business* (2nd ed.). Macmillan Press Ltd.

Hosli, O. M., & Saether, A. (1997). *Free trade agreements and customs unions.* Tacis Information.

Kemp, M. C., & Wan, H., Jr. (1976). An elementary proposition concerning the formation of customs unions. *Journal of International Economics, 6*(February), 95–97.

Krugman, P. (1995). *Growing world trade: Causes and consequences.* [Brookings Papers on Economic Activities]. https://www.brookings.edu/wp-content/uploads/1995/ ... ooper_srinivasan.pdf

Kuc-Czarnecka, M., Saltelli, A., Olczyk, M., & Reinert. E. (2021). The opening of Central and Eastern European countries to free trade: A critical assessment. *Structural Change and Economic Dynamics, 58,* 23–34.

Lages, L. F., & Montgomery, D. B. (2004). Export performance as an antecedent of export commitment and marketing strategy adaptation. *European Journal of Marketing, 38*(9/10), 1186–1214.

Landesmann, M., & Székely, I. P. (Eds.). (2021). *Does EU membership facilitate convergence? The experience of the EU's Eastern enlargement – Volume II. Studies in economic transition.* Springer International Publishing. https://doi.org/10.1007/978-3-030-57702-5

Lipsey, R. G. (1957). The theory of customs unions: Trade diversion and welfare. *Economica, New Series, 24*(93), 40–46. https://doi.org/10.2307/2551626

Mullen, M. R., Doney, P. M., Mrad, S. B., & Sheng, S. Y. (2009). Effects of international trade and economic development on quality of life. *Journal of Macromarketing, 29*(3), 244–258.

Navarro-García, A., & Arenas-Gaitán, J. (2014). External environment and the moderating role of export market orientation. *Journal of Business Research, 67,* 740–745.

Ricardo, D. (2004). *The principles of political economy and taxation.* Dover Publications.

Rose, A. K. (2000). One money, one market: The effect of common currency on trade. *Economic Policy, 15*(30), 7–46.

Rose, A. K., & Van Wincoop, E. (2001). National money as a barrier to international trade: The real case for currency union. *American Economic Review, 91*(2), 386–390.

Rugman, A. M., & Verbeke, A. (2005). Towards a theory of regional multinationals: A transaction cost economics approach. *Management International Review, 45*(1), 5–17.

Samen, S. (2010). *Export development, diversification, and competitiveness: How some developing countries got it right* (28 pp.). Growth and Crisis Unit World Bank Institute. https://blogs.worldbank.org/files/growth/ExportDevDiv&CompetitivenessHowDidSomeDevelopingCountriesGotitRightMarch2010(1).pdf

Samuelson, P. A. (1948). International trade and the equalisation of factor prices. Oxford University Press on behalf of the Royal Economic Society. *The Economic Journal, 58*(230), 163–184.

Šavriņa, B., & Grundey, D. (2008). The impact of economic receptiveness to economic development of Central and Eastern European Countries. *Transformations in Business & Economics, 7*(2, Supplement B), 20–33.

Viner, J. (1950). *The customs union issue*. Carnegie Endowment for International.

World Bank Group. (2018). *Stronger open trade policies enable economic growth for all*. https://www.worldbank.org/en/results/2018/04/03

World Bank Group. (2023). *Regional integration overview*. https://www.worldbank.org/en/topic/regional-integration/overview#1

World Bank Group. (2024). *DataBank. World development indicators*. https://databank.worldbank.org/reports.aspx?source

Yu, D. (1994). Free trade is green, protectionism is not. *Wiley for Society for Conservation Biology, Conservation Biology, 8*(4), 989–996.

CHAPTER 8

FINANCIAL SECTOR DEVELOPMENT IN NEW EU MEMBER STATES

Marina Kudinska, Irina Solovjova and Inna Romānova

University of Latvia, Latvia

ABSTRACT

Purpose: *This chapter analyses the financial sector development indicators of the new European Union (EU) member states, identifying the most important factors affecting their development. It focuses on the 13 new member states of the EU that joined the EU from 2004.*

Need for study: *Financial sector development has a significant impact on any country's economy, supporting faster growth of its national economy. It is essential to study the general development factors and individual characteristics of the financial sector's development in the new EU member countries and evaluate their financial policy decisions during the crisis period.*

Methodology: *The authors examine indicators characterising the development of the financial market, such as assets to gross domestic product (GDP), loans to GDP, market capitalisation to GDP, the number of companies traded in the capital market, and other indicators. Along with the development indicators, the authors analyse those affecting security and resilience, such as bank capital adequacy, non-performing loan (NPL) portfolio, and others. The research*

Economic Development and Resilience by EU Member States
Contemporary Studies in Economic and Financial Analysis, Volume 115, 119–139
Copyright © 2025 by Marina Kudinska, Irina Solovjova and Inna Romānova
Published under exclusive licence by Emerald Publishing Limited
ISSN: 1569-3759/doi:10.1108/S1569-375920240000115008

methodology comprises content analysis, logical, constructive analysis, synthesis methods, and graphic visualisation.

Findings: *This chapter examines development aspects of the financial systems in the new EU member states, concluding that joining the EU contributed to the successful development of the financial markets and that common financial market principles helped the new EU member states cope with the challenges.*

Practical implications: *Helpful for financial sector experts and policymakers, findings provide insight into the development trends of financial and capital markets in the new EU members.*

Keywords: New EU countries; bank activities; lending; EBU; capital market; market capitalisation; CMU

JEL classifications: G01; G21; G15

1. INTRODUCTION

A developed financial sector is a driving force of the economy, providing businesses and households with the necessary financial resources through different channels. The industry undergoes continuous development and constantly interacts with the external environment, exposing its structure to external and internal challenges. As suggested by International Monetary Fund (IMF) research data (IMF, 2023), the European financial sector has a specific structure where banks have the prevailing role in funding the economy (see Fig. 8.1).

This situation is also a characteristic for the countries that joined the EU from 2004. Compared to banks, capital market positions are negligible. On one hand, a well-developed capital market provides for diversifying the structure of the

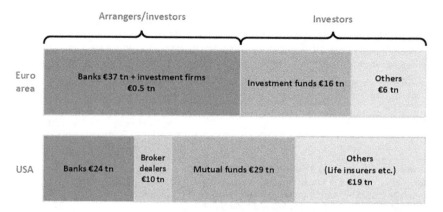

Fig. 8.1. Market Structure of the Euro Area and the United States, 2022.
Source: Adapted from IMF (2023).

Financial Sector Development   121

institutional segment of lending, increasing the flow of financial capital among investors and issuers of securities, and improving the circulation and the rate of return of financial capital in the national economy (Solovjova et al., 2022). On the other hand, we can observe the fragmentation of capital markets, low liquidity, high costs, lack of investor trust, and other issues.

Several studies have focused on the development of financial markets in individual member states after joining the EU. Baudino et al. (2022) analysed the financial crisis in the Baltic states and concluded that foreign banks played a supportive role during the financial crisis in Baltic countries. The foreign ownership of banks allowed for faster growth and financial deepening before the crisis but represented a vulnerability during the crisis (Baudino et al., 2022, p. 35). Cleridesa and Stephanou (2009) examined the development of the banking system in Cyprus, Szikszai et al. (2012) analysed the Hungarian financial system before and after joining the EU, Włodarczyk et al. (2019) studied the role of the financial sector in macroeconomic stability in Poland, and Solovjova et al. (2019) and Romānova and Solovjova (2020) analysed a bank financial health in Latvia. However, there is a lack of studies on the development of the financial market in all new EU member states. This study is designed to assess the development of financial systems in all countries that joined the EU in 2004. The study shows how the common principles and values of the EU influence the financial markets of the new member states.

This chapter aims to analyse the financial sector development indicators of the new EU member states and identify the most important factors affecting their development. The authors examine various indicators to achieve this aim, such as bank assets to GDP, loans to GDP, stock market capitalisation to GDP, and the number of companies traded on the stock market.

The data used for the research cover the period starting from 2004, which marks the accession of Latvia, Lithuania, Estonia, Malta, Cyprus, Poland, the Czech Republic, Slovenia, Slovakia, and Hungary to the EU. Bulgaria and Romania joined the EU in 2007 and Croatia in 2013. In this study, the authors refer to this group of countries as new EU member states. The indicators describing the financial sector's performance have been studied until 2022.

The research methodology comprises content analysis, logical constructive analysis, synthesis methods, and graphic visualisation. This chapter examines the development aspects of the financial systems in the new EU member states.

2. BANKING SYSTEMS OF THE NEW EU MEMBER STATES

Maintaining an efficient and reliable banking system is vital for achieving sustainable economic growth in every country. The ratio of banking assets as a percentage of GDP is the main indicator of the significance of the banking system for the development of the country's economy. However, in the new EU member states, the banking assets to GDP ratio is lower than the EU average (292%). The banking assets to GDP ratio exceeds the EU average only in the banking systems of Cyprus and Malta, where, according to 2020 data, it was 300% and 310%, respectively (see Fig. 8.2).

The common feature of the banking systems of the new EU member states is that commercial banks form the core of the banking systems. However, there are also peculiarities. For example, the Polish banking system is represented by mortgage banks in addition to commercial and retail banks, whereas the banking sectors of the Baltic states and the Czech Republic consist only of commercial banks and branches of foreign commercial banks. Hungary has both commercial banks and specialised credit institutions such as mortgage banks and export–import banks; Malta has Lombard bank regulated as a credit institution and as an investment service provider. Slovakia, Slovenia, and Croatia have specialised savings banks. Another common characteristic of the banking systems analysed is the significant share of foreign investment in bank capital. In several new EU member states, banks were mainly owned by foreign capital. Thus, for example, two-thirds of its banking assets in the Czech Republic belonged to non-residents;

Fig. 8.2. Banking Assets as a Percentage of GDP in the New EU Member States and EU Average in 2020. *Source*: Adapted from Eurostat data (2024a).

in the Baltic states, Scandinavian capital banks played the dominant role throughout the examined period. According to the data of the Central Banks at the end of 2022, the share of Scandinavian capital banks in the banking assets of the Baltic countries was, on average, 68% (in Latvia – 72.5%, in Lithuania – 63%, in Estonia – 69%), and in Bulgaria, foreign banks controlled 70% of bank assets. All the analysed countries have branches or subsidiaries of foreign banks.

All banks in EU countries are members of the European Bank Union (EBU). EBU was established after the crisis of 2008–2009. The economic crisis has had a significant impact on the financial system in the EU. The most important goal of the EBU was to protect taxpayers from the necessity of solving the problems of banks, as between 2008 and 2011, the European taxpayers diverted more than EUR 1 trillion to the rescue of the banking systems. Moreover, the fiscal costs of the financial aid provided throughout 2008–2014 caused the worsening of the euro area budget balance (ECB Economic Bulletin, 2015).

According to the unified principles of the EBU, the following mechanisms are in place in the new EU member states: the European Single Supervisory Mechanism (SSM) and the Single Resolution Mechanism (SRM). Moreover, a single deposit insurance scheme is valid in all EU member states. According to the SSM, some banks registered in the new EU member states are also under the direct supervision of the European Central Bank (ECB): three Estonian banks, three Latvian banks, three Lithuanian banks, two Cypriot banks, three Maltese banks, five Slovenian banks, and one Bulgarian bank (ECB, 2024).

Since 2010, the single EU principles of deposit insurance have been in place in the new EU member states, providing the same amount of insurance coverage for deposits, namely up to 100,000 euros. Until 2010, each new EU country had its own amount of deposit insurance coverage (see Fig. 8.3).

Due to the fight against illegally obtained funds, the deposit structure in the context of the depositors' residence has significantly changed in recent years in

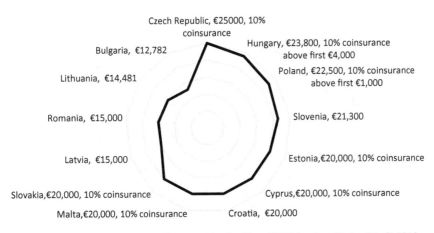

Fig. 8.3. Deposit Insurance Coverage in the New EU Member States Until 2010, Euros. *Source*: Adapted from Laeven et al. (2013).

the countries where banks traditionally worked with non-resident customers. For example, in Latvia, until 2017, the situation of the Latvian banking sector was unique due to the large number of customers from the former Soviet Union countries. At the end of 2015, 56% of total bank deposits belonged to non-residents from CIS countries (Rupeika-Apoga et al., 2020, p. 3). After the collapse of the third largest bank, ABLV, in 2018, wherein non-resident customer services accounted for 80% of the business, the regulator (at that time the Financial and Capital Market Commission) demanded that 11 banks serving non-residents change their business model, reducing the business with high-risk non-residents. Not all banks managed to find new markets; out of 14 banks working in 2018, only 9 remained at the end of 2023. Refusal of banks to serve high-risk clients was also observed in other new EU member states.

Another trend that contributed to the decrease in the number of banks in the new EU member states was the consolidation of the bank capital following the implementation of strict prudential regulations in the EU member states after the financial crisis of 2007–2009. Consequently, the number of banks in the new EU member decreased by 64 banks in the period between 2004 and 2023. The banking systems of the countries have become stronger; their policy is directly aimed at sustainable development. A higher risk tolerance is suggested by the capital adequacy ratio, which, in recent years, has been higher than the EU average in most new EU member states (Fig. 8.4). It should be noted that Tier I capital adequacy in several new EU member states equals total capital adequacy, which comprises the highest-quality capital.

Another important indicator of bank performance that suggests that the banking systems of the new EU member states have become more robust and secure is their liquidity. In 2015, the EU introduced the liquidity coverage ratio (LCR), which is designed to ensure that banks hold a sufficient reserve of high-quality liquid assets (HQLA) to allow them to survive a period of significant liquidity stress lasting for 30 calendar days (BIS, 2018). At the end of 2022, the

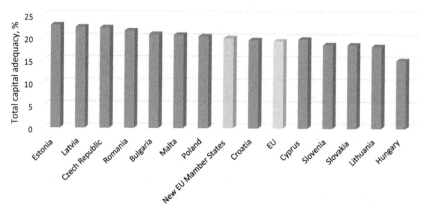

Fig. 8.4. Total Capital Adequacy in the Banking Systems of the New EU Member States and EU Average at the End of 2023, Percentage (ECB, 2023).

Financial Sector Development 125

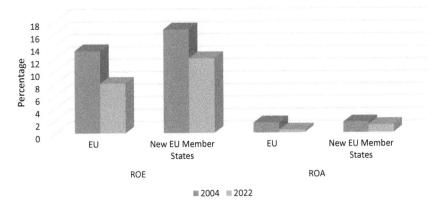

Fig. 8.5. ROE and ROA in the Banking Systems of the New EU Member States and EU Average in 2004 and 2022, Percentage (ECB, 2005, 2023).

average ratio in the new EU member states accounted for 227.17% (the prudential criterion is 100% (Summaries of EU Legislation, 2019)), while the EU average was 161.46%, whereas the highest ratio was that of the banks of Malta (396.14%) and lowest of the Hungarian banks (174.5%).

Prudential requirements for risk management and maintenance of liquid assets have decreased the banks' profitability. As shown in Fig. 8.5, however, the return on equity (ROE) and return on assets (ROA) in the new EU member states still exceed the EU average.

Bank profitability is affected not only by internal factors within the banks but also by external factors, such as the country's inflation rate, changes in interest rates, growth of the national economy, and others. Thus, in 2022, the rise of EURIBOR was the decisive reason for the increase in banks' profitability.

3. LENDING BY THE BANKS IN THE NEW EU MEMBER STATES BEFORE AND AFTER THE FINANCIAL CRISIS

After joining the EU, investments in the real sector in newly admitted countries grew rapidly, especially in production, real estate, and banking. In Bulgaria, capital investment volumes were higher than in the other newly admitted countries (Bekker & Klingen, 2012). Investments in banks activated lending in all new EU member states. It should be noted that before joining the EU, the new member states had a relatively low ratio[1] of bank loans to GDP, which negatively affected the countries' overall economic development. The economic reforms related to joining the EU and the available credit resources of the banks contributed to the development of lending in all newly admitted countries. Loan balances grew especially rapidly in the Baltic countries. The average annual growth rate of loans issued to households from 2004 to 2007 was +58.5% in Estonia, +52% in Latvia, and +66.7% in Lithuania. Figs. 8.6 and 8.7 show that before the global financial crisis, household loan growth rates in these countries were significantly higher than the EU average of +8.45%.

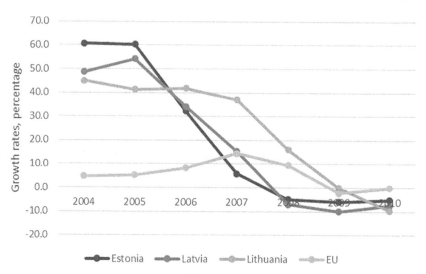

Fig. 8.6. Bank Loans to Non-financial Institution Growth in the Baltic States and EU in 2004–2010, Percentage (ECB, 2005, 2006, 2007, 2008, 2010, 2011). *Source*: Authors' calculations.

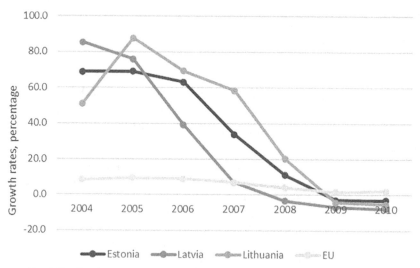

Fig. 8.7. Bank Loans to Households Growth in the Baltic States and EU in 2004–2010, Percentage (ECB, 2005, 2006, 2007, 2008, 2010, 2011). *Source*: Authors' calculations.

Financial Sector Development　　　　　　　　　　　　　　　　　　　　　　127

Before the global financial crisis, borrowing in a foreign currency was facilitated by lower borrowing costs than in national currencies. For example, 75%–80% of the loans issued to households by the banks in the Baltic states were in foreign currencies. Lending contributed to raising the welfare level of the population. From 2000 to 2008, the Baltic states made significant progress in catching up with the European living standards – in 2000, their per capita GDP was around 40% of the EU average, and in 2008, they reached 55%–65% (Baudino et al., 2022, p. 8). The easily accessible loans were mainly directed to consumption and speculative transactions in the real estate market. Due to the growing lending, real estate prices rose sharply. In most new EU member states, real estate prices rose in double digits annually in the first years after joining the EU. Thus, in Cyprus, real estate prices increased by an average of 50% per year in the period from the beginning of 2004 to the end of 2008 (Cleridesa & Stephanou, 2009); in the Baltic states in 2006, the increase in real estate prices was over 40% per year; and in Poland, during 2007, residential prices in Warsaw grew by 48%, while the price of apartments in new housing projects jumped by 65% (Ober-House, 2007). In 2007, several countries introduced strict prudential rules on lending for housing. The financial crisis and prudential restrictions on lending reduced the demand for real estate and mortgage loans, which contributed to a dramatic drop in real estate prices. According to the ECB data, in 2008–2010, the biggest fall in real estate prices in the new EU member states was seen in five countries (see Fig. 8.8).

The Czech Republic, on the other hand, experienced a boom in mortgage lending faster than other newly admitted countries. In the wait to join the EU from 1998 to 2003, the Czech housing price index rose by 64%, facilitated by the government's rapid spending growth as the state budget deficit grew. During this period, the prices of the block apartments in the Czech Republic rose by 118%, while the prices of the individual apartments rose by 91%. Despite joining the

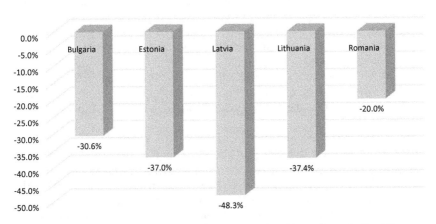

Fig. 8.8. New EU Member States with the Most Significant Drop in Real Estate Prices During 2008–2010 (Eurostat, 2024c). *Source*: Authors' calculation.

EU, EU citizens were barred from buying property for a seven-year transition period until 2009 (Delmendo, 2023).

There are several studies related to the role of European banks in the financial crisis of 2007–2009: Lisandrou (2022) analysed the European banks' role in the financial crisis. Carletti et al. (2024) examined the impact of banks' strength in credit and deposit markets on the credit availability and financial system stability. Leaven and Valencia (2010) analysed the features of the 2007–2009 crisis and common patterns with earlier crises. Cooper and Nikolov (2018) created a model of the feedback loop between banks and sovereigns, etc. Dell'Ariccia et al. (2018) found three interacting channels that linked banks and state budget: banks hold large amounts of sovereign debt, government guarantees protected banks, and the health of banks and government effects. Kudinska (2017) evaluated the post-crisis development of the Latvian banking system and the impact of the Basel III Accord on the further development of the banking sector in Latvia. Maudos and de Guevara (2015) investigated how the global financial crisis has affected economic integration and economic growth. Due to the systemic importance of banks in the stability of the state, in virtually all EU member states, including the new member states, systemic banks were saved during the crisis. According to the IMF data, the level of state support to banks in Latvia in 2007–2009 was 5% of GDP (including 2.5% for Parex bank recapitalisation and 2.5% for maintaining the liquidity of other banks); in Hungary, it was 2.8% of GDP (including 0.1% capital injection in FHB Mortgage Bank (mortgage lender) for recapitalisation and 2.6% for large banks lending); and in Slovenia, 2.8% of GDP were allocated to maintaining bank liquidity.

Due to the slowdown in economic development during the crisis, the quality of bank loan portfolios deteriorated dramatically. The bursting of the housing bubble revealed weaknesses in the regulation of the financial system, which had consequences for the financial sector and the real economy. Loan portfolios were poorly diversified; there was a high concentration of mortgage loans. Therefore, banks were very sensitive to changes in the real estate market. Banks issued loans without seriously analysing the borrower's creditworthiness, creating hidden systemic risks. In several new EU member states, the regulators strengthened the regulatory requirements for credit risk management. As a result, getting loans became no longer easy.

In 2014, the EBA introduced the definition of NPLs, which became a benchmark for monitoring the quality of banking assets in the European banking sector. Fig. 8.9 shows how the NPL ratio has changed in the new EU countries since the definition of NPL.

In 2015, Cyprus demonstrated the highest NPL ratios, reaching 47.75%. It can be explained by a substantial offshore banking sector Cyprus' banking sector had for a long time. By 2012, the banking sector had assets of more than EUR 87 billion in the economy with a GDP of only EUR 17.5 billion, with EUR 43 billion of these assets involving Russian corporate deposits (Gold Heritage Properties, 2017). In 2012, Cyprus banks were forced to write off the Greek debt, resulting in losses of more than EUR 4 billion, which amounted to about 22%

Financial Sector Development

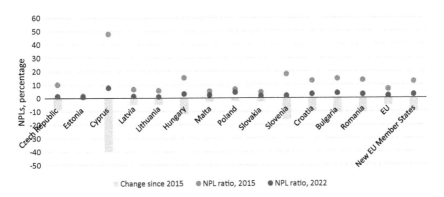

Fig. 8.9. NPL Ratio in the New EU Member States in 2022, Compared to 2015, Percentage (Eurostat, 2024b). *Source*: Authors' calculation.

of the country's GDP (ESM, 2019). Without support, the banking sector could not cope with the losses; the state could not help the financial sector due to the budget deficit of 80% of GDP. In 2012, the Cyprus banking system collapsed. In 2013, the country was declared defaulted on its national debt. In March 2013, Cyprus became the fifth Eurozone country to receive rescue aid from three institutions: the IMF, the ECB, and the European Commission. In total, Cyprus was lent EUR 10 billion with the following significant reforms and downsizing of the Cyprus banking system.

The banks in countries with high NPL rates in 2015 (Cyprus, Hungary, Slovenia, Croatia, Bulgaria, and Romania) managed to reduce the share of bad loans in the loan portfolio faster than in other EU member states. Cypriot and Slovenian banks were under special attention of the ECB and had to reduce NPLs significantly. In Cypriot banks, NPL decreased from 2015 to 2022 by more than 40 pp and in Slovenian banks by 16 pp. In general, in the new EU member states, NPLs were higher than the EU average; however, they decreased faster than the EU average (see Fig. 8.10).

After the crisis, lending rates decreased and, in the following years, grew at moderate rates in all analysed countries. In the period from 2010 to 2022, the fastest development of lending was seen in Poland (the average annual growth rate of lending to households was 16%, and the growth rate of business lending was 7% per year) and in Slovakia (the average annual growth rate of lending to households was 11% year, and the growth rate of business lending was 4.4% per year). A comparison of the activity of banks in the loan market in the new EU member states with the EU average shows that the domestic credit to the private sector as a percentage of GDP ratio is still significantly lower than the average ratio in Europe (see Fig. 8.11).

The worst situation in lending was observed in Latvia, Lithuania, and Romania. At the end of 2022, it was only 52.5% of GDP in Latvia, 51.3% in Lithuania, and 43.3% in Romania. This is much less than in most European countries.

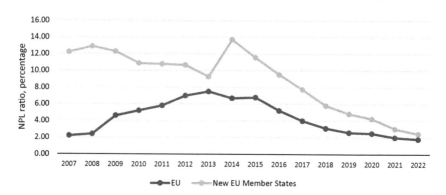

Fig. 8.10. NPLs in the New EU Member States and EU Average During 2007–2022, Percentage (Eurostat, 2024b). *Source*: Authors' calculation.

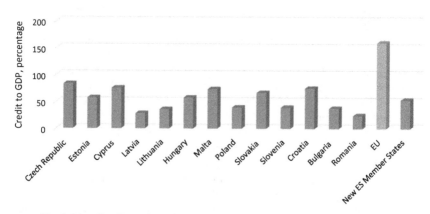

Fig. 8.11. Credit to the Private Sector as a Percentage of GDP Ratio in the New EU Member States and EU Average in 2022 (Eurostat, 2024d). *Source*: Authors' calculation.

In Latvia and Lithuania, the reasons for weak credit growth could be related to the lack of access to loans in regions, structural weaknesses, for example, bureaucratic obstacles related to the construction process, and relatively high interest rates on loans and stringent requirements on borrowers. In Romania, a further significant factor is the weak creditworthiness of potential borrowers. This confirms that more than half of the companies operating in Romania have negative equity.

Thus, despite the significant improvement in the financial situation of households and companies in the new EU member states, lending continued to be weak after the crisis.

Financial Sector Development

4. CAPITAL MARKET DEVELOPMENT IN THE NEW EU COUNTRIES

The capital market is an integral part of the financial sector as it provides for attracting investments necessary for development. Before describing the situation in the new EU member states, it is essential to briefly describe the situation in the EU as a whole. European capital markets are fragmented, and the European capital market picture is very complex. It is possible to make minor adjustments to regulatory details; however, if Europe continues to have 22 distinct stock exchange groups overseeing 35 listing exchanges, 41 trading exchanges, and nearly 40 different central counterparty clearing houses (CCPs) and central securities depositories (CSDs), substantial changes are unlikely (Wright & Hamre, 2021). This means that European companies and citizens cannot fully benefit from the financing and investment opportunities offered by European capital markets. European capital markets are not large, leading to high reliance on bank financing. Banking assets in Europe make up 300% of GDP, which is a higher indicator compared to the United States – 85% of GDP and a smaller one compared to Japan – 500% of GDP (Bhatia et al., 2019). The listed capital accounts for only 68% of GDP, which is much less compared to both the United States (170%) and Japan (120%) (Bhatia et al., 2019). As shown in Fig. 8.12, 28% of the total available funding in Europe is constituted by trading instruments. This figure is also significantly lower than that of the United States, Japan, and the United Kingdom (see Fig. 8.12).

Non-financial corporations in Europe and the new EU member states, in particular, rely mainly on bank financing, while capital markets play a lesser role. In the new member states, bank financing has an almost complete monopoly in financing companies (see Fig. 8.13).

The data in Fig. 8.13 suggest that the most significant reliance on bank financing is observed in Cyprus (98%); Latvia, Slovakia, and Bulgaria are also among the leaders in this respect. However, also the 'old' EU member states have strong bank lending positions (see Fig. 8.13).

The new EU member states are very diverse in terms of capital market development. For example, in Slovakia, only 1% of the listed shares are used for corporate finance, and Bratislava's stock market capitalisation is only 2 billion euros. In contrast, Poland has the most developed stock market in the analysed region, with approximately 22% of corporate capital market financing, close to the EU average. The market capitalisation of the Warsaw Stock Exchange is roughly EUR 138 billion, which is significantly ahead of other stock markets in the region, such as Bucharest (EUR 27 billion), Prague (EUR 27 billion), and Budapest (EUR 22 billion) (CEE Capital Markets Under Development, 2023). There are many reasons for underdeveloped capital markets, including the relatively small size of the economies.

In 2018, the Association for Financial Markets in Europe started a project that evaluates EU countries' development and compliance with the Capital Market Union (CMU) requirements according to seven criteria. The first criterion

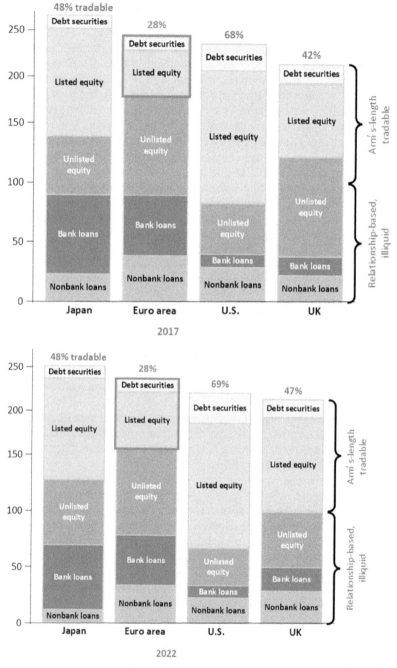

Fig. 8.12. Non-financial Corporations Funding Structure 2017 and 2022, Percentage to GDP. *Source*: Adapted from IMF (2023).

Financial Sector Development

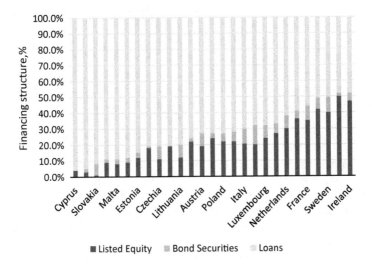

Fig. 8.13. Financing of Non-financial Corporates (NFCs), 2022 (CEE Capital Markets Under Development).

(Market Finance Indicator + Pre-IPO Risk Capital) assesses the availability of financing. Table 8.1 shows the Market Finance Indicator, which measures how easily the NFCs can attract public funding (initial public offerings, bonds, secondary equity offerings).

Table 8.1 suggests that regarding the availability of financing, most of the new EU member states can be found at the bottom of the list – except Malta, Hungary,

Table 8.1. Progress of EU Capital Markets Relative to Key Performance Indicators, Indicator 1 – Market Finance (NFC Equity and Bond Issuance as % of Total NFC Annual Financing), 1 – Higher Rankings, 28 – Lower Rankings.

Country	Year			
	2018	2019	2022	2023
Czech Republic	12	5	2	10
Estonia	22	11	24	28
Cyprus	28	28	25	28
Latvia	23	25	20	20
Lithuania	16	7	16	28
Hungary	21	24	9	6
Malta	28	8	1	1
Poland	15	22	17	15
Slovakia	28	23	23	28
Slovenia	28	28	25	28
Croatia	20	28	25	28

Sources: AFME (2018, 2019, 2022, 2023).

and the Czech Republic. Unfortunately, the ranking of several countries (Croatia, Romania, etc.) tends to worsen.

Market capitalisation to GDP is one of the most important indicators of the securities market's size, scale, and capacity. There are substantial differences in terms of the size of the markets in the EU – more than 200% in France and Sweden and less than 50% in Lithuania and Latvia (Bhatia et al., 2019). According to the data from Fig. 8.14, among the new member states admitted in 2004, we can see an extensive indicator spread, from 4.2% of GDP in Slovakia to 81% of GDP in Cyprus. It should be noted that for a more significant proportion of new entrants in 2004, except Cyprus (81%), this figure is well below the euro area average (42%). The situation in Bulgaria (9.71%), Romania (9.28%), and Croatia (32.33%), which joined the EU in 2007 and 2013, respectively, is very similar. The pre-accession ratio was below the euro area average (see Fig. 8.14).

Examined further is the development of the capital market after joining the EU, which was influenced by various internal and external factors. Undoubtedly, the global financial crisis of 2008 deeply affected the capital market. In 2010, compared to the pre-crisis year of 2007, the market capitalisation index in the Czech Republic decreased by approximately 19%, in Estonia by 16%, Cyprus by 45%, Latvia by 4.3%, Lithuania by 13%, Hungary by 12%, Malta by 25%, Poland by 10%, Slovakia by 3.5%, Slovenia by 40%, Croatia by 74%, Bulgaria by 34%, and Romania by 10%. Respectively, there is a decreasing trend (see Fig. 8.15).

The degree of impact of the financial crisis on various countries depended on their socioeconomic development and specific features of their economy. Capital markets are an essential channel for the best corporate governance practices for new entrants. Listed companies follow higher corporate governance standards and set an example for other companies. Besides, the successful listing is an excellent example for other companies. The global financial crisis mainly affected the capital market in Croatia (↓ 74%). According to Tomislav Rizak (Member of the Board of the Croatian Financial Services Supervisory Agency (HANFA-CFSSA)), Croatian highly leveraged companies faced severe challenges and were

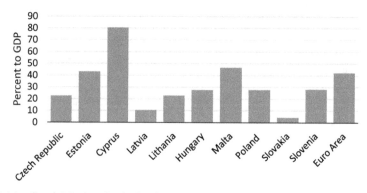

Fig. 8.14. Stock Market Capitalisation to GDP (%) in the New EU Member States, 2004 (CEIC Data; World Bank).

Financial Sector Development

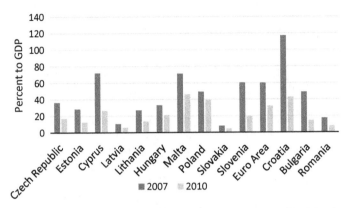

Fig. 8.15. Stock Market Capitalisation to GDP (%) in the New EU Member States, 2007 and 2010 (CEIC Data; World Bank).

forced to adapt to a new reality with limited funding and significant costs (Eurofi, 2020). Well-capitalised companies, on the other hand, handled the recession much better.

The next challenge for the capital markets of the new EU member states came with the COVID-19 pandemic (Fig. 8.16). For most countries, the authors observed a trend towards declining rates. The drop was observed in Latvia – from 2.5% in 2018 to a critically low level of 1.5% in 2022. The biggest fall was observed in Malta (11 percentage points) and Poland (17 percentage points).

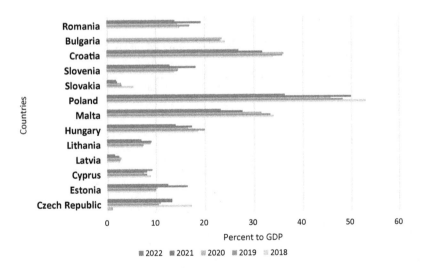

Fig. 8.16. Stock Market Capitalisation to GDP (%) in the New EU Member States, 2018–2022 (CEIC Data; World Bank).

Another indicator of the scale of the capital market is the number of companies listed on the stock exchange. Table 8.2 shows how changes in the indicator may be related to new business entries (as a result of initial public offerings (IPO) or delisting.

When analysing Table 8.2 data, it is necessary to note that the number of listed companies in Malta, Poland, Slovakia, Croatia, etc. has increased after joining the EU in 2004. However, the global financial crisis of 2007 has affected the indicator in various ways. For example, the authors observed a significant increase in Poland from 352 companies in 2007 to 570 in 2010, a substantial decrease in Cyprus from 124 companies in 2007 to 11 in 2010, and Slovakia from 160 companies in 2007 to 90 in 2010. The analysis of the indicators in subsequent periods suggests the improvement and stabilisation of the situation in Cyprus and a positive trend in the Czech Republic and Slovenia. According to the latest data from the World Stock Exchange Federation, the number of companies listed in Malta rose 18.5% year on year in 2022, with 35 listed companies, and 11.1% in Hungary with 50 companies (World Federation of Exchange Statistics Portal, 2022). The number of listed companies in the new EU member states increased by 30% compared to 2004. However, the analysis of the overall situation in the EU shows that the number of listed companies had decreased by 17% from 2009 onwards (by 1,300 companies) until 2022 (Wright & Hamre, 2021).

According to P. Heilbronn (Vice President of the European Bank for Reconstruction and Development Policy and Partnerships), capital markets in the new EU member states faced a number of challenges (Eurofi, 2020) connected essentially with a market size constraint (fragmentation). Markets lack liquidity and investor confidence. A significant problem is giving investors access to local markets and reducing transaction costs. According to experts, local capital

Table 8.2. Number of Listed Companies Per Million People in the New EU Member States, Not Seasonally Adjusted.

Country	Year							
	2004	2007	2010	2011	2013	2018	2019	2020
Czech Republic	33	13	15	17	15	17	17	20
Estonia	No data							
Cyprus	124	124	11	106	95	91	96	92
Latvia	No data							
Lithuania								
Hungary	47	39	48	52	50	43	44	45
Malta	14	16	21	21	23	25	27	27
Poland	211	352	570	757	869	823	798	782
Slovakia	8	160	90	147	67	–	–	–
Slovenia	140	87	72	66	55	31	29	37
Croatia	166	259	240	233	192	127	119	104
Bulgaria	332	369	390	393	381	274	262	259
Romania	55	54	73	77	81	85	81	81
Total	1,130	1,473	1,530	1,869	1,828	1,516	1,473	1,447

Source: World Bank.

markets in the new EU member states do not attract investors or provide support to larger issuers because of their limited scale. Underdeveloped money markets and corporate bond markets are having a negative impact on economic development. Another critical aspect is the risk aversion by investors and the lack of financial literacy. An Organisation for Economic Co-operation and Development (OECD) study (OECD/INFE, 2020) found that the overall level of financial literacy is low in all studied countries. Slovenia has the highest position as the most financially literate among the analysed countries, followed by Estonia and Poland, while Romania has the lowest rate.

5. CONCLUSIONS

The banking industry plays the dominant role in the financial sector of the new EU member states. The number of banks in the new EU countries tends to shrink. This process is influenced by banks' refusal to work with high-risk clients and the consolidation of bank capital due to the introduction of strict prudential regulations in EU countries after the financial crisis of 2007–2009. Key indicators of banking activity show that banking systems in the new EU countries have become more robust, and banking policies are geared towards sustainable development. Banks of the new member states are better capitalised than the EU average and have higher liquidity ratios. Economic reforms linked to the accession to the EU contributed to the development of lending in all newly admitted countries. However, lending to GDP in these countries is still significantly lower than the European average.

EU member states need to continue developing their financial and capital markets to meet the needs of its changing economy, channel private finance towards investment, promote innovation, and improve access to capital funding for the EU companies. The problems existing in the new EU member states, such as market size, liquidity, investor protection, etc., can be addressed by an integrated EU capital market (CMU; Principles for a European Capital Markets Union, 2015). The process and principles for forming the CMU have been validated, and close attention has been paid to transparency, liquidity provision, investor protection, and other conditions of market discipline while exposing systemic actors to intrusive prudential supervision. Political support is vitally necessary to implement this process, thus providing the European economy with the resources needed for development.

NOTE

1. In 2004, the mode of the loans-to-GDP ratio in the new EU member states was 33%.

REFERENCES

AFME. (2018). *Capital Markets Union. Key performance indicators, European capital markets: Scaling up capital markets* (1st ed.). https://www.afme.eu/

AFME. (2019). *Capital Markets Union. Key performance indicators, European capital markets: Scaling up capital markets* (2nd ed.). https://www.afme.eu/

AFME. (2022). *Capital Markets Union. Key performance indicators, European capital markets: Scaling up capital markets* (6th ed.). https://www.afme.eu/

AFME. (2023). *Capital Markets Union. Key performance indicators, European capital markets: Scaling up capital markets* (7th ed.) https://www.afme.eu/

Baudino, P., Lielkalne, O., Reichenbachas, T., Tamm, M., & Vrbaski, R. (2022). *The 2008 financial crises in the Baltic countries* [Financial Stability Institute Working Paper, FSI Crisis Management (Series 3)]. https://www.bis.org/

Bekker, B. B., & Klingen, C. A. (2012). *Bulgaria: Surviving the crisis on its own. How emerging Europe came through the 2008/09 crisis* (Chapter 20). IMF. https://doi.org/10.5089/9781616353810.071

Bhatia, A. V., Mitra, S., Weber, A., Aiyar, S., Almeida, L., Cuervo, C., Santos, A. O., & Gudmundsson, T. (2019). *A Capital Market Union for Europe* [IMF Staff Discussion Note]. https://www.imf.org/en/Publications/

BIS. (2018). *Liquidity coverage ratio (LCR)* [Executive summary]. https://www.bis.org

Carletti, E., Leonello, A., & Marquez, R. (2024). *Market power in banking* [ECB Working Paper No. 2886]. https://www.ecb.europa.eu/

CEE capital markets under development. (2023). Erste Group Research. www.erstegroup.com

CEIC Data Global Database. (2024). https://www.ceicdata.com/

Cleridesa, M., & Stephanou, C. (2009). The financial crisis and the banking system in Cyprus. *Cyprus Economic Policy Review*, *3*(1), 27–50. https://www.researchgate.net/publication/228298868_The_Financial_Crisis_and_the_Banking_System_in_Cyprus

CMU. (2024). https://www.consilium.europa.eu/en/policies/capital-markets-union/

Cooper, R., & Nikolov, K. (2018, November). *Government debt and banking fragility: The spreading of strategic uncertainty* [ECB Working Paper Series No. 2195]. https://www.ecb.europa.eu

Dell'Ariccia, G., Ferreira, C., Jenkinson, N., Laeven, L., Martin, A., Minoiu, C., & Popov, A. (2018). *Managing the sovereign-bank nexus.* https://www.imf.org/en/Publications/

Delmendo, L. C. (2023). *Czech Republic's housing market weakening.* https://www.globalpropertyguide.com

ECB. (2005). Financial stability review. December 2005, https://www.ecb.europa.eu/pub/pdf/fsr/financialstabilityreview200512en.pdf

ECB. (2006). Financial stability review. December 2006, https://www.ecb.europa.eu/pub/pdf/fsr/financialstabilityreview200612en.pdf

ECB. (2007). Financial stability review. December 2007, https://www.ecb.europa.eu/pub/pdf/fsr/financialstabilityreview200712en.pdf

ECB. (2008). Financial stability review. December 2008, https://www.ecb.europa.eu/pub/pdf/fsr/financialstabilityreview200812en.pdf

ECB. (2010). Financial stability review. December 2010, https://www.ecb.europa.eu/pub/pdf/fsr/financialstabilityreview201012en.pdf

ECB. (2011). Financial stability review. December 2010, https://www.ecb.europa.eu/pub/pdf/fsr/financialstabilityreview201112en.pdf

ECB. (2023). ECB annual report on supervisory activities 2023. https://www.bankingsupervision.europa.eu/press/publications/annual-report/html/ssm.ar2023~2def923d71.en.html

ECB. (2024). Supervisory banking statistics, fourth quarter 2023. https://www.bankingsupervision.europa.eu/ecb/pub/pdf/ssm.supervisorybankingstatistics_fourth_quarter_2023_202404~71683cabe2.en.pdf

ECB Economic Bulletin. (2015). *The fiscal impact of financial sector support during the crisis* (Issue 6). https://www.ecb.europa.eu

ESM. (2019). Crisis in Cyprus: No negotiating power, no credibility. In *Safeguarding the euro in times of crisis* (pp. 261–277). ESM Publications. https://www.esm.europa.eu/publications/safeguarding-euro

Eurofi. (2020). *Capital market development in CEE.* https://www.eurofi.net/

Eurostat. (2024a). Bank assets to GDP. https://ec.europa.eu/

Eurostat. (2024b). *Gross non-performing loans, domestic and foreign entities – % of gross loans.* https://ec.europa.eu/

Eurostat. (2024c). *House prices.* https://ec.europa.eu/

Eurostat. (2024d). *Private sector debt: Loans, by sectors, consolidated – % of GDP.* https://ec.europa.eu/

Financial Sector Development

Gold Heritage Properties. (2017). *Cyprus' housing market improving, after dramatic measures encourage buyers*. https://goldheritage.com.cy/

IMF. (2023). *Background note on CMU for Eurogroup*. www.imf.org

Kudinska, M. (2017). Post-crisis evolution and challenges of banking sector: The case of Latvia. In *New challenges of economic and business development – 2017 digital economy* (pp. 362–373). University of Latvia. https://www.bvef.lu.lv/

Laeven, L., Enoch, C., Everaert, L., Tressel, T., & Zhou, J. (2013). *From fragmentation to financial integration in Europe* (Chapter 14, pp. 279–293). IMF. https://doi.org/10.5089/9781484387665.071

Leaven, L., & Valencia, F. (2010). *Resolution of banking crises: The good, the bad, and the ugly* [IMF Working Paper No. 2010/146]. https://www.imf.org/en/Publications

Lisandrou, P. (2022). The European banks' role in the financial crisis of 2007-8: A critical assessment. *New Political Economy, 27*(5), 879–894. https://doi.org/10.1080/13563467.2022.2038115

Maudos, J., & de Guevara, J. F. (2015). The economic impact of European financial integration: The importance of the banking union. *The Spanish Review of Financial Economics, 13*(1), 11–19.

Ober-House. (2007). *Real estate market report* (p. 6). https://www.ober-haus.lt/

OECD/INFE. (2020). *International survey of adult financial literacy*. www.oecd.org

Principles for a European Capital Markets Union: Strengthening capital markets to foster growth. (2015). https://www.deutsche-boerse.com/

Romānova, I., & Solovjova, I. (2020). Bank reliability assessment model: Case of Latvia. *Eurasian Studies in Business and Economics, 12*(2), 285–298. https://doi.org/10.1007/978-3-030-35051-2_19

Rupeika, R., Romānova, I., & Grima, S. (2020). The determinants of bank's stability: Evidence from Latvia, a small post-transition economy. *Contemporary Issues in Business Economics and Finance, 104*, 235–253. https://doi.org/10.1108/S1569-375920200000104016

Solovjova, I., Romanova, I., Rupeika-Apoga, R., Saksonova, S., Kudinska, M., & Joppe A. (2019). *Assessment of bank financial health in Latvia*. https://dspace.lu.lv/

Solovjova, I., Talikovs, K., Golubeva, L., Litvinenko, A., & Svētiņa, R. (2022). Underpricing in a capital market: Case of Latvia. *WSEAS Transactions on Business and Economics, 19*, 638–646. https://wseas.com/journals/bae/2022/b125107-020(2022).pdf

Summaries of EU Legislation. (2019). *Liquidity coverage requirement for credit institutions*. https://eur-lex.europa.eu

Szikszai, S., Badics, T., Raffai, C., Stenger, Z., & Tóthmihály A. (Eds.). (2012). *The Hungarian financial system*. https://www.researchgate.net

Włodarczyk, B., Heller, J., & Ostrowska, A. (2019). *Financial aspects of macroeconomic stability. The case of Poland*. https://www.researchgate.net

World Bank. (2024). https://data.worldbank.org/

World Federation of Exchange Statistics Portal. (2022). *Number of listed companies*. https://statistics.world-exchanges.org/

Wright, W., & Hamre, E. F. (2021). *The problem with European stock market, new financial*. https://newfinancial.org/

CHAPTER 9

THE LEADING INDUSTRIES IN THE NEW EU MEMBER STATES AND THEIR CONTRIBUTION TO INCREASING THE EU'S EXPORT POTENTIAL*

Ileana Tache

Transilvania University of Brasov, Romania

ABSTRACT

Purpose and need for study: *This chapter analyses the leading industries in the new European Union (EU) member states, focusing on automotive, information technology (IT), aerospace, textiles, machinery, chemicals, renewable energy, and food and beverages. It compares the 13 new EU countries that joined in 2004, 2007, and 2013, considering factors like industrial diversity, infrastructure, workforce skills, national economic policies, and geographical position. The aim is to enhance the EU's industrial competitiveness and contribute to overall prosperity and social cohesion.*

Methodology: *The methodological instruments used in this chapter include literature review, EU documents search, historical analysis, comparative study, data handling, and interpretation.*

---

*Disclaimer: Extracts of this chapter have been reused from Dobrowolska, B., Dorożyński, T., & Kuna-Marszałek, A. (2023). The quality of governance and its impact on FDI inflows. A comparative study of EU member states. *Comparative Economic Research*, 26(3), 7–30. https://doi.org/10.18778/1508-2008.26.19.

Economic Development and Resilience by EU Member States
Contemporary Studies in Economic and Financial Analysis, Volume 115, 141–157
Copyright © 2025 by Ileana Tache
Published under exclusive licence by Emerald Publishing Limited
ISSN: 1569-3759/doi:10.1108/S1569-375920240000115009

Findings: *A careful look at the top industries of the new EU states and their capacity to increase the EU export potential shows the need for the following measures: digitalisation (growing e-commerce, digital marketing, and data analytics to meet global market demand), the monitoring of geopolitical factors and dynamics of the internal market, the expansion of external economic relations, and the reduction of barriers in global trade. This study finds that the new EU members confronted several challenges and deficiencies over the years, which are highlighted (e.g. outdated infrastructure, skilled labour shortage, environmental issues, bureaucratic hurdles, and lack of transparency in certain areas), along with the associated solutions and initiatives meant to remedy them.*

Practical implications: *This study derives important practical implications linked to new business opportunities, investment decisions, infrastructure improvement, skills development, and educational policies.*

Keywords: Leading EU industries; European industrial strategy; industrial sectors of new EU member states; EU's export potential; industrial competitiveness; industrial policy

JEL classifications: F10; L50; L60

INTRODUCTION

The EU industry plays a crucial role in driving economic growth, creating employment opportunities, and contributing to the overall prosperity and social cohesion. Starting from the need to enhance the industrial competitiveness of Europe and considering the EU's industrial strategy on the background of the green and digital transitions, this chapter intends to analyse the leading industries in the new EU member states and their contribution to increasing the EU's export potential. More specifically, the following key areas are explored: the automotive industry, IT and electronics, aerospace and defence, textiles and apparel, chemicals and pharmaceuticals, renewable energy, and food and beverages.

The methodological instruments used in this chapter include literature review, EU documents search, historical analysis, comparative study, data handling, and interpretation.

A careful look at the top industries of the new EU states and their capacity to increase the EU's export potential highlights the need for a new approach to industrial competitiveness in the new EU member states. This chapter also highlights important practical implications linked to investment decisions, infrastructure improvement, skills development, and educational policies.

To attain the envisaged objectives, this chapter is organised as follows: the next section contains a brief review of the specialised literature; then, this chapter shows the priorities of the EU's industrial policy and the challenges confronted by the new EU members in complying with them; it goes on with an overview of the industrial landscape and export potential of these countries, concerning their leading industrial sectors; the findings provided by the analysis led to the measures and solutions proposed in the next section, which offers a new approach to industrial competitiveness in the new EU countries, followed by the concluding remarks.

BRIEF LITERATURE REVIEW

There is an extended literature concerning the EU's trade potential. Still, few recent studies have focussed on the new EU member states' industrial production and export issues. However, we have identified some authors deeply concerned about the industrial development and export potential of Central and Eastern Europe (CEE) countries, Cyprus, and Malta.

Xin (2019) provides a brief analysis of the industries in CEE in 2019, enriching the knowledge of the challenges confronted by the region's industrial sectors.

Zavarskà et al. (2023), while showing the rapid convergence of CEE countries with the Western EU members, reveal that the respective industrial growth model is hitting its limits, both endogenous and exogenous, propose a new growth model for creating an EU-CEE version of the entrepreneurial state. The same study suggests that CEE countries should follow successful past examples of effective industrial policy developed by East Asian countries. A new growth model for CEE countries is also proposed by Grieveson et al. (2021) in a study with three components: (a) establishing that the existing growth model is reaching its limit, especially for the region's most developed countries; (b) detailing the global megatrends that impact the region's development; and (c) presenting a set of policy options for a more sustained rate of convergence with Western Europe.

Pellényi (2020), who examines the role of CEE economies within global value chains (GVCs), combines occupation-level employment with an input–output model to analyse the types of jobs sustained by exporting industries and recommends a functional upgrading for improving value-capture by the evolving industries. Other authors are concerned with the low value-added to CEE in GVCs. For example, Kordalska and Olczyk (2023) try to identify patterns of functional specialisation in GVCs and determinants of upgrading them for selected CEE economies. They show that Poland and Slovakia have an unfavourable GVS position and specialise in low-value-added fabrication functions. In contrast, other CEE countries have competitive advantages in high value-added tasks: the Baltic states and Slovenia in management services and the Czech Republic and Slovenia in research development. The above-mentioned study proposes upgrading factors for different types of functional specialisation in GVSs and solutions for escaping the 'factory economies' status and generating higher value-added.

The present stage of the CEE industrial development is suggestively called by Hillebrand (2022) 'the second transition', explaining why CEE needs proactive industrial and innovation policy now: he shows that the CEE's industry-based growth model is forecasted to come under pressure in the coming years, capturing the challenges faced by these countries: the region's economies are CO_2 intensive, less productive, and less automated than Western Europe.

Studies analysing Malta and Cyprus's external trade are not very recent. Instead, the present documentation for these countries can be extracted from the International Monetary Fund (IMF) Country Reports or Communications of the European institutions.

This chapter intends to contribute to the existing literature and stresses the significant economic importance of the new member states in increasing the EU's export potential.

PRIORITIES OF THE EU INDUSTRIAL POLICY AND CHALLENGES CONFRONTED BY THE NEW MEMBER STATES

Industrial policy has become an issue of growing importance in the EU, augmenting the public policy space to shape markets and coordinate economic activity towards more significant societal goals (Mazzucato, 2016). The EU's industrial policy must adapt to the current global challenges, at the centre of which are the twin transitions towards climate neutrality and digital leadership.

According to the European Commission (2020), the key priorities of the new EU industrial strategy are:

- maintaining European industry's global competitiveness;
- making Europe climate neutral by 2050; and
- shaping Europe's digital future.

The first Communication of the European Commission on the new industrial policy dates from 2020, a year marked by the outbreak of the COVID-19 pandemic. This is the reason why the New Industrial Strategy for Europe aimed at a resilient and sustainable post-pandemic recovery. In April 2021, the European Commission published an update on the Communication, stressing the need to protect the single market, promote competitiveness, and foster resilience in the EU industry. Renda and Schaus (2021) show how the shaping of the final EU industrial strategy was put in place by the CEPS[1] Task Force with the adoption of drastic changes, meant to highlight that a truly EU strategy should not be looked at as a standalone initiative but should be considered along with broader EU objectives and policies. The CEPS Task Force conceived a list of specific recommendations, focusing on the European Green Deal and the Digital Transition.

The new industrial strategy proposes actions such as an Intellectual Property Action Plan, a review of EU competition rules, comprehensive measures to modernise and decarbonise energy-intensive industries, an Action Plan in Critical Raw Materials and Pharmaceuticals, a clean hydrogen alliance, further legislation and guidance on green public procurement, and a renewed focus on innovation, investment, and skills.

An essential aspect of implementing the directions of action listed above is how the new member states adapted to the industrial policy of the EU.

As Zavarskà et al. (2023) remark, industrial policy admittedly represents somewhat of an unchartered territory for EU-CEE countries. They experienced a command economy and lacked a constructive approach to industrial policy-making. Indeed, in the ex-communist countries, the government had the role of resource allocation through centralised planning, which hindered entrepreneurship (Grieveson et al., 2021). Some industrial capacities were indeed accumulated through this way of organisation. Still, it is far from the approach of the 'entrepreneurial state', which, even if not replacing the free market, leads the process of industrial development. It was, therefore, a challenge for the new CEE states to comply with the common industrial policy of the EU, which focused on promoting competitiveness, structural change, development of small and medium enterprises, and innovation through research and development (R&D).

Cyprus and Malta were the first ex-colonial territories to join the EU. This means they have inherited the legislative, administrative, and structural characteristics of the former colonial power, the United Kingdom. Even before Brexit, the United Kingdom was most out of step in its views and policies with the status of a federated, continental Europe (Baldacchino, 1996). So, even in the case of these two small islands, an extensive policy reorientation programme was needed to meet the EU requirements.

About 20 years after becoming members of the EU, the new member states achieved an impressive catch-up with Western Europe, supported mainly by the requirements of the EU accession. They managed to overcome the recession of the 1990s and became deeply integrated into the European economy. However, in the case of CEE economies, the great promise of an EU-wide convergence of living standards has got stuck halfway; their economies are still less productive, less automated, and less advanced in many technological sectors (Hillebrand, 2022).

The EU membership creates not only many opportunities – European funds and participation in research networks (such as Horizon 2020) but also constraints – complying with the strictly rule-based framework of the EU economic policies. For example, studies analysing the impact of Horizon 2020 on innovation in Europe, such as Cincera et al. (2015), revealed persistent differences in innovation performance between countries like Sweden, Denmark, Germany, and Finland (the countries with the best results) and the weakest group of countries including Latvia, Bulgaria, Lithuania, and Romania. Despite the generous European funding, there is still a high level of heterogeneity in innovation capacity in the EU. Even though the differences in innovation performance have been slightly reduced recently, they remain significant. According to Eurostat (R&D expenditure, data extracted in December 2023), eight member states reported R&D expenditure that was below 1% of their gross domestic product (GDP) in 2022; each of them was a new member state, with the lowest R&D intensities recorded in Romania (0.46%), Malta (0.65%), and Latvia (0.75%).

During the transition period to the market economy, some CEE countries like Bulgaria, Romania, and Hungary faced challenges related to lack of transparency, corruption, and bureaucratic hurdles. Lack of transparency can significantly affect the volume of foreign investment, as happened in Romania and Bulgaria's cases. In these countries, lack of progress in addressing a high level of corruption, weak and poorly enforced property rights, and inefficient government institutions postponed their entry into the EU in 2007.

The CEE countries have also had the disadvantage of inheriting an outdated infrastructure, especially in the energy sector, with low-efficiency coal-fired units, electricity utilities partially or totally owned by the state, inefficient production and distribution of electricity, and high retail prices set by the government (Ćetković & Buzogány, 2020).

The new member states, especially CEE countries, adopted a successful foreign direct investment (FDI)-driven export model, however, with the disadvantage that FDI profits fly abroad instead of being spent within the national territory.

Another challenge highlighted by various studies (Bykova et al., 2023; Drahokoupil & Piasna, 2017) is that all CEE countries specialise in labour-intensive production. As a result, they still depend on low wages, an issue that diminishes the economic catch-up process with Western Europe; the successful model of the past years is starting to reach its limits.

In addition, the Russian invasion of Ukraine created problems through the brutal decoupling of Russia's fossil fuels (on which CEE countries were still strongly dependent) and the increase in energy prices and inflation; Cyprus and Malta, however, do not heavily depend on Russian energy sources.

OVERVIEW OF THE INDUSTRIAL LANDSCAPE AND EXPORT POTENTIAL OF THE NEW EU COUNTRIES

Central and Eastern members of the EU (CEE), Cyprus, and Malta are growing economies that are very attractive to global investors. The manufacturing opportunities were triggered by lower production and living costs (especially in CEE countries) compared to Western Europe. As a result of the single European market, involving the free movement of goods and services, the economies of CEE have become an industrial hub for Europe. The development of high-tech sectors is supported by an educated workforce, multilingual staff, and access to Western European markets. Cyprus and Malta are small economies, but their strategic geographical position significantly boosts their trade opportunities.

There are many linkages between CEE and eurozone countries in the EU trade. According to the Organisation for Economic Co-operation and Development (OECD)–World Trade Organisation (WTO) Trade in Value-Added (TiVA) database, the euro area countries account for a large share of the external trade of non-euro CEE countries: about one-third of their top 15 trade partners in GVCs are from the euro area, the most important partner being Germany, followed by Italy, France, and Austria. In addition, a large share of the external trade of non-euro CEE countries passes through GVCs in which exporters from these countries are usually located further 'downstream', that is, closer to the customer buying the finished product than their euro area partners (ECB Monthly Bulletin, 2013).

CEE countries have gradually increased their international trade, mainly due to expanding multinational corporations' activities into their national economies. As Bierut and Kuziemska-Pawlak (2016) showed, relatively low labour costs and direct proximity of the largest European markets spurred foreign capital inflow. They resulted in the inclusion of the CEE countries in the European and GVCs, leading to a significant increase in the share of the CEE countries' exports in world exports (Narodowy Bank Polski, 2014). However, CEE countries continue to specialise as 'factory economies', focusing on production, the least profitable part of the value chain (Grieveson et al., 2021).

Exporting goods and services as a percentage of GDP is an important macroeconomic indicator of a national economy's export potential. This indicator reflects openness to global markets, foreign exchange earnings, and job creation. Table 9.1 presents this indicator for the CEE economies, of Cyprus and Malta in 2020–2022.

The countries with the highest percentages are, in all three years, Malta (163.9% in 2022), Slovakia (99.4% in 2022), and Cyprus (95.0% in 2022). However, this indicator should be carefully interpreted because relying too much on exports can make a country vulnerable to global economic crises and external trade disruptions. Instead, countries must diversify their sources of economic growth, ensure export sustainability, and balance their economic strategies for a solid macroeconomic performance and resilience to economic shocks.

Cyprus and Malta have specific features due to their history and insular position. This is the reason why a brief analysis of their industrial potential is needed here (see Table 9.2).

Considering the export potential, comparative advantage, resource endowment, value chain integration, and job creation as general selection criteria, the leading industries of the new EU member states include the automotive industry, IT and electronics, aerospace and defence, textiles and apparel, chemicals and pharmaceuticals, renewable energy, and food and beverages.

The automotive industry is represented mainly by the Czech Republic (with Skoda), Slovakia (with Citroen and Kia), Hungary (with Mercedes-Bentz), and Romania (with Dacia-Renault and Ford). The automotive sector is, in fact,

Table 9.1. Exports of Goods and Services in % of GDP.

Country	2020	2021	2022
Bulgaria	56.1	61.4	69.2
Czech Republic	69.9	72.7	76.5
Estonia	69.2	80.3	85.8
Croatia	41.4	49.7	59.2
Cyprus	80.7	89.4	95.0
Latvia	60.8	64.6	72.0
Lithuania	73.1	80.1	86.8
Hungary	78.7	79.9	91.2
Malta	173.8	166.3	163.9
Poland	53.0	57.7	62.7
Romania	36.9	40.6	43.0
Slovenia	77.8	83.6	94.1
Slovakia	85.1	92.1	99.4

Source of data: Eurostat (nama_10_gdp).

Table 9.2. Cyprus and Malta's Strengths and Weaknesses of the Industrial Potential.

Country	Strengths	Weaknesses
Cyprus	1. Central geographical position, location between Europe, the Middle East, and Africa favours the transhipment industry 2. Rich, unexploited offshore natural gas deposits 3. Skilled, English-speaking labour force	1. Cyprus is divided between the EU-aligned Republic of Cyprus and Turkey-aligned Turkish Republic of Northern Cyprus 2. Slow legal process, poor enforcement of contracts 3. Weak industrial diversification (tourism, construction, natural gas, finance)
Malta	1. At the crossroads of the Suez Canal and Gibraltar, a major Mediterranean transhipment hub 2. Resurging tourism industry 3. Productive, English-speaking, growing, and high-income workforce	1. Poor road infrastructure 2. Inadequate higher education 3. Slow legal process, cronyism, and corruption

Source: Elaborated by the author using materials supplied by Coface Group (https://www.coface.com/news-economy-and-insights/business-risk-dashboard/country-risk-files).

a combination of FDIs and domestic players. Some multinational automobile companies have opened factories in CEE, attracted by the lower labour costs, the vicinity of important markets, the favourable business environment, and government policies (such as tax breaks, subsidies, and grants).

As Table 9.3 indicates, the countries with the highest share in extra EU car exports are the Czech Republic (4.0%), Slovakia (5.8%), Hungary (1.4%), Poland (0.9%), and Romania (0.6%). Of course, these percentages are much lower than Germany's (58.5%), but comparable to countries like Belgium (5.3%), Spain (5.2%), or Italy (5.1%).

Some CEE countries have a relatively high share in total extra EU exports, like Slovakia (45.6%) – the highest in the EU, the Czech Republic (14.9%), and Hungary (7.2%), as Table 9.3 shows. According to the same table, the countries with a positive balance of extra EU trade are the Czech Republic, Croatia, Lithuania, Hungary, Poland, Romania, and Slovakia. In the CEE region, four states have a negative trade balance: Bulgaria, Estonia, Latvia, and Slovenia.

Table 9.3 presents only the export of cars, but CEE countries are also exporters of car components, parts, and accessories. According to Statista 2024 (https://www.statista.com/statistics/1115534/cee-car-components-and-parts-export/), the countries with the biggest exports in this field are the Czech Republic, Poland, Hungary, Slovakia, and Romania; the country with the highest value of exported automotive components in 2022 was Poland, followed by the Czech Republic.

Cyprus and Malta have a negative trade balance in the motor car trade.

Despite the numerous present opportunities in the automotive sector, it also confronts some challenges, represented by increasing global competition, technological disruptions, and environmental restrictions.

IT and electronics. Estonia, Poland, and Romania are countries with emerging IT sectors. Estonia is a key digital leader and provides software, IT outsourcing,

New EU Member States' Contribution to the EU Export Potential

Table 9.3. Extra EU Trade in Motor Cars by Member State, 2022 (EUR Million and %).

	Extra EU Trade (EUR Million)			Share in Extra EU Trade of Cars		Share in Total Extra EU Trade	
	Export	Import	Balance	Export	Import	Export	Import
EU	157,670	61,882	95,788	100.0	100.0	6.1	2.1
Belgium	8,305	15,222	−6,917	5.3	24.6	4.3	6.2
Bulgaria	57	190	−133	0.0	0.3	0.3	0.8
Czech Republic	6,300	448	5,852	4.0	0.7	14.9	0.7
Denmark	164	403	−239	0.1	0.7	0.3	1.0
Germany	92,244	19,879	72,365	58.5	32.1	12.9	3.4
Estonia	40	61	−21	0.0	0.1	0.6	1.1
Ireland	36	832	−796	0.0	1.3	0.0	0.9
Greece	24	395	−372	0.0	0.6	0.1	0.7
Spain	8,198	5,512	2,685	5.2	8.9	5.6	2.4
France	4,356	5,379	−1,023	2.8	8.7	1.7	1.8
Croatia	60	35	25	0.0	0.1	0.8	0.3
Italy	8,090	4,216	3,874	5.1	6.8	2.7	1.3
Cyprus	6	235	−228	0.0	0.4	0.2	5.1
Latvia	17	33	−16	0.0	0.1	0.2	0.5
Lithuania	842	96	745	0.5	0.2	5.0	0.5
Luxembourg	21	15	6	0.0	0.0	0.6	0.6
Hungary	2,251	405	1,847	1.4	0.7	7.2	0.8
Malta	2	66	−64	0.0	0.1	0.1	1.9
Netherlands	3,008	2,211	798	1.9	3.6	1.1	0.4
Austria	3,519	173	3,345	2.2	0.3	5.8	0.3
Poland	1,351	677	674	0.9	1.1	1.6	0.5
Portugal	1,061	362	700	0.7	0.6	4.6	1.1
Romania	944	500	444	0.6	0.8	3.7	1.4
Slovenia	842	2,890	−2,048	0.5	4.7	3.4	9.1
Slovakia	9,200	141	9,059	5.8	0.2	45.6	0.6
Finland	187	315	−128	0.1	0.5	0.5	1.0
Sweden	6,546	1,195	5,351	4.2	1.9	7.6	1.7

Source: Eurostat (online data code: DS-018995).

and related services, contributing to its export potential. The information and communication technology (ICT) sector, including electronics manufacturing, is also a component of Malta's exports.

Cieślik (2024), observing the advance of CEE countries in the field of ICT, recently conducted an interesting study starting from the following question: has the ICT service sector become a cure for lagging behind the rest of EU countries in GVCs? Immediately after becoming EU members, the CEE countries had high positions in GVCs, but over time, they were reduced to factories assembling components or intermediate products. The study mentioned above focuses on ICT services as a potential source for a renewed position of CEE economies in GVCs. The research results proved inconclusive, showing that only selected CEE countries (usually with smaller GDP) performed better in ICT services in GVCs and that the largest economies generally worsened their positions in this field, meaning that further efforts are needed to increase the exports of this field.

Aerospace and defence. The EU aerospace industry is mainly represented by big countries like France, Germany, Italy, and Spain, but it has been developing gradually in the new member states with noteworthy progress. According to ECORYS (2009), the division of labour has increased in the EU, with cost advantages and a well-educated labour force as driving factors; however, wage increases incorporate the risk of losing competitiveness in the long run. Malta and Cyprus do not have a significant presence in the aerospace industry.

The recent high demand for ammunition and services for armoured and artillery systems, which resulted from the Russia–Ukraine war, determined a significant increase in sales for defence firms in CEE. The countries with the highest arms production and exports are Poland, the Czech Republic, Bulgaria, Hungary, Romania, and Slovakia. The results of the military sector are also performant because this region represents NATO's eastern flank countries, unlike the two islands of Malta and Cyprus, which are not NATO members. However, Cyprus has an emerging defence industry with a surprising innovation hub.

Given the very tense political climate due to the war between Russia and Ukraine, the defence sector is becoming increasingly important in the EU. This is why we present a ranking of the defence companies from the CEE countries.

Table 9.4 shows the top 10 defence firms in 2022 and their revenues in 2021 and 2022. It can be seen that in the first place in this table, there is a company located in Poland, the only one from the region appearing in the top 100 defence firms' rankings published by the Defense News website (https://www.defensenews.com).

Table 9.4. Top 10 Defence Firms in CEE in 2022.

Rank	Company	Country	Number of Employees	Revenue, 2022 (USD Millions)	Revenue, 2021 (USD Millions)	Revenue Change 2021–2022 (%)
1	Polish Armaments Group (PGZ)	Poland	18,272	1,874	1,646	13.9
2	Czechoslovak Group (CSG)	Czech Republic	5,450	1,067	666	60.2
3	Colt CZ Group	Czech Republic	2,205	625	493	26.7
4	STV Group	Czech Republic	324	278	64	336.6
5	Vazov Machine-Building Plant (VMZ)	Bulgaria	3,973	273	116	135.3
6	Aero Vodochody AEROSPACE	Czech Republic/ Hungary	1,600	227	114	98.2
7	ROMARM	Romania	1,328	162	32	413.8
8	DMD Group	Slovakia	612	143	131	9.2
9	WB Group	Poland	1,109	135	89	52.0
10	Remontowa Shipbuilding (RSB)	Poland	345	71	129	−44.8

Sources: Annual reports, companies' press releases.

Textiles and apparel. The EU qualifies as one of the largest producers of textile and clothing worldwide, with Italy, Germany, France, and Spain producing 60% of the total value of textile output (Eurostat, 2022). In apparel manufacturing, Western EU countries with high-end luxury products remain the most important players. Products with medium prices for mass consumption are manufactured, especially in CEE countries like Poland, Hungary, and Romania, where wages are lower (Lu, 2022).

Poland, Romania, and Bulgaria are among the European countries that provided 90% of the total EU apparel output in 2019 (Lu, 2022). However, the competitive advantage of CEE countries' low labour costs might be at risk, considering that these costs are becoming scarcer in EU Western countries as automated technologies are increasingly adopted. Other challenges are high inflation and hiking energy costs determined by the Russia–Ukraine war.

Textile and apparel production is not a major sector in the economies of Malta and Cyprus.

Chemicals and pharmaceuticals. The EU exports of chemicals grew strongly between 2021 and 2022, with six member states exporting more than 30 billion euros to countries outside the EU in 2022: Germany, Belgium, Ireland, France, the Netherlands, and Italy (see Table 9.5). From the CEE group of countries, Slovenia's exports of chemicals represented more than half of total exports (54.6%), occupying the second place in the EU after Ireland. Other CEE states with a positive trade balance are the Czech Republic, Latvia, and Lithuania. Malta and Cyprus registered a negative balance (Malta, −218 and Cyprus, −7).

The pharmaceutical industry's production in CEE countries is still much lower than that of the old EU member states. The German pharmaceutical market recorded a turnover of about 50 billion euros in 2021, the highest in the EU, followed by France, 37 billion euros, and Italy, 32.4 billion euros (Sas, 2023); Poland represents the largest pharmaceutical market in the CEE region. According to Statista 2024, Polish exports of pharmaceutical products have grown considerably in the last few years. If in 2008 they amounted to about 1.1 billion euros, they more than doubled in 2021, reaching 2.9 billion euros. The value of the revenues of the pharmaceutical products market in the CEE countries in 2021 is presented in Fig. 9.1; it shows that Poland is followed by Romania, the Czech Republic, and Hungary – as countries with revenues of more than 3 million euros.

Cyprus and Malta are also producers of pharmaceutical products, with exports of 381 million euros and 367 million euros in 2020, respectively. Both countries have a positive trade balance (Eurostat, 2022).

Renewable energy. The EU is firmly committed to promoting sustainable development and addressing environmental issues. The objective of the European Green Deal is that of becoming the world's first climate-neutral continent by 2050. Some EU countries like Germany, Denmark, Sweden, Netherlands, and Finland are global exporters of renewable energy technologies and energy efficiency solutions.

While CEE countries are not as dominant in production and exports as their Western counterparts, they are making efforts to increase their presence in this

Table 9.5. Extra EU Trade in Chemicals by Member State 2022 (EUR Million and %).

	Extra EU Trade (EUR Million)			Share of Total Extra EU Trade (%)	
	Export	Import	Balance	Export	Import
EU	553,005	362,812	190,193	21.5	12.1
Belgium	80,797	53,292	27,505	41.8	21.6
Bulgaria	1,959	2,183	−224	11.9	8.9
Czech Republic	3,124	3,075	49	7.4	4.9
Denmark	19,394	3,567	15,827	35.5	8.8
Germany	141,628	72,454	69,174	19.8	12.4
Estonia	399	498	−99	6.2	9.0
Ireland	70,726	25,272	45,454	57.7	27.8
Greece	1,955	2,778	−823	8.0	5.2
Spain	24,153	27,965	−3,812	16.6	12.0
France	53,417	27,674	25,743	20.6	9.2
Croatia	904	927	−23	11.7	7.2
Italy	42,304	29,898	12,406	14.3	9.3
Cyprus	305	312	−7	10.0	6.8
Latvia	748	626	122	9.5	10.2
Lithuania	2,967	1,828	1,139	17.7	9.5
Luxembourg	262	358	−96	8.2	14.2
Hungary	4,476	6,224	−1,748	14.3	12.5
Malta	188	406	−218	11.6	12.0
Netherlands	49,425	52,659	−3,234	18.7	10.0
Austria	9,794	8,370	1,424	16.0	15.1
Poland	8,625	12,953	−4,328	10.3	9.9
Portugal	2,549	3,139	−590	11.0	9.4
Romania	1,289	4,313	−3,024	5.1	11.7
Slovenia	13,456	12,978	478	54.6	40.6
Slovakia	580	711	−131	2.9	2.9
Finland	3,669	2,519	1,150	10.3	8.0
Sweden	13,914	5,833	8,081	16.1	8.3

Source: Author's compilation adapted from Eurostat (online data code: DS-018995).

sector and contribute to the global focus on sustainability. Poland, for example, even though it has a significant share of coal in its energy capacity, has recently become involved in producing wind turbines and related technologies. Companies from the Czech Republic started to export solar panels and wind components. Hungary has shown a great interest in solar energy and biomass. Romania has also developed wind and solar energy capacities and is interested in bioenergy. Unfortunately, Cyprus and Malta are not engaged in exporting renewable energy; they face challenges in generating this type of energy due to their limited geographical features that are unsuitable for large-scale renewable projects.

Despite all efforts, the statistics related to international trade in green energy products show that the EU imports much more than exports (Eurostat, Comext DS-645593).

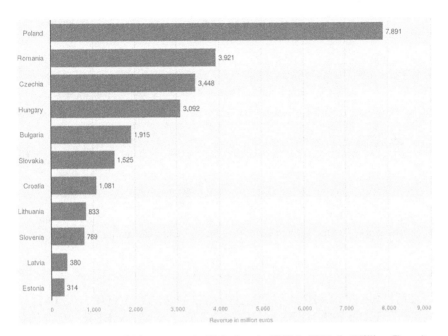

Fig. 9.1. Revenue of Pharmaceutical Markets in CEE in 2021 (in Million Euros). *Source*: Statista 2024.

Food and beverages. Many CEE countries have a strong agricultural sector and a rich culinary heritage that has made an essential contribution to the EU export of food and beverage industries. CEE countries know how to capitalise on their culinary traditions to export unique food products that are highly sought after on international markets. To ensure the competitiveness of their products in the global market, these countries also invest in meeting international quality and safety standards. There is a diversity of CEE country's exports in this sector, including grains, fruits, vegetables, processed food products (dairy products, confectionery, canned goods), alcoholic and non-alcoholic beverages (beer, wine, spirits, fruit juices), cured meats, cheese, and culinary specialities.

Due to its geographical position, Malta has a limited arable surface and a small agricultural sector. It produces and exports processed foods, high-quality beverages, fish, and seafood. Compared to Malta, Cyprus has a richer agricultural sector, with exports including citrus fruits, dairy products, the traditional Halloumi cheese, wine, spirits, and olive oil.

Fig. 9.2, with data regarding the extra EU trade balance for agricultural, fisheries, and food and beverages products, shows that almost all EU new member states (Poland, Romania, Hungary, Lithuania, Bulgaria, Latvia, Croatia, Estonia, the Czech Republic, Malta, Slovakia, Cyprus, and Slovenia) are net exporters. Poland is the third biggest exporter in the EU after France and Italy.

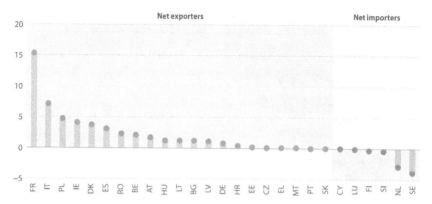

Fig. 9.2. Extra EU Trade Balance for Agricultural, Fisheries, and Food and Beverages Products (€ billion, 2021). *Source*: Eurostat (online data code: DS-045409).

THE NEED FOR A NEW APPROACH TO INDUSTRIAL COMPETITIVENESS IN THE NEW EU MEMBER STATES

The specific characteristics of CEE countries, Malta and Cyprus, the priorities of the new EU industrial strategy, and the features of the industrial landscape presented above call for a new approach to industrial competitiveness meant to increase the new member states' contribution to the EU export potential and involving various economic, regulatory, and innovation factors. Here are some general measures proposed for sustaining their export-oriented production (specific measures depending on each country's unique circumstances, economic structure, and social aspects):

1. The automotive industry (one of the most important industrial sectors in CEE countries) must adapt to the rapid technological progress, orienting production towards electric cars and investing in charging infrastructure.
2. The new EU member states, especially CEE countries, must upgrade transportation and infrastructure, including roads, rail networks, and ports, to facilitate industrial supply chains.
3. Educational programmes must respond to the needs of evolving industries, including promoting vocational training to ensure a skilled workforce.
4. The new EU member countries should ensure regulation transparency, reduce bureaucracy, and facilitate doing business.
5. The new member countries must comply with the twin transitions towards climate neutrality and digitalisation.

   The dependence on coal and other fossil fuels should be considerably diminished, along with reduced CO_2 industrial production. This is the reason why investment in technologies that capture and store carbon emissions from industrial processes is needed. Aligning with the recent developments, the new

EU member states should continue to promote investment in renewable energy sources (solar, wind, hydro, geothermal power) and provide education on sustainable practices and circular economy.

CEE countries have a high potential in IT and digitalisation, but the gap separating them from the EU Western states remains significant. This is why they must implement digital literacy programmes to equip the workforce with the necessary digital skills and expand digital infrastructure. All the new member states must promote science, technology, engineering, and mathematics (STEM) education at all levels.

6. The CEE countries must escape the trap of 'factory economies' that rely on traditional manufacturing and specialise in more lucrative parts of the value chain. They should invest more in R&D, encourage the adoption of advanced technologies, and support industries with higher value-added potential, such as IT, biotechnology, and renewable energy.

7. The new EU member countries should facilitate the growth of e-commerce by simplifying regulations and promoting digital payment solutions; digital marketing, data analytics, and monitoring of geopolitical factors are also needed to meet global market demand.

8. The new member states cannot rely only on market forces to increase the competitiveness of their exports and adapt to the new requirements of the green and digital transitions. Active industrial policies are needed to strengthen the national innovation systems; the absorption of the EU cohesion funds should be maximised, along with a more efficient use of these funds. At the same time, given the FDI-driven export model, FDI incentives in the new member states should be tied to the national industrial strategies.

9. The new EU members can expand their external economic relations by exploring emerging markets and regions with growth potential for exports and participating in global efforts to liberalise trade, such as supporting the initiatives of the World Trade Organization.

CONCLUSIONS

The new EU member states faced some challenges in complying with the requirements of the EU industrial policy. In the case of CEE countries, the transition from planned economic systems to a market economy meant adaptation to entrepreneurship and an active entrepreneurial state; some also inherited a lack of transparency, corruption, bureaucratic hurdles, and outdated infrastructure. Malta and Cyprus, ex-colonial territories of the United Kingdom, inherited views and policies that were out of step with the EU initiatives and economic policies. In addition, all the new members confronted the challenge of complying with the strictly rule-based framework of the EU economic policies.

After their EU accession, the new member states built strong export-oriented manufacturing sectors. CEE countries were included in the European and GVCs, significantly increasing their share in world exports. Malta and Cyprus's strategic geographical position boosted their trade opportunities.

FDI and export potential were triggered by lower labour costs, especially in CEE countries, as compared to Western Europe. However, the competitive advantage of low labour costs might be lost as automated technologies are increasingly adopted by Western countries; in addition, this initial comparative advantage maintains the CEE countries at the level of fabrication tasks, with limited value-added production for export. It is, therefore, necessary to implement a new export production model based on innovation, research, and a highly qualified labour force, which is assured by educational policies focussed on improving skills, including more significant development of vocational schools.

The analysis of the new EU member states' leading industries reveals that they are very successful exporters contributing significantly to the EU's export potential. Still, despite great strides, the gaps with Western Europe persist. As Hillebrand (2022) states, 'The great promise of an EU-wide convergence of living conditions has got stuck halfway'. Besides the adaptation to the recent technological trends to the green and digital transitions (which can boost new business opportunities and investment decisions), these countries must go on improving their infrastructure (without additional investment in infrastructure, the industrial competitiveness might be at risk), get out from the stage of 'factory economies', promote active industrial policies, and implement educational programmes responding to the needs of their evolving industries. A set of nine measures were proposed to increase the industrial competitiveness of the new EU members. As some studies mentioned in the literature review suggest, the new member states could also follow the example of the East Asian countries' successful industrial stories.

The new member states, especially from CEE, should also consider that the availability of structural EU funds will diminish in the long run as the region becomes more prosperous, so private sector investors must be mobilised to replace European funding.

NOTE

1. Centre for European Policy Studies (CEPS) is a prominent think tank in Europe.

REFERENCES

Baldacchino, G. (1996). Cyprus, Malta and the European Union: Lessons for the future. In K. Symeonides & G. Baldacchino (Eds.), *Cyprus–Malta on the threshold of accession to the European Union: Challenges to workers and trade unions; Positions of the main trade unions and reports from two seminars* (pp. 34–39). Ministry of Education.

Bierut, B. K., & Kuziemska-Pawlac, K. (2016). *Competitiveness and export performance of CEE countries* [NBO (Narodowy Bank Polski) Working Paper No. 248]. Economic Institute, Warsaw.

Bykova, A., Dobrinsky, R., Grieveson, R., Grodzicki, M., Hanzl-Weiss, D., Hunya, G., Korpar, N., Leitner, S., Moshammer, B., Sankot, O., Bernd Christoph Ströhm, B. C., Tverdostup, M., & Zavarská, Z. (2023). *Industrial policy for a new growth model – country briefing Hungary.* Friedrich Ebert Stiftung – Politics for Europe.

Ćetković, S., & Buzogány, A. (2020). Between markets, politics and path-dependence: Explaining the growth of solar and wind power in six Central and Eastern European countries. *Energy Policy, 139,* 1–9.

Cieślik, E. (2024). A ray of hope for Central and Eastern Europe: Has the ICT service sector become a cure for lagging behind the rest of EU countries in global value chains? In R. Dekkers & L. Morel (Eds.), *European perspectives on innovation management* (pp., 459–490). Springer. https://doi.org/10.1007/978-3-031-41796-2_17

Cincera, M., Frietsch, R., Leijten, J., Montalvo, C., Pelle, A., Rammer, C., Renda, A., Schubert, T., & Veugelers, R. (2015). The impact of Horizon 2020 on innovation in Europe. *Intereconomics*, *50*(1), 4–30.

Drahokoupil, J., & Piasna, A. (2017). *What drives wage gaps in Europe?* [Working Paper 2017.04]. European Trade Union Institute (ETUI), Brussels.

ECB Monthly Bulletin. (2013, June). *Box 1: The role of Central and Eastern Europe in Pan-European and global value chains.* https://www.ecb.europa.eu/pub/pdf/mobu/mb201306en.pdf

ECORYS. (2009). *Competitiveness of the EU aerospace industry with focus on: Aeronautics industry, within the framework of contract of sectoral competitiveness studies – ENTR/06/054.* https://www.decision.eu/wp-content/uploads/2016/11/FWC-Sector-Competitiveness-Studies-Competitiveness-of-the-EU-Aerospace-Industry-with-focus-on-Aeronautics-Industry.pdf

European Commission. (2020, March 10). *Making Europe's businesses future-ready: A new Industrial Strategy for a global competitive, green and digital Europe* [Press release], Brussels. https://ec.europa.eu/commission/presscorner/detail/en/ip_20_416

Eurostat. (2022, May). *COMEXT database.*

Grieveson, R., Bykova, A., Hanzl-Weiss, D., Hunya, G., Korpar, N., Podkaminer, L., Stehrer, R., & Stöllinger, R. (2021). *Avoiding a trap and embracing the megatrends: Proposals for a* new growth model *in EU-CEE* (No. 458). The Vienna Institute for International Economic Studies, WIIW.

Hillebrand, E. (2022). *The second transition – Why Central Eastern Europe needs proactive industrial and innovation policy now.* Friedrich Ebert Stiftung. https://library.fes.de/pdf-files/bueros/budapest/19511.pdf

Kordalska, A., & Olczyk, M. (2023). Upgrading low value-added activities in global value chains: A functional specialisation approach. *Economic Systems Research, 35*(2), 265–291. https://doi.org/0.1080/09535314.2022.2047011

Lu, S. (2022). *EU textile and apparel industry and trade patterns, Europe, FASH 455 course material global apparel and textile trade and sourcing.* Retrieved January 19, 2024, from https://shenglufashion.com/2022/12/02/eu-textile-and-apparel-industry-and-trade-patterns/

Mazzucato, M. (2016). From market fixing to market-creating: A new framework for innovation policy. *Industry and Innovation, 23*(2), 140–156. Retrieved January 17, 2024, from https://doi.org/10.1080/13662716.2016.1146124

Narodowy Bank Polski. (2014). Foreign trade of the Central and Eastern European countries. In M. Golik, M. Grela, M. Humanicki, M. Kitala, T. Michałek, W. Mroczek, J. Mućk, & E. Rzeszutek (Eds.), *Analysis of the economic situation in the countries of Central and Eastern Europe* (1/14, pp. 25–54). Narodowy Bank Polski.

Pellényi, G. M. (2020). *The role of Central & Eastern Europe in global value chains: Evidence from occupation-level employment data, economic brief 062/December 2020.* Publication Office of the European Union.

Renda, A., & Schaus, M. (Eds.). (2021). *CEPS Task Force report, towards a resilient and sustainable post-pandemic recovery – The new industrial strategy for Europe.* CEPS.

Sas, A. (2023). *Revenue of pharmaceutical markets in Central and Eastern Europe 2021.* Statista. Retrieved January 19, 2024, from https://www.statista.com/statistics/458901/pharmaceutical-markets-turnover-central-and-eastern-european/#statisticContainer

Xin, C. (Ed.). (2019). *Overview of industries in Central and Eastern European countries.* China-CEE Institute.

Zavarskà, Z., Bykova, A., Grieveson, R., Hanzl-Weiss, D., & Sankot, O. (2023). *Industrial policy for a new growth model: A toolbox for EU-CE countries* (No. 469). The Vienna Institute for International Economic Studies, WIIW.

CHAPTER 10

MANAGING CLIMATE CHANGE RISKS AND ENVIRONMENTAL CHALLENGES TOWARDS SUSTAINABLE DEVELOPMENT WITHIN THE EUROPEAN UNION*

Marilen-Gabriel Pirtea[a], Graţiela Georgiana Noja[b], Nicoleta-Claudia Moldovan[a], Irina-Maria Grecu[c] and Alexandra-Mădălina Ţăran[a]

[a] West University of Timisoara, Faculty of Economics and Business Administration, Timisoara, Romania
[b] West University of Timisoara, Faculty of Economics and Business Administration, East-European Center for Research in Economics and Business, Timisoara, Romania
[c] West University of Timisoara, Doctoral School of Economics and Business Administration, Timisoara, Romania

ABSTRACT

Purpose: *This study aims to examine the inferences of climate change risks on the natural environment within the European Union (EU) and to explore how*

---

*This work was supported by a grant from the Romanian Ministry of Research, Innovation, and Digitalization, the project with the title 'Economics and Policy Options for Climate Change Risk and Global Environmental Governance' (CF 193/28.11.2022, Funding Contract No. 760078/23.05.2023), within Romania's National Recovery and Resilience Plan (PNRR) – Pillar III, Component C9, Investment I8 (PNRR/2022/C9/MCID/I8) – Development of a programme to attract highly specialised human resources from abroad in research, development and innovation activities.

Economic Development and Resilience by EU Member States
Contemporary Studies in Economic and Financial Analysis, Volume 115, 159–176
Copyright © 2025 by Marilen-Gabriel Pirtea, Graţiela Georgiana Noja, Nicoleta-Claudia Moldovan, Irina-Maria Grecu and Alexandra-Mădălina Ţăran
Published under exclusive licence by Emerald Publishing Limited
ISSN: 1569-3759/doi:10.1108/S1569-375920240000115010

environmental governance initiatives that prioritise sustainability and are globally agreed upon can help mitigate these adverse effects of climate change. This study conducted an in-depth systematic review and comprehensive bibliometric analysis of the scientific literature identifying the theoretical underpinnings of climate change risks and global environmental governance.

Need for study: *Climate swaps pose significant risks to the environment, sustainability, and socioeconomic systems at the EU and global levels. Nowadays, every industry, company, and region worldwide is exposed to varying degrees of climate risk, which is only expected to increase as climate change accelerates.*

Methodology: *An extensive collection of articles, books, and book chapters available through Web of Science and Scopus was analysed, gathering key ideas, theories, directions for future research, authors, research organisations/ institutes, nations, and co-citation histories. The research methodology involved was extracting information from 1,586 documents on Scopus and 1,024 papers on Web of Science and processing the data in VOSviewer. The following keywords were used for basic searches and further extraction: 'climate', 'politics', 'risk', 'global', 'environment', and 'governance'.*

Findings: *Governance/management becomes even more important when studying climate change risks along with resilience, adaptation, vulnerability, uncertainty, and sustainability/sustainable development among EU member states.*

Practical implications: *This study emphasises climate change's most significant environmental effects and risks at the EU and global levels and highlights the importance of addressing these risks through effective environmental governance initiatives.*

Keywords: Climate change risks; sustainability; environmental governance; European Union; bibliometric analysis; network analysis

JEL classifications: Q50; Q54; Q56; G38

1. INTRODUCTION

Climate swaps pose significant risks to the environment, sustainability, and socioeconomic systems at the European Union (EU) and global levels. Nowadays, every industry, company, and region worldwide is exposed to varying degrees of climate risk, which is only expected to increase as climate change accelerates. Average global temperatures have increased by about 1.1°C. This was confirmed by studying satellite measurements and observations from tens of thousands of independent weather stations worldwide. Moreover, scientists confirm that the ice on the planet's surface is melting rapidly and that they have more evidence. The rate of warming observed today is at least 10 times the rate observed in the paleoclimate record over the past 65 million years. A recent evaluation of 105 nations representing 90% of the world's population and 90% of the world's gross domestic product (GDP) indicates that all of them 'are expected to experience an increase in at least one major type of impact on their stock of human, physical, and natural capital by 2030' (Woetzel et al., 2020).

These impacts could be severe, affecting people and physical capital, economic activity, and global stocks of natural capital. The extent of these consequences will depend on how well-equipped individuals, groups, authorities, and governments are to comprehend climate risks and implement sensible adaptation measures to mitigate them.

Taking into consideration the EU member states, the problematic topic of managing climate change risks gets a deeper substrate, as the governments and the responsible European institutions must find reliable solutions to avoid the spread of the risks, also trying to keep together all the 27 EU countries, supporting peace, communion, and unity between them.

This study aims to examine the inferences of climate change risks on the natural environment in EU member states and explore how environmental governance initiatives prioritising sustainability are globally agreed upon and how they can help mitigate the adverse effects of climate change. A rigorous systematic review and bibliometric analysis of the existing scientific literature were employed in this chapter to identify the theoretical underpinnings of climate change risks, associated threats, and global environmental governance. This research reveals if and how the EU member states, working together, based on sustainable governance and the environment-friendly policies and governance applied immediately and kept long term, will be able to maintain the climate change inevitable risks that can rapidly spread their multiple effects under control.

2. BRIEF LITERATURE REVIEW

2.1. Climate Change Risks

Climate risk refers to the possibility of adverse effects caused by climate change on ecological or social systems (Cervest, 2022). This includes impact on people's lives, means of subsistence, health, and well-being, as well as investments in economic, social, political, and cultural resources, infrastructure links, services, natural ecosystems, and endangered species. It is essential to note that every business, regardless of the industry or location, faces different degrees of climate risk. As climate change accelerates, so does this risk (Cervest, 2022). The climate change categories can be split into two, as follows:

(a) Transition risks: risks associated with the multiple transitions to a low-carbon economy.

Transition climate risk represents the business risks associated with transitioning from fossil fuels and other different greenhouse gas (GHG) emitting activities. Article 6 of the Paris Agreement contributes to an advanced and new global carbon market, which needs to be managed by a United Nations agency to ensure trading in emissions reductions, respectively, through the introduction of carbon markets as a representative mechanism to offset and reduce carbon and other GHG emissions (Salman et al., 2022). Long-term climate stabilisation requires decarbonisation, which brings about economic, social, and political changes. The costs of decarbonising facilities and operations represent transition risk. Otherwise, companies that choose not to decarbonise also risk losing their reputation and market share, respectively, breaking the law. Moreover, following the Pigouvian theory, Manta et al. (2023) examined within the EU countries the viability of environmental taxes to mitigate and reduce GHG emissions. The results suggest that by integrating various measures, decision-makers can follow the path towards climate neutrality and adequately combat climate change. At the centre of transition risk is the energy industry. Fossil fuels account for over 80% of the energy used worldwide today. Institutions that produce or rely on these energy sources face transition risks due to the quick shift from them by the middle of the century. Energy producers must contend with the diminishing value of their fuel sources and run the risk of abandoning infrastructure like pipelines, drilling rigs, and power plants. Companies that rely on fossil fuels and downstream energy sources are at risk of supply chain and operational disruptions, with notable impacts on financial performance (Pirtea et al., 2015).

Examples of transition climate risks:

- Stranded assets and depreciation, such as the decreased value of buildings with inefficient energy use.
- Reduced consumer demand and loss of market share.
- Increased capital expenditures, such as those resulting from insulating buildings or updating equipment.
- Increased costs, such as those resulting from supply chain effects or increases in the price of raw materials.
- Financial risk, such as being uninsurable or unable to obtain financing as a result of failing to adhere to stricter policy.
- Financial risk, such as being uninsurable or unable to obtain financing as a result of failing to adhere to stricter policy.
- Legal liability stemming from failure to comply with regulatory criteria.

(a) Physical risks: risks associated with the physical impacts of climate change.

The multiple actions implemented and held to mitigate the impact of climate change are associated with climate-related opportunities. In this light, these actions can be characterised by resource efficiency and cost savings, using low-emission energy sources, creating new goods and services, penetrating new markets, and developing supply chain resilience.

Physical climate risk refers to the possibility of both material losses and bodily harm due to a person's increased exposure to climate risks due to climate change. Physical climate risks can be either shocks or stresses. Therefore, shocks, like floods, storms, or wildfires, are sudden, devastating and usually pass quickly. Stresses such as seasonal fluctuations, temperature increases, and variations in precipitation have gradual onsets. The supply chains, property value, and insurability may all be impacted by these prolonged changes in climate patterns in the long run (United States Environmental Protection Agency, 2023). There is an increasing physical risk associated with a changing environment. Seven characteristics stand out; hence, physical climate risk can be (Woetzel et al., 2020):

- *Increasing*: by 2030 and again by 2050, the level of physical climate hazard will increase in each of our nine examples. Based on all our observations, the socioeconomic impact will grow 2–20 times by 2050 compared to current levels. Additionally, we found that physical climate risks are increasing globally in all the countries we examined (such as the expected increase regarding the agricultural outputs in developing countries, such as Canada).
- *Spatial:* climate hazards manifest locally. Therefore, there is a need to understand the direct impact produced by physical climate risks within the framework of a specific geographical area. There are differences both within and between countries.
- *Nonlinear:* in the context that the Earth continues to warm, the physical climate risks are constantly changing or not fixed. The next 10 years of warming will be 'blocked' by the physical inertia of the geophysical system. According to climate science, achieving net-zero GHG emissions is the only way to avoid further warming and increased risks. Additionally, some warming is likely to continue after net-zero emissions are achieved due to the thermal inertia of the Earth system.
- *Nonlinear*: Socioeconomic effects are anticipated to spread nonlinearly as risks exceed the points at which the impacted biological, artificial, or ecological systems function poorly or cease to function thoroughly. This is because such systems have changed or improved in past climates.
- *Systemic*: Although the immediate effects of climate change are local, they can spread to other areas and industries due to the interdependence of socioeconomic and financial systems.
- *Regressive*: In each scenario, the most vulnerable groups tend to be the localities and populations with the lowest incomes. Spatial inequality results from climate risk since some places may profit while others suffer.
- *Under-prepared*: Although businesses and communities have begun making adaptations to lessen climate risk, it is likely that these efforts will need to be significantly enhanced if climate risks are to be managed. Adaptation will likely come with increased spending and difficult decisions, such as investing in strengthening or moving people and assets.

The EU has made significant progress in adopting policies that, if effectively implemented, would result in emission reductions going beyond its Nationally Determined Contributions (NDC) target, which means the EU should present a more robust target. This progress has occurred more than a year after Russia's illegitimate invasion of Ukraine and the ensuing energy crisis. The EU's efforts to reduce carbon emissions are jeopardised by ongoing investments in new fossil fuel infrastructure, particularly liquefied natural gas (LNG) terminals and fossil gas pipelines. The EU's total climate action is deemed 'Insufficient' by the Climate

Action Tracker (CAT). Moreover, geopolitical and climate factors can increase European natural gas bubbles, with climate change being considered a primary driver of natural gas bubbles (Su et al., 2023).

The 'Fit for 55' package and the RePowerEU plan, which include most of the legislation, aim to reduce emissions by 60%–61% below the 1990 levels by 2030. This target would surpass the EU's current target of 'at least 55%'. The key measures of the plan include:

- Increasing the EU Emissions Trading Scheme's (EU ETS) targets to reduce emissions from electricity, industry, and aviation from 43% to 63% below 2005 levels.
- Raising the mandatory emission reduction targets for the building, transportation, and agricultural sectors from 30% to 40% under the Effort Sharing Regulation.
- Extending the scope of the EU ETS to include buildings and transport in a parallel scheme from 2027.
- Strengthening the goal for the proportion of renewable energy in 2030 from 32% to 42.5%, with speculation of raising it to 45%.
- Strengthening energy efficiency objectives, such as the target for energy usage that should not exceed 763 Mtoe.
- Increasing the land use and forestry sector sink to 310 MtCO2e.

To continue improving its climate action, the EU should:

- Stop funding new LNG capacity and concentrate your efforts on the switch to renewable energy.
- Submit an additional update to its NDC, raising its domestic goal to a 1.5°C global least cost compatible level of at least 61%, excluding land use, land use change and forestry (LULUCF) below 1990 levels by 2030.
- Substantially increase its climate finance contributions.
- Update its strategy for reaching its net-zero target.

Following its Climate Law, the EU is now formulating its 2040 target, which will be announced in 2024. The CAT concludes that to satisfy its minimum contribution under 1.5°C global least-cost pathways, the EU should propose a domestic emission reduction target for 2040 of at least 80% below 1990 levels (excluding LULUCF). The EU must, however, support much deeper emission reductions and enhance its climate financing commitment to reach its 1.5°C fair share contribution. The anticipated switch back to coal did not occur in the winter of 2022–2023, and the bloc was successful in reducing its reliance on fossil gas, ending the season with more fossil gas in storage than in prior winters. While doing so, it puts the world's efforts to combat climate change in danger of carbon lock-in and LNG development. In late 2022 and early 2023, the EU strengthened its climate legislation by adopting various targets. These include raising the EU ETS 2030 emission reduction goal from 43% to 62% below 2005 levels and raising the Effort Sharing Regulation's 2030 emission reduction goal from 30% to

40% below 2005 levels. The EU also strengthened its renewable energy objective for 2030 from 32% to 42.5% of total energy, with an additional 2.5% 'indicative' target. Additionally, the EU aims to cut its final energy demand from 846 Mtoe to 763 Mtoe in 2030 and expand the size of its land sector sink target from 225 MtCO2e to 310 MtCO2e. Furthermore, the EU plans to develop a separate programme under the EU ETS from 2027 onwards, including buildings and transportation (European Commission, 2024). Member states still need to pass laws to carry out these objectives. They are required to include their national goals for energy consumption and the share of renewable energy in their National Energy and Climate Plans (NECPs), which must at least meet the goals outlined in the relevant directive for the EU as a whole. The initial drafts of these plans were presented at the end of June 2023. The EU has streamlined the permitting processes for investments in batteries, renewable energy, and the expansion of the power system in addition to the significant policy reforms. The results of these actions won't be seen until the following years, but by 2022, investments in renewable energy will have significantly increased, particularly in solar energy and heat pumps. However, despite a rise in both offshore and onshore wind energy installed capacity, there has been a sharp decline in new investments, signalling a short-term recession in the industry. The anticipated return to coal, particularly during the winter of 2022–2023, did not occur due to the rapid deployment of renewable energy and energy savings, which were primarily fuelled by high energy prices. The EU heavily relies on imports from other nations in the case of the majority of low-carbon technology, particularly solar panels, wind turbines, and batteries. If trade flows are disrupted, this could worsen bottlenecks.

The Net-Zero Industry Act, which establishes the objective of covering at least 40% of chosen low-carbon technologies with domestic manufacture, was recommended by the Commission in March 2023 to address this issue. This is a positive step because it will improve the availability of the products needed to achieve the EU's carbon reduction targets while lowering their costs due to economies of scale (CAT, 2023).

2.2. Global Environmental Governance

'Global environmental governance' refers to all the practices, laws, and organisations that guide efforts to safeguard the environment worldwide (International Institute for Sustainable Development, 2006). In the early 1970s, environmental issues were placed on the international agenda. Since then, politics and policies have evolved incredibly swiftly, far outpacing their initial intent and laying the groundwork for a coordinated effort to make fundamental, long-lasting changes to the global environment.

'The United Nations Environment Programme', also known as 'UNEP', plays an essential role in global environmental governance by working with governments to develop sound environmental policies and legal frameworks that respect human rights obligations, protect the environment, and fulfil their ecological commitments. This involves providing environmental information to government decision-makers and citizens who need to know their rights; supporting the development and enforcement of national and international environmental laws; promoting, protecting, and enforcing environmental rights; promoting global and regional cooperation; promoting cooperation between government and civil society; and supporting regional dialogue on the goals set out in international environmental agreements. The sustainable development goals and the broader goals of the 2030 Agenda are further promoted by UNEP's function as environmental stakeholder coordinator (UNEP, 2023).

At the EU level, numerous initiatives for environmental governance include:

- 'The European Green Deal': achieve net-zero emissions by 2050. The EU has established a net-zero emissions target by 2050 and climate neutrality binding EU law in 2021. By 2030, it established an interim goal of 55% emission reduction. The climate law makes these net-zero emission objectives a legal requirement. The European Green Deal is the EU's road plan for achieving carbon neutrality by 2050.
- 'The Sustainable European Investment Plan', which aims to attract at least €1 trillion in public and private investment over the next 10 years, was launched by the European Commission in January 2020 to finance the EU.
- 'The Just Transition Fund', part of the investment plan, is intended to assist towns and areas that would be most negatively impacted by a green transition, such as those highly dependent on coal (European Parliament, 2023).

Globally, the 'Intergovernmental Panel on Climate Change (IPCC)' has identified several concerns for the future, including: (i) irreversible impacts on ecosystems and coral reefs, especially in the Arctic, even if global temperatures change more modestly; (ii) extreme weather events; (iii) adverse effects on the world's most vulnerable and poor people; (iv) environmental and economic damage; (v) large-scale discrete phenomena (e.g., sea-level rise caused by the melting of the giant ice sheets in Greenland and Antarctica). Nevertheless, extreme weather risks also have a significant impact on food prices (Cai et al., 2023).

So that institutions and organisations established for global environmental governance to be able to identify the best and viable methods of combating climate change, the irreversible nature of these changes, and the propagation of effects and risks in the cascade towards all systems must be considered, as well as the affected domains. Thus, everything must be foreseen in the minor details, being necessary simulations, variants, variations, and fluctuations of climate changes and the scope of implementation of policies dedicated to combating them so that the results reported at a particular level in each country, but also in general, at the level of the entire globe, to be the expected ones or as close as possible to them.

The use of brand-new technology can help achieve practical solutions in combating the risks and environmental effects of the inevitable climate changes in the coming years. This will have a crucial role in the evolution of climate governance. Climate change represents a fundamental and essential problem related to the environment but also a development problem interconnected with the changing character and permanent and continuous development of human society. Around

Managing Climate Change Risks and Environmental Challenges 167

90% of CO_2 emissions result from the processing, producing, and using energy, placing the energy sector at the core of efforts to reduce climate change.

In this case, governments have a crucial, essential role, which should be capitalised to identify the relationship between business actors and information technology. In this context, ecological modernisation theory has been used as the basis for numerous studies on the influence of political, technological, economic, and other factors on environmental policy. In return, economic actors and technological innovation can encourage and influence governments to take a more proactive approach to climate policy through technological advances and diverse power resources (Kuriakose et al., 2022).

2.3. Sustainable Development

The term 'sustainable development' is mainly used by representatives of developed states to manage and control sustainable and unsustainable environmental principles, practices, and policies in developing countries. In this case, it becomes crucial to grant substantial financial aid, which ensures the maintenance and expansion of conservation areas in rural regions but also supports campaigns to raise awareness among the population, the promotion of which highlights the importance of maintaining protected areas and conservation natural resources and more (Medeiros et al., 2022).

Climate change has the greatest negative impact, especially in the areas and regions of the globe where governance capacity is fragile, as well as where the citizens have not formed a culture and awareness regarding the protection of the environment and resources, so they are challenging to adapt to any measure or policy aimed at reducing the risks caused by climate change but encouraging a sustainable lifestyle. In developing countries, implementing government measures and mechanisms regarding the environment should cross national borders and become a concept and action specific to several nations, working together to achieve the desired effects and reduce the impact of climate change (Herath, 2013).

Sustainable development is 100% dependent on major industries' abilities to transition and produce based on green technologies, being not limited to gradual variations and changes in how a product is manufactured. Instead, a conceptual shift in management, manufacturing diverse processes, and delivery channels brings about the recognition that products are part of an overall ecosystem.

3. SYSTEMATIC AND BIBLIOMETRIC REVIEW OF THE SCIENTIFIC LITERATURE

Through rigorous bibliometric analysis, this study delves into the theoretical fundamentals of climate change risks and global environmental governance. It, therefore, captures the main theories, concepts, research directions, authors, organisations/institutes, countries, and co-citation history that are extracted from a large sample of scientific articles, books, and book chapters available in Web of Science and Scopus. Hence, we extracted information from 1,586 documents available in Scopus and other 1,024 papers from Web of Science for the period 2010–2022. Following the same methodology for the comprehensive literature review as Lobonț, Țăran, Vătavu, & Para (2023), Crăciun et al. (2023), Varadi et al. (2023), Lobonț, Trip, Țăran, Mihit, & Moldovan (2023), Vătavu et al. (2022), and Lobonț et al. (2020), the identified large amount of data was being processed in VOSviewer software.

The Scopus search and further extraction were made based on the following keywords: 'climate', 'policy', 'environment', and 'governance'. The co-occurrence map resulting after processing the data is presented in Fig. 10.1 and entails that climate change, environmental policy, sustainability, governance, and adaptive management were the main topics approached in recent studies published on this topical subject. If we analyse the sample of 1,024 scientific documents (articles, book chapter) extracted from Web of Science based on the following keywords: 'climate', 'risks', 'global', 'environment', and 'governance', we note that governance/management becomes even more relevant in the study of climate change risks, together with resilience, adaptation, vulnerability, uncertainty, and policy (Figs. 10.2(a) and 10.2(b)).

When we restrict the search to at least 10 appearances of keywords in the analysed sample of 1,586 documents available in Scopus, we note that climate change remains at the core of the studies, along with sustainability/sustainable development (Figs. 10.3(a) and 10.3(b)).

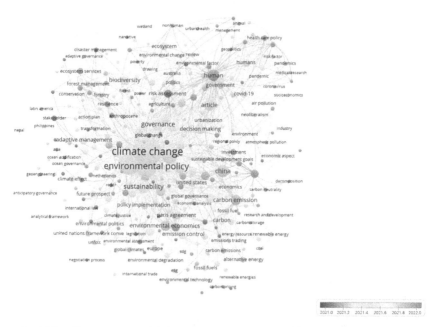

Fig. 10.1. Co-occurrence, Links, and Clustering of Terms/Keywords Approached in Recent Literature About Climate Change Risks and Environmental Governance.
Source: Designed by authors in VOSviewer, using Scopus-indexed articles.

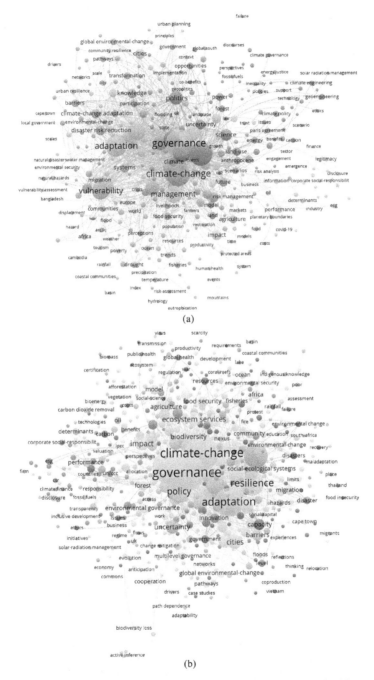

Fig. 10.2. Co-occurrence, Links, and Clustering of Terms Approached in Recent Literature About Climate Change Risks and Environmental Governance: (a) All Keywords and (b) Author Keywords. *Source*: Designed by authors in VOSviewer, using Web of Science-indexed articles.

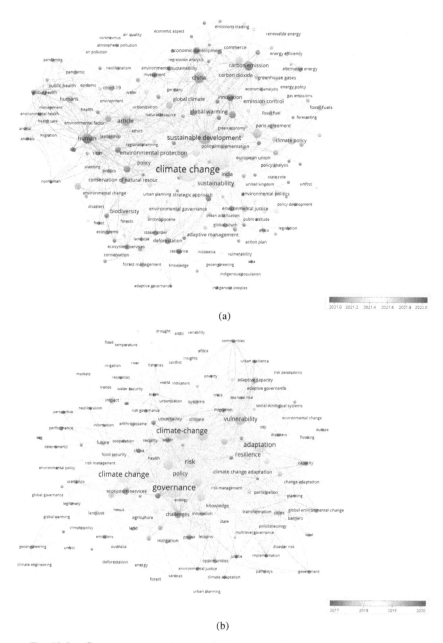

Fig. 10.3. Co-occurrence, Links, and Clustering of Terms/Keywords (at Least 10 Appearances) Approached in Recent Literature About Climate Change Risks and Environmental Governance: (a) All Keywords and (b) Author Keywords. *Source*: Designed by authors in VOSviewer, using Web of Science and Scopus-indexed articles

Fig. 10.3 also reveals the principal terms used by the authors analysed in the published texts, namely: 'climate change' or 'climate change' (a structure already known in both forms in specialised literature), 'governance', 'risks', 'resilience', but also 'adaptation', the latter must be recognised and desired by people so that the effects and risks generated by climate change can be reduced as much as possible in the coming years.

Analysing Figs. 10.4(a) and 10.4(b), it can be observed that, in recent years, starting with the analysis year 2021 and until the beginning of 2022, the authors interested in the subject of climate change and environmental governance come from countries such as Great Britain and the United States, as well as from China, Canada, or some member states of the EU, both in the case of Web of Science and Scopus publications.

Recent literature attests that all the discussions and research ideas within the articles submitted for analysis are focused on climate change. In addition to explaining the urgent concerns regarding the risks generated by climate change, the authors express opinions regarding sustainable development and sustainability, conservation of natural resources but also focus attention on humans, their needs, and human behaviour in recent decades, whose effects can be observed on the environment, and which determines to a certain extent the triggering and threat of climate change.

Fig. 10.5 highlights the leading educational institutions and research institutes where the authors whose articles had climate change and environmental governance as their main themes are working. Thus, not only environmental or economic sciences schools are interested in these subjects but also numerous research and development centres, natural resource conservation institutes, as well as sociology and political science faculties, the subject being addressed as a far-reaching, multidisciplinary one of national interest, approached and analysed on a global scale.

Authors, researchers, employees in the field, authorities, and governments all together propose ideas, changes, methods, and policies aimed to minimise the risks of climate change but which are supposed to increase the involvement of everyone towards the sustainable development of the environment and economies. Only everyone's efforts will be able to make a difference in the future and give future generations access to the natural resources they need, as well as a life based on sustainable development and environmental governance.

However, although governments are increasingly involved and propose measures and models of action to combat the effects generated by climate change, there is still a high degree of uncertainty regarding the form of these measures and their application and implementation, especially from the perspective of the period in which they are implemented, their magnitude, and the anticipated consequences. In reality, it has yet to be discovered precisely how climate change will evolve and what the future trends regarding the effects and risks created by it will be. To ensure the credibility of tackling climate change, draft climate change policies must include enough credible commitments to motivate investors to make changes (Lin & Zhao, 2023).

After an in-depth assessment of the scientific literature on this topical subject, through a systematic and bibliometric analysis, we note that there is a growing

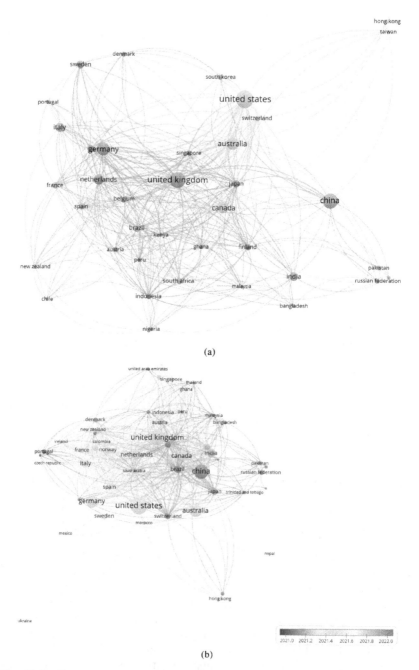

Fig. 10.4. Co-occurrence, Links, and Clustering Of Countries: (a) Web of Science-indexed Articles and (b) Scopus-indexed Articles. *Source*: Designed by authors in VOSviewer, using Web of Science- and Scopus-indexed articles.

Fig. 10.5. Co-occurrence, Links, and Clustering of Institutions. *Source*: Designed by authors in VOSviewer, using Web of Science- and Scopus-indexed articles.

interest in climate change and its risks and challenges, as evidenced by the vast literature and research findings. This research focused on policies and directives to prevent the accentuation and expansion of climate change risks, improve environmental, water, and air quality and reduce pollution in large cities worldwide. These measures aim to protect citizens and plant and animal species, ensuring the safety and security of natural resources for future generations.

All the EU 27 member states must adhere to the new environmental and sustainable economic development policies, respecting the stipulated terms and conditions and implementing environmentally friendly practices. Sustainable development has been defined differently throughout history, but its fundamental principles are common and collective efforts that all 27 member states should support and encourage.

Future research should investigate the social and economic impacts of green economy transition and transformation, such as industry competitiveness and job creation, to provide valuable insights to policymakers in the EU and researchers. This will help strengthen the EU's environmental policies and advance the transition to a sustainable and environmentally responsible economy. The new results will also help researchers update the literature and extend their studies to new opportunities and challenges.

4. CONCLUSIONS

Global environmental governance involves policies and cooperation among countries, institutions, and other essential parts that extend beyond some specific regions and impact the environment alongside the multiple natural resources across different areas or entire nations worldwide. World politics includes various environmental problems that highlight a significant awareness of the numerous tensions accumulated by the various human activities exerted on the Earth's resources and life support systems.

Environmental policy typically targets negotiating and implementing multilateral agreements and other collaborative structures and mechanisms to ensure the security of the environment and natural resources. Thus, some of the agreements are fundamental to global environmental regimes with varying effects that aim to regulate or control the behaviour of states.

Different economic, political, and environmental interests can result in legitimate differences, making it a political and diplomatic challenge to achieve unanimity among countries responsible for or directly affected by environmental issues. There is often an opportunity for one or more countries to block or undermine multilateral agreements, and finding ways to break such impasses is of great concern.

Assessing the complex risks of climate change is a critical and pressing demand. The cumulative experiences highlight the significance of collaborative operators of climate change risk and interactions between various risks, but the risk assessments need to be completed and consistent. Furthermore, integrating responses into climate risk frameworks can help improve the understanding and relevance of climate change risk assessments to different decision-makers and help conceptualise risk trade-offs.

Although climate change risk assessments generally begin at low levels of complexity, there is a need to frequently update and revise the risk assessments based on new and advanced insights regarding the interacting risk factors and risks. As the environmental, social, and engineering sciences collectively progress towards these goals, they will provide more informed risk assessments and detailed decision-making to address emerging complex climate change risks.

Ecological, social, and economic inclusiveness must be ensured in the green economy and sustainable development. Green economic policies should, therefore, be at the core of economic development, prioritising human well-being and social justice, as well as the rational use and preservation of natural and human resources. While integrating and developing green measures, we must consider these three aspects and perspectives of sustainable development mentioned above.

Various climate change risks and associated threats, such as those presented in this chapter, significantly impact sustainable development. Governments and policymakers must harden diplomatic efforts and dispute-resolution mechanisms to reduce these risks and prioritise efforts focused on strengthening economic development. One way to foster sustainable economic growth is by investing in alternative sectors like the service industry and renewable energy. Countries that rely heavily on extractive industries and resource imports can collaborate to transform this sector into a driver of sustainable development. This can be achieved by prioritising low carbon emissions, climate resilience, inclusiveness, and long-term viability. Policymakers and governments can work towards a more sustainable and equitable future by reducing our carbon footprint, building resilience, promoting inclusiveness, and taking a forward-thinking approach.

According to the main findings of this research, Europe is expected to experience a significant increase in temperature, with some regions getting drier and others getting wetter. This could lead to a differentiated impact on EU member states. As a result, new EU countries should take action by designing specific policies to counteract the effect of these environmental changes on people's health. The ecosystem we depend on may also be affected, and therefore, the new EU countries are preparing to live with a changing climate through various adaptation measures. These measures may include the implementation of new technologies, the development of sustainable practices, and the promotion of renewable energy sources. Moreover, policymakers ought to consider the recommendations outlined in this research, which emphasise the importance of proactive measures to mitigate the adverse effects of climate change, such as improving water management, increasing forest resilience, and promoting sustainable agriculture. By doing so, the new EU countries can ensure that they are better equipped to deal with the challenges of a changing climate while safeguarding the health and well-being of their citizens and protecting the environment that we all rely on.

REFERENCES

Cai, Y., Chang, H., Chang, T., Țăran, A., & Pirtea, M. (2023). Time-varying causal impacts of the continental US weather risks on food price. *Applied Economics Letters, 31*(14), 1298–1304. https://doi.org/10.1080/13504851.2023.2186344

Cervest. (2022). *What is climate risk, and what does it mean for your organisation.* https://cervest.earth/news/what-is-climate-risk-and-what-does-it-mean-for-your-organization

Climate Action Tracker. (2023). *CAT: Climate target update tracker.* https://climateactiontracker.org/climate-target-update-tracker-2022/

Crăciun, A., Răcătăian, R., Țăran, A., & Moldovan, N. (2023). Is there any obvious relationship between taxation and economic growth? *Studies in Business and Economics, 18*(1), 69–89. https://doi.org/10.2478/sbe-2023-0004

European Commission. (2024). *Energy, climate change, environment, causes of climate change. Consequences of climate change.* https://climate.ec.europa.eu/climate-change_en

European Parliament. (2023). *Fact sheets on the European Union, just transition fund.* https://www.europarl.europa.eu/factsheets/en/sheet/214/just-transition-fund

Herath, G. (2013). Climate change and global environmental governance: The Asian experience. In H. Ha & T. N. Dhakal (Eds.), *Governance approaches to mitigation of and adaptation to climate change in Asia.* Energy, Climate and the Environment Series (pp. 68–83). Palgrave Macmillan. https://doi.org/10.1057/9781137325211_5

International Institute for Sustainable Development. (2006). *Sustaining excellence: The 2005–2006 annual report of the International Institute for Sustainable Development* (pp. 1–38). International Institute for

Sustainable Development. https://www.iisd.org/publications/annual-report/sustaining-excellen
ce-2005-2006-annual-report-international-institute

Kuriakose, J., Jones, C. D., Anderson, K., McLachlan, C., & Broderick, J. (2022). What does the Paris climate change agreement mean for local policy? Downscaling the remaining global carbon budget to sub-national areas. *Renewable and Sustainable Energy Transition, 2*, 100030. https:// doi.org/10.1016/j.rset.2022.100030

Lin, B., & Zhao, H. (2023). Tracking policy uncertainty under climate change. *Resources Policy, 83*, 103699. https://doi.org/10.1016/j.resourpol.2023.103699

Lobonț, O., Țăran, A., & Costea, F. (2020). E-government research still matter? A bibliometric analysis. *Annals of Dunarea De Jos University. Fascicle I: Economics and Applied Informatics, 26*(2), 58–63. https://doi.org/10.35219/eai15840409106

Lobonț, O., Țăran, A., Vătavu, S., & Para, I. (2023). Scientific radiography of healthcare system process efficiency digitalisation. *Zagreb International Review of Economics and Business, 26*(2), 113–136. https://doi.org/10.2478/zireb-2023-0017

Lobonț, O., Trip, A., Țăran, A., Mihit, L., & Moldovan, N. C. (2023). Science mapping and country clustering regarding challenges of public governance to ensure societal well-being. *Broad Research in Artificial Intelligence Neuroscience, 14*(2), 257–284. https://doi.org/10.18662/ brain/14.2/454

Manta, A. G., Doran, N. M., Bădîrcea, R. M., Areu, G. B., & Țăran, A. (2023). Does the implementation of a Pigouvian tax be considered an effective approach to address climate change mitigation? *Economic Analysis and Policy, 80*, 1719–1731. https://doi.org/10.1016/j.eap.2023.11.002

Medeiros, E., Valente, B., Gonçalves, V., & Castro, P. (2022). How impactful are public policies on environmental sustainability? Debating the Portuguese case of PO SEUR 2014–2020. *Sustainability, 14*(13), 7917. https://doi.org/10.3390/su14137917

Pirtea, M., Nicolescu, C., Botoc, C., & Lobont, O. (2015). Board gender and firm value: an empirical analysis. *Economic Computation and Economic Cybernetics Studies and Research, 49*(4), 21–32.

Salman, M., Long, X., Wang, G., & Zha, D. (2022). Paris climate agreement and global environmental efficiency: New evidence from fuzzy regression discontinuity design. *Energy Policy, 168*, 113128. https://doi.org/10.1016/j.enpol.2022.113128

Su, C., Qin, M., Chang, H., & Țăran, A. (2023). Which risks drive European natural gas bubbles? Novel evidence from geopolitics and climate. *Resources Policy, 81*, 103381. https://doi.org/10.1016/ j.resourpol.2023.103381

United Nations Environment Programme. (2023). *Climate action.* https://www.unep.org/topics/climate-action

United States Environmental Protection Agency. (2023). *Climate change.* https://www.epa.gov/climate-change

Varadi, A., Țăran, A., Vătavu, S., & Lobonț, O. (2023). European Union's portrayal of health expenditure funding challenges in pandemic crises. In A. M. Dima & E. R. Danescu (Eds.), *Fostering recovery through metaverse business modelling* (pp. 221–233). Springer. https://doi. org/10.1007/978-3-031-28255-3_17

Vătavu, S., Țăran, A., Moldovan, N., & Lobonț, O. (2022). Does technical and democratic governance have the potential to enhance health spending allocations? *Studies in Business and Economics, 17*(3), 251–268. https://doi.org/10.2478/sbe-2022-0059

Woetzel, J., Pinner, D., Samandari, H., Engel, H., Krishnan, M., Brodie Boland, B., & Powis, C. (2020). *Climate risk and response: Physical hazards and socioeconomic impacts* (pp. 1–164). McKinsey Global Institute.

CHAPTER 11

QUALITY OF LIFE IN THE EUROPEAN UNION

Kesra Nermend[a] and Simon Grima[b,c]

[a]Department of Decision Support Methods and Cognitive Neuroscience, Institute of Management, University of Szczecin, Poland
[b]Department of Insurance and Risk Management, Faculty of Economics, Management and Accountancy, University of Malta, Malta
[c]Faculty of Business, Management and Economics, University of Latvia, Latvia

ABSTRACT

Purpose: *This study aims to investigate the complex and multifaceted issue of changes in the quality of life of residents of the European Union (EU) member states from a dynamic perspective. This issue encompasses various social, economic, and political dimensions.*

Methodology: *This study uses the vector measure construction method (VMCM) to compare the quality of life in 27 EU countries since 2004. The VMCM approach, based on vector calculus properties, uses a scalar product to analyse the actual objects of analysis. Indicators such as per capita income, housing conditions, healthcare, education, and social and environmental inequality will be identified. The aggregate measure and available data will be used to create a ranking of the quality of life in each EU country, with the top-ranked country serving as a benchmark for comparison in the second phase.*

Results: *This study reveals that Ireland, Greece, Cyprus, and Luxembourg are the top performers in quality of life, while Hungary and Bulgaria consistently rank lower. Malta and Estonia show improvements in education, gross domestic product (GDP) per capita, income, and employment rates, while Poland*

Economic Development and Resilience by EU Member States
Contemporary Studies in Economic and Financial Analysis, Volume 115, 177–200
Copyright © 2025 by Kesra Nermend and Simon Grima
Published under exclusive licence by Emerald Publishing Limited
ISSN: 1569-3759/doi:10.1108/S1569-375920240000115011

and Spain experience declines. Slovenia is the top performer, followed by Malta and Lithuania, which have improved their ranking over time.
Practical implications: *This study underscores the dynamic nature of quality of life and provides valuable insights for policymakers and researchers alike.*

Keywords: VMCM; quality of life; MCDA – multicriteria decision-making; MCA – multidimensional comparative analysis; aggregate measure; quality of life in the EU

JEL classifications: D15; J17

INTRODUCTION

Our expectations for a high quality of life rise as civilisation progresses. Thirty years ago, most tangible and intangible goods and services – such as cell phones, internet access, banking services, and medical services – were considered luxury items connected to a high quality of life in a particular society. Meanwhile, many people still struggle to access clean water or healthcare in many different parts of the world today. As a result, determining the world's quality of life using a single metric is exceedingly challenging. As a result, determining the quality of life is difficult because it depends on various factors, including the location in which we live. As a result, determining the quality of life is a difficult task influenced by a wide range of variables depending on the region under study. The methodology for evaluating the quality of life in Africa should be customised since the factors that influence this evaluation differ significantly from those in Asia or Europe. The question of quality of life has gained significant attention from researchers across various disciplines in recent decades. The quantity of publications in various fields with the phrase 'Quality of life' in the title – a number that has risen over time – proves this.

The concept of quality of life is widely used in scientific literature, journalism, and in everyday conversations (Bańka, 2005; Bańka et al., 1995; Borys & Ostasiewicz, 2004; Jankowiak et al., 2017; Oleś, 2010). Nevertheless, it is not easy to find a clear, generally satisfactory definition of the term (Wnuk et al., 2013). A researcher who diagnoses the social situation must use an established system of terms that will enable him to conduct scientific discussions and comparisons. In the case of the term 'quality of life', however, we encounter a variety of definitions and ways of conceptualisation (Zandecki, 1999). These definitions are not contradictory or incompatible with each other. They focus on different aspects, emphasise different spheres of reality, and are based on different foundations.

Some researchers try to emphasise unique aspects of quality of life and attribute them to different fields of knowledge (Rybczyńska, 1998; Zandecki, 1999). Accordingly, sociologists deal with quality of life in the context of social lifestyles and principles. In this context, the concept of quality of life is equated with a sense of happiness and satisfaction with life, which refers to the environment in which human needs are met, both environmental and social (Kaleta, 1982).

Quality of Life in the EU

Psychologists focus on feelings of satisfaction, happiness, or well-being (Bańka, 2005; Czapiński, 1994; Czapiński et al., 2015; Kaleta, 1988), and educators analyse values, goals, and aspirations related to the quality of life (Daszykowska-Tobiasz, 2007; Kusterka-Jefmańska, 2010; Wysocka, 2014). An analysis of the available literature indicates that such generalisations are justified and have adequate explanatory power only to a certain extent. Thus, they fulfil the postulate of the aspiration of the various scientific fields to exact specialisation. Nevertheless, a complex and interdisciplinary concept of quality of life often eludes researchers, who put it too narrowly.

In colloquial communication, we frequently rely on our interpretations and perceptions or intuitive understanding, but in a scientific setting, definitions that permit a clear understanding of the term must be sought after. Nevertheless, these definitions often share a common starting point as they attempt to answer questions such as how people experience life. How do they evaluate their everyday life? Are they satisfied with their situation? This is particularly important when comparing the quality of life of residents of different European countries.

The topic's popularity of quality of life dates back to the early 1930s. However, due to the rapid progress of civilisation, it has taken on quite a different dimension. This research was not the same as the quality-of-life research that A. Campbell conducted in the 1960s. To gather data on the quality of life in society, he critically examined the current state of research and theoretical studies on social indicators (Merelman, 1981). Participation in quality-of-life research was important given the general disenchantment with economic growth and the conviction that accumulating wealth does not by itself enhance people's quality of life (GUS, 2020, 2021; Zenka-Zganiacz, 2017). Numerous studies have also discovered that life satisfaction depends not only on material possessions but especially on the ability to realise higher needs, such as a sense of security, self-realisation, and state of mind, so nowadays in the literature, we can find numerous publications on quality of life (Borys & Ostasiewicz, 2004; Gierszewski et al., 2023; Rokicka, 2013; Ślęczek-Czakon, 2019).

In the context of this study, it is necessary to look for an appropriate set of indicators that could be considered universally identical for different countries in Europe and in line with their specific development characteristics (Biskup & Ostasiewicz, 2002; Wachowiak & Wyższa Szkoła Pedagogiczna with Tadeusza Kotarbińskiego (Zielona Góra), 2001). The literature distinguishes between two approaches to the quality of life: the objective one, which is based on objective conditions of life, and the subjective one, which is identified with the level of satisfaction individuals derive from various areas of their lives.

E. Skrzypek (2007) wrote extensively about this in her research, which defines the quality of life as a comprehensive set of elements, including objective and subjective aspects. Among the determinants of quality of life, the author distinguishes three objective elements: economic conditions, leisure time, housing conditions, and the individual's environment, which collectively contribute to the overall well-being and satisfaction of individuals. In addition, the three subjective conditions, as perceived individually by each person, mainly focus on well-being. Therefore, evaluating living conditions and considering satisfaction, happiness, anxiety, and feelings of loneliness play a key role. A similar characterisation is provided by The World Health Organization (WHO) (WHOQOL, 2024), emerging six basic areas that relate to quality of life:

1. Physical dimension: pain, discomfort, energy, fatigue, sleep, rest.
2. Psychological dimension: positive feelings, negative feelings, cognitive functioning.
3. Independence: motor independence, activities of daily living, communication skills, performance at work.
4. Social relationships: personal ties, social support, and behaviours that support others.
5. Environment: home environment, physical freedoms and security, job satisfaction, financial resources, participation in recreation and leisure activities.
6. Spiritual dimension: personal beliefs.

From here, it can be concluded that the study of quality of life in the modern world is very important and is not a trivial issue because it allows you to assess the important determinants that can make a society more or less satisfied with the level of its quality of life (Biskup & Ostasiewicz, 2002; Grotowska-Leder & Rokicka, 2013). This study should cover objective and subjective aspects of individuals and households. Both aspects should determine the inclusion of different indicators, which should be treated as complementary.

The Central Statistical Offices' global approach to measuring quality of life aims to integrate with the extensive body of research on quality of life worldwide and international recommendations. The idea is predicated on the statistical assessment of life quality, accounting for the concept's multifaceted nature. Its premise is that subjective quality of life, subjective well-being, and objective living conditions are included in this measurement. Many facets of life are examined; these are called domains. These include material circumstances, the primary activity, employment, health, education, leisure, and social interactions; economic and physical security; the state and fundamental rights; civic engagement; and the standard of one's living environment and subjective well-being. Assessing an individual's perceived quality of life, or the satisfaction they get from different aspects of their lives, is part of measuring their subjective well-being (WHOQOL, 2024).

A set of European indicators for evaluating quality of life was developed in Europe as a result of several demands, including the need to consider the multidimensionality of the study of quality of life, the perspective of households, and the distribution (diversity) of income, consumption, and wealth, as well as environmental sustainability. The model of quality of life developed by the experts includes nine spheres, known as the 8 + 1 model. The first eight areas focus on capabilities (capabilities), which form a complex of resources. According to their notions, access to these resources is the foundation for citizens' achievement of well-being. The spheres that are part of the analysis of quality of life in European statistics are material conditions, productive/primary activities, education, health, leisure and social relations, economic security, power and basic rights, living environment, and the natural environment, the overall experience of life (Eurostat, 2024). Surveys in European countries are conducted and published by Eurostat. However, most of these surveys or analyses presented by Eurostat

Quality of Life in the EU

are single-criteria surveys and cover one year or the dynamics of change for one country over time. There is still a lack of a multicriteria dynamic approach to surveys. Such an approach would make it possible to monitor the quality of life for different periods and any set of criteria from different areas.

The purpose of this study is to use the selected multicriteria/multidimensional analysis method to solve the problem in the context of the study of the quality-of-life level in EU countries over time. The study presents three case studies. The first case will build an aggregate measure to assess the quality of life over time according to the selected criteria concerning the base year, which, in this case, is 2010. The second case is to assess the level of quality of life in the year 2022 by identifying the best and worst countries as reference points for the selected countries (Bulgaria, Cyprus, the Czech Republic, Estonia, Hungary, Latvia, Lithuania, Malta, Poland, Romania, Slovakia, Slovenia). The goal is to determine when each selected country will achieve a quality of life level comparable to or similar to the 2022 reference points. The author utilized the Vector Measure Construction Method (VMCM), which possesses all the necessary features for this study. Unlike other multicriteria methods in this class, such as Topsis or Vikor, VMCM uniquely meets all the requirements needed for this analysis. Many authors have used the VMCM to solve similar issues, such as the assessment of the dynamics of change in the development of the information society in the EU countries (Ogonowski, 2020), assessment of the level of renewable energy in the EU countries (Ogonowski, 2021), study on the level of poverty in the EU countries (Miłaszewicz, 2017), analysis of the dynamics of change in the investment attractiveness of the region (Marchewka, 2021), assessments of the level of housing attractiveness of municipalities (Szaja, 2021), make complex decisions in management business processes (Piwowarski & Nermend, 2022), multicriteria assessment of bureaucracy in a selected country, for example, Poland (Klimek, 2020), study on the level of healthcare capacity in European countries on COVID-19 infections and mortality (Borawski et al., 2021), and measurement of economic growth factors (Fatima et al., 2023). Multicriteria methods were also applied to studying edutainment in the broadest sense. They are used for analysis in e-learning training design and decision support (Korniejenko, 2017) or in optimising the selection of e-learning courses (Miłaszewicz et al., 2020). In most studies where multi-criteria decision analysis (MCDA) methods were used to measure the complex socioeconomic process, they were limited to only one year.

The study's authors use a new approach, using the possibilities given by the VMCM, to study the changes in the quality-of-life level with a dynamic approach. For the research procedure, the WHO's definition of quality of life was adopted, which is defined as 'full physical, mental, and social well-being and not merely the absence of disease'. Thus, quality of life is an individual's perception of the position of life of residents in the context of the culture and value system in which they live and about their goals, expectations, and standards (Kowalczewska-Grabowska, 2013). Using indicators from Eurostat, the authors examined differences in the quality of life of residents of EU member states. Soft indicators from the database, such as mental and social status, were not selected because the scope of the data was limited to one year only. The VMCM was used for the analysis (Nermend, 2009).

MATERIALS AND METHODS

The VMCM was employed in the study as a methodical tool to evaluate the issue of changes in the quality of life in countries that are members of the EU. Three cases were presented in this study. First, the quality-of-life level in each country that made up the EU in 2022 will be measured using specific criteria from the Eurostat database's quality-of-life section. This information will be used in subsequent research to identify which countries are the best and worst in terms of quality of life. Based on the established criteria, the second case will evaluate each country in the EU's quality of life using a dynamic approach throughout the time frame (2010–2022). Utilising the data from 2010 as a point of reference, the pattern and the anti-pattern objects (so-called artificial pattern) were computed. In the third case, which is founded on an actual pattern and will verify the anti-pattern, it will be checked as to which of the 12 countries (Bulgaria, Cyprus, the Czech Republic, Estonia, Hungary, Latvia, Lithuania, Malta, Poland, Romania, Slovakia, Slovenia) is most similar to the nation that ranked highest in the first instance for quality of life. The overall goal of this research concept is to make it possible to rank all the EU's member states according to their respective quality of life and to compare the outcomes of those rankings for each nation separately over a period spanning from 2010 to 2022. The criteria used in this research were selected from the quality-of-life area from the Eurostat database:

x_1 – Population by educational attainment level, sex, and age (%) – main indicators.

x_2 – Self-perceived health by sex, age, and educational attainment level.

x_3 – Inactive population as a percentage of the total population by sex and age (%).

x_4 – Long working hours in the main job by sex, age, professional status, and occupation.

x_5 – Employment rates by sex, age, and educational attainment level (%)

x_6 – Unemployment rates by sex, age, and educational attainment level (%).

x_7 – Long-term unemployment by sex – annual data.

x_8 – Share of people living in under-occupied dwellings by household type and income quintile – total population – European Union Statistics on Income and Living Conditions (EU-SILC) survey.

x_9 – Main GDP aggregates per capita.

x_{10} – At-risk-of-poverty rate by poverty threshold, age, and sex – EU-SILC and European Community Household Panel (ECHP) surveys.

x_{11} – Mean and median income by age and sex – EU-SILC and ECHP surveys.

x_{12} – Self-perceived health by sex, age, and groups of country of citizenship.

x_{13} – People having a long-standing illness or health problem by sex, age, and groups of the country of citizenship.

x_{14} – Self-reported unmet needs for medical examination by sex, age, main reason declared, and groups of country of citizenship.

The analysed selected countries (decision variants) were Austria (AT), Belgium (BE), Bulgaria (BG), Cyprus (CY), the Czech Republic (CZ), Denmark (DK), Estonia (EE), Finland (FI), France (FR), Germany (DE), Greece (EL), Hungary (HU), Ireland (IE), Italy (IT), Latvia (LV), Lithuania (LT), Luxembourg (LU), Malta (MT), the Netherlands (NL), Norway (NO), Poland (PL), Portugal (PT), Romania(RO), Slovakia (SK), Slovenia (SI), Spain (ES), and Sweden (SE). Data referred to the year 2010–2022 and were obtained from the Eurostat database. This gave a picture of how 12 EU countries joining since 2004 (i.e. Bulgaria (BG), Cyprus (CY), the Czech Republic (CZ), Estonia (EE), Hungary (HU), Latvia (LV), Lithuania (LT), Malta (MT), Poland (PL), Romania (RO), Slovakia (SK),

Quality of Life in the EU 183

and Slovenia (SI)) compared with each other. Iceland (IS) and Croatia (HR) that were not included in the analysis due to a lack of data for most of the adopted criteria.

The time frame from 2010 to 2022 was particularly relevant due to significant events and changes occurring within the EU during this period. For instance, the global financial crisis of 2008 had profound impacts on economies worldwide, including those within the EU, which was felt later in the years. Additionally, notable policy changes and developments within the EU during these years could have influenced the quality of life indicators.

Moreover, gathering and analysing data over a too-broad time frame might pose logistical challenges or result in too diverse data to draw meaningful conclusions. Focusing on a narrower time frame could help mitigate these challenges and provide more focussed insights.

DESCRIPTION OF VMCM

The VMCM is a multicriteria approach developed relatively recently. The methodological basis was developed in 2009 by Nermend (2009). A detailed description of the method and its applications has been described by Nermend (2023). It utilises the properties of vector calculus to create vector aggregate measures based on the definition of an inner product. This approach enables the ranking and classification of objects and the analysis of changes over time. The VMCM involves eight stages of procedure.

Stages 1 and 2. Selection of Variables and Elimination of Variables

The study's criteria were chosen using two methods: one that involved selecting items based on logic and substance and the other that involved removing variables with high levels of collinearity (Grabiński, n.d.; Nermend, 2017). Elimination of variables is carried out by using the significance coefficient of features (Kukuła, 2000):

$$V_{x_i} = \frac{\sigma_i}{\bar{x}_i} \tag{1}$$

where x_i is ith variable, σ_i is standard deviation of the ith variable, and $\bar{x}_i$ is mean value of the ith variable.

Variables for which significance coefficient values are within the range $\langle 0;0,1 \rangle$ are quasi-constant, and such variables should be eliminated from the set of variables under consideration (Kukuła, 2000; Nermend, 2007a,b).

Stage 3. Defining the Diagnostic Variables Character

The criteria can be stimulants (benefits), destimulants (no benefit), and nominants (natural, interval). Stimulants (benefits) are such criteria in which greater values mean a higher level of benefits. Destimulants are such criteria in which smaller values mean a higher level of benefits, while nominants are criteria in which desired values are within a specific range. In the study, the criteria (x_1, x_2, x_5, x_8, x_9, x_{11}, x_{12}) had character stimulants (benefits) and (x_3, x_4, x_6, x_7, x_{10}, x_{13}, x_{14}) was destimulants (no benefit).

Stage 4. Assigning Weights to Diagnostic Variables

In the study, five experts from different universities in Poland (Szczecin, Warsaw, Koszalin, Łódź, and Częstochowa) were asked to determine the importance of criteria on a scale (Grabiński, n.d.; Kolenda, 2006; Kukuła, 2000; Nermend, 2007, 2009, 2012, 2017, n.d.; Nermend & Borawski, 2014; Panek & Zwierzchowski, 2013). The average rating of the experts' evaluation showed that the criteria were $(x_1 - [7], x_2 - [10], x_3 - [6], x_4 - [7], x_5 - [8], x_6 - [8], x_7 - [9], x_8 - [7], x_9 - [10], x_{10} - [10], x_{11} - [9], x_{12} - [10], x_{13} - [8], x_{14} - [9])$. In the next step, the weights were normalised according to the formula:

$$w_i = \frac{w_i}{\sum_{j=1}^{m} w_j} \tag{2}$$

Depending on the greatness of the weight w_i. Intended for a given criterion, its share will be greater or minor in the value of the aggregate measure. However, it should be remembered that the weights are to be positive and meet the following condition:

$$\sum_{i=1}^{m} w_i = 1 \tag{3}$$

In practice, various approaches can be used to weigh the criteria, for example, statistical weights, the Monte Carlo method, or using a relative value metre, etc. (Panek & Zwierzchowski, 2013). An example of such an approach is:

$$w_i = \frac{V_{x_i}}{\sum_{k=1}^{m} V_{x_k}} \tag{4}$$

where w_i means the variable's weight.

Nevertheless, regardless of the system adopted, the weights should be normalised.

Stage 5. Normalisation of Variables

The criteria come in different units of measurement, which can make any arithmetic difficult. Therefore, the studies' criteria should be normalised at this stage. This process leads not only to the elimination of units of measurement but also to the equalisation of criteria values. Standardisation is the most used normalisation technique:

$$x'_{ij} = \frac{a_i}{\sigma_i} \tag{5}$$

where nominator a_i can be defined in any way, for example:

$$a_i = x_{ij} - \bar{x}_i \tag{6}$$

where x'_{ij} is the normalised value of the ith variable for the jth object.

Quality of Life in the EU 185

Stage 6. Determination of Pattern and Anti-pattern

The VMCM allows you to use patterns and anti-patterns as real-life objects, or it can be automatically determined based on the first and third quartiles. The study is used for both approaches (Kolenda, 2006). Where stimulants (benefit) values of the third quartile and for destimulants (no benefit) values of the first quartile are taken as coordinates of the pattern accordingly:

$$x'_{i\,w} = \begin{cases} x'_{i_{qIII}} & \text{for stimulants} \\ x'_{i_{qI}} & \text{for destimulants} \end{cases} \tag{7}$$

where $x'_{i\,w}$ is the value of the ith normalised variable for the pattern, $x'_{i_{qI}}$ – the value of the ith normalised variable for the first quartile, and $x'_{i_{qIII}}$ – the value of the ith normalised variable for the third quartile. In the case of an anti-pattern, the procedure is inversed. Values in the first quartile are anti-pattern coordinates for stimulants, and values in the third quartile for destimulants:

$$x'_{i\,aw} = \begin{cases} x'_{i_{qI}} & \text{for stimulants} \\ x'_{i_{qIII}} & \text{for destimulants} \end{cases} \tag{8}$$

where $x'_{i\,aw}$ means the value of the ith normalised variable for anti-pattern.

Stage 7. Construction of the Synthetic Measure

The values of the variables of the examined objects in the vector space are interpreted as vector coordinates. Each object, therefore, determines a specific direction in space. The pattern and anti-pattern difference is also a vector determining a certain direction in space. Along this direction, the aggregate measure value for each object is calculated. This difference can be treated as a monodimensional coordinate system in which the coordinates are calculated based on the formula (Nermend, 2007, 2009):

$$c = \frac{\left(\vec{A}, \vec{B}\right)}{\left(\vec{B}, \vec{B}\right)} \tag{9}$$

In turn, $\vec{A}$ and $\vec{B}$ are vectors and $\left(\vec{A}, \vec{B}\right)$ is the scalar product, which can be defined as follows:

$$\left(\vec{A}, \vec{B}\right) = \sum_{k=1}^{n} a_k b_k \tag{10}$$

where a_k and b_k are coordinates of the appropriate vectors $\vec{A}$ and $\vec{B}$.

We consider the $\vec{B}$ vector as the monodimensional coordinates system. Thus, it represents a difference between the pattern and anti-pattern. By entering the coordinates of the pattern and anti-pattern as well as the object into the formula (11), the result is as follows:

$$m_{aj} = \frac{\sum_{i=1}^{m}\left(x'_{ij} - x'_{i\,aw}\right)\left(x'_{i\,w} - x'_{i\,aw}\right)}{\sum_{i=1}^{m}\left(x'_{i\,w} - x'_{i\,aw}\right)^2} \tag{11}$$

Stage 8. Classification of Objects

The last step of the VMCM is decision variant rankings, which depend on the obtained aggregate measure values. Thus, it is possible to determine which of them are 'better' and which are 'worse'. They also allow for determining which are like each other in terms of adopted criteria. Decision variants can be divided into classes with similar measurement values to better visualise the results of calculations. In the simplest case, objects can be classified based on mean value $\overline{m}_{m_{a0}}$ and standard deviation of the aggregate measure $\sigma_{m_{a0}}$. Objects are classified into four classes (Nermend, 2009):

$$\begin{cases} 1 \text{ for } m_{aj} \in (\overline{m}_{m_{a0}} + \sigma_{m_{a0}}; \infty), \\ 2 \text{ for } m_{aj} \in (\overline{m}_{m_{a0}}; \overline{m}_{m_{a0}} + \sigma_{m_{a0}}), \\ 3 \text{ for } m_{aj} \in (\overline{m}_{m_{a0}} - \sigma_{m_{a0}}; \overline{m}_{m_{a0}}), \\ 4 \text{ for } m_{aj} \in (-\infty; \overline{m}_{m_{a0}} - \sigma_{m_{a0}}). \end{cases} \tag{12}$$

RESEARCH RESULTS

Research Study 1

The VMCM was used to assess the dynamics of change in the quality-of-life level in EU countries in the period spanning from 2010 to 2022. The results of the aggregated measure and their specific class membership were illustrated in tables. For each year, values of the aggregate measure are calculated separately, and as a reference point, the artificial pattern was built based on data from the base year 2010.

Table 11.1 shows the results of the classification of EU countries according to the quality-of-life level obtained in EU countries based on data from 2010 and 2014. The created ranking in 2010 shows that six countries were classified into Class 1: Ireland, Cyprus, Greece, Spain, Luxembourg, and Sweden. Ireland is the leading country in this ranking because in 2010, all criteria were good, but the criteria x_1 – population by educational attainment level, sex, and age (%) – main indicators 33.9% and x_8 – share of people living in under-occupied dwellings by household type and income quintile – total population – EU-SILC survey 72.5% had the highest value of all countries. The situation in 2014 in the first and second classes is stable; the changes are not great, and only Greece moves to the first place in the ranking. Greece changed their ranking from Place 3 to 1. Greece potentially provides the best environment for quality of life in EU countries. Latvia, on the other hand, in relation to 2010, was in Position 15 in this ranking.

Quality of Life in the EU 187

Table 11.1. Ranking of EU Countries in 2010 and 2014 in Respect of the Level of Quality of Life by the VMCM.

Country	Measure Value	Class	Country	Measure Value	Class
Pattern from 2010 and Data (2010)			Pattern from 2010 and Data (2014)		
Ireland	0.066	1	Greece	0.069	1
Cyprus	0.062	1	Cyprus	0.067	1
Greece	0.058	1	Ireland	0.065	1
Spain	0.056	1	Spain	0.057	1
Luxembourg	0.053	1	Luxembourg	0.055	2
Sweden	0.053	1	Sweden	0.054	2
Norway	0.047	2	Norway	0.053	2
Finland	0.047	2	Belgium	0.051	2
Belgium	0.046	2	Finland	0.049	2
France	0.044	2	France	0.046	2
Denmark	0.039	2	Austria	0.045	2
Austria	0.039	2	Denmark	0.041	2
Germany	0.038	2	Germany	0.040	2
The Netherlands	0.033	3	Netherlands	0.036	3
Latvia	0.029	3	Portugal	0.035	3
Poland	0.028	3	Estonia	0.033	3
Slovakia	0.028	3	Malta	0.030	3
Italy	0.028	3	Italy	0.029	3
Portugal	0.028	3	Poland	0.028	3
Estonia	0.026	3	Slovenia	0.027	3
Malta	0.024	3	Latvia	0.027	3
Slovenia	0.021	3	Lithuania	0.024	3
Lithuania	0.019	4	Slovakia	0.024	3
Bulgaria	0.018	4	Bulgaria	0.018	4
Romania	0.016	4	Romania	0.017	4
Czech Republic	0.013	4	Czech Republic	0.014	4
Hungary	0.012	4	Hungary	0.012	4

Source: Authors compilation.

It moved down to Position 21 in 2014. These changes result from the fact that in 2014, in Latvia, the value of the criteria x_5 – employment rates by sex, age, and educational attainment level (%) increased by 6.4%, x_6 – unemployment rates by sex, age, and educational attainment level (%) decreased and amounted to 8.7%, x_8 increased by 6.6%, x_9 – main GDP aggregates per capita increased by 18.29%, and x_{11} – mean and median income by age and sex – EU-SILC and ECHP surveys increased by 13.74%.

Portugal changed its ranking from 19 to 15 in 2014. These changes result from the fact that in 2014, in Portugal, the value of the criteria x_1 – increased by 5.8% and x_8 increased by 13.6%. Meanwhile, Estonia changed its ranking from Class 4 to Class 3. These changes result from the fact that in 2014, in Estonia, the value of the criteria x_5 increased by 7.5%, x_6 decreased and amounted to 9.6%, x_7 – long-term unemployment by sex – annual data decreased and amounted to 4.2%, x_8 increased by 18.3%, x_9 increased by 17.87%, and x_{11} increased by 20.65%. Lithuania changed their ranking from Class 4 to Class 3. These changes result from the fact that in 2014, in Lithuania, the value of the criteria x_1 was 4.5%, x_3 – inactive population as a percentage of the total population, by sex and age (%), increased by 3.5%, x_5 increased by 7.5%, x_8 increased by 10.5%, x_9 increased by 20.26%, and x_{11} increased by 16.44%. This process positively impacted the quality of life in these countries. The opposite pole (Class 4) includes four countries, of which Bulgaria, Romania, the Czech Republic, and Hungary had the lowest ranking.

Table 11.2 shows the results of the classification of EU countries according to the quality of life obtained based on data from 2015 and 2019; two differences in class assignments can be observed. Cyprus changed its position in 2010 from second to first in 2019, while Sweden and Spain changed their position in 2010 from class first to second class in 2019. These changes result from the fact that in 2019, in Sweden, the value of the criteria x_2 – self-perceived health by sex, age, and educational attainment level, x_{10} – at-risk-of-poverty rate by poverty threshold, age, and sex – EU-SILC and ECHP surveys, x_{12} – self-perceived health by sex, age, and groups of country of citizenship, and x_{13} – people having a long-standing illness or health problem, by sex, age, and groups of the country of citizenship decreased and amounted to 9%, 2.3%, 9.4%, and 5.8%. Meanwhile,

Table 11.2. Ranking of EU Countries in 2015 and 2019 Regarding the Quality of Life by the VMCM.

Country	Measure Value	Class	Country	Measure Value	Class
Pattern from 2010 and Data (2015)			Pattern from 2010 and Data (2019)		
Greece	0.070	1	Cyprus	0.068	1
Cyprus	0.068	1	Greece	0.066	1
Ireland	0.065	1	Ireland	0.066	1
Spain	0.057	1	Luxembourg	0.065	1
Luxembourg	0.057	1	Norway	0.059	1
Sweden	0.055	2	Sweden	0.056	2
Norway	0.054	2	Spain	0.055	2
Belgium	0.051	2	Belgium	0.053	2
Finland	0.049	2	Finland	0.051	2
France	0.047	2	France	0.051	2
Austria	0.047	2	Austria	0.051	2
Denmark	0.042	2	Denmark	0.046	2
Germany	0.041	2	Netherlands	0.043	2
The Netherlands	0.037	3	Germany	0.042	2
Portugal	0.036	3	Estonia	0.042	2
Estonia	0.035	3	Portugal	0.037	3
Malta	0.031	3	Malta	0.037	3
Italy	0.030	3	Slovenia	0.032	3
Slovenia	0.028	3	Lithuania	0.031	3
Poland	0.027	3	Italy	0.030	3
Latvia	0.027	3	Latvia	0.028	3
Lithuania	0.025	3	Poland	0.026	3
Slovakia	0.023	3	Slovakia	0.023	4
Bulgaria	0.018	4	Romania	0.020	4
Romania	0.018	4	Czech Republic	0.019	4
Czech Republic	0.015	4	Bulgaria	0.017	4
Hungary	0.012	4	Hungary	0,014	4

Source: Authors compilation.

Quality of Life in the EU 189

Spain's criterion x_8 decreased to 6.6%. However, criteria x_2, x_{12}, and x_{13} in Poland have decreased by 2.6%, 2.6%, and 5.8% compared to 2010, which was in Position 16 in this country's ranking, moving down to Position 22. In contrast, Slovakia changed their ranking from Class 3 to Class 4. However, criteria x_2 and x_{12} in Slovakia have decreased by 1% and 1%, respectively, compared to 2010. This is bad news because the quality of life in these countries has deteriorated. The situation in Norway is quite the opposite, as criteria x_1, x_4, x_9, and x_{11} increased by 6.3%, 0.7%, 10.97%, and 17.19%, changing their ranking from Class 2 to Class 1.

Table 11.3 shows the results of classifying EU countries according to the quality-of-life level obtained based on data from 2020 and 2022. Most countries retained their position as of 2019, except for a minor change at the end of the ranking. Poland moved from Class 3 to 4 and changed its position to 22. These changes result from the fact that in 2022, in Poland, the value of the criteria x_2 and x_{12} decreased and amounted to 2.4% and 2.5%, which means the station of self-perceived health is generally becoming worse. In contrast, Spain moved down from Position 4 to 10 in 2010. These changes result from the fact that in 2022,

Table 11.3. Ranking of EU Countries in 2020 and 2022 Regarding the Quality of Life by the VMCM.

Country	Measure value	Class	Country	Measure value	Class
Pattern from 2010 and Data (2020)			Pattern from 2010 and Data (2022)		
Luxembourg	0.068	1	Luxembourg	0.074	1
Cyprus	0.068	1	Ireland	0.068	1
Ireland	0.066	1	Cyprus	0.066	1
Greece	0.063	1	Norway	0.063	1
Norway	0.060	1	Sweden	0.057	2
Sweden	0.056	2	France	0.056	2
Spain	0.055	2	Greece	0.055	2
Belgium	0.054	2	Belgium	0.053	2
France	0.053	2	Finland	0.053	2
Finland	0.052	2	Spain	0.053	2
Austria	0.052	2	Austria	0.053	2
Denmark	0.047	2	Denmark	0.050	2
The Netherlands	0,045	2	Netherlands	0.048	2
Estonia	0.043	2	Estonia	0.047	2
Germany	0.042	2	Germany	0.043	3
Malta	0.038	3	Malta	0.040	3
Portugal	0.036	3	Lithuania	0.036	3
Slovenia	0.033	3	Slovenia	0.035	3
Lithuania	0.033	3	Portugal	0.034	3
Italy	0.030	3	Latvia	0.031	3
Latvia	0.029	3	Italy	0.030	3
Poland	0.025	4	Slovakia	0.025	4
Slovakia	0.023	4	Poland	0.023	4
Romania	0.021	4	Romania	0.023	4
Czech Republic	0.020	4	Czech Republic	0.022	4
Bulgaria	0.017	4	Hungary	0.017	4
Hungary	0.015	4	Bulgaria	0.016	4

Source: Authors compilation.

in Poland, the value of the criteria x_2, x_8, and x_{13} decreased and amounted to 1%, 3.8%, and 8.6%, which means that the level of education, the share of people living in under-occupied dwellings by household, and people having a long-standing illness or health problem become worse. Greece moved from Class 1 to 2 and changed its position to 7. These modifications stem from the fact that in Greece, in 2022, the values of the criteria x_2, x_{11}, x_{13}, and x_{14} fell and totalled 3.3%, 25.66%, 1.9%, and 5.6%. This indicates that the country's standing in terms of self-reported unmet medical examination needs, individuals with long-term illnesses or health conditions, and mean income worsened compared to 2010. Furthermore, in 2010, the stations in Malta and Estonia improved their relationship. Malta moved from Position 21 to 16 and Estonia from 20 to 14. These changes result from the fact that in 2022, in Estonia, the value of the criteria x_1, x_2, x_5, x_9, x_{11}, and x_{12} increased by 6.7%, 5.2%, 15.1%, 45.25%, 61.37%, and 5.6%. The unemployment rates, main GDP aggregates per capita, and mean income are impressively changed, that means the level of quality of life is better related to 2010. The station in Malta is also better related to the year 2010. The criteria x_1, x_9, x_{11}, x_5, and x_3, the population by educational attainment level (14.7%), main GDP aggregates per capita (24.25%), and mean income (45.52%) and employment rates (21%) are impressively changed, that means the level of quality of life is better related to 2010. At the same time, the inactive population as a percentage of the total population (19.6%) decreases.

Fig. 11.1 shows the dynamics of changes in the quality-of-life level. In the first class, Sweden has changed its position in the ranking. The value of Sweden's aggregate measure changed from 0.053 to 0.057 in 2022, but it moved from the first class to the second class. At the same time, Norway moved from second in the 2010 class to first in 2022. The value of Norway is an aggregate measure that changed from 0.047 to 0,063 in 2022. At the same time, Luxembourg has changed its aggregate measure from 0.053 to 0.074 to become the leading country in this ranking (2010–2022).

According to Fig. 11.2, there have been changes in the ranking of the quality-of-life level. In the second category, Estonia and the Netherlands have moved up to the second class, with Estonia's aggregate measure increasing from 0.026 to 0.047 and the Netherlands from 0.033 to 0.048 in 2022. Meanwhile, Germany has dropped from second to third class in 2022, with its aggregate measure changing from 0.038 to 0.043. Greece has also shifted from first to second class, decreasing its aggregate measure value from 0.058 in 2010 to 0.055 in 2022. Sweden is now the second-leading country in the category, with Estonia ranking last from 2010 to 2022.

Fig. 11.3 shows the dynamics of changes in the quality-of-life level. In the third class, Lithuania has changed its position in the ranking. The value of Lithuania's aggregate measure changed from 0.019 to 0.036 in 2022, and it moved from the fourth class in 2010 to the third class in 2022. At the same time, the Netherlands moved from third class in 2010 to second class in 2022. The value of the Netherlands' aggregate measure changed from 0.033 to 0.048 in 2022. At the same time, Germany changed its aggregate measure from 0.038 to 0.043 and dropped from Class 2 in 2010 to Class 3 in 2022, becoming the leading country

Quality of Life in the EU

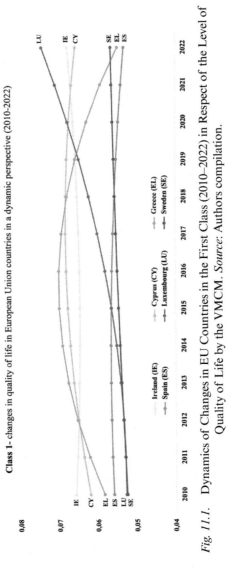

Fig. 11.1. Dynamics of Changes in EU Countries in the First Class (2010–2022) in Respect of the Level of Quality of Life by the VMCM. *Source*: Authors compilation.

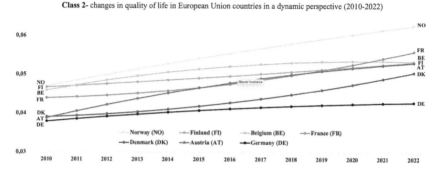

Fig. 11.2. Dynamics of Changes in EU Countries in the Second Class (2010–2022) in Respect of the Level of Quality of Life by the VMCM. *Source*: Authors compilation.

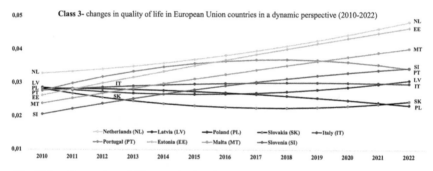

Fig. 11.3. Dynamics of Changes in EU Countries in the Third Class (2010–2022) in Respect of the Level of Quality of Life by the VMCM. *Source*: Authors compilation.

in this ranking in Class 3 (2010–2022). At the same time, Italy is the last country in the ranking.

According to Fig. 11.4, there have been changes in the ranking of the quality-of-life level. In the fourth category, Poland and Slovakia have moved down to the fourth class, with Poland's aggregate measure decreasing from 0.028 to 0.023 and Slovakia's from 0.028 to 0.025 in 2022. Meanwhile, Slovakia is now the leading country in the fourth category, with Bulgaria ranking last from 2010 to 2022.

Research Study 2

Table 11.4 shows the results of the classification of EU countries according to the level of quality of life obtained based on data from 2022 and the pattern and anti-pattern based on data from 2022 as reference points. The ranking is different compared with the result from 2022, where the reference point is from 2010. For example, Greece ranked second and was included in the first class, with an aggregate measure value of 0.070. It was in second position in the first class. In the first ranking, when the data and the reference point from 2022 are in the second

Quality of Life in the EU

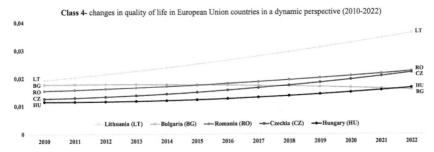

Fig. 11.4. Dynamics of Changes in EU Countries in the Fourth Class (2010–2022) in Respect of the Level of Quality of Life by the VMCM. *Source*: Authors compilation.

class, the value of the aggregate measure is 0.055 and becomes Position 7 in the ranking, etc. This means that the calcification results depend largely on reference points (pattern and anti-pattern).

Research Study 3

In the second study (based on the adopted criteria), EU countries were ranked according to the artificial pattern. Then, the selected countries were assessed, including those that have recently joined the EU structures, such as Bulgaria, Cyprus, the Czech Republic, Estonia, Hungary, Latvia, Lithuania, Malta, Poland, Romania, Slovakia, and Slovenia, where two real objects were selected: a pattern and an anti-pattern. In our case, the best country (Luxembourg) in the ranking became the pattern. The anti-pattern was the last country (Bulgaria)

Table 11.4. Ranking of EU Countries in 2022 with Respect to the Level of Quality of Life by the VMCM.

Country	Measure Value	Class	Country	Measure Value	Class
Pattern From 2022 and Data (2022)			Pattern From 2022 and Data (2022)		
Luxembourg	0.074	1	The Netherlands	0.035	3
Greece	0.070	1	Portugal	0.030	3
Ireland	0.066	1	Germany	0.029	3
Cyprus	0.065	1	Malta	0.029	3
Norway	0.058	1	Italy	0.028	3
France	0.053	2	Slovenia	0.026	3
Spain	0.053	2	Lithuania	0.022	3
Belgium	0.050	2	Latvia	0.021	3
Sweden	0.049	2	Romania	0.020	3
Finland	0.045	2	Slovakia	0.020	3
Austria	0.043	2	Poland	0.013	4
Denmark	0.043	2	Czech Republic	0.010	4
Estonia	0.041	2	Hungary	0.005	4
			Bulgaria	0.005	4

Source: Authors compilation.

in the ranking. The purpose of this research concept was to enable the general ranking of the selected countries and the possibility of making comparisons concerning the selected real object (Luxembourg, Bulgaria), which was the pattern. To show which of these selected countries has improved the quality of life, the analysis compares how close each country is to Luxembourg's level and how far it is from Bulgaria's level.

Table 11.5 shows the results of the classification of selected EU countries according to the quality-of-life level obtained based on data from 2010 and 2014. The information is shared in Table 11.5. It seems that Malta and Slovenia are leading countries in terms of quality of life among the selected EU countries, based on data from 2010 and 2014, the real pattern and anti-pattern (Luxembourg and Bulgaria) based on data from 2022 as reference points in 2022. It's interesting to note that these countries have been identified as the closest to Luxembourg in terms of quality of life. It's good to see that the stations in other countries are stable and have undergone little change. Malta and Slovenia are leading countries in terms of ranking in both stations. At the same time, the stations of the rest of the countries are stable and have undergone little change. Malta and Slovenia have been identified as the countries closest to Luxembourg in terms of quality of life among the 12 countries considered.

Table 11.6 demonstrates the outcomes of the classification of certain EU countries based on their quality-of-life level, which has been calculated using data from 2015 and 2019. Among the selected EU countries, Malta and Slovenia are still leading in terms of quality of life, based on the data from both 2015 and 2019. Luxembourg and Bulgaria have been considered as the real pattern and anti-pattern, respectively, based on the data from 2022, which means that these countries have been identified as those closest to Luxembourg in terms of quality of life. The situation in the second class has undergone some changes. Slovakia's aggregate measure has changed from -0.003 to 0.004 in 2019, which has caused it to drop from Class 2 in 2010 to Class 3 in 2022.

Table 11.5. Ranking of EU Countries in 2010 and 2012 Regarding the Quality of Life by the VMCM.

Country	Measure Value	Class	Country	Measure Value	Class
Pattern From 2022 and Data (2010)			Pattern From 2022 and Data (2014)		
Malta	0.008	1	Malta	0.011	1
Slovenia	0.007	1	Slovenia	0.008	1
Czech Republic	0.002	2	Czech Republic	0.004	2
Poland	-0.002	2	Poland	0.000	2
Slovakia	-0.003	2	Estonia	-0.001	2
Estonia	-0.007	3	Slovakia	-0.001	2
Hungary	-0.007	3	Lithuania	-0.002	3
Lithuania	-0.008	3	Hungary	-0.006	3
Romania	-0.009	3	Latvia	-0.007	3
Latvia	-0.012	4	Romania	-0.008	4
Bulgaria	-0.012	4	Bulgaria	-0.012	4

Source: Authors compilation.

Quality of Life in the EU

Table 11.6. Ranking of EU Countries in 2015 and 2019 Regarding the Quality of Life by the VMCM.

Country	Measure Value	Class	Country	Measure Value	Class
Pattern From 2022 and Data (2015)			Pattern From 2022 and Data (2019)		
Malta	0.012	1	Malta	0.017	1
Slovenia	0.008	1	Slovenia	0.014	1
Czech Republic	0.005	2	Czech Republic	0.010	2
Poland	0.001	2	Estonia	0.008	2
Estonia	0.001	2	Lithuania	0.008	2
Lithuania	0.000	2	Poland	0.006	2
Slovakia	0.000	3	Slovakia	0.004	3
Hungary	−0.005	3	Latvia	0.001	3
Latvia	−0.005	3	Romania	0.000	3
Romania	−0.007	4	Hungary	0.000	3
Bulgaria	−0.011	4	Bulgaria	−0.006	4

Source: Authors compilation.

Conversely, Latvia has moved from the fourth to the third class, and its aggregate measure has changed from −0.012 in 2010 to 0.001 in 2019. Meanwhile, Estonia has moved from the third class to the second, and its aggregate measures have changed from −0.007 to 0.008. This means that Estonia and Latvia have become closer to Luxembourg in terms of quality of life in 2019 compared to the 12 countries considered.

According to Table 11.7, which shows the results of the classification of selected EU countries based on data from 2020 and 2022, Slovenia is the leading country in terms of quality of life among the selected EU countries. The classification is based on the real pattern and anti-pattern (Luxembourg and Bulgaria) using data from 2022 as reference points. Malta secured the second position in

Table 11.7. Ranking of EU Countries in 2020 and 2022 Regarding the Quality of Life by the VMCM.

Country	Measure Value	Class	Country	Measure Value	Class
Pattern From 2022 and Data (2020)			Pattern From 2022 and Data (2022)		
Malta	0.018	1	Slovenia	0.022	1
Slovenia	0.017	1	Malta	0.021	1
Czech Republic	0.012	2	Czech Republic	0.015	2
Estonia	0.010	2	Lithuania	0.015	2
Lithuania	0.010	2	Estonia	0.015	2
Poland	0.008	2	Poland	0.012	2
Slovakia	0.006	3	Slovakia	0.009	3
Latvia	0.003	3	Romania	0.009	3
Romania	0.002	3	Latvia	0.006	3
Hungary	0.001	3	Hungary	0.005	3
Bulgaria	−0.005	4	Bulgaria	−0.001	4

Source: Authors compilation.

this ranking, while Lithuania moved up from Position 8 in 2010 to Position 4 in 2022. Lithuania's aggregate measure improved from −0.008 to 0.015 in 2022, indicating friendly conditions for quality of life between the 10 countries and identifying them as the closest to Luxembourg regarding quality of life. The situation in other countries has not changed since 2019. Overall, these 12 countries were considered to be the closest to Luxembourg in terms of quality of life.

Fig. 11.5 seems quite interesting as it shows how the quality of life has changed in some EU countries from 2010 to 2022. It seems that the figure is based on actual patterns and anti-patterns, showing that Malta and Slovenia consistently ranked as the top countries in all periods of the analysis. However, Slovenia managed to grab the first position in the ranking last year. The figure also mentions that the aggregate measure has increased for both Slovenia and Malta, which means they are closest to Luxembourg in terms of quality of life. Moreover, Lithuania's aggregate measure improved in 2022, while Hungary became nearest to Bulgaria as the anti-pattern. The figure concludes that Bulgaria and Hungary provide the worst quality-of-life conditions for inhabitants of the 13 analysed countries in terms of selected criteria for analysis.

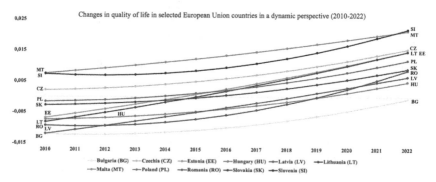

Fig. 11.5. Dynamics of Changes in Selected EU Countries in (2010–2022) With Respect to the Level of Quality of Life by the VMCM. *Source*: Authors compilation.

CONCLUSION

This novel methodology uses multicriteria techniques to assess how people's lives have changed across several EU nations. Because it considers a wide range of socioeconomic factors that may impact people's quality of life, the author's VMCM is especially intriguing. Seeing how this type of methodology can be applied to acquire an understanding of intricate phenomena is fascinating. The results of the study show that there were significant differences in the quality of life across the European nations that were examined. Every year, the aggregate measure value produced was split into four classes.

Ireland had the highest quality of life from 2010 to 2011, but Greece topped the list from 2012 to 2017. During this time, Ireland moved down to the third position

*Quality of Life in the EU*197

in the ranking. In 2018–2019, Cyprus took the lead in the ranking, while Greece dropped to second. At the same time, Luxemburg held the top spot in the ranking from 2020 to 2022, while Greece moved down to the seventh position in the ranking. It appears that from 2010 to 2021, Hungary held the last position in the ranking. However, in 2022, Bulgaria moved down and became the last country in the ranking. This situation seems to result from significant changes in the criteria x_9 – main GDP aggregates per capita by age and the x_{11} – mean income in Luxemburg and Greece. According to the data provided, there was an increase of 16.30% and 27.65% in these criteria in Luxemburg between 2012 and 2022, respectively.

In contrast, Greece saw a more considerable increase of 20.30% in x_9 but only a small growth of 0.007 in x_{11} during the same period. Ireland seems to have performed exceptionally well in the ranking due to its overall good performance, particularly because of its high scores in two specific criteria. According to the data, the indicators x_1 and x_8, which measure the population by educational attainment level and the share of people living in under-occupied dwellings, respectively, were very high in Ireland, with the latter being the highest among all countries surveyed. It's interesting to note that Malta and Estonia have significantly improved their quality of life since 2010. The stations in both countries have increased their rankings, with Malta moving from Position 21 to 16 and Estonia from 20 to 14. Estonia has seen impressive improvements in criteria such as $x_1, x_2, x_5, x_9, x_{11}$, and x_{12}, which have led to lower unemployment rates, higher main GDP per capita, and increased mean income.

Similarly, Malta has also seen improvements in criteria like population by educational attainment level, main GDP per capita, mean income, and employment rates, which have contributed to an overall improvement in the quality of life. It's great that the inactive population percentage has also decreased in Malta. The positioning of Poland and Spain has changed in relation to certain criteria. Poland moved from Class 3 to 4 and is now in Position 22 due to a decrease in the value of certain criteria x_2 and x_{12} by 2.4% and 2.5%, respectively, indicating that self-perceived health is declining. On the other hand, Spain moved down from Position 4 to 10 compared to 2010, as the value of criteria x_2, x_8, and x_{13} decreased by 1%, 3.8%, and 8.6%, respectively, indicating a decline in the level of education, the share of people living in under-occupied dwellings by household, and people having a long-standing illness or health problem. The next step was to choose two real objects, a pattern and an anti-pattern, so that comparisons and a general ranking of the chosen countries could be made. Here, Luxembourg, the top-ranked nation, was designated as the pattern, and Bulgaria, the bottom-ranked nation, was designated as the anti-pattern.

The objective was to demonstrate which of the chosen nations had higher living standards, as well as how much it differed from Bulgarian standards and how close it was to Luxembourg. In this instance, the 13 nations were compared to see which had a higher quality of life than Luxembourg. Of the chosen EU nations, Slovenia had the best quality of life. Malta took the second spot, and Lithuania, whose quality of life has improved, moving up from Position 8 in 2010 to Position 4 in 2022. It's interesting to note that Lithuania is currently among the nations closest to Luxembourg in terms of living standards. Since 2019, the circumstances in other nations have not changed.

Regarding the third study, Malta and Slovenia have been identified as the countries closest to Luxembourg in terms of quality of life among the 12 countries considered, based on data from 2010 and 2022. The reference points were collected based on data from 2022 regarding two objects (Luxembourg and Bulgaria) as a real pattern (the best country in the ranking from Case 2) and anti-pattern (the last country in the ranking from Case 2). Latvia has moved from the fourth to the third class based on data from 2015 and 2019, while Estonia has moved from the third class to the second. This means that Estonia and Latvia have come closer to Luxembourg in terms of quality of life in 2019 compared to the 12 countries considered, while Lithuania moved up from Position 8 in 2010 to Position 4 in 2022. Slovenia has become the leading country in terms of quality of life among the selected EU countries based on data from 2020 and 2022.

REFERENCES

Bańka, A. (Ed.). (2005). *Psychology of quality of life*. Association of Psychology and Architecture.

Bańka, A., Derbis, R., Adam Mickiewicz University (Poznań), & Higher Pedagogical School (Częstochowa) (Eds.). (1995). *Measurement and sense of quality of life among the employed and unemployed*. Central European Center for Social and Economic Action.

Biskup, D., & Ostasiewicz, W. (Eds.). (2002). *Methodology of measuring quality of life*. Publishing House of the Oskar Lange Academy of Economics.

Borawski, M., Duda, J., & Biercewicz, K. (2021). Impact of the healthcare potential in European countries on infections and mortality caused by Covid-19. *Procedia Computer Science, 192*, 4037–4046.

Borys, T., & Ostasiewicz, W. (Eds.). (2004). *Assessment and analysis of quality of life*. Publishing House of the Oskar Lange Academy of Economics.

Czapiński, J. (1994). *Psychology of happiness: Overview of research and outline of the onion theory*. Psychological Tests Laboratory, Polish Psychological Association.

Czapiński, J., Kowalczewska, J., Radzicki, J., Suchecki, J., Szuster, M., & Tarłowski, A. (Eds.). (2015). *Positive psychology: Science of happiness, health, strength, and virtues of human beings* (1st ed., 4th corr.). PWN Scientific Publishers.

Daszykowska-Tobiasz, J. (2007). *Quality of life from a pedagogical perspective*. Impulse Publishing House.

Eurostat. (2024). *Statistics explained*. https://ec.europa.eu/eurostat/statistics-explained/index.php?title=Main_Page

Fatima, M., Sherwani, N. U. K., & Singh, V. (2023). Comparative analysis among doctors working in private and government hospitals in identifying and prioritising essential stress factors during COVID-19: An AHP-TOPSIS approach. *Intelligent Pharmacy, 1*(1), 17–25.

Gierszewski, J., Pieczywok, A., & Piestrzyński, W. (Eds.). (2023). *Measurement of quality of life and sense of security at the local level: Example of the Chojnicki county* (1st ed.). Difin.

Grabiński, T. (n.d.). *Methods of international statistics*. PWE.

Grotowska-Leder, J., & Rokicka, E. (Eds.). (2013). *New order? Dynamics of social structures in contemporary societies: Commemorative book dedicated to Professor Wielisława Warzywoda-Kruszyńska on the occasion of her 45th anniversary of scientific and didactic work*. University of Łódź Publishing House.

GUS. (2020). *Quality of life and social capital in Poland: Results of the 2018 social cohesion survey*. https://stat.gov.pl/en/topics/living-conditions/living-conditions/quality-of-life-and-social-capital-in-poland-results-of-the-social-cohesion-survey-2018,13,3.html

GUS. (2021). *Towards a better life: Poland in the OECD*. https://stat.gov.pl/en/topics/other-studies/other-aggregated-studies/towards-better-lives-poland-in-the-oecd,29,1.html

Quality of Life in the EU 199

Jankowiak, B., Kowalewska, B., Krajewska-Kułak, E., Rolka, H., & Faculty of Health Sciences (Medical University of Białystok) (Eds.). (2017). *Quality of life in medical and social sciences: Collective work* (Vol. 1). Medical University of Białystok.

Kaleta, A. (1982). Quality of life as a category of humanistic sociology. *Acta Universitatis Nicolai Copernici. Sociology of Education, 4*(135), 93–105. https://bazhum.muzhp.pl/media/files/Acta_Universitatis_Nicolai_Copernici_Socjologia_Wychowania/Acta_Universitatis_Nicolai_Copernici_Socjologia_Wychowania-r1982-t4_(135)/Acta_Universitatis_Nicolai_Copernici_Socjologia_Wychowania-r1982-t4_(135)-s93-105/Acta_Universitatis_Nicolai_Copernici_Socjologia_Wychowania-r1982-t4_(135)-s93-105.pdf

Kaleta, A. (1988). *Quality of life of rural and urban youth: Study of inter-environmental similarities and differences.* UMK Publishing House.

Klimek, J. A. (2020). Multicriteria assessment of bureaucracy in Poland – The individual decision-making aspect. *Procedia Computer Science, 176,* 2434–2444.

Kolenda, M. (2006). *Numerical taxonomy: Classification, ordering, and analysis of multi-featured objects.* Publishing House of the Oskar Lange Academy of Economics in Wrocław.

Korniejenko, K. (2017). *Possibilities of using multicriteria methods in e-learning design* [Scientific papers, No. 52]. Faculty of Electrical Engineering and Automation of the Gdańsk University of Technology. https://ejournals.eu/pliki_artykulu_czasopisma/pelny_tekst/fcea29c8-2eef-412e-9a5e-707c87c1408e/pobierz

Kowalczewska-Grabowska, K. (2013). *Health promotion in the local environment: Theoretical and practical assumptions: Pedagogical perspective.* University of Silesia Publishing House.

Kukuła, K. (2000). *Zero-based unitarisation method.* Scientific Publisher PWN.

Kusterka-Jefmańska, M. (2010). High quality of life as the overriding goal of local, sustainable development strategies. *ZARZĄDZANIE PUBLICZNE, 4*(12), 2010. Zeszyty Naukowe Instytutu Spraw Publicznych Uniwersytetu Jagiellońskiego. file:///E:/Desktops/Desktop%202018/Papers/New%20Paper%20proposals/1.%20Published/Book%20Series/Book%20Series%20Proposals%20Accepted/Emerald/221.%20Inna%20%20EU%20after%2020%20years%20CSEF%20Vol%20115%205-March%202024/8-zarzadzanie%20publiczne_4_12_10.pdf

Marchewka, A. (2021). Applying vector measure construction method (VMCM) to analyse change dynamics of investment attractiveness of the region. *Procedia Computer Science, 192,* 3252–3261. https://doi.org/10.1016/j.procs.2021.09.098

Merelman, R. M. (1981). *The sense of well-being in America: Recent patterns and trends.* By Angus Campbell (New York: McGraw-Hill, 1981. pp. xiii + 263. $14.95.). *American Political Science Review, 75*(3), 763–764. https://doi.org/10.2307/1960993

Miłaszewicz, D. (2017). Change of the paradigm and method of modern economics – The role of behavioral economics. *Studia i Prace WNEiZ, 47,* 65–82. https://doi.org/10.18276/sip.2017.47/3-06

Miłaszewicz, D., Piwowarski, M., & Nermend, K. (2020). Application of vector measure construction methods to estimate growth factors of fundamental importance for the economy on the example of nations in transition. *Procedia Computer Science, 176,* 2913–2922. https://doi.org/10.1016/j.procs.2020.09.262

Nermend, K. (2007a). *Examination of the properties of normalisation methods used in ranking socio-economic objects* [Scientific papers]. University of Szczecin; Economic Service Problems (pp. 171–186).

Nermend, K. (2007b). Taxonomic vector measure of region development (TWMRR). *Polish Journal of Environmental Studies, 4A,* 171–186.

Nermend, K. (2009). *Vector calculus in regional development analysis: Comparative regional analysis using the example of Poland.* Physica-Verlag.

Nermend, K. (2012). Properties of normalisation methods used in the construction of aggregate measures. *Folia Oeconomica Stetinensia, 12*(2), 31–45. https://doi.org/10.2478/v10031-012-0030-9

Nermend, K. (2017). *Metody analizy wielokryterialnej i wielowymiarowej we wspomaganiu decyzji.* Wydawnictwo Naukowe PWN.

Nermend, K. (2023). *Multicriteria and multidimensional analysis in decisions: Decision making with preference vector methods (PVM) and vector measure construction methods (VMCM).* Springer Nature Switzerland. https://doi.org/10.1007/978-3-031-40538-9

Nermend, K., & Borawski, M. (2014). Modelling user's preferences in the decision support system. *Indian Journal of Fundamental and Applied Life Sciences, 4*(S1), 1480–1491.

Ogonowski, P. (2020). Application of VMCM to investigate the dynamics of changes information society development. *Procedia Computer Science, 176*, 3182–3190. https://doi.org/10.1016/j.procs.2020.09.131

Ogonowski, P. (2021). Application of VMCM to assess of renewable energy impact in European Union countries. *Procedia Computer Science, 192*, 4762–4769. https://doi.org/10.1016/j.procs.2021.09.254

Oleś, M. (2010). *Jakość życia młodzieży: W zdrowiu i w chorobie.* Wydawn. KUL.

Panek, T., & Zwierzchowski, J. (2013). *Statistical methods of multidimensional comparative analysis: Theory and applications* (1st ed. (rev.)). Warsaw School of Economics. Publishing Office.

Piwowarski, M., & Nermend, K. (2022). Issues of multicriteria methods applicability supporting complex business process decision-making in management. *Procedia Computer Science, 207*, 4161–4170. https://doi.org/10.1016/j.procs.2022.09.479

Rokicka, E. (2013). Quality of life – Contexts, concepts, interpretations. In J. Grotowska-Leder & E. Rokicka (Eds.), *New order? Dynamics of social structures in contemporary societies. Commemorative book dedicated to Professor Wielisława Warzywoda-Kruszyńska on the occasion of her 45th anniversary of scientific and didactic work* (pp. 159–177). University of Lodz Publishing House. https://doi.org/10.18778/7525-967-4.10

Rybczyńska, D. (1998). *Jakość życia młodzieży z rodzin ubogich.* Wyższa Szkoła Pedagogiczna im. Tadeusza Kotarbińskiego.

Skrzypek, E. (Ed.). (2007). *Determinants of quality of life in an information society* (Vol. 2). Department of Quality Economics and Knowledge Management, Faculty of Economics. Maria Curie-Skłodowska University.

Ślęczek-Czakon, D. (2019). The concept of quality of life: Medical and bioethical aspects. *Studia Philosophica Wratislaviensia, 13*(4), 19–31.

Szaja, M. (2021). Applying the VMCM method to assess the level of residential attractiveness of municipalities in the West Pomeranian Voivodeship. *Procedia Computer Science, 192*, 4701–4710. https://doi.org/10.1016/j.procs.2021.09.248

Wachowiak, A., & Wyższa Szkoła Pedagogiczna with Tadeusza Kotarbińskiego (Zielona Góra) (Eds.). (2001). *How to live? Selected issues of quality of life.* Humaniora Foundation.

WHOQOL. (2024). *Measuring quality of life.* The World Health Organization.

Wnuk, M., Zielonka, D., Purandare, B., Kaniewski, A., Klimberg, A., Ulatowska-Szostak, E., Palicka, E., Zarzycki, A., Kaminiarz, E., Higieny, Z., Katedra, M., Społecznej, U., Medyczny, I., & Marcinkowskiego. (2013). *Review of Concepts of Quality of Life in Social Sciences, 2013*, 10–16.

Wysocka, E. (2014). Quality of life as a pedagogical category – Experiencing life by the young generation in a theoretical perspective. *Chowanna, 1*, 21–43.

Zandecki, A. (1999). *Education and quality of life: Dynamics of orientation of high school youth.* Editor.

Zenka-Zganiacz, A. (2017). Quality of life in economic, social, and public statistics research. In *Studia i Materiały Wydziału Zarządzania i Administracji Wyższej Szkoły Pedagogicznej im. Jana Kochanowskiego w Kielcach* (Vol. 21, No. 3, Part 1: Measurement of Quality of Life in Regional and National Systems: Dilemmas and Challenges, pp. 93–105). WZiA WSP.

CHAPTER 12

DIGITALISATION AND PRODUCTIVITY IMPROVEMENT

Vida Davidaviciene and Alma Maciulyte-Sniukiene

Department of Business Technologies and Entrepreneurship, Faculty of Business Management, Vilnius Gediminas Technical University, Vilnius, Lithuania

ABSTRACT

Purpose: *The primary purpose is to discuss the productivity and digitalisation interaction at the theoretical level, analyse the productivity and digitalisation differences between the European Union (EU)-14 and EU-13 countries, and evaluate the digitalisation impact on the manufacturing sector labour productivity of the EU countries.*

Need for study: *The average added value created per capita in new EU countries (EU-13) is one-third lower than in old EU countries (EU-14). To increase productivity, manufacturing companies must adapt to modern trends and take advantage of industrial digitisation opportunities. Digitisation can improve production efficiency, reduce costs, and improve product quality, allowing continuous monitoring and analysis of production data, enabling informed decisions and faster problem-solving.*

Methodology: *Analysis of scientific literature, comparing viewpoints, insights, and conclusions. The empirical study includes calculating rates of change of indicators, differences between EU-14 and EU-13, and structural analysis. The impact of digitisation on the productivity of EU countries is studied by creating a correlation matrix and using regression analysis: ordinary least square models.*

Economic Development and Resilience by EU Member States
Contemporary Studies in Economic and Financial Analysis, Volume 115, 201–230
Copyright © 2025 by Vida Davidaviciene and Alma Maciulyte-Sniukiene
Published under exclusive licence by Emerald Publishing Limited
ISSN: 1569-3759/doi:10.1108/S1569-375920240000115012

Findings: *EU-13 countries are behind EU-14 in labour productivity and manufacturing digitalisation. Digitalisation positively impacts productivity per employee. A faster increase in digitisation, industrial robot use, and e-commerce sales could significantly increase productivity in EU-13, reducing productivity differences between countries.*

Practical implications: *This study highlights the need for policy promoting digitisation innovation, particularly in EU-13 countries, to be implemented by both national and EU-based economic development and regional and cohesion institutions.*

Keywords: Productivity; digitalisation; manufacturing industry; cohesion; twin transition;

JEL classifications: L60; O14; O30; O33; O52; Q55

1. INTRODUCTION

1.1. Green and Digital Transition

The transition of the European Union (EU) industry and its ecosystems to green and digital technologies involves digitalising industries, green jobs, and the challenges sectors face. Presenting the importance of digitisation, the scientist observed that new technologies have a significant impact on the operations, products, services, and business models of companies as they open up new ways of working, collaborating, connecting, automating, and providing access to untapped data sources (Almeida et al., 2020; Ren et al., 2023; Warner & Wäger, 2019). In the context of the digital world, the rapid generation and collection of information are vital considerations. The readiness of industries for digital transition, financial capabilities, and the digital divide within the EU are essential factors to address (Atik & Ünlü, 2020; Cruz-Jesus et al., 2016). Moreover, developing innovative ecosystems in the EU contributes to the growth of knowledge-intensive enterprises (Shyshkovskyi et al., 2022). Regulations stipulated by the EU and its member states drive changes in platforms and ecosystems, affecting roles, relations, and power structures (Bazarhanova et al., 2020). The swift transition of the EU industry and its ecosystems to green and digital technologies requires a comprehensive approach that considers gender equality, biodiversity protection, sustainable energy, digital divide, and ecosystem preservation.

On the one hand, the concept of sustainable manufacturing has gained significant attention in recent years. It involves the creation of manufactured products through processes that minimise negative environmental impacts, conserve energy and natural resources, ensure the safety of employees, communities, and consumers, and are economically sound (Ahmad et al., 2019). The move towards sustainable manufacturing aligns with the principles of sustainable development, as outlined in the Brundtland Report, and involves exploring tools and techniques to conduct sustainable manufacturing (Kravchenko et al., 2019). Sustainable manufacturing encompasses various environmental, economic, and social dimensions. It involves the assessment of the environmental sustainability of industrial systems, consolidating leading sustainability-related performance indicators, and implementing sustainable production principles in practice (Alayón et al., 2017; Angelakoglou & Gaidajis, 2015). It can be claimed that the digitalisation of industry will probably lead to more sustainable manufacturing.

Additionally, economic sustainability plays a significant role in the manufacturing industry, and assessing key performance indicators is crucial for economic sustainability (Nawaz et al., 2020). Frameworks and methodologies have been proposed to evaluate and measure sustainable manufacturing practices. These include sustainability metric frameworks, grey-based approaches for sustainability evaluation, and the development of sustainability indicators and performance measurement systems (Agrawal & Vinodh, 2020; Lucato et al., 2017; Martins et al., 2006). Furthermore, the integration of sustainability principles in small- and medium-sized manufacturing enterprises has been studied, emphasising the need for sustainability reporting standards and indicator sets to measure sustainability in manufacturing processes (Franciosi et al., 2021; Garbie, 2016). The assessment of redundancies in environmental performance measures for supply chains, benchmarking supply chain sustainability, and the analysis of sustainability practices in the context of road freight transport provide insights into the broader application of sustainability in manufacturing and supply chain operations (Colicchia et al., 2011; Fürst & Oberhofer, 2012; Genovese et al., 2017).

Moreover, designing sustainable development indicators and setting a course in corporate sustainability performance measurement contribute to developing robust frameworks for evaluating and monitoring sustainability in manufacturing and business operations (Searcy, 2009; Searcy et al., 2005). In conclusion, sustainable manufacturing involves a comprehensive approach that integrates environmental, economic, and social dimensions. Developing and applying sustainability indicators, performance measurement systems, and frameworks play a crucial role in advancing sustainable manufacturing practices. On the other hand, in line with these indicators stands the digitalisation of industry and its impact on sustainability and labour productivity.

The digitalisation of industry has a significant impact on sustainability and labour productivity. Sustainable manufacturing practices have been shown to significantly impact all elements of sustainability, indicating the potential for digitalisation to contribute to sustainable outcomes. However, the digital divide across the EU presents a multidimensional issue that needs to be addressed to ensure equitable access to digital technologies and opportunities. An integrated approach to sustainable and smart manufacturing highlights the importance of sustainability assessment measures, indicating the need for comprehensive strategies to integrate digitalisation and sustainability in manufacturing. These scholars highlight the multifaceted impact of digitalisation on sustainability and labour productivity in the manufacturing industry, emphasising the need for comprehensive strategies to address the challenges and leverage the opportunities presented by the digital transition. The conclusion is that digitalisation and digital technologies, data to generate income, improve business, change/transform business processes, and create an environment for digitalised business, where digitalisation information is the most important.

The pandemic has accelerated digitalisation across various sectors, including businesses, driving the adoption of digital technologies globally (Amankwah-Amoah et al., 2021). It is considered that the industry, digital technology adoption, and digital dynamic capability significantly impact digital transformation performance, with digital innovation orientation playing a positive-moderating role. Moreover, the spatial implications of the digital economy on urban innovation have been evidenced, with the digital economy influencing urban innovation within a specific spatial spillover range and threshold (Huang et al., 2022). Artificial intelligence adoption and digital innovation are interconnected, with digital resilience playing a crucial role in the current digitalised world (Zeng et al., 2022). Different authors investigated various industry specifics, which will be discussed shortly. In the agricultural sector, the adoption and use of digital technologies have intensified, leading to increased studies on adopting digital and precision agriculture technologies in crop production and livestock farming (Gabriel & Gandorfer, 2023). Furthermore, the impact of digital technology adoption on the sustainable development performance of strategic emerging industries has been a research subject, highlighting the need for a comprehensive investigation into the micro mechanism of this impact (Shen et al., 2022). The adoption of digital technologies across different life spans, including in distance education, has been studied, emphasising the importance of understanding the use of digital technologies in educational settings (Jelfs & Richardson, 2013). The coupling mechanism of the digital innovation ecosystem and value co-creation has been explored, emphasising the significance of digital innovation ecosystems in creating value from a digital innovation perspective (Xiaoli et al., 2023). Additionally, the adoption of digital technologies in construction projects has been investigated, highlighting the pressure faced by main contractor firms to adopt digital technologies to improve logistics processes and project performance (Gholami, 2023). The role of digital technology adoption in strategy renewal has been empirically assessed, indicating a potential association between adopting new digital technologies and changes to firm strategy (Van Zeebroeck et al., 2023). The digitalisation of businesses has varied, with some adopting digital technology before the pandemic while others began adoption during the pandemic, showcasing different adoption timelines across businesses (Samsami & Schøtt, 2022). Furthermore, the adoption of digital technologies and the move to a digital business, known as digitalisation, have been focal points in various industries, including the oil and gas sector (Wanasinghe et al., 2020). The impact of manufacturing digital innovation resources on knowledge creation has been studied, emphasising the mediation effect of the digital innovation ecosystem in forming a comprehensive digital innovation ecosystem (Wang et al., 2022). In the context of micro and small enterprises, the ease of usage of digital technologies has been linked to a positive intention to adopt digital technologies, highlighting the importance of usability in digital technology adoption (Kimuli et al., 2021). However, despite the perceived importance of digitalisation in the waste management sector, the actual adoption of advanced digital technologies has fallen notably behind reported intentions, indicating a gap between intention and actual adoption (Borchard et al., 2022). The concept of digital health innovation ecosystems has emerged in the health-care sector, emphasising the importance of digital health, innovation, and digital ecosystems in the administration and delivery of health-care services (Iyawa et al., 2017). The influence of technology usability on digital banking adoption has been studied, indicating that the high usability of digital technologies increases the likelihood of digital banking technology adoption (Kiplagat et al., 2019). Moreover, the antecedents of digital innovativeness have been explored, linking individual characteristics to digital innovativeness and emphasising the need to appropriately understand and train the workforce (Mancha & Shankaranarayanan, 2021). The adoption of digital payments by small retail stores has been studied, with consumers keen on adopting digital technologies to make more informed choices in buying (Seethamraju & Diatha, 2018). Additionally, environmental factors influencing the adoption of digitalisation technologies in automotive supply chains have been identified, emphasising the need to understand the environmental factors that influence the adoption of digitalisation technologies in supply chains (Simoes et al., 2019). The drivers of digital transformation in SMEs have been identified, guiding practitioners adopting digital technologies in SMEs and suggesting an assessment of firms' readiness before investing in digital technology (Omrani et al., 2022). The adoption of information technology (IT) among small and medium enterprises has been linked to digital transformation, with the target year for digital transformation set as 2020, highlighting the need to successfully adopt IT to realise digital transformation (Sridevi et al., 2019). Furthermore, the role of technological innovation in achieving social and environmental sustainability has been explored, indicating the strong role of attitude towards technological innovation in organisational innovation, digital entrepreneurship, and sustainability (Xiao & Su, 2022).

Fu et al. (2023) offer insights into the impact of managerial capabilities on the digital transformation of enterprises, enriching the literature about executives and providing practical significance for the implementation of digitalisation in enterprises. Conceptual clarity provides several authors and proposes clear definitions specifying the unit of analysis, degree of digitalisation, and the sociotechnical nature of digital platforms (De Reuver et al., 2018; Jiang et al., 2021). From an industrial application standpoint, a digital twin is the virtual replica of a real-world product, system, community, or city that is continuously updated with data from its physical counterpart and its environment, offering a perspective on digitalisation (Bali, 2019; Jiang et al., 2021). Bali (2019) and Shoker and Abdullah (2022) reimagine digital literacies from a feminist perspective in a postcolonial context, providing a unique viewpoint on digitalisation and its implications in the context of literacy and gender studies. More research is needed to better understand and implement digital sovereignty from different perspectives, emphasising technological, economic, and geopolitical importance and considering other viewpoints in defining digitalisation strategies, as noted by Shoker and Abdullah (2022). These references offer diverse perspectives on digitalisation, ranging from managerial capabilities and digital platforms to digital twins, digital literacy, and digital sovereignty, providing a comprehensive understanding of digitalisation from various angles. In general, digitalisation has become an integral part of the development of organisations, industry, and society, and its role in the development and implementation of the concept of sustainability is indisputable. The question arises of how strongly and whether the digitisation of industrial companies impacts labour productivity. The following section presents an analysis of scientific studies in this field in more detail.

2. DIGITALISATION AND LABOUR PRODUCTIVITY

At the theoretical level, many authors have discussed the impact of information and communication technologies (ICTs) on productivity and/or economic growth. However, digitalisation could have been analysed more deeply, and a lack of data is observed. This chapter will present studies of digitalisation's impact on labour productivity, and research assumptions will be proposed.

The impact of managerial capabilities on the digital transformation of enterprises is a crucial aspect to consider when examining the relevance of labour productivity dependence on digitalisation. Fu et al. (2023) provide valuable insights into this relationship, emphasising the significance of managerial ability in driving digital transformation within enterprises. The study delves into the perspective of managerial heterogeneity and empirically tests the influence of managerial capabilities on the digital transformation of enterprises in the context of China. This research sheds light on the pivotal role of managerial capabilities in steering the digitalisation process within organisations, which, in turn, can have implications for labour productivity dependence on digitalisation.

The relevance of ICT capital to labour productivity and its dependence on digitalisation can be comprehensively assessed by synthesising the following examples of the impact ICT capital has on economic growth in the EU-15 and EU-12 countries (Hanclova et al., 2015). This study provides insights into the relationship between ICT capital and economic growth, which is essential for understanding the potential impact on labour productivity (Ceccobelli et al., 2012). The direct and indirect impact of ICT on the EU's productivity growth, emphasising the importance of ICT capital deepening and total factor productivity (TFP) growth in shaping productivity dynamics, was revealed particularly in the most developed EU economies (Mlynarzewska-Borowiec, 2021). This research provides a nuanced perspective on the role of ICT capital in driving productivity growth, offering valuable insights into its potential impact on labour productivity dependence from digitalisation (Van Ark & Piatkowski, 2004). It is necessary to investigate the role of digitalisation in labour productivity growth in old and new EU countries. This study offers insights into the differential impact of digitalisation capital on labour productivity growth across different regions, providing valuable implications for labour productivity dependence on digitalisation.

It is not easy to evaluate the cause–effect and impact of technological, economic, and social development to prove that digitalisation is the factor of economic increase in efficiency, productivity, and growth. Davidavičienė (2008) suggests that the significant advancements in ICT have likely been the primary driver of economic transformations in businesses and entire nations, mainly manifesting in increased labour productivity. The author emphasises the escalating significance of ICT-based information systems, which many enterprises have increasingly adopted. The more efficient processing of information through communication technologies has the potential to enhance the overall efficiency of the contemporary economic system, thereby instigating changes in the economies of businesses, industries, and nations, ultimately impacting the growth of added value. Several scholars have also highlighted the influence of ICT progress on economic development, including the augmentation of labour productivity, at a theoretical level (Davidavičiene, 2008).

The ICT revolution is characterised by higher productivity growth in industries producing ICT, driven by rapid technological progress, particularly the rapidly increasing computing power of new ICT products, such as memory chips. These performance increases are equivalent to rapid TFP growth in ICT-producing sectors, which raises the economy's average TFP growth. Various studies support the relevance of this research. For instance, Leo (n.d.) discusses the influence of ICT on economic growth, emphasising the impact of ICT on TFP growth in the sector producing ICT. Additionally, Mlynarzewska-Borowiec (2021) aims to verify the hypothesis of a significant direct and indirect ICT impact on the EU's productivity changes. Furthermore, Bergeaud et al. (2016) provide insights into the role of production factor quality and technology diffusion in 20th-century productivity growth, which aligns with the channels through which ICT influences productivity growth.

In this chapter, the research targets labour productivity in the manufacturing sector, which depends on digitalisation. The use of the internet of things (IoT) promises to solve the problem of poor communication in the implementation of projects (Ammar et al., 2018; Crnjacas et al., 2017). Also, big data analytics promises better predictions of future construction project delivery by identifying patterns from past projects and making informed decisions early before the project begins (Aghimien et al., 2022). Three-dimensional (3D) printing and autonomous robots promise to reduce labour and material costs, reduce on-site injuries and fatalities, improve labour productivity, and create more job opportunities (Fonseca, 2018; Sakin & Kiroglu, 2017). In fact, García De Soto et al. (2019) argued that autonomous robots work alongside the traditional construction system to create greater job variability and create new roles for construction workers. In addition to these, other digitisation functions are distinguished, such as cloud computing, where the exchange of IT-related capabilities is provided as a service over the internet to several external customers, and augmented reality, which is an innovation that provides an expanded view of objects or designs using specific apps. In addition, García De Soto et al. (2019) noted the importance of digitisation technologies in improving construction delivery with a digitisation building system that can help projects succeed from site selection for construction to project handover. Yu et al. (2023) discuss the research model on TFP in Chinese manufacturing firms and the role of e-commerce adoption. It provides a direct and current insight into the specific relationship between e-commerce adoption and TFP in Chinese manufacturing firms. Similar aspects were analysed by Liu et al. (2013) when the impact of e-commerce and research and development (R&D) on firm-level productivity, especially within the specific context of Taiwan, was evaluated. Song et al. (2022) offer empirical evidence and findings that demonstrate the promotional effect of digitalisation on labour productivity in China, with a significant portion of this effect attributed to the transmission and influence on human capital. The impact of robots on labour productivity, as it employs a panel data approach covering multiple industries and countries, was analysed by Jungmittag and Pesole (2019). Using panel data allows for a comprehensive analysis of the relationship between robot adoption and labour productivity across different sectors and countries. Still, it does not provide a large picture of digitalisation's impact.

After analysing existing sources, the impact of digitalisation on labour productivity and economic growth involving those three channels was formed for empirical research (see Fig. 12.1).

The use of industrial robots, IoT, and e-commerce in the manufacturing industry are the three factors that are considered as most important for expressing manufacturing industry change and important for evaluating impact on labour productivity. It should be noted that the analysis of scientific sources in this chapter assumes that as the general level of digitisation of manufacturing enterprises' increases, the labour productivity of the manufacturing sector increases. Therefore, the digitalisation intensity index is another indicator used in researching relationships between digitalisation and labour productivity. Methodology of the research is presented in the next section.

3. RESEARCH METHODOLOGY AND DATA

This study begins with an analysis of the added value created in EU countries and their changes in the period 2015–2022, comparing the situation between EU-14 countries that were members of the EU prior to 2004 and EU-13 countries that joined the EU in 2004 and later. This analysis made it possible to highlight the differences in economic well-being between these groups of countries. The beginning of the analysis period was chosen, considering that in the Eurostat database, some of the indicators are presented as indices by equating the 2015 data to 100. Although indices were not used in the study, the selection of the period ensured the availability of productivity statistics.

In the following, labour productivity expressed in value added per worker is calculated, analysed, and compared between EU-14 and EU-13. Considering the terminology used by Eurostat, it is named in the study as productivity per employee. This analysis partially confirmed the insights about existing productivity gaps between the old and new EU countries.

The value-added structure by industry in EU countries was analysed to identify the most significant sectors that create the most added value in the country. Labour productivity of industries and its changes are also calculated and compared between EU-14 and EU-13 countries. Continuing the logical sequence

Digitalisation and Productivity Improvement

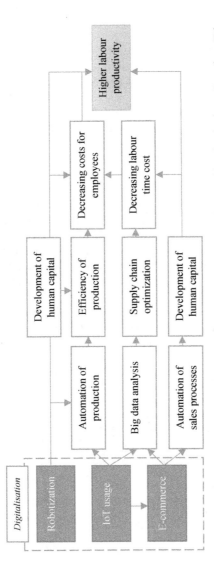

Fig. 12.1. Channels of Digitalisation Factors Impact on Labour Productivity (Formed by the Authors Based on Eder et al., 2023; Falk & Hagsten, 2015; Mollins & Taskin, 2023; Song et al., 2022; Yu et al., 2023).

leads to the analysis of manufacturing productivity per employee differences between country groups. Considering the theoretical assumptions that differences in labour productivity in the manufacturing sector between groups of countries can be determined by digitalisation, the following analysis of indicators reflecting digitalisation, the statistics of which are freely available in the Eurostat database, is carried out. Analysed indicators:

- Percentage of enterprises with basic digitisation intensity.
- Percentage of manufacturing enterprises that use the IoT, that is, interconnected devices or systems that can be monitored or remotely controlled via the internet.
- Percentage of manufacturing enterprises using industrial robots.
- Manufacturing enterprises with e-commerce sales.

These digitisation indicators were accumulated only from 2021, and the Eurostat database only provides data for 2021 and 2023. Data from the most recent period, 2023, were selected to analyse the digitisation level.

The last stage of the study examines the interrelationships between manufacturing sector labour productivity and digitisation in EU-26 countries. Belgium was eliminated from the sample due to the large productivity gap with other countries. Due to the lack of data on indicators reflecting digitisation, it was not possible to use time series or panel-type data for the study, so cross-sectional data for 2021 have been used since these statistics are available for all indicators (Table 12.1).

First, a correlation matrix was created to determine the relationships between the indicators. The closer the obtained value of the correlation coefficient is to unity, the stronger the relationship between the indicators. A negative value indicates an inverse relationship.

Table 12.1. Research Variables and Summary Statistics.

Notation	Variable	Mean	Median	Standard Deviation (SD)	Minimum	Maximum
VAemp	Value added per employee	64,300	50,000	37,900	22,100	189,000
IoT	Percentage of enterprises that use the IoT	29.5	27.9	11.2	9.40	53.4
DI_basic	Percentage of enterprises with basic digitisation intensity	55.1	53.0	15.5	21.9	87.5
Ecomm	Percentage of manufacturing enterprises with e-commerce sales	22.1	20.0	10.4	8.00	50.8
Ind_Rob	Percentage of enterprises that use industrial robots	17.0	16.3	7.29	6.30	36.9

Source: Compiled by the authors based on Eurostat data, using software package Gretl.

The examination of the impact of digitalisation on labour productivity is based on ordinary least squares (OLS) regression models:

$$\ln(VAemp_t) = \alpha_t + \beta_t \, \mathrm{IoT}_t + \varepsilon t \qquad (1)$$

where t stands for the period, in this research 2021. The dependent variable *VAemp* is value added per employee; β is parameters to be estimated; IoT – percentage of manufacturing enterprises that use the IoT; ε is the idiosyncratic error term.

$$\ln(Vaemp_t) = \alpha_t + \beta_t \, DI\_basic_t + \varepsilon_t \qquad (2)$$

where *DI_basic* – percentage of manufacturing enterprises with basic digitisation intensity;

$$\ln(Vaemp_t) = \alpha_t + \beta_t \, Ecomm_t + \varepsilon_t \qquad (3)$$

where *Ecomm* – percentage of manufacturing enterprises with e-commerce sales;

$$\ln(Vaemp_t) = \alpha_t + \beta_t \, Ind\_Rob_t + \varepsilon_t \qquad (4)$$

where *DI_basic* – percentage of manufacturing enterprises that use industrial robots.

Logarithmisation of added value allows results to be interpreted as changes.

Applied regression models cover cross-sectional data, and the absorption is treated independently. Therefore, based on Lebanon and Rosenhal (1975) approach, OLS estimates can be considered efficient. This insight is confirmed by the tests carried out.

Many authors (e.g. Du & Jiang, 2022; Jungmittag & Pesole, 2019; Akhmadalieva & Akhmadalieva, 2022) use this method to study the relationship between productivity and digitisation due to its advantages and easy interpretation of the results. In the OLS method, the estimated beta coefficients are linear and unbiased, which means that neither homoscedastic nor heteroscedastic errors affect the unbiasedness of the estimates. Nevertheless, the model was tested for heteroscedasticity to ensure that the forecast had the slightest variance in the unbiased estimates.

As per the Gauss–Markov theorem, assuming certain conditions of the linear regression model (including linearity in parameters, random sampling of observations, conditional mean equal to zero, absence of multicollinearity, and homoscedasticity of errors), the OLS estimators α and β emerge as the optimal linear unbiased estimators (BLUE) for the actual values of α and β.

The open-access cross-platform software package Gretl is used for the research.

4. PRODUCTIVITY AND ITS DIFFERENCES BETWEEN EU-14 AND EU-13 COUNTRIES

One of the EU's goals is the convergence of countries and regions. Productivity is one of the sources of economic growth, so to reduce differences in economic development between countries, it is necessary to ensure productivity growth in lagging regions. Eurostat data show 497,016 million EUR of added value was created in EU countries in 2022. It is 33.14% more than in 2015. Despite the positive trends, the volume of added value created and its growth tempo vary between EU countries. The fastest rates of created added value are recorded in the new EU countries (EU-13) (see Fig. 12.2), but the higher volumes of created added value remain in the old EU countries (EU-14) (see Fig. 12.3).

In EU countries, the added value in 2022 compared to 2015 grew by 48.74% on average. In only one EU-14 country, Ireland, the change was higher than the EU average at 97%. In that period, the change in added value was higher than the EU average in all beneficiary EU countries except for Slovakia. In the EU-14 countries, the added value increased by an average of 34.09% over seven years, and in the EU-13 group of countries, it increased by 64.51%. These changing trends reduce differences in added value between EU countries. Nevertheless, the volume of added value of the new EU countries remains lower than the old countries. In the EU-14 group of countries, 529,863 million EUR of 2022 value added were created in 2022, and in the EU-13 group of countries, only 124,794 million EUR. Nevertheless, given that countries' populations differ, comparing them based on a relative indicator – value added per capita or employee – is more appropriate. This indicator reflects the country's productivity.

The productivity per employee of the new EU countries and the total added value lag behind the old EU countries (see Fig 12.3).

In the EU-14 group of countries, almost all countries except Greece, Spain, and Portugal exceeded the EU average of productivity per employee in 2022. In the group of EU-13 countries, productivity per employee did not reach the EU average in all countries. In 2022, one working person in EU countries created an average of 65,527 EUR added value. In the old EU countries, one employee created an average of 89,180 EUR of added value, while in the new ones, only 40,054 EUR, that is, in the group of EU-13 countries, productivity is 2.2 times lower.

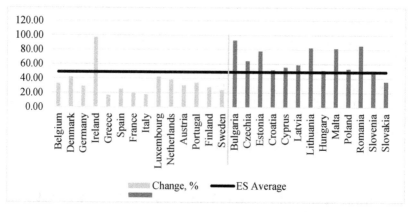

Fig. 12.2. Change in Added Value During 2015–2022 in EU Countries, %.
Source: Compiled by the authors based on Eurostat data.

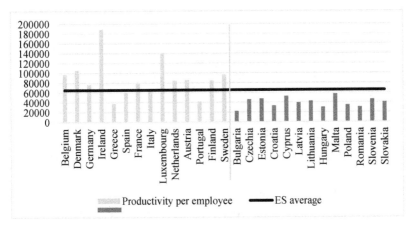

Fig. 12.3. Productivity Per Employee 2022 in EU Countries, EUR.
Source: Compiled by the authors based on Eurostat data.

It should be noted that productivity in 2022, compared to 2015, increased by an average of 19.66% in the EU-14 group of countries and by an average of 50.14% in the EU-13 group of countries, which led to a decrease in the difference in productivity per employee between the EU-14 and the EU-13. However, as mentioned, the differences remain large, so it is necessary to search for sources of the increase in countries lagging in productivity. However, before that, analysing the productivity situation in different sectors is appropriate. As Tan et al. (2020) indicated, weak local industrial structures negatively limit the potential for economic resilience.

Fig. 12.4 shows the structure of added value in EU countries.

In almost all EU countries, the most added value is created by the industry sector; wholesale and retail trade, transport, accommodation, and food service activities; and public administration, defence, education, human health, and social work activities. Martins et al. (2006) state that the industrial sector plays a fundamental role in the economy; therefore, this sector must be given special attention. In Ireland, the most significant part of the added value, as much as 41.35% of the total added value, is created precisely in the industry sector. The smallest share of added value among the EU-14 countries is made in Luxembourg, as here, the largest share of added value is created by the financial sector. The largest part of the added value of the industry sector among the EU-13 countries is fixed in the Czech Republic, where this sector created 27.02% of the country's added value in 2022. About 25% of the country's added value is created by the industrial sector in Poland, Slovenia, and Slovakia. The smallest part of added value created in industry is characterised by Cyprus (8.31%).

On average, 80% of the added value of the industry sector in EU countries is created in manufacturing. Many scientific publications emphasise the importance of the manufacturing sector for the country's economy. According to Sallam (2021), 'manufacturing is essential to growth and development'. This industrial

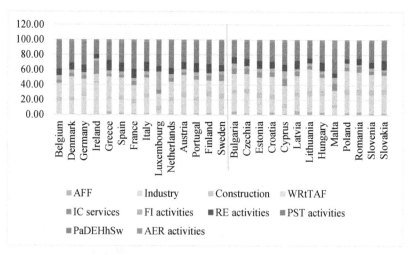

Fig. 12.4. Value-Added Structure by Sector in EU Countries 2022, %.
Source: Compiled by the authors based on Eurostat data.
Note: AFF – agriculture, forestry, and fishing; WRtTAF – wholesale and retail trade, transport, accommodation, and food; IC – information and communication; FI – financial and insurance; RE – real estate; PST – professional, scientific, and technical activities; administrative and support service activities; PaDeHhSw – public administration, defence, education, human health, and social work; AER – arts, entertainment and recreation; other service activities; activities of household and extra-territorial organisations and bodies.

sector is highly productive, technologically advanced, and closely integrated with other sectors, such as the service sector. It provides opportunities to enter international markets unavailable to agricultural and primary production countries. Compared to the spatially dispersed capital of the agricultural sector, the manufacturing sector allows for more accessible capital accumulation. Therefore, it is important to analyse productivity in this particular sector, which will be done further.

This study also revealed that the manufacturing sector is characterised by high productivity. Fig. 12.5 shows productivity per employee in EU countries by sector. It should be noted that the largest amount of added value per employee is created in the real estate sector: in 2022, as much as 17,643,557 EUR. Due to the large gap with other sectors, this sector is eliminated from the sample.

More value added per employee than in the manufacturing sector is created only in the financial and IC sectors. The industrial sector includes manufacturing, so manufacturing productivity primarily determines its productivity. The productivity of all sectors increased in 2020 compared to 2015. Agriculture, forestry, and fishing productivity increased the most (52%) but remained among the lowest. The manufacturing sector is in the third position in terms of productivity growth. Productivity in this sector increased by an average of 35.46%. In the industry sector, which includes manufacturing, productivity increased by 36.18%.

Digitalisation and Productivity Improvement 215

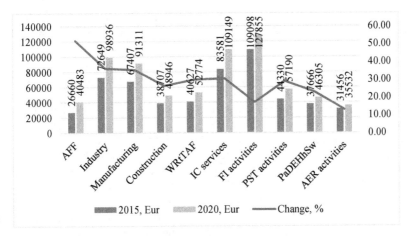

Fig. 12.5. Average Productivity Per Employee by Sector in EU Countries 2015 and 2022, EUR and Its Change, %. *Source*: Compiled by the authors based on Eurostat data. *Note*: AFF – agriculture, forestry and fishing; WRtTAF – wholesale and retail trade, transport, accommodation and food; IC – information and communication; FI – financial and insurance; RE – real estate; PST – professional, scientific, and technical activities; administrative and support service activities; PaDeHhSw – public administration, defence, education, human health, and social work; AER – arts, entertainment and recreation; other service activities; activities of household and extra-territorial organisations and bodies.

Although the overall productivity of the manufacturing sector in EU countries is relatively high, the problem is the differences between countries (see Fig. 12.6).

The highest manufacturing sector productivity per employee in 2022 was achieved in Ireland, where one employee created an average of 672,827 EUR of

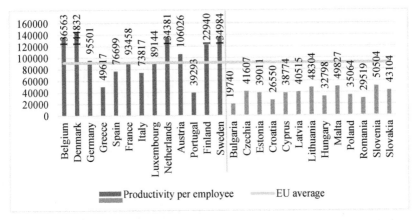

Fig. 12.6. Manufacturing Productivity Per Employee in EU Countries 2022, EUR. *Source*: Compiled by the authors based on Eurostat data.

added value. Due to the large gap with other countries on this indicator, Ireland was eliminated from the sample when forming the figure. The lowest manufacturing productivity per employee in 2022 is recorded in Bulgaria, where one employee created an average of 19,740 EUR of added value, that is, even 30 times less than in Ireland. As can be seen, there is a vast manufacturing sector productivity gap between EU-14 and EU-13 countries. In 2022, in the EU-14 group of countries, in the manufacturing sector, an average of 140,720 EUR of added value per employee was created, while in the EU-13 group of countries, only 38,101 EUR, that is, 3.69 times less. All EU-13 countries do not reach the EU average (91,311 EUR). It is optimistic that the productivity of the manufacturing sector is growing faster in the EU-13 group of countries. From 2015 to 2022, it grew by 46.62% on average and 22.99% in the EU-14 countries. The faster growth of EU-13 manufacturing sector productivity per employee reduces the differences between EU countries, but searching for sources of its increase is necessary. One of the sources of productivity increase mentioned by scientists and practitioners is the implementation of Industry 4.0 technologies and digitisation. Therefore, studying the manufacturing sector in the EU-14 and EI-13 country groups is appropriate according to these factors.

5. DIGITALISATION OF THE MANUFACTURING

One of the indicators defining the degree of digitalisation is the digitalisation intensity index. To compare manufacturing digitalisation between EU-14 and EU-15 country groups and inside a group, Fig. 12.7 presents data on the percentage of companies with basic digitisation intensity and how many are with very low. It should be noted that the base intensity index includes very high-, high-, and low-intensity levels.

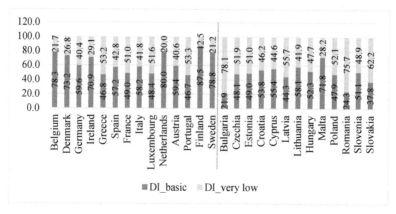

Fig. 12.7. EU-14 and EU-13 Country's Digitalisation Level in 2023.
Source: Compiled by the authors based on Eurostat data.

The graphically displayed data reveal that Finland digitises production most intensively in the old EU countries, where as many as 87.5% of enterprises have reached the basic level of digitalisation, and only 12.5% have low digitisation intensity. The countries with the lowest digitalisation intensity of manufacturing enterprises in the EU-14 group are Portugal and Greece, where 53.3% and 53.2% of enterprises have very low digitalisation intensity, respectively. Nevertheless, the intensity of digitisation in the new EU countries is significantly lower (see Fig. 12.8), which may be one of the reasons for lower productivity. In the EU-14 group of countries, on average, 63.86% of manufacturing enterprises have reached the basic digitisation intensity. In the EU-13 group of countries, only 47.37%, that is, more than half of manufacturing companies, have a very low digitisation intensity.

Among the new EU countries, production is digitalised most intensively in Malta, where 71.8% of manufacturing enterprises have reached the basic level of digitalisation, and only 28.2% of companies have a very low digitalisation intensity. Bulgaria and Romania have achieved the lowest intensity of digitisation of production in this group of countries. Even 78.1% of manufacturing enterprises in Bulgaria have a very low digitisation intensity. It is as much as 24.8 percentage points more than Portugal – the EU-14 group of countries with the lowest digitisation level.

The degree of implementation of Industry 4.0 and digitisation is reflected by the IoT, that is, interconnected devices or systems that can be monitored or remotely controlled via the internet. Figs. 12.8 and 12.9 show the percentage of manufacturing companies using IoT.

According to the use of IoT in the manufacturing sector, the differences between EU-14 and EU-13 countries are not so significant. An average of 32.2% of manufacturing sector companies use IoT in the EU-14 group of countries and an average of 26.92% in the EU-14. Another indicator reflecting the

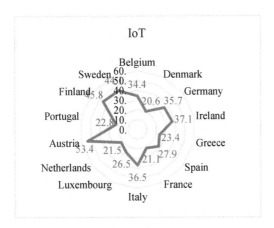

Fig. 12.8. Percentage of Manufacturing Enterprises in EU-14 Countries That Use IoT, 2021. *Source*: Compiled by the authors based on Eurostat data.

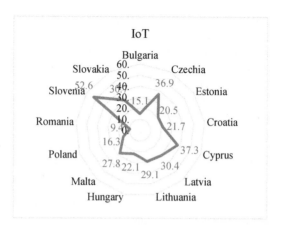

Fig. 12.9. Percentage of Manufacturing Enterprises in EU-13 Countries That Use IoT, 2021. *Source*: Compiled by the authors based on Eurostat data.

degree of Industry 4.0 technology usage and digitisation is the use of industrial robots. Most manufacturing enterprises (53.4% of all companies) use IoT in Austria, which belongs to the EU-14 group of countries, followed by Slovenia, which belongs to the EU-13 group. In the EU-13 group, Romania and Bulgaria are countries with the lowest IoT adoption, with 9.4% and 15.1%, respectively, in 2021.

Another indicator reflecting the degree of implementation of Industry 4.0 technologies and digitisation is the usage of industrial robots. Fig. 12.10 shows the percentage of manufacturing companies employing 10 persons or more that use industrial robots.

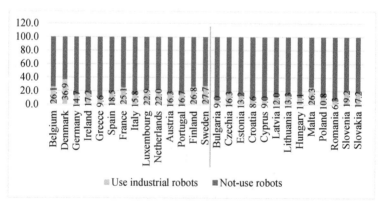

Fig. 12.10. Percentage of Manufacturing Enterprises in EU-14 and EU-13 Countries That Use Industrial Robots, 2023. *Source*: Compiled by the authors based on Eurostat data.

The data show that the degree of use of industrial robots is shallow in the whole EU but slightly higher in the EU-14 group of countries compared to the new EU countries. In the EU-14 group of countries, industrial robots are used by an average of 21.16% of manufacturing enterprises, while in the EU-13 group of countries, an average of 13.25% of companies use them. Industrial robots are primarily used in production by Danish enterprises (36.9% of all manufacturing companies), while Romania (6.3% of companies), Bulgaria (9% of companies), and Cyprus (9% of companies) use them the least. Since using robots is associated with productivity growth, EU-14 and EU-13 countries have a high potential for productivity growth.

An indicator of e-commerce intensity is also associated with digitisation. Fig. 12.11 shows the percentage of manufacturing companies with e-commerce sales (percentage of enterprises).

In the EU-14 group of countries, 26.01% of manufacturing enterprises develop e-commerce and in the EU-13 group an average of 20.55% of manufacturing enterprises. Thus, the gap according to this indicator in the old and new EU countries is insignificant. The most significant number of manufacturing enterprises with e-commerce sales in 2023 was in Sweden (41.7% of enterprises), and the smallest was in Bulgaria (10% of enterprises).

The analysis revealed that the EU-13 countries need to catch up to the old EU countries in terms of productivity and the degree of digitisation. By using the possibilities of Industry 4.0 technologies and digitisation, it is possible to increase the productivity of these countries' manufacturing sectors and, at the same time, their overall productivity. This assumption can be tested by analysing the relationships between productivity and digitisation.

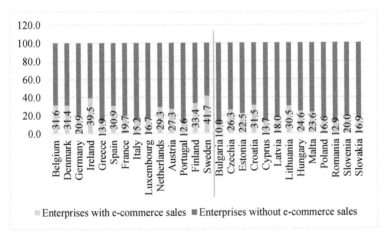

Fig. 12.11. Percentage of Manufacturing Enterprises with E-Commerce in EU-14 and EU-13, 2023. *Source*: Compiled by the authors based on Eurostat data.

6. INTERACTION BETWEEN MANUFACTURING DIGITALISATION AND PRODUCTIVITY

To determine the relationship between productivity per employee and manufacturing digitalisation, first of all, using the open-access Gretl program, a correlation matrix was created that included the following variables: manufacturing sector value added per employee (VAemp), percentage of manufacturing enterprises that use IoT; digitalisation level (percentage of manufacturing enterprises that have achieved basic digitalisation level); percentage of enterprises with e-commerce sales; percentage of enterprises that use industrial robots. Intergroup data of EU countries in 2021 are used. The obtained results are reflected in Table 12.2. It should be noted that Belgium was eliminated from the sample due to the high productivity per employee gap with other countries.

A 5% critical value of 0.3882 shows the coefficient size from which the correlation is considered significant. Thus, with 95% confidence, there is a statistically significant positive relationship between productivity per employee and the percentage of manufacturing enterprises with e-commerce sales, the percentage of manufacturing enterprises that have achieved a basic digitalisation level, and the percentage of enterprises that use industrial robots. The correlation between productivity per employee and the percentage of manufacturing enterprises that use IoT is positive but statistically insignificant.

A statistically significant mutual correlation was also established between factors determining productivity: between the use of IoT and the degree of digitisation of manufacturing enterprises, IoT usage and e-commerce, digitisation degree and e-commerce, degree of digitisation and use of industrial robots, and the use of industrial robots and e-commerce.

The strongest correlation was found between values added per employee and the percentage of manufacturing enterprises with e-commerce sales. After constructing and implementing the OLS model for a more detailed study of interrelationships, the results obtained are reflected in Table 12.3.

The study results reveal that if the percentage of manufacturing enterprises with e-commerce sales in EU countries increases by one percentage point, manufacturing sector productivity per employee will increase by 3.32% if the Ceteris Paribus assumption is applied to other factors. These results align with other

Table 12.2. Correlation Matrix of Productivity per Employee and its Factors.

Correlation Coefficients, Using the Observations 1–26					
5% Critical Value (Two-Tailed) = 0.3882 for $n = 26$					
VAemp	IoT	DI_basic	Ecomm	Ind_Rob	
1	0.3274	0.5603	0.691	0.5552	VAemp
	1	0.4693	0.3994	0.2646	IoT
		1	0.6955	0.6727	DI_basic
			1	0.5054	Ecomm
				1	Ind_Rob

Source: Compiled by the authors based on Eurostat data, using software package Gretl.

Digitalisation and Productivity Improvement

Table 12.3. Estimation Results on The Relationship Between Manufacturing Sector Productivity per Employee and the Percentage of Manufacturing Enterprises With E-Commerce Sales.

Model 1: OLS, Using Observations 1–26				
Dependent Variable: l_VAemp				
	Coefficient	Standard Error (SE)	t-Ratio	p-Value	
const	10.20150	0.183320	55.650	<0.0001	***
Ecomm	0.03316	0.007526	4.407	0.0002	***
Mean dependent var		10.93530	SD dependent var		0.51518
Sum squared resid		3.66774	SE of regression		0.39093
R^2		0.44724	Adjusted R^2		0.42421
$F(1, 24)$		19.41824	p-value (F)		0.00019
Log-likelihood		−11.43161	Akaike criterion		26.86323
Schwarz criterion		29.37942	Hannan–Quinn		27.58780

Source: Compiled by the authors based on Eurostat data, using software package Gretl.
Notes: *** indicates significance at the 1 percent level.

research findings on the relationship between productivity and e-commerce. These results align with other research findings on the relationship between productivity and e-commerce. For example, Liu et al. (2013) investigated the impact of e-commerce on Taiwanese manufacturing firms' productivity using 1999–2002 panel data and applying the generalised method of moment (GMM) technique and concluded that e-commerce has a positive influence on productivity.

Falk and Hagsten (2015) also found a positive statistically significant relationship between e-commerce sales and productivity in EU-14 countries applying OLS and GMM estimators using firm-level data during the 2002–2010 period. Falk and Hagsten (2015) also found a positive statistically significant relationship between e-commerce sales and productivity in EU-14 countries applying OLS and GMM estimators using firm-level data during the 2002–2010 period. The authors' estimations revealed that an increase in e-sales by one percentage point led to a growth of labour productivity by 0.3 percentage points. Moreover, the authors concluded that labour productivity in the EU-14 countries increased by 18% during the analysed period due to e-commerce sales growth.

Yu et al. (2023) explored the connection between e-commerce usage and TFP within manufacturing firms utilising data from 178 A-share listed companies in China spanning from 2015 to 2021. They examine whether and in what manner the direct utilisation of e-commerce by manufacturing firms contributes to their growth in productivity. The findings indicate that the impact of e-commerce on TFP growth in the manufacturing sector is positive and substantial. Additionally, the study reveals that the influence of intra-firm human capital spillovers and the impact of inter-firm market competition are pivotal in connecting e-commerce to TFP growth at the firm level. More specifically, e-commerce contributes significantly to TFP growth by attracting high-quality human capital to manufacturing enterprises rather than low-quality human capital. Moreover, it enhances TFP growth by improving market concentration appropriately, as opposed to intensifying market competition.

The study results (Table 12.4) show that if the percentage of manufacturing enterprises that have achieved basic digitalisation levels increases by one percentage point in the EU countries, the manufacturing sector productivity per employee will increase by 2.28% if the Ceteris Paribus assumption is applied to other factors. It is in line with Gal et al.'s (2019) findings that digital adoption in an industry is associated with productivity gains at the firm level. However, the relationship was not confirmed at the sector level in their study. Nevertheless, it is impossible to directly compare the study results because the authors use different indicators to reflect the digitisation level than our study used. Digitalisation's promotional effect on labour productivity at the enterprise level was also found by Song et al. (2022) in China's case. Mollins and Taskin (2023), based on a review and study of retrospective studies, concluded that digitisation positively affects productivity both at the firm level and at the sector level and identified the main impact transmission channels. They claim that digitalisation promotes productivity through the availability of data and information, automation, and more efficient capital. The authors (Mollins & Taskin, 2023) made another fundamental insight that the influence of digitisation on productivity becomes more pronounced when coupled with other supportive assets. As the effective coordination and integration of complementary elements require time, the realisation of productivity gains may experience a delay. The presence of skilled human capital and the implementation of efficient management practices enhance the overall impact of digitisation on productivity. This chapter will not investigate how these factors influence the impact of digitisation on productivity, but this could be a direction for further research.

Based on the results (Table 12.5) of the study presented in the table, it can be asserted that if the percentage of manufacturing enterprises that use industrial robots in EU countries increases by one percentage point, the manufacturing sector productivity per employee will increase by 4.81% if the Ceteris Paribus assumption is applied to other factors. These findings align with Jungmittag and

Table 12.4. Estimation Results on the Relationship Between Manufacturing Sector Productivity per Employee and the Percentage of Manufacturing Enterprises That Have Achieved Basic Digitalisation Level.

Model 2: OLS, Using Observations 1–26				
Dependent Variable: l_VAemp				
	Coefficient	SE	t-Ratio	p-Value
const	9.67923	0.282025	34.320	<0.0001	***
DI_basic	0.02281	0.004938	4.620	0.0001	***
Mean dependent var		10.93530	SD dependent var		0.515181
Sum squared resid		3.511781	SE of regression		0.382523
R^2		0.470741	Adjusted R^2		0.448688
$F(1, 24)$		21.34640	p-value (F)		0.000109
Log-likelihood		−10.86675	Akaike criterion		25.73350
Schwarz criterion		28.24969	Hannan–Quinn		26.45807

Source: Compiled by the authors based on Eurostat data, using software package Gretl.
Notes: *** indicates significance at the 1 percent level.

Digitalisation and Productivity Improvement

Table 12.5. Estimation Results on the Relationship Between Manufacturing Sector Productivity per Employee and the Percentage of Manufacturing Enterprises That Use Industrial Robots.

		Model 3: OLS, Using Observations 1–26			
		Dependent Variable: l_VAemp			
	Coefficient	SE	*t*-Ratio	*p*-Value	
const	10.11590	0.195050	51.86	<0.0001	***
Ind_rob	0.04815	0.010567	4.556	0.0001	***
Mean dependent var		10.93530	SD dependent var		0.51518
Sum squared resid		3.55776	SE of regression		0.38502
R^2		0.46381	Adjusted R^2		0.44147
$F(1, 24)$		20.76036	*p*-value (F)		0.00013
Log-likelihood		−11.03585	Akaike criterion		26.07170
Schwarz criterion		28.58789	Hannan–Quinn		26.79627

Source: Compiled by the authors based on Eurostat data, using software package Gretl.
Notes: *** indicates significance at the 1 percent level.

Pesole's (2019) research results. The authors used data from 12 EU countries and 9 manufacturing industries to estimate the impact of robot usage on labour productivity. The study covers the time period of 1993–2015. They found that increased robot use positively contributes to labour productivity in each manufacturing industry. According to Jungmittag and Pesole (2019), it is conceivable that the anticipated increases in productivity and employment will be limited to nations and sectors already possessing a substantial supply of industrial robots. The favourable effects on other areas will be influenced by the level of complexity involved in the automation process across various industries and countries. Eder et al. (2023) investigated the contribution of industrial robots to labour productivity growth in 19 developed and 16 emerging countries from 1999 to 2019. They found a positive contribution of robotisation to labour productivity growth for all countries, but the effect is stronger in emerging countries compared with developed countries. According to Eder et al. (2023), 'the effect of robot capital deepening on the shift of the entire labour productivity distribution is rather modest and dominated by other growth factors, such as technological change'. Şahin (2020) examines the impact of the number of industrial robots on productivity and other indicators (employment, minimum wage) by applying the panel pooled mean group estimator method and using Organisation for Economic Co-operation and Development (OECD) country's 2006–2017 period data. Estimated results revealed that the number of industrial robots positively impacts OECD countries' productivity.

Robotics is one of the features of the current economic development. Kasych et al. (2022) predict that the pace of robotisation will accelerate in all countries, including developing countries. According to the authors, the rapid growth of the labour force and the challenges of the development of the manufacturing industry will be the engines that will lead to the development of robotisation and the development of the world economy. Countries that robotise the manufacturing sector are expected to win the competition of competitiveness.

224   VIDA DAVIDAVICIENE AND ALMA MAČIULYTĖ-ŠNIUKIENĖ

Table 12.6.   Estimation Results on the Relationship Between Manufacturing Sector Productivity per Employee and the Percentage of Manufacturing Enterprises That Use IoT.

Model 4: OLS, Using Observations 1–26					
Dependent Variable: l_VAemp					
	Coefficient	SE	t-Ratio	p-Value	
const	10.346700	0.265876	38.92	3.37e-023	***
IoT	0.0199707	0.008452	2.363	0.0266	**
Mean dependent var		10.93530	SD dependent var		0.51518
Sum squared resid		3.38319	SE of regression		0.47360
R^2		0.18870	Adjusted R^2		0.15489
$F(1, 24)$		5.58219	p-Value (F)		0.02659
Log-likelihood		−16.41980	Akaike criterion		36.83961
Schwarz criterion		39.35580	Hannan–Quinn		37.56418

Source: Compiled by the authors based on Eurostat data, using software package Gretl.
Notes: *** indicates significance at the 1 percent level.

Correlation analysis (see Table 12.2) revealed that the relationship between labour productivity and IoT is positive but statistically insignificant. Nevertheless, a regression analysis was additionally performed, substantiating this primary result (see Table 12.6).

The regression analysis results repeatedly confirmed that the relationship between IoT and labour productivity is positive but statistically insignificant ($p > 0.05$). However, these results do not refute the theoretical assumptions that IoT is a source of increasing labour productivity. Because IoT is only used by an average of 30% of manufacturing companies, this effect is insignificant, but the relationship is likely to become statistically significant as IoT usage increases.

7. CONCLUSIONS

Based on the analysis of scientific literature, digitalisation is one of the modern trends linked to the sustainability of companies, especially production, and determines efficiency and productivity. One of the positive effects of digitisation is the increase in labour productivity.

The use of IoT can increase the productivity of manufacturing enterprises through the automation of production processes, which is the use of IoT devices; through the positive benefits of gathering and analysing data on production processes, allowing for reasonable optimisation decisions; through improved equipment maintenance, as it will enable predicting failures in advance and thereby shortening the time of unwanted equipment downtime; and through impact on the supply chain, energy efficiency, and quality control.

Robotisation increases labour productivity by increasing the speed of work processes, ensuring high-quality work results, and reducing production costs in the long term. In addition, robots can be integrated with other automation systems and IoT devices, creating a better coordinated, synchronised work environment.

E-commerce, based on digitisation technologies and solutions, also impacts labour productivity. This effect manifests through more efficient operations management, as e-commerce platforms and systems enable the automation of supply chain and sales processes. E-commerce increases the actual demand for a product, which can lead to an increase in production efficiency and a decrease in average costs.

These intermediate conclusions suggest that the labour productivity of manufacturing companies and the entire sector depends on the overall degree of digitisation. Thus, if the degree of digitalisation of manufacturing in one group of countries is lower, this will likely lead to lower labour productivity.

The analysis results show that the new EU countries (E-13) lag behind the old EU countries (E-14) in terms of labour productivity and the degree of digitalisation.

After researching to empirically check the relationship between the general degree of digitalisation and individual indicators reflecting the state of digitalisation with the productivity of EU countries, a positive statistically significant relationship was established between productivity per employee and the percentage of manufacturing enterprises with e-commerce sales, the percentage of manufacturing enterprises that have achieved a basic digitisation level, and the percentage of enterprises that use industrial robots. The correlation between productivity per employee and the percentage of manufacturing enterprises that use IoT is positive but statistically insignificant. Nevertheless, if more manufacturing companies in EU countries took advantage of IoT opportunities, their impact would probably become statistically significant. But this is only an assumption that has yet to be verified in the future.

Considering these results, it can be concluded that if the digitisation of the manufacturing sector in the EU-13 countries is faster compared to the EU-14, the gap between the new countries and the new countries will decrease not only in terms of digitisation indicators but also in terms of labour productivity.

Although the study revealed specific interactions between digitisation and productivity, the study has limitations. First, due to the lack of long-term digitalisation statistics, the simple research methods applied in the work did not allow us to fully reveal the differences between the EU-13 and EU-14 country groups on the effects of digitalisation on labour productivity and to reveal possible delayed effects. In addition, the work assumes that other factors do not change (ceteris paribus assumption). Still, in practice, the effect of several factors co-occurs, which can strengthen or reduce the impact of the indicator reflecting digitalisation. It could be the direction of further research when the statistics of the indicators reflecting the digitalisation of a more extended period are accumulated.

Despite these work limitations, it could be concluded that national and EU-level economic development and cohesion policymakers should encourage manufacturing companies, especially in the EU-13 group of countries, to implement digital technologies through tax incentives and support programmes.

REFERENCES

Aghimien, D., Aigbavboa, C., Oke, A., Thwala, W., & Moripe, P. (2022). Digitalization of construction organisations – A case for digital partnering. *International Journal of Construction Management*, *22*(10), 1950–1959. https://doi.org/10.1080/15623599.2020.1745134

Agrawal, R., & Vinodh, S. (2020). Sustainability evaluation of additive manufacturing processes using grey-based approach. *Grey Systems*, *10*(4), 393–412. https://doi.org/10.1108/GS-08-2019-0028/FULL/PDF

Ahmad, S., Wong, K. Y., & Rajoo, S. (2019). Sustainability indicators for manufacturing sectors: A literature survey and maturity analysis from the triple-bottom line perspective. *Journal of Manufacturing Technology Management*, *30*(2), 312–334. https://doi.org/10.1108/JMTM-03-2018-0091/FULL/PDF

Akhmadalieva, Z., & Akhmadalieva, Z. (2022). Impact of digitalization on firms' productivity. *ICFNDS'22 Proceedings of the 6th Intenational Conference on Future Networks & Distributed Systems*. (pp. 364–369) December 2022. https://doi.org/10.1145/3584254

Alayón, C., Säfsten, K., & Johansson, G. (2017). Conceptual sustainable production principles in practice: Do they reflect what companies do? *Journal of Cleaner Production*, *141*, 693–701. https://doi.org/10.1016/J.JCLEPRO.2016.09.079

Almeida, F., Duarte Santos, J., & Augusto Monteiro, J. (2020). The challenges and opportunities in the digitalization of companies in a post-COVID-19 world. *IEEE Engineering Management Review*, *48*(3), 97–103. https://doi.org/10.1109/EMR.2020.3013206

Amankwah-Amoah, J., Khan, Z., Wood, G., & Knight, G. (2021). COVID-19 and digitalization: The great acceleration. *Journal of Business Research*, *136*, 602–611. https://doi.org/10.1016/J.JBUSRES.2021.08.011

Ammar, M., Russello, G., & Crispo, B. (2018). Internet of things: A survey on the security of IoT frameworks. *Journal of Information Security and Applications*, *38*, 8–27. https://doi.org/10.1016/J.JISA.2017.11.002

Angelakoglou, K., & Gaidajis, G. (2015). A review of methods contributing to the assessment of the environmental sustainability of industrial systems. *Journal of Cleaner Production*, *108*, 725–747. https://doi.org/10.1016/J.JCLEPRO.2015.06.094

Atik, H., & Ünlü, F. (2020). Industry 4.0-related digital divide in enterprises: An Analysis for the European Union-28. *Sosyoekonomi*, *28*(45), 225–244. https://doi.org/10.17233/SOSYOEKONOMI.2020.03.13

Bali, M. (2019). Reimagining digital literacies from a feminist perspective in a postcolonial context. *Media and Communication*, *7*(2), 69–81. https://doi.org/10.17645/MAC.V7I2.1935

Bazarhanova, A., Yli-Huumo, J., & Smolander, K. (2020). From platform dominance to weakened ownership: How external regulation changed Finnish e-identification. *Electronic Markets*, *30*(3), 525–538. https://doi.org/10.1007/S12525-019-00331-4/FIGURES/7

Bergeaud, A., Cette, G., & Lecat, R. (2016). The role of production factor quality and technology diffusion in 20th century productivity growth. *SSRN Electronic Journal*. https://doi.org/10.2139/SSRN.2759837

Borchard, R., Zeiss, R., & Recker, J. (2022). Digitalization of waste management: Insights from German private and public waste management firms. *Waste Management and Research*, *40*(6), 775–792. https://doi.org/10.1177/0734242X211029173/ASSET/IMAGES/LARGE/10.1177_0734242X211029173-FIG7.JPEG

Ceccobelli, M., Gitto, S., & Mancuso, P. (2012). ICT capital and labour productivity growth: A non-parametric analysis of 14 OECD countries. *Telecommunications Policy*, *36*(4), 282–292. https://doi.org/10.1016/J.TELPOL.2011.12.012

Colicchia, C., Melacini, M., & Perotti, S. (2011). Benchmarking supply chain sustainability: Insights from a field study. *Benchmarking*, *18*(5), 705–732. https://doi.org/10.1108/14635771111166839/FULL/PDF

Crnjac, M., Veza, I., Banduka, N. (2017). From concept to the introduction of Industry 4.0. *International Journal of Industry Engineering Management (IJIEM)*, *8*(1), 21–30.

Cruz-Jesus, F., Vicente, M. R., Bacao, F., & Oliveira, T. (2016). The education-related digital divide: An analysis for the EU-28. *Computers in Human Behavior*, *56*, 72–82. https://doi.org/10.1016/J.CHB.2015.11.027

Digitalisation and Productivity Improvement

Davidavičiene, V. (2008). Change management decisions in the information age. *Journal of Business Economics and Management, 9*(4), 299–307. https://doi.org/10.3846/1611-1699.2008.9.299-307

De Reuver, M., Sørensen, C., & Basole, R. C. (2018). The digital platform: A research agenda. *Journal of Information Technology, 33*(2), 124–135. https://doi.org/10.1057/S41265-016-0033-3

Du, X., & Jiang, K. (2022). Promoting enterprise productivity: The role of digital transformation. *Borsa Instambul Review, 22*(6), 1165–1181. https://doi.org/10.1016/j.bir.2022.08.005

Eder, A., Koller, W., Mahlberg, B. (2023). The contribution of industrial robots to labour productivity growth and economic convergence: A production frontier approach. *Journal of Productivity Analysis.* https://doi.org/10.1007/s11123-023-00707-x

Falk, M., & Hagsten, E. (2015). E-commerce trends and impacts across Europe. *International Journal of Production Economics, 170*(Part A), 357–369. https://doi.org/10.1016/j/ijpe.2015.10.003

Fonseca, L. M. (2018). Industry 4.0 and the digital society: Concepts, dimensions and envisioned benefits. *Proceedings of the International Conference on Business Excellence, 12*(1), 386–397. https://doi.org/10.2478/PICBE-2018-0034

Franciosi, C., Roda, I., Voisin, A., Miranda, S., Macchi, M., & Iung, B. (2021). Sustainable maintenance performances and EN 15341:2019: An integration proposal. *IFIP Advances in Information and Communication Technology, 633 IFIP*, 401–409. https://doi.org/10.1007/978-3-030-85910-7_42/ COVER

Fu, J., Zhang, N., & Li, F. (2023). Research on the impact of managerial capabilities on the digital transformation of enterprises. *Journal of Business Economics and Management, 24*(4), 614-632–614–632. https://doi.org/10.3846/JBEM.2023.19915

Fürst, E., & Oberhofer, P. (2012). Greening road freight transport: Evidence from an empirical project in Austria. *Journal of Cleaner Production, 33*, 67–73. https://doi.org/10.1016/ J.JCLEPRO.2012.05.027

Gabriel, A., & Gandorfer, M. (2023). Adoption of digital technologies in agriculture – An inventory in a European small-scale farming region. *Precision Agriculture, 24*(1), 68–91. https://doi.org/ 10.1007/S11119-022-09931-1/TABLES/5

Gal, P., Nicoletti, G., von Rüden, Ch., Sorbe, S., Renault, T. (2019). Digitalization and productivity: In search of the holy grail – Firm-level empirical evidence from European countries. *International Productivity Monitor, 37*, 1–71.

Garbie, I. (2016). Sustainability in small and medium-sized manufacturing enterprises: An empirical study. *The Journal of Engineering Research (TJER), 13*(1), 42–57. https://doi.org/10.24200/ TJER.VOL13ISS1PP42-57

García De Soto, B., Agustí-Juan, I., Joss, S., & Hunhevicz, J. (2019). Implications of Construction 4.0 to the workforce and organizational structures. *International Journal of Construction Management, 22*(2), 205–217. https://doi.org/10.1080/15623599.2019.1616414

Genovese, A., Morris, J., Piccolo, C., & Koh, S. C. L. (2017). Assessing redundancies in environmental performance measures for supply chains. *Journal of Cleaner Production, 167*, 1290–1302. https://doi.org/10.1016/J.JCLEPRO.2017.05.186

Gholami, Y. (2023). *Investigating ddoption of digital technologies in construction projects.* Linköping University, Department of Science and Technology, Norrköping, Sweden.

Hanclova, J., Doucek, P., Fischer, J., & Vltavska, K. (2015). Does ICT capital affect economic growth in the EU-15 and EU-12 countries? *Journal of Business Economics and Management, 16*(2), 387–406. https://doi.org/10.3846/16111699.2012.754375

Huang, X., Zhou, J., & Zhou, Y. (2022). Digital economy's spatial implications on urban innovation and its threshold: Evidence from China. *Complexity, 2022*, 1–25. https://doi.org/10.1155/2022/3436741

Iyawa, G. E., Herselman, M., & Botha, A. (2017). Identifying essential components of a digital health innovation ecosystem for the Namibian context: Findings from a Delphi study. *The Electronic Journal of Information Systems in Developing Countries, 82*(1), 1–40. https://doi. org/10.1002/J.1681-4835.2017.TB00601.X

Jelfs, A., & Richardson, J. T. E. (2013). The use of digital technologies across the adult life span in distance education. *British Journal of Educational Technology, 44*(2), 338–351. https://doi.org/ 10.1111/J.1467-8535.2012.01308.X

Jiang, Y., Yin, S., Li, K., Luo, H., & Kaynak, O. (2021). Industrial applications of digital twins. *Philosophical Transactions of the Royal Society A, 379*(2207), 1–15. https://doi.org/10.1098/ RSTA.2020.0360

Jungmittag, A., Pesole, A. (2019). *The impact of robots on labour productivity: A panel data approach covering 9 industries and 12 countries*. JRC Working Papers Series on Labour, Education and Technology No. 2019/08. European Commission, Joint Research Centre (JRC), Seville.

Kasych, A., Glukhova, V., Buhas, N., & Nefedova, T. (2022). Key factors of production robotization and its impact on labor productivity. *IEEE 4th International Conference on Modern Electrical and Energy System (MEES)*, 2022 October, Kremenchuk, Ukraine. doi: 10.1109/MEES58014.2022.10005707

Kimuli, S. N. L., Sendawula, K., & Nagujja, S. (2021). Digital technologies in micro and small enterprise: Evidence from Uganda's informal sector during the COVID-19 pandemic. *World Journal of Science, Technology and Sustainable Development, 18*(2), 93–108. https://doi.org/10.1108/WJSTSD-02-2021-0017/FULL/XML

Kiplagat, R., Gesimba, P., & Gichuhi, D. (2019). Influence of technology usability on digital banking adoption by customers of selected commercial banks in Nakuru town, Kenya. *Editon Consortium Journal of Economics and Development Studies, 1*(1), 28–39. https://doi.org/10.51317/ECJEDS.V1I1.68

Kravchenko, M., Pigosso, D. C., & McAloone, T. C. (2019). Towards the ex-ante sustainability screening of circular economy initiatives in manufacturing companies: Consolidation of leading sustainability-related performance indicators. *Journal of Cleaner Production, 241*, 118318. https://doi.org/10.1016/J.JCLEPRO.2019.118318

Lebanon, A., & Rosenthal, H. (1975). Least squares estimation for models of cross sectional correlation. *Political Methodology, 2*(2), 221–244.

Leo, J. G. (n.d.). *Impact of information and communication technology on public sector productivity growth in Nigeria*. Retrieved February 11, 2024, from www.rsisinternational.org

Liu, T.-K., Chen, J.-R., Huang, C. C. J., Yang, C.-H. (2013). E-commerce, R&D, and productivity: Firm-level evidence from Taiwan. *Information Economics and Policy, 25*, 272–283. http://dx.doi.org/10.1016/j.infoecopol.2013.07.001

Lucato, W. C., Santos, J. C. da S., & Pacchini, A. P. T. (2017). Measuring the sustainability of a manufacturing process: A conceptual framework. *Sustainability, 10*(1), 81. https://doi.org/10.3390/SU10010081

Mancha, R., & Shankaranarayanan, G. (2021). Making a digital innovator: Antecedents of innovativeness with digital technologies. *Information Technology and People, 34*(1), 318–335. https://doi.org/10.1108/ITP-12-2018-0577/FULL/PDF

Martins, A. A., Mata, T. M., Costa, C. A. V., & Sikdar, S. K. (2006). Framework for sustainability metrics. *Industrial and Engineering Chemistry Research, 46*(10), 2962–2973. https://doi.org/10.1021/IE060692L

Mlynarzewska-Borowiec, I. (2021). Direct and indirect impact of ICT on EU's productivity growth. *European Research Studies Journal, XXIV* (Special Issue 4), 278–287. https://doi.org/10.35808/ERSJ/2689

Mollins, J., & Taskin, T. (2023). *Digitalization: Productivity*. Staff Discussion Paper 2023-17. Bank of Canada. https://doi.org/10.34989/sdp-2023-17. ISSN 1914-0568.

Nawaz, R., Hussain, I., Noor, S., Habib, T., & Omair, M. (2020). The significant impact of the economic sustainability on the cement industry by the assessment of the key performance indicators using Taguchi signal to noise ratio. *Cogent Engineering, 7*(1), 1–20. https://doi.org/10.1080/23311916.2020.1810383

Omrani, N., Rejeb, N., Maalaoui, A., Dabic, M., & Kraus, S. (2022). Drivers of digital transformation in SMEs. *IEEE Transactions on Engineering Management, 7*, 1–20 https://doi.org/10.1109/TEM.2022.3215727

Ren, Y., Li, B., & Liang, D. (2023). Impact of digital transformation on renewable energy companies' performance: Evidence from China. *Frontiers in Environmental Science, 10*, 1105686. https://doi.org/10.3389/FENVS.2022.1105686/BIBTEX

Şahin, L. (2020). Impacts of industrial robots usage on international labour markets and productivity: Evidence from 22 OECD countries. *Journal of International Studies, 3*, 59–67.

Sakin, M., & Kiroglu, Y. C. (2017). 3D printing of buildings: Construction of the sustainable houses of the future by BIM. *Energy Procedia, 134*, 702–711. https://doi.org/10.1016/J.EGYPRO.2017.09.562

Sallam, M. A. M. (2021). The role of the manufacturing sector in promoting economic growth in the Saudi economy: A cointegration and VECM approach. *Journal of Asian Finance, Economics and Business, 8*(7), 21–31. doi:10.13106/jafeb.2021.vol8.no7.0021

Samsami, M., & Schøtt, T. (2022). Past, present, and intended digitalization around the world: Leading, catching up, forging ahead, and falling behind. *Naše Gospodarstvo/Our Economy, 68*(3), 1–9. https://doi.org/10.2478/NGOE-2022-0013

Searcy, C. (2009). Setting a course in corporate sustainability performance measurement. *Measuring Business Excellence, 13*(3), 49–57. https://doi.org/10.1108/13683040910984329/FULL/PDF

Searcy, C., Karapetrovic, S., & McCartney, D. (2005). Designing sustainable development indicators: Analysis for a case utility. *Measuring Business Excellence, 9*(2), 33–41. https://doi.org/10.1108/13683040510602867/FULL/PDF

Seethamraju, R., & Diatha, K. S. (2018). Adoption of digital payments by small retail stores. *ACIS 2018 – 29th Australasian Conference on Information Systems*. https://doi.org/10.5130/ACIS2018. AS/DOWNLOAD/3685/

Shen, L., Zhang, X., & Liu, H. (2022). Digital technology adoption, digital dynamic capability, and digital transformation performance of textile industry: Moderating role of digital innovation orientation. *Managerial and Decision Economics, 43*(6), 2038–2054. https://doi.org/10.1002/MDE.3507

Shoker, A., & Abdullah, K. (2022). Digital sovereignty strategies for every nation. *Applied Cybersecurity & Internet Governance, 1*(1), 1–17. https://doi.org/10.5604/01.3001.0016.0943

Shyshkovskyi, S., Semkiv, I., & Kashuba, A. (2022). Research of the development of the electronic industry and economy on the example of Ukraine. *Technology Audit and Production Reserves, 5*(4(67)), 22–25. https://doi.org/10.15587/2706-5448.2022.266606

Simoes, A., Oliveira, L., Rodrigues, J. C., Simas, O., Dalmarco, G., & Barros, A. C. (2019). Environmental factors influencing the adoption of digitalization technologies in automotive supply chains. *Proceedings – 2019 IEEE International Conference on Engineering, Technology and Innovation, ICE/ITMC 2019*. https://doi.org/10.1109/ICE.2019.8792639

Song, M., Tao, W., & Shen, Z. (2022). The impact of digitalization on labour productivity evolution: Evidence from China. *Journal of Hospitality and Tourism Technology, 5*(4), 2–17. https://doi.org/10.1108/JHTT-03-2022-0075

Sridevi, K. B., Shyamala, P., & Nagarenitha, M. (2019). Adoption of information technology among small and medium enterprises in Indian context. *International Journal of Innovative Technology and Exploring Engineering, 8*(12), 2242–2247. https://doi.org/10.35940/IJITEE. L2492.1081219

Tan, J., Hu, X, Hassink, R., & Ni, J. (2020). Industrial structure or egency: What affect regional economic resilience? Evidence from resource-based cities in China. *Cities, 106*, 102906. https://doi.org/10.1016/j.cities.2020.102906

Van Ark, B., & Piatkowski, M. (2004). Productivity, innovation and ICT in old and new Europe. *International Economics and Economic Policy 2004 1:2, 1*(2), 215–246. https://doi.org/10.1007/S10368-004-0012-Y

Van Zeebroeck, N., Kretschmer, T., & Bughin, J. (2023). Digital 'is' strategy: The role of digital technology adoption in strategy renewal. *IEEE Transactions on Engineering Management, 70*(9), 3183–3197. https://doi.org/10.1109/TEM.2021.3079347

Wanasinghe, T. R., Wroblewski, L., Petersen, B. K., Gosine, R. G., James, L. A., De Silva, O., Mann, G. K. I., & Warrian, P. J. (2020). Digital twin for the oil and gas industry: Overview, research trends, opportunities, and challenges. *IEEE Access, 8*, 104175–104197. https://doi.org/10.1109/ACCESS.2020.2998723

Wang, Y., Liu, S., Liu, Y., & Wu, J. (2022). Research on the impact of manufacturing digital innovation resources on knowledge creation based on SmartPIS: The mediation effect of digital innovation ecosystem. In *2022 2nd International conference on management science and software engineering (ICMSSE 2022)* (pp. 744–752). https://doi.org/10.2991/978-94-6463-056-5_108

Warner, K. S. R., & Wäger, M. (2019). Building dynamic capabilities for digital transformation: An ongoing process of strategic renewal. *Long Range Planning, 52*(3), 326–349. https://doi.org/10.1016/J.LRP.2018.12.001

Xiao, D., & Su, J. (2022). Role of technological innovation in achieving social and environmental sustainability: Mediating roles of organizational innovation and digital entrepreneurship. *Frontiers in Public Health, 10*, 850172. https://doi.org/10.3389/FPUBH.2022.850172/BIBTEX

Xiaoli, X., Xiangyang, M., Nan, T., & Shi, Y. (2023). The coupling mechanism of the digital innovation ecosystem and value co-creation. *Advances in Environmental and Engineering Research, 4*(1), 1–9. https://doi.org/10.21926/AEER.2301013

Yu, W., Du, B., Guo, X., & Marinova, D. (2023). Total factor productivity in Chinese manufacturing firms: The role of E-commerce adoption. *Electronic Commerce Research, 2023*, 1–27. https://doi.org/10.1007/s10660-023-09711-7

Zeng, X., Li, S., & Yousaf, Z. (2022). Artificial intelligence adoption and digital innovation: How does digital resilience act as a mediator and training protocols as a moderator? *Sustainability, 14*, 1–14. https://doi.org/10.3390/SU14148286

CHAPTER 13

THE LABOUR MARKET, HUMAN CAPITAL AND MIGRATION: AGEING AND STRATIFICATION OF SOCIETY

Biruta Sloka, Ilze Buligina, Ginta Tora,
Juris Dzelme, Ilze Brante, Anna Angena
and Kristīne Liepiņa

University of Latvia, Latvia

ABSTRACT

Purpose*: This chapter analyses the labour market and human capital development in 13 European Union (EU)-adopted countries. It discusses innovative activities for various target groups, addressing demographic challenges and social issues related to labour market developments, highlighting positive experiences and practical solutions for improved human capital development.*

Need for study*: Demographic challenges, such as ageing societies and information and communication technology (ICT), are causing further stratification in Europe and increasing pressure on human capital development. Positive experiences reduce economic imbalances and achieve sustainability goals in human capital development, including successful application of the 'silver economy'.*

Methodology*: Representative data from randomly selected households implemented in all EU and candidate countries using the same Eurostat*

Economic Development and Resilience by EU Member States
Contemporary Studies in Economic and Financial Analysis, Volume 115, 231–247
Copyright © 2025 by Biruta Sloka, Ilze Buligina, Ginta Tora, Juris Dzelme, Ilze Brante, Anna Angena and Kristīne Liepiņa
Published under exclusive licence by Emerald Publishing Limited
ISSN: 1569-3759/doi:10.1108/S1569-375920240000115013

methodology, and Household Finance and Consumption Surveys conducted in all Eurozone countries, Hungary, and Poland, implemented by national banks and supervised by the European Central Bank, where representative survey data are available for comparative studies.

Findings*: Academic researchers are focusing on human capital development for the elderly population, exploring demographic processes and the silver economy to support their labour market involvement. Increased adult education and internet usage in new EU countries show significant income increases, with the highest increase in countries with larger adult education shares. Health issues are also being studied for elderly labour market retention.*

Practical implications*: This study suggests policy measures to address human capital development issues, particularly in the context of demographic challenges, investing in all age groups, avoiding economic bottlenecks, and preventing burnout to maximise labour market retention. These solutions could enhance Europe's competitiveness.*

Keywords: Human capital development; investment in education; economic activity support; retention in employment; silver economy

JEL classifications: E24; E26; G51; G38; I13; I15; I24; I31

INTRODUCTION

Demographic trends with an increase in the elderly share of the population in Europe demand long-term innovative solutions in the development of national economies, balance these demographic changes, and provide reasonable contributions to welfare systems since the share of the older population in most of the European countries is increasing, and this requires specific policy solutions for labour market stability: qualified and motivated labour force development according to the needs of high technology solutions in national economies. Older workers are also more exposed to the risk of skills obsolescence, and this requires solutions in the context of lifelong learning policy as well as training in the provision of different sectors and digital skills, thus preserving their employability and their competitive activities in the labour market and fulfilling ageing. This chapter attempts to analyse various factors and aspects related to human capital development, especially in relation to the elderly part of the population. It includes involvement in lifelong learning, ICT competence, health issues, income level, etc. The authors believe that investing in these aspects can contribute to more effective development of human capital and its retention in the labour market, with a particular focus on the silver economy. Available data are used in the analysis: some indicators have longer time series. The authors intended to use as several data as available to analyse the current development tendencies, thus contributing to a more comprehensive understanding of current societal developments.

THEORETICAL FINDINGS

Academic researchers worldwide seek innovative solutions to motivate and retain older people in the labour market (Crossen-White et al., 2020) and propose adequate policy approaches. Researchers are offering solutions (Meiners, 2014) analysing varied aspects (Labit & Dubost, 2016) with innovative and creative solutions (Bogataj et al., 2023; Marcucci et al., 2021; Pavia et al, 2021; Solovjova & Romānova, 2020; Vinichenko et al., 2021) including preparation of virtual competence assistant (Liutkevičius & Yahia, 2022). The new part of the economy, the so-called silver economy, is developing with significant attention from several social partners and academic researchers. Social and solidarity economy is on the agenda of academic researchers (Borzaga et al., 2019), with practical recommendations for real applications. Addressing the ageing persons' sustained competence is still a challenge for companies and their innovations (Barska & Śnihur, 2017) to keep those persons as knowledgeable customers. Aged persons are also a challenging issue for pension systems (Bogataj et al., 2019; European Commission, 2021), and the new situation has to be addressed. Older people are producers, consumers, and decision-makers (Poland, 2014), and their needs must be respected as, in many cases, they can purchase products and services more often than the younger part of the population. Information technologies and digitalisation requirements must also be taught to elderly employees (European Commission, 2023a; Finn & Wright, 2011; Mason et al., 2023; Sowa-Kofta et al., 2021). Transportation solutions are considered for practical applications in *the silver economy* (Cirella et al., 2019). Adjusted training programmes have to be developed and implemented to be successful for employment (Bolton et al., 2018) and knowledgeable customers. Work-based learning is very efficient, where employees' involvement is important for realising work-based learning (Brante & Sloka, 2022; Buligina & Sloka, 2013, 2019, 2022). Students at risk to drop out from the education and/ or social exclusion, especially in vocational education, it is very important to keep in education to train those students as successful future employees (Bruin et al., 2023; Sloka et al., 2023; Tūtlys et al., 2022) and excellent and active members of society. Work and time management for elderly inhabitants require special solutions and innovative approaches (Csoba & Ladancsik, 2023) to keep this part of the population interested in educational activities. Healthcare requires effective solutions (van Zaalen et al., 2018) and innovative solutions (Zgonec, 2021) to keep older people in economic activity and employment. Income differences in several regions play an essential role (Sloka et al., 2019), where the differences are statistically significant, and education plays an important role (Sloka et al., 2022). Health-care aspects are of great importance, including health self-evaluations (Sloka & Angena, 2022a, 2022b) and health-care financing aspects (Sloka & Angena, 2022c; Walczak et al., 2018), including attracting foreign patients (Behmane et al., 2021) to keep medical personnel qualified and well paid. The long-term care (LTC) reforms of the European member states also play an important role in addressing the medical needs of LTC and improving the care of older adults (European Commission, 2021, 2023a). Europe's silver economy (population over 50), the third largest economy in the world, is behind only the United States and

China, and it will only get bigger. Forecasts show that the silver economy in the EU will increase over the next 10 years, and its contribution to GDP will reach €6.4 trillion and 88 million jobs by 2025, which would be equivalent to 32% of EU gross domestic product (GDP) and 38% of EU employment (European Commission, 2018). Those findings need to be taken into account, especially by policymakers.

Researchers worldwide apply various research methods and data analysis methods, including multivariate statistics, and in many cases, factor analysis (Wiktorowicz, 2017) was also applied. Researchers in Baltic countries (Aidukaite & Blaziene, 2022) have concluded that longer working lives bring several challenges to which academic researchers must also pay attention. Free time activities are essential for ageing persons (Krekula et al., 2017), for example, with special dancing activities. Involvement in different activities (Salaj & Senior, 2021) makes older people feel like co-creators and supports their well-being. Some researchers have reminded us that particular attention should be paid to changes in the social structure, intensification of intergenerational cooperation, and knowledge transfer between generations in education (European Commission, 2023b). Education needs to be strengthened in relation to digital change and due to the steadily accelerating adoption of artificial intelligence (AI) in the economy (Dzelme, 2023). Human-level general AI may be able to replace humans in a few years (Salkovska et al., 2023). The chance of unaided machines outperforming humans in every possible task was estimated at 10% by 2027 and 50% by 2047 (Grace et al., 2024). The latter estimate is 13 years earlier than that reached in a similar survey only one year earlier (Grace et al., 2022). AI will likely lead to a shift towards the use of unconditional basic income (UBI). Transforming the whole social system will be necessary, mainly through education. Special attention will have to be paid to adult education in this respect, with specially targeted and comprehensive academic research on this.

PRACTICAL RESEARCH FINDINGS

In many countries, economic activity support is well connected with involvement in adult education. This information is collected annually in the Labour Force Survey (LFS) in all EU and candidate countries using the same methodology. The situation of older people's (part of the silver economy) involvement in education and training was very different in the analysed new EU countries (see Table 13.1).

Data indicate that in Slovenia and Estonia, involvement in adult education was much higher than in other analysed countries. In most analysed countries, the situation in adult education was different for female and male persons – in almost all cases, female persons were involved in adult education and training more than male persons (see Tables 13.2 and 13.3).

Data indicate that the biggest share of male persons involved in adult education in new EU countries was in Slovenia and Estonia, where this share was much bigger than in some countries where it was even five times less during the analysed period. The share of involvement in adult education was very low in Bulgaria and Romania, but in Romania, during the last several years, it has been increasing.

Labour Market, Human Capital and Migration 235

Table 13.1. Participation Rate (in %) in Adult Education and Training (Last Four Weeks) 2014–2022 in New EU Countries.

Country	2014	2015	2016	2017	2018	2019	2020	2021	2022
Bulgaria	2.1	2.0	2.2	2.3	2.5	2.0	1.6	1.8	1.7
Czechia	9.6	8.5	8.8	9.8	8.5	8.1	5.5	5.8	9.4
Estonia	11.6	11.9	15.3	16.8	19.3	19.6	16.6	18.4	21.1
Croatia	2.8	3.1	3.0	2.3	2.9	3.5	3.2	5.1	4.4
Cyprus	7.1	7.5	6.9	6.9	6.7	5.9	4.7	9.7	10.5
Latvia	5.6	5.7	7.3	7.5	6.7	7.4	6.6	8.6	9.7
Lithuania	5.1	5.8	6.0	5.9	6.6	7.0	7.2	8.5	8.5
Hungary	3.3	7.1	6.3	6.2	6.0	5.8	5.1	5.9	7.9
Malta	7.7	7.4	7.8	10.6	10.9	11.9	11.0	13.9	12.8
Poland	4.0	3.5	3.7	4.0	5.7	4.8	3.7	5.4	7.6
Romania	1.5	1.3	1.2	1.1	0.9	1.3	1.0	4.9	5.4
Slovenia	12.1	11.9	11.6	12.0	11.4	11.2	8.4	18.9	22.3
Slovakia	3.1	3.1	2.9	3.4	4.0	3.6	2.8	4.8	12.8

Source: Author's construction based on Eurostat data based on LFSs.

Table 13.2. Participation Rate (in %) of Male Persons in Adult Education and Training (Last Four Weeks) 2014–2022 in New EU Countries.

Country	2014	2015	2016	2017	2018	2019	2020	2021	2022
Bulgaria	1.8	1.9	2.1	2.2	2.4	1.8	1.4	1.7	1.6
Czechia	9.3	8.3	8.6	9.6	8.3	8.1	5.6	5.6	9.3
Estonia	9.2	9.8	12.2	13.1	15.7	16.3	12.6	14.4	16.7
Croatia	2.6	2.7	3.1	2.1	2.4	3.2	2.6	3.7	3.9
Cyprus	6.7	6.9	6.7	6.7	6.8	5.6	4.9	9.9	10.4
Latvia	4.9	4.1	6.1	6.0	4.8	5.4	4.6	5.5	6.6
Lithuania	4.6	5.1	5.1	4.4	4.9	5.5	5.6	6.7	6.8
Hungary	3.0	6.8	5.6	5.9	5.6	5.6	4.4	5.8	6.7
Malta	7.3	6.9	7.0	9.5	9.4	10.7	9.6	12.9	12.1
Poland	3.6	3.3	3.4	3.5	5.1	4.2	3.1	5.0	7.0
Romania	1.7	1.3	1.2	1.1	1.0	1.4	1.0	5.2	5.6
Slovenia	10.5	10.7	10.2	10.0	9.4	9.7	7.4	17.4	20.8
Slovakia	3.0	2.7	2.6	3.5	4.2	3.6	2.6	4.6	12.9

Source: Author's construction based on Eurostat data based on LFSs.

The share of female involvement in adult education during the last decade in all new EU member countries was higher than that of male participants. Data indicate that the biggest share of female participants in adult education was in Slovenia and Estonia.

The employment rate has increased during the last decade in all new EU countries, with the highest in Estonia and the lowest in Romania in 2022 (Table 13.4).

For the silver economy, it is important to be involved in labour market activities for persons aged 66–64, which are often problematic. Table 13.5 presents employment rate tendencies for persons aged 55–64 in new EU countries.

Data indicate that the employment rate for older persons aged 55–64 in all new EU countries increases, with the highest employment rate for this age group in

Table 13.3. Participation Rate (in %) of Female Persons in Adult Education and Training (Last Four Weeks) 2014–2022 in New EU Countries.

Country	2014	2015	2016	2017	2018	2019	2020	2021	2022
Bulgaria	2.3	2.1	2.3	2.4	2.6	2.1	1.7	1.9	1.8
Czechia	9.8	8.6	9.0	10.0	8.7	8.1	5.5	5.9	9.4
Estonia	13.9	13.9	18.2	20.4	22.9	22.9	20.6	22.5	25.5
Croatia	3.0	3.6	2.9	2.6	3.4	3.7	3.8	6.4	5.0
Cyprus	7.5	7.9	7.1	7.1	6.6	6.2	4.5	9.5	10.5
Latvia	6.3	7.2	8.5	8.8	8.4	9.3	8.4	11.5	12.5
Lithuania	5.6	6.5	6.8	7.3	8.3	8.5	8.7	10.2	10.2
Hungary	3.6	7.5	7.0	6.4	6.4	6.0	5.7	5.9	9.2
Malta	8.1	7.9	8.7	11.9	12.5	13.4	12.6	14.9	13.6
Poland	4.3	3.8	4.0	4.4	6.3	5.4	4.3	5.9	8.3
Romania	1.4	1.3	1.2	1.0	0.9	1.2	1.0	4.7	5.2
Slovenia	13.8	13.3	13.2	14.1	13.5	12.8	9.5	20.6	24.0
Slovakia	3.2	3.4	3.2	3.3	3.8	3.6	3.0	4.9	12.8

Source: Author's construction based on Eurostat data based on LFSs.

Table 13.4. Employment Rate (in %) 2014–2022 in New EU Countries.

Country	2014	2015	2016	2017	2018	2019	2020	2021	2022
Bulgaria	64.4	66.5	67.0	70.6	71.7	74.3	72.7	73.2	75.7
Czechia	73.5	74.8	76.7	78.5	79.9	80.3	79.7	80.0	81.3
Estonia	75.0	76.7	77.0	79.2	79.7	80.5	79.1	79.3	81.9
Croatia	59.2	60.6	61.4	63.6	65.2	66.7	66.9	68.2	69.7
Cyprus	67.6	67.9	68.7	70.8	73.9	75.7	74.9	75.9	77.9
Latvia	70.6	72.5	73.0	74.6	76.8	77.3	76.9	75.3	77.0
Lithuania	71.8	73.3	75.2	76.0	77.8	78.2	76.7	77.4	79.0
Hungary	68.7	70.9	73.7	75.4	76.7	77.6	77.5	78.8	80.2
Malta	67.9	69.0	71.1	73.0	75.5	76.8	77.3	79.1	81.1
Poland	64.9	66.3	68.2	70.0	71.4	72.3	72.7	75.4	76.7
Romania	58.0	59.2	60.3	62.7	63.9	65.1	65.2	67.1	68.5
Slovenia	67.3	68.6	69.5	72.9	74.9	75.9	74.8	76.1	77.9
Slovakia	67.8	69.6	71.8	73.2	74.5	75.6	74.6	74.6	76.7

Source: Author's construction based on Eurostat data.

Estonia, Czechia, Lithuania, and Latvia and the lowest in Romania and Croatia. Internet use is an important part of employment in many fields. Data on the internet use rate for individuals in new EU countries are reflected in Table 13.6.

The internet use rate for individuals has increased during the last decade in all new EU countries, with the highest rate for individuals in Estonia and the lowest rate for individuals in Bulgaria, Croatia, Romania, and Poland in 2022. Trend analysis results for new EU member countries on the internet use rate for individuals in the last three months of 2014–2022 are included in Table 13.7.

Results of trend analysis for new EU member countries on internet use rate for individuals in the last three months in 2014–2022 indicate that during the analysed time, the most significant average annual increase is for Romania by 4.08%, and the smallest average yearly increase is for Estonia by 1.18%.

Labour Market, Human Capital and Migration

Table 13.5. Employment Rate (in %) for Persons Aged 55–64 During 2014–2022 in New EU Countries.

Country	2014	2015	2016	2017	2018	2019	2020	2021	2022
Bulgaria	49.3	52.2	53.8	57.4	59.9	63.5	63.4	64.8	68.2
Czechia	54.0	55.5	58.5	62.1	65.1	66.7	68.2	69.8	72.9
Estonia	64.0	64.1	65.0	67.9	68.4	71.9	71.3	71.6	73.7
Croatia	36.2	39.2	38.1	40.3	42.8	43.9	45.5	48.6	50.1
Cyprus	46.9	48.5	52.2	55.3	60.9	61.1	61.0	63.4	65.0
Latvia	56.3	59.4	61.2	62.2	65.3	67.3	68.4	67.8	69.5
Lithuania	56.2	60.4	64.6	66.1	68.5	68.4	67.6	68.0	69.8
Hungary	41.8	45.3	49.8	51.7	54.4	56.7	59.6	62.8	65.6
Malta	39.5	42.3	45.8	47.2	50.2	51.1	52.7	52.3	54.5
Poland	40.5	42.5	44.5	46.9	47.7	48.3	50.4	54.7	56.4
Romania	33.0	32.7	35.3	36.9	38.6	40.4	41.5	43.8	46.7
Slovenia	35.1	36.3	38.2	42.4	46.7	48.2	49.9	52.7	55.2
Slovakia	46.0	48.3	50.5	54.6	55.9	58.8	60.2	60.6	64.1

Source: Author's construction based on Eurostat data.

Table 13.6. Internet Use Rate (in %) for Individuals in the Last Three Months 2014–2022 in New EU Countries.

Country	2014	2015	2016	2017	2018	2019	2020	2021	2022
Bulgaria	55.49	56.66	59.47	63.41	64.78	67.95	70.16	75.27	79.13
Czechia	79.71	81.30	82.17	84.64	86.50	87.03	87.60	88.85	90.64
Estonia	84.24	88.41	87.24	88.10	89.36	90.23	89.06	90.98	91.50
Croatia	68.57	69.80	72.70	67.10	75.29	79.08	78.32	81.25	82.07
Cyprus	69.33	71.72	75.90	80.74	84.43	86.06	90.80	90.76	89.60
Latvia	75.83	79.20	79.84	81.32	83.58	86.14	88.90	91.30	91.31
Lithuania	72.13	71.38	74.38	77.62	79.72	81.58	83.06	86.93	87.72
Hungary	75.65	72.83	79.26	76.75	76.07	80.37	84.77	88.64	89.14
Malta	73.63	76.77	78.08	80.75	81.66	85.78	86.86	87.47	91.54
Poland	66.60	68.00	73.30	75.99	77.54	80.44	83.18	85.37	86.94
Romania	54.08	55.76	59.50	63.75	70.68	73.66	78.46	83.59	85.50
Slovenia	71.59	73.10	75.50	78.89	79.75	83.11	86.60	89.00	88.91
Slovakia	79.98	77.63	80.48	81.63	80.45	82.85	89.92	88.93	89.07

Source: Author's construction based on Eurostat data.

Every year in all EU countries and candidate countries, the EU-SILC – Survey on Income and Living Conditions is organised as a representative survey by the same methodology where several questions related to health self-evaluations are asked on a scale of 1–5 where 1 – very good; 2 – good; 3 – fair; 4 – bad; 5 – very bad. The share of the population of self-evaluations of health as very good in analysed countries in 2012–2022 is reflected in Table 13.8.

Data indicate that the self-evaluations of health are very different in new EU countries: the lowest share of evaluations as very good was in the Baltic countries; in Latvia, this share was the weakest during the last decade, but the most significant share where inhabitants evaluated health as very good during

Table 13.7. Analytical Trends for 2014–2022 on Internet Use Rate for Individuals in the Last Three Months in New EU Countries.

Country	Trend	R^2
Bulgaria	$y = 2.73x + 47.061$	0.983
Czechia	$y = 1.5988x + 73.671$	0.9507
Estonia	$y = 1.1813x + 79.79$	0.8193
Croatia	$y = 1.8623x + 61.751$	0.9078
Cyprus	$y = 2.9117x + 60.799$	0.9397
Latvia	$y = 1.8671x + 71.039$	0.9846
Lithuania	$y = 2.1142x + 64.395$	0.9863
Hungary	$y = 1.8763x + 67.606$	0.8982
Malta	$y = 2.2063x + 66.69$	0.9833
Poland	$y = 2.4901x + 59.558$	0.9758
Romania	$y = 4.0827x + 40.947$	0.9931
Slovenia	$y = 2.103x + 66.152$	0.9727
Slovakia	$y = 1.2106x + 74.859$	0.8212

Source: Author's calculations based on Eurostat data.

Table 13.8. Self-perceived Health Evaluations as *Very Good* in 2014–2022 in New EU Countries (Share in %).

Country	2014	2015	2016	2017	2018	2019	2020	2021	2022
Bulgaria	17.3	18.8	19.1	21.8	19.7	16.8	17.4	18.2	14.8
Czechia	19.0	18.9	18.6	20.3	19.9	20.1	21.3	26.8	26.1
Estonia	10.6	9.4	9.3	11.0	8.8	12.5	15.1	13.3	13.5
Croatia	24.8	26.2	25.5	28.2	28.7	28.4	31.0	31.4	31.2
Cyprus	45.3	55.8	44.1	49.8	46.7	46.8	45.3	46.1	47.6
Latvia	4.6	4.8	5.1	3.5	5.5	4.7	4.8	5.3	4.4
Lithuania	7.4	6.6	6.6	7.3	6.9	7.6	8.9	9.1	7.6
Hungary	18.1	18.1	17.6	17.1	16.3	16.4	17.7	17.9	17.4
Malta	20.2	24.6	22.3	28.7	24.4	21.1	23.2	22.1	24.1
Poland	17.3	16.3	15.9	16.2	15.5	15.4	14.4	15.7	15.6
Romania	26.9	26.7	26.6	27.9	26.4	28.0	31.7	31.8	32.7
Slovenia	21.2	21.7	20.3	21.4	20.1	21.9	22.8	25.7	22.1
Slovakia	20.5	21.2	22.4	23.3	22.3	20.8	20.3	20.3	21.2

Source: Author's construction based on Eurostat data based on EU-SILC.

last decade was in Cyprus; a substantial increase of the share of inhabitants considering health as very good was in Croatia. The share of the population of self-evaluations of health as very bad in analysed countries in 2014–2022 is reflected in Table 13.9.

Data indicate that the self-evaluations of health are very different in new EU countries: the lowest share of evaluations as very bad was in Malta and Cyprus during the analysed period (2014–2022), but the most significant share where inhabitants evaluate health as very bad during analysed period was in Croatia, Slovakia, Latvia, and Hungary; considerable decrease of share of inhabitants

Labour Market, Human Capital and Migration 239

Table 13.9. Self-Perceived Health Evaluations as *Very Bad* in 2014–2022 in New EU Countries (Share in %).

Country	2014	2015	2016	2017	2018	2019	2020	2021	2022
Bulgaria	2.9	2.8	2.3	2.5	2.2	1.6	1.7	1.4	1.1
Czechia	2.0	1.9	2.0	2.0	1.5	1.6	1.3	1.4	1.5
Estonia	2.7	2.2	1.9	2.1	2.5	1.9	1.5	1.6	2.4
Croatia	3.8	4.2	3.8	3.9	3.6	3.7	3.1	2.8	2.8
Cyprus	1.0	1.0	0.7	0.9	1.1	1.1	0.7	0.7	0.9
Latvia	3.5	3.2	3.0	3.1	3.1	2.3	2.3	2.1	2.8
Lithuania	2.9	2.7	2.7	3.1	2.9	3.0	2.5	2.1	2.0
Hungary	3.4	3.3	2.8	3.2	3.2	3.1	2.3	1.8	2.5
Malta	0.3	0.4	0.5	0.5	0.6	0.7	0.7	0.6	0.5
Poland	2.3	2.4	2.6	2.7	2.5	2.4	1.8	1.7	1.5
Romania	1.7	1.4	1.2	1.3	1.2	1.3	1.3	1.4	1.2
Slovenia	2.0	2.2	1.7	1.5	2.0	1.9	1.7	1.7	1.1
Slovakia	2.3	2.4	2.6	2.3	2.5	2.7	2.9	3.0	2.8

Source: Author's construction based on Eurostat data based on EU-SILC.

considering health was very bad in Croatia, in other new EU countries, the share of the evaluations was relatively stable.

Many academic publications note that income and changes in income are essential to maintaining social activities and a certain standard of living. For comparative analysis, median income is used. Median indicates that half of the population in the respective country has income as median or lower and half of the population in the respective country has income as median or more. This indicator is used because arithmetic means are significantly influenced, especially by significant income, often for part of the population. Median income in analysed new EU countries in the analysed period 2014–2022 is included in Table 13.10.

Table 13.10. Median Income (in EUR) in New EU Countries in 2014–2022.

Country	2014	2015	2016	2017	2018	2019	2020	2021	2022
Bulgaria	3,311	3,332	3,151	3,590	3,590	4,224	4,612	5,157	5,378
Czechia	7,622	7,423	7,838	8,282	9,088	9,995	10,627	10,625	12,146
Estonia	7,217	7,889	8,645	9,384	10,524	11,461	12,228	12,623	14,827
Croatia	5,225	5,453	5,726	6,210	6,659	7,306	7,892	8,061	8,760
Cyprus	14,400	13,793	14,020	14,497	15,336	16,215	16,704	16,686	17,856
Latvia	5,203	5,828	6,365	6,607	7,333	8,187	8,827	9,437	10,258
Lithuania	4,823	5,180	5,645	6,134	6,895	7,586	8,606	9,669	10,195
Hungary	4,512	4,556	4,768	4,988	5,424	5,852	6,478	6,619	6,975
Malta	12,808	13,551	13,617	14,522	14,781	15,354	16,240	17,036	18,155
Poland	5,336	5,556	5,884	5,945	6,574	7,124	8,022	8,297	8,946
Romania	2,155	2,315	2,448	2,742	3,284	3,851	4,267	4,830	5,512
Slovenia	11,909	12,332	12,327	12,713	13,244	14,067	14,774	15,415	16,544
Slovakia	6,809	6,930	6,951	7,183	7,462	8,119	8,703	8,473	8,819

Source: Author's construction based on Eurostat data based on EU-SILC.

Data indicate that median income increased in all analysed new EU countries from 2014 to 2022, with the most significant values for Malta, Cyprus, and Estonia and the lowest median income for Bulgaria and Romania. Fig. 13.1 shows the tendencies of changes – increase in median income in new EU countries from 2014 to 2022.

Data indicate that Cyprus had the highest median income among the analysed new EU countries in 2014–2022, Estonia had the most significant increase in the analysed period (with an average annual growth in the median by 898 EUR), and Slovakia had the lowest (with an average yearly increase in the median by 285 EUR). To compare those changes in detail, median income trends for all new EU countries were calculated. Data analysis results are included in Table 13.11.

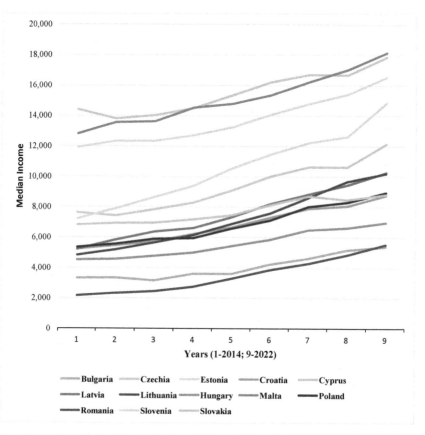

Fig. 13.1. Tendencies of Median Income in New EU Countries in 2014–2022.
Source: Author's construction based on Eurostat data based on EU-SILC (years 1-2014; 9-2022).

Labour Market, Human Capital and Migration

Table 13.11. Median Income Trends (in EUR) in New EU Countries in 2014–2022.

Country	Trend in 2014–2022	R^2
Bulgaria	$y = 288.32x + 2596.8$	0.8864
Czechia	$y = 705.48x + 3665.1$	0.9769
Estonia	$y = 898.08x + 6042.7$	0.9794
Croatia	$y = 456.53x + 4527.6$	0.985
Cyprus	$y = 493.15x + 13035$	0.8971
Latvia	$y = 625.85x + 4431.3$	0.9898
Lithuania	$y = 705.48x + 3665.1$	0.9769
Hungary	$y = 338.75x + 3880.9$	0.9658
Malta	$y = 632.02x + 11958$	0.9691
Poland	$y = 468.63x + 4510.6$	0.9597
Romania	$y = 428.67x + 1346$	0.9613
Slovenia	$y = 567.28x + 10866$	0.9435
Slovakia	$y = 285.15x + 6290.8$	0.9204

Source: Author's calculations based on Eurostat data based on EU-SILC.

Data indicate that the median income increase is related to better-educated persons, especially those active in adult education in the analysed new EU countries during the last decade.

Data on population changes in new EU countries indicate that the situation is quite different, as Table 13.12 indicates.

Data from Table 13.12 indicate that there are considerable differences in population changes in new EU countries: for some countries, there is a noticeable increase in the population (Czechia, Estonia, Cyprus, Malta, Slovenia, and Slovakia), but for many countries, there is a considerable decrease in population (Bulgaria, Latvia, Lithuania, Hungary, Poland, and Romania). To find more precise tendencies in all new EU countries, linear trends in population changes were calculated in the analyses of new EU countries in 2014–2022. The results of the data analysis are included in Table 13.13.

The countries with the highest population reduction, mainly due to the emigration to Western European countries, were Latvia, Bulgaria, Romania, Lithuania, Croatia, and Hungary. New EU countries Malta, Cyprus, Estonia, and Slovenia, during the period 2014–2022, experienced significant population growth. In the other countries – Slovakia and Poland – the changes were modest. Population migration exacerbates the social and economic challenges, as mainly young people emigrate. Countries from which the population migrates (donors) will exacerbate the challenges of an ageing population. Adult education and the *silver economy* deserve particular attention in these countries. Digitisation and robotics could solve some of the challenges of migration and ageing, but targeted measures are needed to use information technologies and AI. Cooperation between national governments, the EU, and businesses and the timely development of appropriate policies are required.

Table 13.12. Population in New EU Countries in 2014–2022.

Country	2014	2015	2016	2017	2018	2019	2020	2021	2022
Bulgaria	7,245,677	7,202,198	7,153,784	7,101,859	7,050,034	7,000,039	6,951,482	6,916,548	6,838,937
Czechia	10,512,419	10,538,275	10,553,843	10,578,820	10,610,055	10,649,800	10,693,939	10,494,836	10,516,707
Estonia	1,315,819	1,314,870	1,315,944	1,315,635	1,319,133	1,324,820	1,328,976	1,330,068	1,331,796
Croatia	4,246,809	4,225,316	4,190,669	4,154,213	4,105,493	4,076,246	4,058,165	4,036,355	3,862,305
Cyprus	858,000	847,008	848,319	854,802	864,236	875,899	888,005	896,007	904,705
Latvia	2,001,468	1,986,096	1,968,957	1,950,116	1,934,379	1,919,968	1,907,675	1,893,223	1,875,757
Lithuania	2,943,472	2,921,262	2,888,558	2,847,904	2,808,901	2,794,184	2,794,090	2,795,680	2,805,998
Hungary	9,877,365	9,855,571	9,830,485	9,797,561	9,778,371	9,772,756	9,769,526	9,730,772	9,689,010
Malta	429,424	439,691	450,415	460,297	475,701	493,559	514,564	516,100	520,971
Poland	38,017,856	38,005,614	37,967,209	37,972,964	37,976,687	37,972,812	37,958,138	37,840,001	37,654,247
Romania	19,947,311	19,870,647	19,760,585	19,643,949	19,533,481	19,414,458	19,328,838	19,201,662	19,042,455
Slovenia	2,061,085	2,062,874	2,064,188	2,065,895	2,066,880	2,080,908	2,095,861	2,108,977	2,107,180
Slovakia	5,415,949	5,421,349	5,426,252	5,435,343	5,443,120	5,450,421	5,457,873	5,459,781	5,434,712

Source: Author's construction based on Eurostat data.

Labour Market, Human Capital and Migration

Table 13.13. Trends of Population Changes in New EU Countries in 2014–2022.

Country	Trend in 2014–2022	R^2
Bulgaria	$y = -49,839x + 7E06$	0.9972
Czechia	$y = 3,966.8x + 1E07$	0.0259
Estonia	$y = 2,412.5x + 1E06$	0.8908
Croatia	$y = -40,798x + 4E06$	0.900
Cyprus	$y = 7,238.1x + 834585$	0.8623
Latvia	$y = -15,570x + 2E06$	0.9973
Lithuania	$y = -19,498x + 3E06$	0.8183
Hungary	$y = -21,242x + 1E07$	0.9608
Malta	$y = 12,616x + 414777$	0.9761
Poland	$y = -3,2826x + 4E07$	0.6122
Romania	$y = -111,989x + 2E07$	0.9959
Slovenia	$y = 6,684.1x + 2E06$	0.8651
Slovakia	$y = 4,477.8x + 5E06$	0.6112

Source: Author's calculations based on Eurostat data.

CONCLUSIONS

Demographic processes, such as an increase in the elderly population, require innovative solutions to retain or involve at least some of them in economic activities. This is reflected in many academic research results by scientists in different countries.

The European Commission (2023a) also calls for supporting healthy and active old age and contributing to society and the economy. Various EU countries have found and applied a range of approaches to this, including measures by the so-called *silver economy*. This is often related to the general development tendencies for adult education.

Success in human capital development is largely related to adult education policies, which are part of the silver economy. In recent years, interventions on digital issues have become particularly important, as the digital divide is a major obstacle to active involvement in economic activity.

Another issue to be addressed is the overall health situation of the population since the tendency towards low levels of health in some countries can gradually increase overall economic productivity.

National health-care expenditures are increasing in long-term forecasts. If in 2019 in the EU it was 6.6% of GDP, then forecasts show that in 2070, it may increase to 7.7% of GDP, in connection with demographic ageing (European Commission, 2021). Alongside this, the broader social situation implications cannot be disregarded since this is related to various risks of social exclusion of various target groups, which consequently may have an adverse impact on the economic activity of citizens and human capital capacity.

During the last decade, females have been much more active in adult education in all the countries analysed. The largest share of involvement in adult education has a statistically significant correlation with GDP growth. This is an essential implication for policymakers regarding the country's overall economic activity and human capital development.

Digitalisation currently reduces demand in the labour market for intermediate qualifications but temporarily increases demand for high-skilled workers. Therefore, the increase in qualifications through adult education and digitalisation correlates with the rise in income and GDP.

The employment of low-skilled workers is also slightly increasing, which provides additional opportunities for developing the silver economy. From a further perspective, however, an increase in automation and robotics is expected, which will require significant changes in the nature and social structure of work, and adaptation will be possible through adult education. Mutual assistance and support are of greater importance, mainly in addressing health problems.

Including all citizens in networks of cooperation, including through employment and education, is becoming more critical. The silver economy will increasingly perform social functions, ensuring the inclusion of older people in collaboration. The development of physical and virtual social networks facilitates the provision of social assistance and support and creates conditions for implementing UBI.

Countries with low health assessment levels (Latvia and Lithuania) should pay increased attention to citizens' involvement in adult education and social networks, as low self-assessment of health is related to an insufficient level of mutual assistance and active participation in the labour market.

REFERENCES

Aidukaite, J., & Blaziene, I. (2022). Longer working lives – What do they mean in practice – A case of the Baltic countries. *International Journal of Sociology and Social Policy*, *42*(5/6), 526–542. https://doi.org/10.1108/IJSSP-02-2021-0049

Barska, A., & Śnihur, J. (2017). Senior as a challenge for innovative enterprises. *Procedia Engineering*, *182*, 58–65. https://doi.org/10.1016/j.proeng.2017.03.115

Behmane, D., Rutitis, D., & Batraga, A. (2021). Conceptual framework for attracting foreign patients to health care services. *Eurasian Studies in Business and Economics*, *19*, 259–275. https://doi.org/10.1007/978-3-030-77438-7_16

Bogataj, D., Battini, D., Calzavara, M., & Persona, A. (2019). The ageing workforce challenge: Investments in collaborative robots or contribution to pension schemes, from the multi-echelon perspective. *International Journal of Production Economics*, *210*, 97–106. https://doi.org/10.1016/j.ijpe.2018.12.016

Bogataj, M., Bogataj, D., & Drobne, S. (2023). Planning and managing public housing stock in the silver economy. *International Journal of Production Economics*, *260*, 108848. https://doi.org/10.1016/j.ijpe.2023.108848

Bolton, R. N., McColl-Kennedy, J. R., Cheung, L., Gallan, A., Orsingher, C., Witell, L., & Zaki, M. (2018). Customer experience challenges: Bringing together digital, physical and social realms. *Journal of Service Management*, *29*(5), 776–808. https://doi.org/10.1108/JOSM-04-2018-0113

Borzaga, C., Salvatori, G., & Bodini, R. (2019). Social and solidarity economy and the future of work. *Journal of Entrepreneurship and Innovation in Emerging Economies*, *5*(1), 37–57. https://doi.org/10.1177/2393957518815300

Brante, I., & Sloka, B. (2022). Selection of companies for student involvement in work-based learning. *Research for Rural Development*, *37*, 143–149. https://doi.org/10.22616/rrd.28.2022.021

Buligina, I., & Sloka, B. (2013). Matching vocational training and labour market demands – The opinion of public administrations. *Economic Research-Ekonomska Istrazivanja, 26*, 299–310. https://doi.org/10.1080/1331677X.2013.11517653

Buligina, I., & Sloka, B. (2019). Development of strategic partnerships for work-based learning. *Eurasian Business Perspectives, 10*(1), 199–210. https://doi.org/10.1007/978-3-030-11872-3_13

Buligina, I., & Sloka, B. (2022). Importance of digital skills for competitive labour force challenges in work-based learning in Latvia. In J. Stankevičienė & V. Skvarciany (Eds.), *Proceedings of 12th International conference of business and management 2022*, Vilnius Gediminas Technical University (pp. 634–640). https://doi.org/10.3846/bm.2022.855

Bruin, M., Tutlys, V., Ümarik, M., Loogma, K., Kaminskiené, L., Bentsalo, I., Väljataga, T., Sloka, B., & Buligina, I. (2023). Participation and learning in Vocational education and training – A cross-national analysis of the perspectives of youth at risk for social exclusion. *Journal of Vocational Education & Training.* https://doi.org/10.1080/13636820.2023.2283745

Cirella, G. T., Bąk, M., Kozlak, A., Pawłowska, B., & Borkowski, P. (2019). Transport innovations for elderly people. *Research in Transportation Business & Management, 30*, 100381. https://doi.org/10.1016/j.rtbm.2019.100381

Crossen-White, H. L., Hemingway, A., & Ladkin, A. (2020). The application of social innovation as it relates to older people and the implications for future policymaking: A scoping review. *Quality in Ageing and Older Adults, 21*(3), 143–153. https://doi.org/10.1108/QAOA-04-2020-0014

Csoba, J., & Ladancsik, T. (2023). The silver generation in the labor market: Work and time management of the 65+ age group in North-Eastern Hungary. *Journal of Women and Aging, 35*(4), 319–342. https://doi.org/10.1080/08952841.2022.2048591

Dzelme, J. (2023). Global cognition and modelling tasks in arts and education. In L. Daniela Riga (Ed.), *Proceedings of scientific papers. Human, technologies and quality of education* (pp. 769–782). University of Latvia. https://doi.org/10.22364/htqe.2023

European Commission. (2018). *The silver economy – Final report* (p. 55). Publications Office of the European Union. https://doi.org/10.2759/640936

European Commission. (2021). *The 2021 ageing report – Economic & budgetary projections for the EU member states (2019–2070)* (375 pp.). Publications Office of the European Union, Directorate-General for Economic and Financial Affairs. https://doi.org/10.2765/84455 and https://data.europa.eu/doi/10.2765/84455

European Commission. (2023a). *Proposal for a joint employment report from the Commission and the Council.* COM (2023a) 904, CELEX number i 52023DC0904, 21-11-2023.

European Commission. (2023b). *Communication from the Commission: Demographic change in Europe: A toolbox for action.* COM (2023b) 577 final.

Finn, R. L., & Wright, D. (2011). Mechanisms for stakeholder co-ordination in ICT and ageing. *Journal of Information, Communication and Ethics in Society, 9*(4), 265–286. https://doi.org/10.1108/14779961111191066

Grace, K., Stein-Perlman, Z., Weinstein-Raun, B., & Salvatier, J. (2022, August 3). *2022 Expert survey on progress in AI.* AI impacts. https://aiimpacts.org/2022-expert-survey-on-progress-in-ai/

Grace, K., Stewart, H., Sandkuhler, J. F., Thomas, S., Weinstein-Raum, B., & Bruner, J. (2024). *Thousands of AI authors on the future of AI.* Cornel University. https://doi.org/10.48550/arXiv.2401.02843

Krekula, C., Arvidson, M., Heikkinen, S., Henriksson, A., & Olsson, E. (2017). On gray dancing: Constructions of age-normality through choreography and temporal codes. *Journal of Aging Studies, 42*, 38–45. https://doi.org/10.1016/j.jaging.2017.07.001

Labit, A., & Dubost, N. (2016). Housing and ageing in France and Germany: The intergenerational solution. *Housing, Care and Support, 19*(2), 45–54. https://doi.org/10.1108/HCS-08-2016-0007

Liutkevičius, M., & Yahia, S. B. (2022). Research roadmap for designing a virtual competence assistant for the European labour market. *Procedia Computer Science, 207*, 2404–2413. https://doi.org/10.1016/j.procs.2022.09.299

Marcucci, G., Ciarapica, F., Poler, R., & Sanchis, R. (2021). A bibliometric analysis of the emerging trends in silver economy. *IFAC-PapersOnLine, 54*(1), 936–941. https://doi.org/10.1016/j.ifacol.2021.08.190

Mason, M. C., Zamparo, G., & Pauluzzo, R. (2023). Amidst technology, environment and human touch. Understanding elderly customers in the bank retail sector. *International Journal of Bank Marketing, 41*(3), 572–600. https://doi.org/10.1108/IJBM-06-2022-0256

Meiners, N. (2014). Economics of ageing: Research area and perspectives. *Quality in Ageing and Older Adults, 15*(2), 63–75. https://doi.org/10.1108/QAOA-07-2013-0020

Pavia, L., Grima, S., Romanova, I., & Spiteri, J. V. (2021). Fine art insurance policies and risk perceptions: The case of Malta. *Journal of Risk and Financial Management, 14*(2), 66. https://doi.org/10.3390/jrfm14020066

Poland, F. (2014). Older people as producers, consumers and decision makers. *Quality in Ageing and Older Adults, 15*(2). https://doi.org/10.1108/QAOA-04-2014-0004

Salaj, A. T., & Senior, C. (2021). Co-creators of wellbeing – Smarter engagement of older residents. *IFAC-PapersOnLine, 54*(13), 669–674. https://doi.org/10.1016/j.ifacol.2021.10.528

Salkovska, J., Batraga, A., Kaibe, L., & Kellerte, K. (2023). Use of artificial intelligence in the digital marketing strategy of Latvian companies. *Lecture Notes in Networks and Systems, 694*, 785–797. https://doi.org/10.1007/978-981-99-3091-3_64

Sloka, B., & Angena, A. (2022a). Challenges for health care financing in Latvia – Comparison with other Baltic countries. *Journal of Service, Innovation and Sustainable Development, 3*(2), 143–152. https://doi.org/10.33168/SISD.2022.0210

Sloka, B., & Angena, A. (2022b). Do health self-evaluations in urban and rural areas in Latvia differ? *Humanities and Social Sciences. Latvia, 30*(1, 2), 143–149. https://doi.org/10.22364/hssl.30.10

Sloka, B., & Angena, A. (2022c). Tendencies in health self-evaluation in Latvia. *Balkan and Near Eastern Journal of Social Sciences, 8*(3), 124–128. https://www.ibaness.org/bnejss-archive/2022-08-03

Sloka, B., Buligina, I., Tora, G., Dzelme, J., Brante, I., Liepina, K., & Angena, A. (2023). Good practice of support to students at risk in vocational education. In C. Nägele, N. Kersh, & B. E. Stalder (Eds.), *Trends in vocational education and training research, Vol. VI. Proceedings of the European conference on educational research (ECER), vocational education and training network (VETNET)* (pp. 59–66). Glasgow. https://doi.org/10.5281/10.5281/zenodo.8269449

Sloka, B., Jekabsone, I., Cipane, K., & Vasina, S. A. (2019). Income differences in regions of Latvia – Problems and challenges. *European Integration Studies, 13*, 52–60. https://doi.org/10.5755/j01.eis.0.13.23562

Sloka, B., Tora, G., Buligina, I., & Dzelme, J. (2022). Role of education in income inequalities in Latvia. *Research for Rural Development, 37*, 328–334. https://doi.org/10.22616/rrd.28.2022.047

Solovjova, I., & Romānova, I. (2020). Bank reliability assessment model: Case of Latvia. *Eurasian Studies in Business and Economics, 12*(2), 285–298. https://doi.org/10.1007/978-3-030-35051-2_19

Sowa-Kofta, A., Marcinkowska, I., Ruzik-Sierdzińska, A., Mackevičiūtė, R. (2021). *Ageing policies – Access to services in different member states* (133 pp.). Publication for the Committee on Employment and Social Affairs, Policy Department for Economic, Scientific and Quality of Life Policies, European Parliament. https://doi.org/10.2861/568600

Tūtlys, V., Buligina, I., Dzelme, J., Gedvilienė, K., Loogma, K., Sloka, B., Tikkanen, T., Tora, G., Vaitkute, L., Valjataga, T., & Ümarik, M. (2022). VET ecosystems and labour market integration of at-risk youth in the Baltic countries: Implications of Baltic neoliberalism. *Education and Training, 64*(2), 190–213.

van Zaalen, Y., McDonnell, M., Mikołajczyk, B., Buttigieg, S., Requena, M. d. C., & Holtkamp, F. (2018). Technology implementation in delivery of healthcare to older people: How can the least voiced in society be heard? *Journal of Enabling Technologies, 12*(2), 76–90. https://doi.org/10.1108/JET-10-2017-0041

Vinichenko, M. V., Rybakova, M. V., Chulanova, O. L., Barkov, S. A., Makushkin, S. A., & Karacsony, P. (2021). Views on working with information in a semi-digital society: Its possibility to develop as open innovation culture. *Journal of Open Innovation: Technology, Market, and Complexity, 7*(2), 160. https://doi.org/10.3390/joitmc7020160

Walczak, R., Piekut, M., Kludacz-Alessandri, M., Sloka, B., Šimanskiene, L., & Paas, T. (2018). Health care spending structures in Poland, Latvia, Lithuania and Estonia over the years as compared to other EU countries. *Foundations of Management, 10*(1), 45–58. https://doi.org/10.2478/fman-2018-0005

Wiktorowicz, J. (2017). Competencies as a factor of economic deactivation: Application of exploratory factor analysis. *International Journal of Social Economics*, *44*(5), 605–619. https://doi.org/10.1108/IJSE-08-2015-0198

Zgonec, S. (2021). Mobile apps supporting people with dementia and their carers: Literature review and research agenda. *IFAC-PapersOnLine*, *54*(13), 663–668. https://doi.org/10.1016/j.ifacol.2021.10.527

CHAPTER 14

FUTURE CHALLENGES ON THE WAY TO THE FULL CONVERGENCE

Andrea Imperia[a] and Loredana Mirra[b]

[a]Sapienza University of Rome, Italy
[b]Tor Vergata University of Rome, Italy

ABSTRACT

Purpose: *This chapter aims to understand what convergence means and why it is considered so crucial for the full admission of a state to the European Economic and Monetary Union. Doing this will help understand what considerations of economic theory it is based on.*

Need for study: *To look into the Maastricht architecture, to point out its fragility during the last crises and the capability of the reforms adopted to reduce it, and to make European monetary union (EMU) more attractive for European Union (EU) members still outside it.*

Methodology: *The experiences of some countries that joined the EU from 2004 to today will be analysed to propose a synthesis from both a qualitative and quantitative perspective that highlights the paths taken by individual states and the processes currently underway.*

Findings: *The fragility of the EMU architecture became apparent during recent crises. The European Central Bank (ECB) took on new functions, and it became necessary to establish new financial institutions to operate beyond the Maastricht Treaty. Public budget control rules were suspended during the pandemic crisis, and a one-off transfer among states (Next-Generation EU)*

Economic Development and Resilience by EU Member States
Contemporary Studies in Economic and Financial Analysis, Volume 115, 249–272
Copyright © 2025 by Andrea Imperia and Loredana Mirra
Published under exclusive licence by Emerald Publishing Limited
ISSN: 1569-3759/doi:10.1108/S1569-375920240000115014

was adopted. This was an important precedent, but it was still far from the redistribution among states necessary for a political union.

Practical implications: *In Maastricht architecture, there is no room for what is needed most by old and new members, that is, coordinated fiscal policies to stimulate aggregate demand, ensuring persistently high employment and production levels. The paths towards the welfare of European citizens, the increase in the sense of belonging to the same community, attracting new members and supporting financial stability all "converge" on the denominator of the Maastricht fiscal parameters.*

Keywords: Central and Eastern countries; economic convergence; European Economic and Monetary Union; euro; European political unification process; financial stability; Maastricht parameters

JEL classifications: E5; E6; F3; G01

1. INTRODUCTION

The European monetary union (EMU) is a political construction. Not in the 20th-century sense of the term, often repeated and now almost ritual, according to which it would represent a crucial step towards political union and would thus be functional to the noble goal of the founding fathers of the European integration process to definitively end the very possibility of a war on the continent (Schuman, 1950). The thesis that monetary union could act as a catalyst for political union, criticised by some observers even before the process was concluded (Pivetti, 1998), is, in the current context, even more difficult to sustain a quarter of a century after the introduction of the euro. Two world-scale crises have endangered the survival of the EMU, showing the inadequacy of the financial architecture created at Maastricht, its rules, and the national and supranational response capabilities they allow. One of its most important members, the United Kingdom, has even left the European Union (EU) and regained its full political and economic sovereignty. The unification process among more than double the number of countries is far from even being defined. A war that was unimaginable just a few years ago dangerously presses on the EU's borders, has pushed back political relations and economic cooperation with the Russian Federation to the times of the Cold War, and has created new dangerous international polarisations that risk opening a new phase of political and economic subordination for the EU. It has generated tensions between European states and posed new global political, economic, and financial problems. Since the second post-war period, there has perhaps not been a period in which a political union among European countries would have been more necessary, urgent, and unrealistic.

The EMU is a political construction in a weaker and less ideal sense than that inherent in its supposed catalytic function. However, it is closer to reality and, for this reason, more significant. It is so because of the way it was achieved. Each of its characteristics is the result of choices that could have led in entirely different directions: the timing for the liberalisation of international capital movements, the role and functions assigned to the European Central Bank (ECB), the economic and legislative requirements for joining and remaining into the union; the possibility of being admitted and remaining members in exception to those requirements.

It is not difficult to give content to these statements. Constraints on international capital movements were eliminated at the beginning of the monetary unification process, even before exchange rates between the different currencies were fixed (Bakker, 2012). When this occurred, the monetary sovereignty of individual countries (considered to be the ability to set the interest rate to stimulate employment and production independently and contain the growth of national public debt) was consequently lost (Obstfeld et al., 2005). The fiscal independence of individual countries was also heavily limited, even before and autonomously, from the imposition of the public finance constraints provided by the Maastricht Treaty and its protocols. Full capital liberalisation indeed imposed strong constraints on the levels and composition of the tax revenues of individual countries not to incentivise capital outflows in search of more favourable conditions. Fiscal policy was thus deprived from the beginning of the possibility of being effective, playing its redistributive function, and stimulating economic activity (Pivetti, 1998).

As for the political nature of the choice of the central bank model, it is enough to recall that at the time of the Maastricht Treaty, the so-called Anglo-French model prevailed in almost all European countries. According to it, a multiplicity of objectives considered of equal importance were assigned to the central bank: a high level of employment, the stabilisation of the economic cycle, and financial and price stability. In the German model – adopted for the ECB – price stability is instead considered the fundamental objective, prevailing over all others. This does not exclude the fact that the ECB can pursue other objectives (including high employment), but only if the measures to be adopted do not interfere with the goal of price stability. Moreover, in the Anglo-French model, the central bank is subordinated to political power. All monetary policy decisions must be approved by the government. In the German model, on the contrary, the central bank is independent of political power. It is extremely significant that at this point, it was even decided to go beyond the German model by providing the ECB with a degree of independence higher than that of the Bundesbank. In fact, according to the German constitution, decisions about the exchange rate are a prerogative of the federal government; government representatives have the right to participate in the meetings of the bank's council, to have items included on the agenda and request the suspension of resolutions (Pivetti, 1995). Moreover, the Bundesbank's statute can be amended by the ordinary parliamentary majorities, while amending the ECB's statute would require a revision of the Maastricht Treaty to be unanimously approved by the countries of the EU, including those outside the euro area (De Grauwe, 2022).

It has been observed that the adoption of the German model of the central bank is due to two causes: the hegemony conquered by monetarism over Keynesian theory in the second half of the last century (the so-called monetarist counterrevolution) and the predominant role played by Germany in the process of forming the EMU (De Grauwe, 2022). This explains both the centrality of the price stability objective and the independence of the ECB from political power. If monetary policy cannot permanently influence real variables, the role of the central bank is just to control the inflation rate. To perform this function best, it has to act independently from political power since this, by setting short-term objectives to manage consensus, would inevitably push for the adoption of expansionary measures that could only have, in the long run, inflationary effects. Since monetary policy has, once short-term adjustments have already occurred, no effect on real variables, when it is correctly oriented towards price stability, it becomes a technical function. The main difference between monetary and political choices relies exactly on this point. This is why they must always be subject, in a democratic country, to voters' judgement. No economic policy measures that affect real variables (the population's living conditions, like employment levels, production, and income distribution) can be implemented in a democratic state by an authority that does not respond to the electorate. For the dominant theoretical approach, monetary policy is not among these, at least when long-term effects are considered. On the contrary, for those who do not share the view of money neutrality, a central bank independent from political power appears to be an institution lacking the necessary democratic legitimacy. The hegemonic role of Germany in negotiations for the EMU helps to understand the successful attempt to make the ECB even more bounded to price stability and more independent from political power than the Bundesbank was.

Even the timing, phases, and requirements for joining the EMU provided by the Maastricht Treaty (which we will discuss shortly) were not without alternatives (see Werner, 1970).[1] It is worth recalling that the German monetary union was realised in six months without any convergence criteria. If such a solution was never even discussed for European countries, it is because it would have required net transfers in favour of the economically weaker countries, the extent of which was not conceivable without the conclusion of a political unification project.

2. THE MAASTRICHT CONVERGENCE CRITERIA

The path chosen for the realisation of the EMU was outlined by the Delors Report and the successive Maastricht Treaty, which entered into force in 1993 after a problematic ratification process by the EU countries.[2] The requirements that each country must fulfil to adopt the euro according to this Treaty (and its protocols) are well known. If we deal with them, it is mainly because of their importance in analysing the convergence processes of the countries that entered the EU in 2004 and 2007.

There are two perspectives from which the Maastricht parameters can be examined: the first, qualitative, concerns the function they have in ensuring the sustainability of euro adoption and the pursuit of the price stability objective assigned to the ECB; the second, quantitative, concerns the reasons that led to choosing specific threshold values and not others. We will focus mainly on the first aspect, which is more relevant to our analysis, limiting ourselves to some brief considerations about the second.

The first requirement is to keep inflation close to that of the countries with the best results within the euro area (not higher than the simple arithmetic average of the three lowest inflation rates, increased by 1.5 percentage points). The second consists of participating in the European exchange rate mechanism (ERM II) for at least two years without devaluation. Considering the two parameters together, the logic behind them emerges clearly. The euro is equivalent to a fixed exchange rate regime among the currencies of the participating countries, without fluctuations and adjustments in parities. An inflation rate that deviated upwards compared to that of other countries would cause current account deficits that would be incompatible in the long run with the adoption of the single currency. Maintaining the exchange rate with the euro within a fluctuation band for a sufficiently long period and having at the same time an inflation rate close to that of the countries with the best inflationary results is thus an index of the sustainability of adopting the euro. The third parameter relates to the nominal interest rate on long-term securities (10 years): it must not exceed by more than 2% the average of the rates of the three member states with the best results in terms of price stability. It responds to the same logic as the previous two parameters. In a fixed exchange rate regime (or a single currency) and perfect capital mobility, the domestic interest rate equals the sum of the foreign interest rate and risk premium. A divergence between the foreign and domestic interest rates is thus an index of the confidence of the financial markets about the adoption of the single currency.

Finally, we come to the requirements related to public finance, which is probably the most controversial among economists (Buiter, 2005; De Grauwe & Schnabl, 2005; Pasinetti, 1998). Since they are mathematically connected, we will deal with them jointly. In order to adopt the euro, the national public debt-to-gross domestic product (GDP) and the public deficit-to-GDP ratios must not exceed 60% and 3%, respectively. There is widespread consensus that the first threshold was chosen because it was close to the average of the values assumed in European countries at the time of the negotiations. Politics played a fundamental role: the 60% parameter was particularly convenient for the two most powerful countries, France and Germany. Because their debt-to-GDP ratios were close to that level, their fiscal policies were not immediately affected. Other countries etc. The most accredited viewpoint for the choice of a 3% threshold is that such a value is consistent with maintaining the debt-to-GDP ratio at 60% under the assumption of a nominal GDP growth rate of 5% (the average value of the time),[3] although there are alternative explanations.[4] Even among politicians who played a central role in the negotiations, there is broad consensus that neither of the two values can be justified by economic theory.[5]

The hostility for public spending in deficit and its consequent accumulation into public debt stock arises from the thesis that the economic system tends spontaneously towards full employment or, in more modern terms, towards the natural rate of unemployment and the corresponding potential output. In such conditions, public expenditure adds to that of the private sector, which can already absorb the full-employment production and thus generate an increase in the inflation rate, contrary to price stability, the primary objective of the ECB. According to the dominant theoretical approach, there is a second negative aspect of the public deficit. It partially absorbs the savings the private sector would have fully invested. Thus, the part of public spending financed in deficit not oriented towards investments will generate a reduction in the overall investment and the growth rate; the corresponding public debt stock accumulated in this way can, therefore, be suggestively interpreted, as the savings subtracted from the private sector over time, hence a measure of the investments that the latter would have otherwise realised. The reduction of the public debt stock achievable by austerity policies would free part of that savings, allowing it to flow back to its original function. It is worth recalling that for any economist who does not consider full employment the normal condition of the economic system, the interpretations of deficit spending and public debt we have just indicated appear meaningless (Ciccone, 2013).

We began this chapter by stating that the EMU is a political construction, meaning that its characteristics could be completely different. The choice to assign the ECB price stability as its primary objective, prevailing over all others, was not without alternatives, nor was it the decision to give it an unprecedented degree of independence from political power. Also, the preventive, total liberalisation of capital movements with the consequences we have described for the national economic policies was not a necessary outcome of the negotiation. Finally, it was not mandatory to impose strong constraints on the national fiscal policies of individual countries without assuming their traditional objectives at the central level.

So far, we have cited the monetarist counterrevolution and the hegemonic role of Germany in European negotiations to explain the causes that led to the current architecture of the EMU. However, as important as they may seem, they are insufficient to explain such a crucial political process. From a historical point of view, it is possible to say that the main causal relationship between economic theory and political action often proceeds from the latter to the former.[6] Politics, as the holder of the power to define and pursue general objectives, selects the economic theory that best fits its vision.

Once the primacy of politics over economic theory in the construction of the EMU has been recognised, the thesis of the decisive role of German hegemony becomes less convincing. Because of profoundly different alternatives, it would have been impossible, even for a powerful country like Germany, to impose its vision on all the others without the consensus, at that historical moment, of the hegemonic political classes and economic elites in Europe. The origin of the European architecture, as we have described it, is therefore not to be found in the role of this or that country in the negotiations, even though the attempt of Germany and France to promote and defend their national interests was undoubtedly significant. Instead, the adherence of the hegemonic classes of all the European countries to the project and their ability to create popular consensus around it can be considered the crucial cause. A project that consciously excluded the very possibility of pursuing the objectives of full employment and distributive equity that would have sharply shifted the action of political and monetary institutions from pursuing the welfare of the working classes to promoting national

Future Challenges on the Way to the Full Convergence

economic competitiveness. A project, in summary, that would impose severe discipline on European working classes, including those of the hegemonic countries, in the name of the national interest and promise of future increases in well-being.

3. THE EMU ARCHITECTURE AND THE CRISES

Over the last 15 years, the EMU faced severe economic and financial crises of global dimensions: the recession that began in the United States in 2007, largely unforeseen by almost all economists (Imperia & Maffeo, 2013); the European banking system crisis[7]; the Eurozone sovereign debt crisis; finally, the COVID-19 pandemic crisis (Pochet, 2022). The measures adopted to address these crises are clear evidence of what many economists theorised about the fragility of the EMU architecture. Not for their extraordinariness, since similar measures were necessary in many countries, but for their unprecedented nature, in several respects: because they required the ECB to exercise functions never assumed before, whose compatibility with the Treaties has been heavily questioned (as in the case of the Quantitative Easing programme and the more recent Public Sector Purchase Program)[8]; or because they led to the creation of new institutions capable of operating outside the constraints imposed by the treaties (as in the case of the European stability mechanism, ESM); or, finally, because they required the suspension of public budget control rules (Fiscal Compact) and the adoption of centrally coordinated stimulus policies (next-generation EU (NGEU)).

It is beyond the scope of this work to reconstruct, even summarily, the origin of the 2007 crisis.[9] It will suffice to remember that the severe difficulties of the American financial system were at the origin of the European banking crisis and that this, through the worsening of public finances due to the recession and the bailout plans implemented in many countries, was among the main causes of the sovereign debt crisis.[10] More important for our purposes is to highlight that the ECB, which for the first 10 years oriented monetary policy to the control of the short-term interest rate, assumed for the first time the function of lender of last resort (Praet, 2016), promptly to provide liquidity to the European banking system (Trichet, 2009), slowly and with many constraints to help governments.

In July 2012, during the so-called sovereign debt crisis, ECB President Mario Draghi announced that the bank was ready, within its mandate, to do whatever it takes to preserve the euro. In September of the same year, the ECB materialised Draghi's announcement, launching the Outright Monetary Transactions (OMT) programme with which it committed to making unlimited purchases of state securities on the secondary markets, thus providing liquidity to holders (not directly to states, an operation expressly prohibited by the Treaties).[11] In this way, the ECB declared, albeit preferring less explicit terminology, to assume the role of lender of last resort also on the public securities markets, guaranteeing the holders reimbursement at maturity. The effect on interest rates was extremely rapid. Between 2012 and 2013, despite no significant changes in debt-to-GDP ratios nor in the external indebtedness of the countries in greater difficulty, the differentials of interest rates on 10-year securities decreased drastically

(De Grauwe & Ji, 2013). To give a significant example, the spread of Greece on 10 years securities went in six months from over 25% to less than 10%. This happened without implementing the OMT programme: the guarantee of total reimbursement of public securities at maturity provided by the ECB was sufficient.

It is important to emphasise that the innovative nature of the OMT programme is strongly limited by its conditionality. If a country requests its activation (which has not yet happened), it must implement a fiscal austerity programme supervised by the ESM. This financial institution was created by European countries under private law, operational since 2012, during the sovereign debt crisis, to which all EMU members must adhere.[12] Regardless of the OMT programme, the ESM provides financial assistance to member countries that request it, setting the conditions for the fiscal policies they must respect. It is essential to clarify that the scope of the ESM is different from that of the ECB, as the ESM can carry out operations prohibited to the ECB by the Treaties, including the direct purchase of public debt securities (the monetisation of public deficit).

The OMT can be activated if a country in difficulty requests it, provided it accepts fiscal austerity measures. This characteristic is difficult to understand in the framework of European solidarity. As the interventions of the International Monetary Fund (IMF) have demonstrated, similar measures have significant social costs: they worsen the recession, increase unemployment, and through the reduction of tax revenues can even accentuate a country's solvency problems. This usually provokes a deep hostility towards the institution that imposes it and popular and political reactions that the EU should carefully avoid. Moreover, if the OMT programme or financial assistance provided by the ESM were activated for a country large enough to endanger the euro's very survival, conditionality would lose much of its credibility (Cesaratto, 2019).

At the beginning of 2015, five years after the major countries' central banks took similar measures, and when the inflation rate of the euro area became negative, the ECB started a massive programme of purchases on the secondary markets (known as quantitative easing, QE) aimed mainly, but not exclusively, at the public debt securities of European countries.[13] The goal was twofold: on the one hand, to provide liquidity to the economic system to stimulate aggregate demand and bring the inflation rate close to the 2% target; on the other hand, to alleviate the situation of public finance of some European countries, both through the reduction of interest rates caused by the increase in the demand for securities and through a second, slightly more complex mechanism. When the central bank purchases public debt securities, the government that issued them pays interest to it; since the central bank typically returns the interest received to the government, that programme had a second significant effect on public finances. If the purchases had been made directly by the ECB, there would have been the possibility of fiscal transfers among countries. To minimise such a possibility, in order to overcome the opposition of Finland, Germany, and the Netherlands, the purchase programme was organised in the following way. Each central bank purchased exclusively public debt securities of its own country and maintained 80% of them on its own balance sheet. Therefore, only the interest on the remaining 20%, transferred to the ECB, could generate net transfers (De Grauwe, 2022).

In order to face the severity of the crises, the ECB was able to follow unprecedented paths (albeit absolutely normal for other central banks) to which the overcoming of the most acute problems of the European financial system is due. The so-called unconventional measures, nothing more than purchases of securities on the secondary markets, exceptional for the amounts, not for their nature, are now part of the monetary policy instruments that the ECB can use. It has assumed, albeit not without controversies, the role of lender of last resort. This undoubtedly represents a step forward to face crises that hit the entire financial system, not to stimulate employment and activity levels under ordinary conditions. If such objectives were assigned to the ECB, it would assume a role similar to that of the Federal Reserve Bank for the United States.

After 30 years, the 60% and 3% thresholds still have a pivotal role in the governance of national public finance. Initially envisaged as a condition for the adoption of the euro – still valid for candidate countries – they were included in the Stability and Growth Pact (SGP) of 1997, strongly supported by Germany (and France) to bind the public finances of the countries already members of the EMU. Since their introduction, they have not been challenged. It is worth remembering that France and Germany, in 2005, instead of being sanctioned for their excessive deficit, secured a favorable change in the SGP rules despite the objections of smaller, fiscally responsible countries. The two parameters were not questioned during the 2010-13 revisions of the SGP, all oriented towards a progressive tightening of fiscal discipline. They were confirmed in the very recent agreement to modify economic governance (Council of Europe, 2024), which at the time of writing is still in the process of final approval. It requires an annual correction of at least one percentage point of GDP for 4–7 years if the debt-to-GDP ratio exceeds 90% and 0.5 percentage points in case it is between 60% and 90%. This is a step forward compared to the previous obligation to reduce the differential by 1/20 every year with the reference value of 60%. However, it is nothing new for those who expected a real reform of European fiscal governance.

Finally, we come to the NGEU plan introduced to counter the negative effects of the COVID-19 pandemic crisis. Supported by France, Italy, and Spain, it was approved in July 2020 thanks to the decisive support of Angela Merkel, which allowed overcoming the opposition of several countries (Austria, Denmark, Finland, Sweden, and especially the Netherlands). It has a total value of 750 billion euros, of which 390 are non-repayable grants and 360 (at most) are very long-term loans at particularly low-interest rates.

Some consider the NGEU plan a first important step towards the centralisation of fiscal policy and, therefore, towards the completion of the EMU that is now supported even by important personalities of the financial sector. Two reasons support such optimism: the plan is financed by European public securities; resources have been distributed according to the needs of the states hit by the pandemic. Indeed, such hopes appear premature. The plan is undoubtedly an important precedent, but it realises one-off transfers, whose amount appears small compared to those necessary for the redistributive function among different states that a central budget would be called to perform. Such a function would require centralising a significant part of the European countries' tax revenues and public spending, hence necessarily realising a political union.

Is this a realistic perspective? The willingness to make income transfers, for the sacrifices they imply, requires a deep sense of belonging to a single community, a social perimeter defined by centuries of history, speaking the same language, and having common culture and traditions. Sometimes, this is not even enough, as hostilities between regions of the same country demonstrate it. Such a spirit is difficult to conceive for citizens of countries whose history is characterised by deep rivalries and bloody conflicts, where the most widespread language, paradoxically, is that of a country that has chosen to leave that community. Even without the policy of progressive enlargements, which increases economic and cultural heterogeneity, the sense of belonging to the EU remains primarily dominant and is on the verge of being overwhelmed by the national spirit.[14]

3. THE CONVERGENCE PROCESS IN CENTRAL AND EASTERN EUROPE

During the last 20 years, 13 new countries joined the EU (in 2004: Cyprus, the Czech Republic, Estonia, Hungary, Latvia, Lithuania, Malta, Poland, Slovakia, Slovenia; in 2007: Bulgaria, Romania; in 2013: Croatia). However, only eight fulfilled the Maastricht criteria and adopted the European common currency. Some of them, Cyprus, Malta, Slovakia, and Slovenia, were in more suitable conditions from the outset and could adopt the euro rapidly. Other countries that had to make significant adjustments did so over a more extended period, like Estonia, Latvia, Lithuania, and Croatia. The latter joined the eurozone in 2023, precisely a decade after entering the EU. Hence, after a period ranging from 14 to 20 years, the enlargement of the euro area is still an ongoing and unfinished process. Five Central and Eastern European (CEE) countries (Bulgaria, the Czech Republic, Hungary, Poland, Romania) are still outside the eurozone.

After the pandemic crisis, the declining interest in the enlargement process has regained momentum, returning to the centre of the European debate. Bulgaria and Romania are displaying a significant commitment to adopting the euro. Conversely, three of the four Visegrad countries – the Czech Republic, Hungary, and Poland (from now on V3 countries) – each influenced by specific monetary and political factors, are deferring the decision to leave their national currencies. For these three countries, the delay in leaving a floating currency regime is not only a matter of incomplete attainment of the Maastricht Treaty target, as we will see later in this section.

Croatia and Bulgaria were the last countries to enter the ERM II in July 2020, during the economic crisis caused by the coronavirus pandemic.

It is interesting to analyse the whole path towards convergence for the 13 countries we have introduced, looking at the possible differences between those already in the eurozone (in-EA countries) and those committed to entering as soon as they fulfil the convergence criteria (non-EA). To this aim, Tables 14.1 and 14.2 allow for an overall view and a glance analysis of the path towards the convergence exploiting information from the ECB convergence reports from 2004 to 2022.

Future Challenges on the Way to the Full Convergence

Table 14.1. Convergence Criteria Fulfilment for Countries in the Euro Area (in-EA); 2004–2022.

	2004	2006	2007	2008	2010	2012	2013	2014	2016	2018	2020	2022
Price stability												
Croatia								F	F	F	F	F
Cyprus	F	F	F									
Estonia	F	F		F	F							
Latvia	NO	F		NO	F		F					
Lithuania	F	F		NO				F				
Malta	NO	NO	F									
Slovakia	NO	NO		F								
Slovenia	NO	F										
Long-term interest rate												
Croatia								F	F	F	F	F
Cyprus	NO	F	F									
Estonia												
Latvia	NO	F		F	NO	F	F					
Lithuania	F	F		F		F		F				
Malta	F	F	F									
Slovakia	NO	F		F								
Slovenia	NO	F										
Deficit-to-GDP												
Croatia								NO	NO	F	F	F
Cyprus	NO	F	F									
Estonia	F	F		F	F							
Latvia	F	F		F	NO	NO	F					
Lithuania	F	F		NO	NO	NO		F				
Malta	NO	NO	F									
Slovakia	NO	NO		F								
Slovenia	F	F										
Debt-to-GDP												
Croatia								NO	NO	NO		NO
Cyprus	NO	NO	NO									
Estonia	F	F		F	F							
Latvia	F	F		F	F	F	F					
Lithuania	F	F		F	F	F		F				
Malta	NO	NO	NO									
Slovakia	F	F		F								
Slovenia	F	F										
Exchange rate	In ERM II from:											
Croatia	July 2020											
Cyprus	May 2005											
Estonia	June 2004											
Latvia	May 2005											
Lithuania	June 2004											
Malta	May 2005											
Slovakia	November 2005											
Slovenia	June 2004											

Source: ECB Convergence Reports (European Central Bank, 2004, 2006, 2007, 2008, 2010, 2012, 2013, 2014, 2016, 2018, 2020, 2022); F = fulfilled; NO = not fulfilled; and empty cell = data not in the report or country out of EU or already in EA.

Table 14.2. Convergence Criteria Fulfilment for Countries Still Outside the Euro Area (Non-EA), 2004–2022.

	2004	2006	2008	2010	2012	2014	2016	2018	2020	2022
Price stability										
Bulgaria			NO	NO	F	F	F	F	NO	NO
Czech Republic	F	F	NO	F	NO	F	F	F	NO	NO
Hungary	NO	NO	NO	NO	NO	F	F	NO	NO	NO
Poland	NO	NO	F	F	NO	F	F	F	NO	NO
Romania		F	F	NO	NO	F	NO	NO	NO	
Long-term interest rate										
Bulgaria			F	NO	NO	F	F	F	F	F
Czech Republic	F	F	F	F	F	F	F	F	F	F
Hungary	NO	NO	NO	NO	NO	F	F	F	F	NO
Poland	NO	F	F	NO	F	F	F	NO	F	NO
Romania			NO	NO	NO	F	F	NO	NO	NO
Deficit-to-GDP ratio										
Bulgaria			F	NO	F	NO	F	F	F	F
Czech Republic	NO	NO	F	NO	NO	F	F	F	F	F
Hungary	NO	NO	NO	NO	NO	F	F	F	F	F
Poland	NO	F	F	NO	NO	NO	F	F	F	F
Romania			F	NO	NO	F	F	F	NO	NO
Debt-to-GDP ratio										
Bulgaria			F	F	F	F	F	F	F	F
Czech Republic	F	F	F	F	F	F	F	F	F	F
Hungary	F	NO	NO	NO	NO	NO	NO	NO	F	F
Poland	F	F	F	F	F	F	F	F	F	F
Romania			F	F	F	F	F	F	F	F
Exchange rate										
Bulgaria					In ERM II from July 2020					
Czech Republic										
Hungary										
Poland					Not in ERM II					
Romania										

Source: ECB convergence reports (European Central Bank, 2004, 2006, 2007, 2008, 2010, 2012, 2013, 2014, 2016, 2018, 2020, 2022); F = fulfilled; NO = not fulfilled; and empty cell = data not in the report or country out of EU.

The purpose of this work is not to describe the steps that led to the adoption of the euro for each country and the criteria over the various years. From Table 14.1, it is relatively straightforward that the process towards the euro unfolded at different speeds and following different tracks. What is very noticeable is that, in the second decade of the EMU, the financial crisis evolving into the sovereign debt crisis had varying impacts on member countries, with the Baltic states (Estonia, but particularly Latvia and Lithuania) being severely affected. International organisations advised these countries to adopt floating currencies primarily due to significant deviations from the Maastricht targets and a notable economic downturn. Specifically, the Baltic states experienced considerable price overheating, which began as early as 2006 (as illustrated in Fig. 14.1), along with a deterioration in the general government balances for Lithuania and Latvia. Both countries had a deficit-to-GDP ratio exceeding the 3% reference value from 2008 to 2012 (Fig. 14.2).

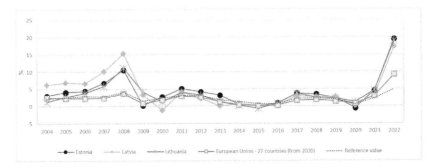

Fig. 14.1. HIPC Inflation Rate for Baltic Republics
(2004–2022). *Source*: Eurostat database.

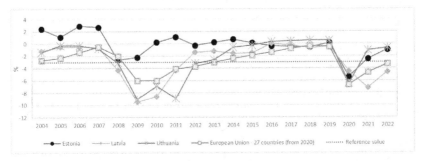

Fig. 14.2. Deficit-to-GDP (%) Baltic
Republics (2004–2022). *Source*: Eurostat database.

The IMF endorsed the advantages of a possible devaluation of the currencies of the Baltic states (Åslund & Dombrovskis, 2011; Purfield & Rosenberg, 2010).[15] However, the three countries accelerated their efforts to join the Eurozone. They maintained fixed exchange rates conforming to the ERM-II conditions (Dandashly & Verdun 2018, 2021).

In 2009, the Baltic countries experienced a considerable GDP reduction compared to other European member states; the decline in EU countries' average GDP growth in 2009 was just above 4% (Fig. 14.3). After a demand-driven boom, this significant crisis hit Estonia, Latvia, and Lithuania more than the larger EU-2004 member states. The dramatic recession was mainly related to their condition of small open economies with large export sectors and excessive financial openness (Staehr, 2013, 2015).

Substantial net capital inflows led to rapid credit growth, which, in turn, stimulated consumption and investment (Bakker & Gulde, 2010; Brixiova et al., 2010; Randveer & Staehr, 2021). For various reasons, the governments of all three countries swiftly and decisively opted to address the crisis through internal rather than currency devaluation. This approach has been mainly recognised as highly effective even if not exempt from negative consequences with economic and social costs such as progressively declining unit labour cost, increasing unemployment, and emigration.

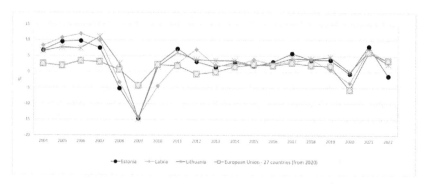

Fig. 14.3. GDP Growth in Baltic Republics (2004–2022). *Source*: World Development Indicators.

Weisbrot and Ray (2011), describing the Latvian case, assert that the remarkable economic recovery in Latvia was not entirely due to internal devaluation. Conversely, they argue that, after a procyclical fiscal policy in 2008 and 2009, the subsequent growth boost stemmed from the government's decision not to adopt the fiscal contraction recommended by the IMF for 2010, alongside an expansionary monetary policy triggered by persistently high inflation. The crisis management strategies implemented by the Baltic states, along with their remarkable economic recovery, motivated supporters of austerity to hold these countries as exemplars, particularly for Southern EMU member states coping with prolonged recessions. However, it is imperative to acknowledge that the factors underpinning this relatively successful recovery were context specific (Blanchard et al., 2013). Kattel and Raudla (2013) underline the peculiarity of the Baltic republics' economic and structural factors, such as the high level of economic globalisation and the solid dependence on the neighbouring Scandinavian countries that experienced a good recovery from the recession. Therefore, the approach adopted by the Baltic states must be cautiously recommended to other economically challenged EU member states.

Why Baltic states' governments decided to accelerate the process of joining the euro in the middle of the financial and sovereign debt crises is still an intriguing question, especially considering the external and internal pressures to maintain the status quo from political opposition parties and public opinion of the respective countries.[16]

The main message to endorse the acceleration in joining the eurozone was centred on the challenge for these three countries to achieve closer alignment with the core of the EU, maintain credibility, and avoid wasting the sacrifices and political costs endured up to that point. Additionally, an external devaluation was depicted as excessively detrimental for residents and companies indebted to foreign currency (mostly euros), who had based their decisions on the government's commitment to the stability of the national currency (i.e. entering the ERM II).

Dandashly and Verdun (2021), through a domestic politics explanation, illustrate how significantly the government choices of these small member states,

Future Challenges on the Way to the Full Convergence 263

often influenced by the electoral cycle, have contributed to accelerating the process leading to the adoption of the euro, irrespective of external pressures and show that there is not only a unique way to cope with a financial crisis. Hence, the decisions made by states to adhere to a different monetary system are related not only to their economic and financial capabilities but also to their political perspective, which may not always align.

As previously noted, five CEE countries remain outside the eurozone at the time of writing, following markedly divergent approaches. Bulgaria and Romania are keen to join the single currency, while the V3 states are more hesitant.

From Table 14.2 and Fig. 14.4, it is possible to infer the long path of the non-EA countries in terms of fulfilment of the convergence criteria from 2004 to 2022.

Bulgaria has been meeting all the economic criteria since 2016, except for inflation, as many other European countries have, because of the war in Ukraine. On 10 July 2020, Bulgaria joined ERM II together with Croatia. The initial target date for entry into the Eurozone was 1 January 2024. However, it was delayed to 1 January 2025 to allow the adoption of the Personal Bankruptcy Act, some revisions to the anti-money laundering act, and the insurance code related to the European Green Card. The Bulgarian Prime Minister, Nikolay Denkov, announced in January 2024 that Bulgaria, despite its efforts, could potentially fail to meet the target entry date of 2025 into the eurozone (Van Der Haegen, 2024), citing inflation as the primary obstacle and reassuring about the government's commitment to address this issue to meet the deadline. Furthermore, a proposal for a referendum against euro adoption, put forth by the pro-Kremlin minority party Vuzrazhdane, was rejected by the Parliament in 2023 and, more recently, in February 2024, by the Bulgarian Constitutional Court.

In Romania, adopting the euro has consistently remained a priority on the country's political agenda and public opinion preferences, even when financial conditions were far from optimal.

According to official statements, Romania initially chose 2014 as a target for euro adoption, but this goal was successively deferred to 2019, then 2024, and ultimately to 2029. The latest Convergence Programme emphasises that Romania is committed to joining the eurozone without specifying a particular year (Schipor, 2020).

Although Romania met all the convergence criteria in 2016,[17] it could not sustain the achieved targets for a prolonged period (see Table 14.2 and Fig. 14.4). According to Dăianu et al. (2017), meeting convergence criteria consistently over time is more complicated than just doing so at a specific moment. Moreover, they argue that accession to the monetary union should rely on a real structural convergence ex-ante rather than only on nominal convergence, especially for countries lagging like Romania.

At present, Romania is subject to an excessive deficit procedure from 2020, experiencing a rise in public debt (although below 60% of GDP) and facing a negative outlook regarding inflation and interest rates, as indicated by the ECB (2022) and the European Commission (2023). There is a need for thorough structural reforms with higher public and private investments in capital and technology, research and development (R&D) and innovation, as well as healthcare and education to

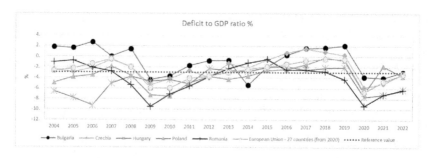
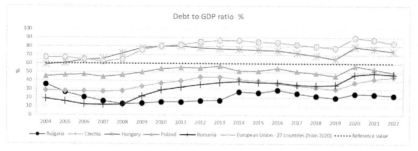
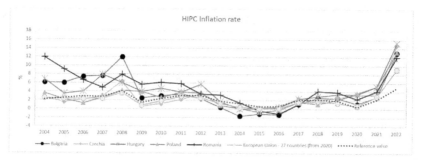
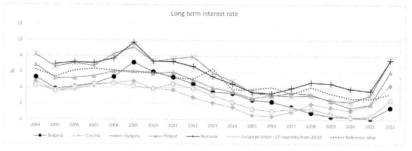

Fig. 14.4. Convergence Indicators for Countries Still Outside the Euro Area (Non-EA) in 2004–2022. *Source*: Eurostat database.

Future Challenges on the Way to the Full Convergence

exploit better domestic resources, enhancing competitiveness (Dăianu et al., 2017). Nevertheless, the Romanian population is experiencing an enhanced quality of life and living standards, attributed to the benefits of the Common Agricultural Policy and Cohesion Policy initiatives (Oehler-Şincai, 2023).

Dandashly and Verdun (2018, p. 385) refer to the V3 countries as 'laggards by default and laggards by choice'. The Czech Republic, Hungary, and Poland had opportunities at various times, especially between 2014 and 2019, to take the final step or implement measures to fulfil all the requirements for eurozone accession (see Table 14.2 and Fig. 14.4). However, despite public opinion being convinced of the benefits of accession to the euro area for their countries, governments of the V3 states adopted a 'wait-and-see' approach (Bod et al., 2021a, p. 546). Also, the stakeholders in the business sector are in favour of joining the Eurozone mainly because of the extensive use of the euro in trade transactions.

CEE economies are progressively moving towards the euroisation of trade and finance. Industries are deeply integrated into global value chains, with Europe as the primary centre of gravity. As a result, transactions within these global value chains are predominantly conducted in euros. Public finance is also subject to euroisation at different extents in these countries, with transactions often denominated in euros. Local banks frequently operate in euros as well.

The application of monetary sovereignty by countries that have maintained exchange rate flexibility is not always feasible due to the presence of the euro in all sectors. As the level of euroisation within a country increases, the effectiveness of the domestic monetary policy decreases, undermining the justification for sticking to the national currency, especially for countries such as Hungary, with a relatively low sovereign credit rating (Bod et al., 2021a).

Maintaining a national currency is mainly a political decision, given monetary authorities' limited manoeuvring room. The significant volatility experienced by floating currencies during challenging times, coupled with the use of the euro as a parallel currency, suggests that being outside the Eurozone offers scarce advantages (Bod et al., 2021b).

The Czech Republic has an increasing degree of integration with the euro area with a national currency (the Czech koruna) characterised by durable stability. Poland has become deeply integrated with the euro area, with solid trade linkages to the Eurozone (Karnowski & Rzońca, 2023). However, the exchange rate of the Polish zloty is not as stable as the Czech koruna. Hungary has quite a relevant degree of euroisation (Palánkai, 2020), a volatile currency (the forint), high inflation, and a high debt-to-GDP ratio. For different reasons, the V3 countries would benefit from the accession to the euro area on different grounds. Nonetheless, they still declare their intention to stay outside, to 'wait and see'. At the time of writing, none of the three countries fulfils all the Maastricht requirements; they are 'laggards by default' but also 'by choice', that is, a political decision made by governments based on specific political interests, national or with supranational ramifications and influences, such as Orbanism in Hungary.

After various political ups and downs, the Czech Republic's stance on joining the eurozone has remained somewhat ambivalent. While there have been debates and discussions within the government and among the public, concrete steps towards adopting the euro have not been consistently pursued. The cabinet, which came into power after the 2021 legislative election, with Petr Fiala as prime minister, continued the previous government's stance of not adopting the euro during its term, citing it as 'disadvantageous' for the Czech Republic. This position, however, was supported only by the Civic Democratic Party (ODS), one of the ruling cabinet parties. In contrast, the other four parties encouraged the initiation of the euro-adoption process. Czech President Petr Pavel has also expressed this pro-euro position in his New Year's speech for 2024 (*Czechia-to-take-concrete-steps-to-adopt-the-euro, 2024*), immediately followed by a counter announcement from the prime minister replying that Czechia's adoption of the euro was going to be definitively off the table at least until the country's next general election at the end of 2025 (*Why Czech PM Is Saying 'Not Yet', 2024*).

After a strategic move from the European Affairs minister, Martin Dvorak, who designated his advisor Petr Zahradnik as his delegate for euro adoption, Fiala has been forced to organise an extraordinary 'conciliation meeting' between coalition leaders and cancel the new position of commissioner for euro adoption with a promise from leaders of the centre-right coalition to request expert panel advice by October 2024 on the possibility of joining the ERM II (Eisenchteter, 2024).

Immediately after accession to the EU, the Polish government committed itself to adopting the euro, but any action was delayed because of the 2008 crisis. Until 2015, successive governments in Poland cautiously approached eurozone membership, aiming to maintain a foothold in the EMU. Poland promoted inclusive eurozone reforms to avoid marginalisation and constant preparatory work.

However, in 2015, the newly elected Law and Justice Party (PiS) government unequivocally rejected joining the eurozone, retaining the Polish currency as a matter of sovereignty despite high inflation rates. Moreover, membership would have subjected Poland to increased fiscal and banking oversight, which was against the Law and Justice agenda. The emergence of a Eurosceptic coalition led by the PiS was surprising, given Poland's pro-European stance (Smoleńska & Tokarski, 2023).

The 2023 election had significant implications for Poland's economic and institutional direction. There was a risk of further distancing from the EU core, exacerbating economic nationalism, deepening rule-of-law issues, and hindering sustainability efforts. Donald Tusk's return as Polish premier, leading the liberal Civic Coalition (KO) after eight years of PiS rule, seemed to anticipate his engagement for Poland's inclusion in the eurozone, especially considering his co-authorship of the prominent 2015 report on 'Completing Europe's Economic and Monetary Union' (Juncker et al., 2015). However, Tusk's priorities have changed. While emphasising closer ties with Europe, euro adoption is not central to his agenda. Coalition discord and the constitutional requirement for a two-thirds majority are challenging for Tusk and his coalition to make significant steps towards euro adoption (Briancon, 2024).

The case of Hungary has particular characteristics. Despite the potential advantages of joining the eurozone due to less stable currency and persistent inflation, there was a lack of political determination before the financial crisis. When

Future Challenges on the Way to the Full Convergence 267

Orbán assumed power in 2010, he defended a pro-sovereignty position, opposing early eurozone entry and introducing additional prerequisites. As outlined by Orbán, these prerequisites included waiting until Hungary's debt-to-GDP ratio dropped below 50% and its purchasing power parity-weighted GDP per capita had reached 90% of the eurozone average. These conditions, coupled with arguments from the Hungarian central bank in favour of a 'wait-and-see' approach, would significantly postpone Hungary's adoption of the euro, possibly for decades, even if it managed to fulfil all the Maastricht criteria. This suggests that Hungary has effectively established new, self-imposed conditions more stringent than those outlined in the Maastricht Treaty, potentially as a strategy to delay or circumvent eurozone entry altogether (Bod et al., 2021b).

In the middle of the pandemic crisis, the potential veto by Hungary and Poland on the Recovery Fund in 2020 brought to attention two views regarding the role of the EU and member states in development and governance. On the one hand, some encourage a more cohesive and integrated EU, which seeks to promote common policies and greater harmonisation among member states. This perspective often sees the EU as an entity that should have a more prominent role in shaping and implementing development and other socioeconomic policies. On the other hand, some view the nation-state as the primary actor in development and governance, with greater importance than the EU. This view tends to emphasise the sovereignty of member states and defend their ability to independently decide their development, economic, and social policies without excessive interference or imposition from above.

These debates reflect the broader challenges that the EU faces in balancing the divergent interests of its member states and in seeking to build a more cohesive and effective union.

4. CONCLUSIONS

As we have seen, an ambivalent attitude towards joining the euro area characterises the political debate in some important CEE countries, partly motivated by economic and social concerns. The idea that sacrificing monetary and fiscal independence would have a negative impact on national well-being, reinforced by the last crises, gave strength to the opportunism of nationalist parties. This posed new challenges that the European institutions do not seem entirely ready for. There is nothing substantially new in the European architecture: monetary policy will continue to be oriented towards price stability, and fiscal policy will be substantially entrusted to individual countries and constrained by the 60% and 3% parameters established 30 years ago. In the little world of Maastricht, there is no room for what is most needed by old and new members: coordinated policies to stimulate aggregate demand, ensuring persistently high levels of employment and production. The paths towards the welfare of European citizens, the increase in the sense of belonging to the same community, attracting new members and supporting financial stability all 'converge' on the denominator of the Maastricht fiscal parameters. After so many years of fiscal austerity, this should be evident.

This consideration well defines the challenges EU countries are called to face to continue along the same path and eventually join new partners.

Over the last 15 years, the EMU has faced severe economic and financial crises of global dimensions. The measures adopted to address these crises are clear evidence of the fragility of the EMU architecture. The ECB was forced to exercise functions never assumed before. It was necessary to create new institutions capable of operating outside the constraints imposed by the Maastricht Treaty. Finally, facing the pandemic crisis's wrecking and unpredictable effects required suspending public budget control rules and adopting centrally coordinated stimulus policies through the NGEU plan. This is undoubtedly an important precedent. However, it realises one-off transfers, whose amount appears small compared to those necessary for the redistributive function among different states that a central budget would be called to perform. Such a function would require a political union to centralise most European countries' tax revenues and public spending.

The steps described above are insufficient to redirect European monetary and fiscal policies towards supporting and stimulating aggregate demand, activity, and employment levels and, hence, to make the EMU attractive for new members.

From a socio-political perspective, it is challenging to understand what has driven some CEE countries to make any effort to adopt the euro and, in contrast, others, after 20 years, remain hesitant. Data to measure the pulse of society are scarce, and many refer to Eurobarometer surveys. Future research could exploit the big data analysis tools to determine societies' orientation towards euro adoption and their impact on political decisions.

NOTES

1. The Werner Plan of 1970 planned monetary unification by 1980 and placed the liberalisation of capital movements in the third and final stage, along with the centralisation of fiscal policy.

2. The negative outcome of the Danish referendum in June 1992, and especially the narrow victory in the French referendum in September 1992, jeopardised the entire process. This was followed by heavy speculative attacks on weaker currencies, leading the British pound, the Italian lira, and the Spanish peseta to exit the European monetary system. Meanwhile, the French franc, thanks to the support of the Bundesbank, managed to avoid devaluation.

3. See Bini Smaghi et al. (1995); for an interesting analysis, see Priewe (2020).

4. There is an explanation according to which the parameter related to the deficit-to-GDP ratio originated from the 3% rule proposed in 1981 by the French economist Guy Abeille to slow down the public deficit growth caused by the maintenance of electoral promises by Mitterand (*Interview to Guy Abeille*, 2012). See also *Wie das Maastricht-Kriterium im Louvre entstand* (2013, September 26).

5. It has been argued that these rules are senseless and should therefore be eliminated (Buiter, 1997).

6. An important example is the marginalist revolution of the second half of the 1800s.

7. Provoking some sudden conversions of economists from the virtues of free markets to those of public bailouts. See, for Italy, Imperia (2008).

8. The Germany's Federal Constitutional Court (Bundesverfassunggericht) has affirmed on several occasions that the purchases of government debt securities made by the ECB through QE violated the treaties.

9. For an interesting explanation that attributes its origin not to the US financial sector but to the persistent worsening of income distribution to the detriment of wage earners, see Barba and Pivetti (2009).

Future Challenges on the Way to the Full Convergence 269

10. The crisis in Europe first hit Northern Rock, a British bank specialised in mortgages, which experienced a bank run in September 2007 and was later nationalised. Public bank rescue plans were implemented in many European countries (Belgium, Denmark, France, Germany, Greece, Luxembourg, the Netherlands, Portugal, Sweden), totalling over 3 trillion euros.

11. In 2015, the Court of Justice of the European Union expressed its support for the compatibility of the Outright Monetary Transactions (OMT) programme with the ECB's statute (see Court of Justice of the European Union, 2015a, 2015b; De Grauwe et al., 2017).

12. At the time of writing (February 2024), Italy is the only country that has not ratified the agreement yet.

13. Officially, the programme is named the Asset Purchase Programme (APP) by the ECB. It is composed of four programmes: the Asset-Backed Securities and Covered Bonds Purchase Programmes (ABSPP and CBPP3) launched in September 2014, the Public Sector Purchase Programme (PSPP), and the Corporate Sector Purchase Programme (CSPP). See Claeys et al. (2015).

14. It is worth to remember that at the beginning of the pandemic crisis, the national selfishness seemed to prevail, with potentially destructive effects on the very idea of the EU. We refer, in particular, to the ban on exporting protective equipment, decided in early March 2020 by some countries to address future national needs, just at the moment when other ones were severely affected by the pandemic. See Tsang (2020).

15. For example, in the request for stand-by arrangement for the Republic of Latvia (IMF, 2009), the IMF acknowledges that the 'unequivocal commitment to the exchange rate peg' by the Latvian 'brings difficult consequences, including the need for fiscal tightening and the possibility that recession could be protracted, perhaps more so than if an alternative strategy had been adopted'.

16. Cf. Eurobarometer data (European Commission, 2010).

17. Between 2015 and 2017, Romania did not take advantage of the opportunity to join the ERM II.

REFERENCES

Åslund, A., & Dombrovskis, V. (2011). *How Latvia came through the financial crisis* (Vol. 17). Peterson Institute.

Bakker, A. F. (2012). *The liberalisation of capital movements in Europe: The monetary committee and financial integration 1958–1994* (Vol. 29). Springer Science & Business Media.

Bakker, B. B., & Gulde, A. M. (2010). *The credit boom in the EU's new member states: Bad luck or bad policies?* IMF Working Paper 130. Washington: International Monetary Fund.

Barba, A., & Pivetti, M. (2009). Rising household debt: Its causes and macroeconomic implications – A long-period analysis. *Cambridge Journal of Economics, 33*(1), 113–137.

Bini Smaghi, L., Padoa Schioppa, T., & Papadia, F. (1995). *The transition to EMU in the Maastricht Treaty* (No. 194). International Economics Section, Department of Economics Princeton University.

Blanchard, O. J., Griffiths, M., & Gruss, B. (2013). Boom, bust, recovery: Forensics of the Latvia crisis. *Brookings Papers on Economic Activity, 2013*(2), 325–388.

Bod, P. Á., Pócsik, O., & Neszmélyi, G. I. (2021a). Varieties of euro adoption strategies in Visegrad countries before the pandemic crisis. *Acta Oeconomica, 71*(4), 519–550.

Bod, P. Á., Pócsik, O., & Neszmélyi, G. I. (2021b). Political and policy dilemmas of euro adoption in CEE countries: What next when a crisis hits? *European Policy Analysis, 7*(2), 470–485.

Briancon, P. (2024, January 16). *Poland's path to euro will be long and arduous.* Ruters.com. https://www.reuters.com/breakingviews/polands-path-euro-will-be-long-arduous-2024-01-16/

Brixiova, Z., Vartia, L., & Wörgötter, A. (2010). Capital flows and the boom–bust cycle: The case of Estonia. *Economic Systems, 34*(1), 55–72.

Buiter, W. H. (1997). The economic case for monetary union in the European Union. *Review of International Economics, 5*, 10–35.

Buiter, W. H. (2005). To purgatory and beyond. In F. Breuss & Hochreiter E. (Eds.), *Challenges for central banks in an enlarged EMU* (pp. 145–186). Springer.

Cesaratto, S. (2019). *Sei lezioni di economia: Conoscenze necessarie per capire la crisi più lunga (e come uscirne)*. Diarkos.

Ciccone, R. (2013). Public debt and aggregate demand: Some unconventional analytics. In E. S. Levrero, A. Palumbo & A. Stirati (Eds.), *Sraffa and the reconstruction of economic theory: Volume two: Aggregate demand, policy analysis and growth* (pp. 15–43). Palgrave Macmillan UK.

Claeys, G., Leandro, Á., & Mandra, A. (2015). *European Central Bank quantitative easing: The detailed manual.* https://www.bruegel.org/sites/default/files/wp_attachments/pc_2015_02_110315.pdf

Council of Europe. (2024). *Proposal for a regulation of the European Parliament and of the council on the effective coordination of economic policies and multilateral budgetary surveillance and repealing Council.* Regulation (EC) No. 1466/97. https://www.consilium.europa.eu/media/70386/st06645-re01-en24.pdf

Court of Justice of the European Union. (2015a, January 14). *Press Release No. 2/15, Luxembourg.* https://curia.europa.eu/jcms/upload/docs/application/pdf/2015-01/cp150002en.pdf

Court of Justice of the European Union. (2015b, June 16). Press Release No. 70/15, Luxembourg. https://curia.europa.eu/jcms/upload/docs/application/pdf/2015-06/cp150070en.pdf

Czechia-to-take-concrete-steps-to-adopt-the-euro. (2024, January 1). brusselstimes.com. https://www.brusselstimes.com/858918/czechia-to-take-concrete-steps-to-adopt-the-euro

Dăianu, D., Kállai, E., Mihailovici, G., & Socol, A. (2017). Romania's euro area accession: The question is under what terms! *Romanian Journal of European Affairs, 17*(2), 5–29.

Dandashly, A., & Verdun, A. (2018). Euro adoption in the Czech Republic, Hungary and Poland: Laggards by default and laggards by choice. *Comparative European Politics, 16*, 385–412.

Dandashly, A., & Verdun, A. (2021). Euro adoption policies in the second decade - The remarkable cases of the Baltic States. In D. Howarth & A. Verdun (Eds.), *Economic and monetary union at twenty* (pp. 93–109). Routledge.

De Grauwe, P. (2022). *Economics of monetary union.* Oxford University Press.

De Grauwe, P., & Ji, Y. (2013). From panic-driven austerity to symmetric macroeconomic policies in the Eurozone. *Journal of Common Market Studies, 51*, 31.

De Grauwe, P., Ji, Y., & Steinbach, A. (2017). The EU debt crisis: Testing and revisiting conventional legal doctrine. *International Review of Law and Economics, 51*, 29–37.

De Grauwe, P., & Schnabl, G. (2005). Nominal versus real convergence – EMU entry scenarios for the new member states. *Kyklos, 58*(4), 537–555.

Eisenchteter, J. (2024, February 13). *Czechia and the single currency: Euro-division.* balkaninsight.com. https://balkaninsight.com/2024/02/13/czechia-and-the-single-currency-euro-division/

European Central Bank. (2004). *Convergence report.* ECB. https://www.ecb.europa.eu/pub/pdf/conrep/cr2004en.pdf

European Central Bank. (2006, May). *Convergence report.* ECB. https://www.ecb.europa.eu/pub/pdf/conrep/cr2006en.pdf

European Central Bank. (2007, May). *Convergence report.* ECB. https://www.ecb.europa.eu/pub/pdf/conrep/cr200705en.pdf

European Central Bank. (2008, May). *Convergence report.* ECB. https://www.ecb.europa.eu/pub/pdf/conrep/cr200805en.pdf

European Central Bank. (2010, May). *Convergence report.* ECB. https://www.ecb.europa.eu/pub/pdf/conrep/cr201005en.pdf

European Central Bank. (2012, May). *Convergence report.* ECB. https://www.ecb.europa.eu/pub/pdf/conrep/cr201205en.pdf

European Central Bank. (2013, June). *Convergence report on Latvia.* ECB. https://www.ecb.europa.eu/pub/pdf/conrep/cr201306en.pdf

European Central Bank. (2014, June). *Convergence report.* ECB. https://www.ecb.europa.eu/pub/pdf/conrep/cr201406en.pdf

European Central Bank. (2016, June). *Convergence report.* ECB. https://www.ecb.europa.eu/pub/pdf/conrep/cr201606.en.pdf

European Central Bank. (2018, May). *Convergence report.* ECB. https://www.ecb.europa.eu/pub/pdf/conrep/ecb.cr201805.en.pdf

Future Challenges on the Way to the Full Convergence

European Central Bank. (2020, June). *Convergence report*. ECB. https://www.ecb.europa.eu/pub/pdf/conrep/ecb.cr202006~9fefc8d4c0.en.pdf

European Central Bank. (2022, June). *Convergence report*. ECB. https://www.ecb.europa.eu/pub/pdf/conrep/ecb.cr202206~e0fe4e1874.en.pdf

European Commission. (2010). *Eurobarometer 74. Public opinion in the European Union*. EC. https://europa.eu/eurobarometer/surveys/detail/918

European Commission. (2023 June) *Country Report Romania*. Institutional paper 247.https://economy-finance.ec.europa.eu/system/files/2023-06/ip247_en.pdf

Imperia, A. (2008). *Chi paga la crisi finanziaria?* www.sdlintercategoriale.it/content/view/2250/2/lang,it/

Imperia, A., & Maffeo, V. (2013). As if nothing were going to happen: A search in vain for warnings about the current crisis in economic journals with the highest impact factors. In E. Brancaccio & G. Fontana (Eds.), *The global economic crisis* (pp. 83–101). Routledge.

International Monetary Fund (IMF). (2009). *Republic of Latvia: Request for stand-by arrangement-staff report*. Staff Supplement; Press release on the executive board discussion; and Statement by the Executive Director for the Republic of Latvia. http://www.imf.org/external/pubs/ft/scr/2009/cr0903.pdf.

Interview to Guy Abeille. (2012, September 28). *Le Pariesenne*. https://www.leparisien.fr/economie/3-de-deficit-le-chiffre-est-ne-sur-un-coin-de-table-28-09-2012-2186743.php

Juncker, J. C., Tusk, D., Dijsselbloem, J., Draghi, M., & Schulz, M. (2015, June). *Completing Europe's economic and monetary union*. https://ec.europa.eu/commission/sites/beta-political/files/5-presidents-report_en.pdf.

Karnowski, J., & Rzonca, A. (2023). Should Poland join the euro area? The challenge of the boom-bust cycle. *Argumenta Oeconomica, 1*(50), 227–262.

Kattel, R., & Raudla, R. (2013). The Baltic Republics and the crisis of 2008–2011. *Europe-Asia Studies, 65*(3), 426–449.

Obstfeld, M., Shambaugh, J. C., & Taylor, A. M. (2005). The trilemma in history: Tradeoffs among exchange rates, monetary policies, and capital mobility. *Review of Economics and Statistics, 87*(3), 423–438.

Oehler-Şincai, I. M. (2023). Romania: A case of differentiated integration into the European Union. *Comparative Southeast European Studies, 71*(3), 333–356.

Palánkai, T. (2020). Some questions of the introduction of euro in Hungary. *Köz-gazdaság, 15*(2), 30–37.

Pasinetti, L. L. (1998). The myth (or folly) of the 3% deficit/GDP Maastricht 'parameter'. *Cambridge Journal of Economics, 22*(1), 103–116.

Pivetti, M. (1995). Maastricht e l'indipendenza politica delle banche centrali: Teoria e fatti. *Studi Economici, 50*(55), 5–33.

Pivetti, M. (1998). Monetary versus political unification in Europe. On Maastricht as an exercise in 'vulgar' political economy. *Review of Political Economy, 10*(1), 5–26.

Pochet, P. (2022). From one crisis to another: Changes in the governance of the Economic and Monetary Union (EMU). *Transfer: European Review of Labour and Research, 28*(1), 119–133.

Praet, P. (2016, February 10). *Speech at the committee on capital markets regulation conference on the lender of last resort*. ECB Press. https://www.ecb.europa.eu/press/key/date/2016/html/sp160210.en.html

Priewe, J. (2020). Why 3 and 60 per cent? The rationale of the reference values for fiscal deficits and debt in the European Economic and Monetary Union. *European Journal of Economics and Economic Policies: Intervention, 17*(2), 111–126.

Purfield, M., & Rosenberg, M. C. B. (2010). *Adjustment under a currency peg: Estonia, Latvia and Lithuania during the global financial crisis 2008-09*. International Monetary Fund.

Randveer, M., & Staehr, K. (2021). Macroeconomic trends in the Baltic states before and after accession to the EU. In M. Landesmann & I. P. Székely (Eds.), *Does EU membership facilitate convergence? The experience of the EU's eastern enlargement – Volume I: Overall trends and country experiences* (pp. 211–237). Springer.

Schipor, G. L. (2020). Euro adoption in Romania: An exploration of convergence criteria. *Ovidius University Annals, Economic Sciences Series, 20*(2), 190–199.

Schuman, R. (1950). *The Schuman Declaration*. Speech, May 9, 1950. https://european-union.europa.eu/principles-countries-history/history-eu/1945-59/schuman-declaration-may-1950_en.

Smoleńska, A. & Tokarski, P. (2023, September 21). *The elephant in the room in Poland's election? Joining the euro.* https://blogs.lse.ac.uk/europpblog/2023/09/21/the-elephant-in-the-room-in-polands-election-joining-the-euro/

Staehr, K. (2013). Austerity in the Baltic states during the global financial crisis. *Intereconomics, 48*(5), 293–302.

Staehr, K. (2015). Exchange rate policies in the Baltic states: From extreme inflation to euro membership. In *CESifo forum* (Vol. 16, No. 4, pp. 9–18). München: Ifo Institut-Leibniz-Institut für Wirtschaftsforschung an der Universität München.

Trichet, J. C. (2009 June 13). *Keynote address at the University of Munich: The ECB's enhanced credit support.* ECB Press. https://www.ecb.europa.eu/press/key/date/2009/html/sp090713.en.html

Tsang, A. (2020). EU seeks solidarity as nations restrict medical exports. *New York Times*, 7.

Van Der Haegen, J. (2024, January 20). *Bulgarian PM hints country may miss eurozone entry date.* Politico. https://www.politico.eu/article/bulgaria-pm-hints-country-miss-eurozone-entry-date-nikolay-denkov/

Weisbrot, M., & Ray, R. (2011). *Latvia's internal devaluation: A success story?* Center for Economic and Policy Research.

Werner, P. (1970, October 8). Report to the Council and the Commission on the realisation by stages of Economic and Monetary Union in the community – "Werner Report" (definitive text). *Bulletin of the European Communities*, Supplement 11.

Why Czech PM is saying 'not yet' to euro adoption. (2024, January 4). EXPATS.cz. https://www.expats.cz/czech-news/article/fiala-czechia-is-not-yet-ready-for-euro-adoption

Wie das Maastricht-Kriterium im Louvre entstand. (2013, September 26). *Frankfurter Allgemeine Zeitung.* https://www.faz.net/aktuell/wirtschaft/wirtschaftswissen/3-prozent-defizitgrenze-wie-das-maastricht-kriterium-im-louvre-entstand-12591473.html

CHAPTER 15

HIGHER EDUCATION INSTITUTIONS' RESPONSES TO DIGITAL TRANSFORMATION WITHIN THE EUROPEAN UNION: SKILLS DEVELOPMENT AND SMART SPECIALISATION*

Graţiela Georgiana Noja[a], Ciprian Pânzaru[b], Mirela Cristea[c] and Eleftherios Thalassinos[d,e]

[a]Department of Marketing, International Business and Economics, Faculty of Economics and Business Administration, East-European Center for Research in Economics and Business, West University of Timisoara, Timisoara, Romania
[b]Department of Sociology, Faculty of Sociology and Psychology, West University of Timisoara, Timisoara, Romania
[c]Corresponding author, Department of Finance, Banking and Economic Analysis, Faculty of Economics and Business Administration, University of Craiova, Craiova, Romania
[d]University of Piraeus, Greece
[e]University of Malta, Malta[l]

ABSTRACT

Purpose: *This study aims to explore universities' vital role in providing educators, teachers, and learners with the necessary smart specialisation and digital skills to adapt to the learning requirements of the digital era. Additionally,*

---

*This work was supported by the Erasmus+ Project 2019-1-RO01-KA203-063214 entitled 'Coordinated higher institutions responses to digitalisation' (ESCALATE).

Economic Development and Resilience by EU Member States
Contemporary Studies in Economic and Financial Analysis, Volume 115, 273–288
Copyright © 2025 by Graţiela Georgiana Noja, Ciprian Pânzaru, Mirela Cristea and Eleftherios Thalassinos
Published under exclusive licence by Emerald Publishing Limited
ISSN: 1569-3759/doi:10.1108/S1569-375920240000115015

the research aims to evaluate the effects of digitalisation on higher education institutions (HEIs) and analyse their responses to it.

Need for study: *Digitalisation is significantly altering the skills demanded by Europe's workforce for the global economy. As the labour market is reshaped, critical challenges emerge that require a strategic response, in which HEIs have a vital role in providing digital skills.*

Methodology: *Employed a thorough desk research methodology, scrutinising secondary data from diverse public and private sources. In-depth qualitative interviews were carried out with information and communication technology (ICT) employers, HEI representatives, and policymakers. A bibliometric analysis was also employed to grasp better this topic's pivotal approach in relevant scientific literature. The Escalator methodology was followed by integrating qualitative and quantitative research using a rigorous five-step approach.*

Findings: *HEIs can reduce the digital skills gap and labour shortages to meet the demands of the local labour market. They can monitor skills gaps and inform policymakers to make informed decisions.*

Practical implications: *HEIs can tackle the digital skills gap within the European Union with two measures. Tracer studies can be conducted to monitor labour market dynamics and the insertion of graduates into the labour market. Employer skills surveys can be carried out to assess the skills needs of the industry, overcoming the skills gap and enabling the local labour market to thrive.*

Keywords: Tertiary education; digital skills; smart specialisation; European Union; higher education institutions; Erasmus+ projects

JEL classifications: J24; A20; I23

1. INTRODUCTION – THE POTENTIAL IMPACT OF DIGITALISATION

Digitalisation has emerged as a transformative force, revolutionising industries and reshaping the world of work. Its pervasive influence extends to the labour market, where it is poised to profoundly impact employment patterns, skill requirements, and work arrangements (Popelo et al., 2021). While digitalisation presents opportunities for job creation and productivity gains, it also raises concerns about job displacement, skill obsolescence, and the potential for widening income inequality. Therefore, digital transformation generated a fierce debate among education providers, policymakers, economists, and industry leaders, raising pivotal concerns about employment, wage structures, socioeconomic disparities, public health, resource optimisation, and security frameworks. As digital technologies reshape the nature of work, the World Economic Forum (2018) projected potential global job losses of up to 2 billion by 2030 due to automation and digital advancements.

Skills Development and Smart Specialisation 275

In this context, acquiring advanced digital skills emerges as an indispensable cornerstone, helping individuals navigate, adapt, and thrive within the evolving digital landscape. However, digital disparities are still present. The European Commission's Digital Economy and Society Index (DESI, 2023a) underscores the gap in digital performance across European Union (EU) member states, with countries like Ireland, the Netherlands, Malta, and Spain making considerable progress, while others, including Romania, Greece, and Bulgaria, lag significantly behind the EU average. In 2009, the European Commission outlined eight competencies vital in our knowledge-based society and should be constantly improved through lifelong learning strategies (Gordon et al., 2009). Among these competencies, digital competence is particularly crucial since it involves the confident and critical use of information and communication technology (ICT) for communication, work, and leisure purposes. Besides the ability to process information using computers, being digitally competent requires the capability to participate and be involved in collaborative networks via the internet (Ilomäki et al., 2011).

As digitalisation continues to reshape the labour market, it presents three critical challenges that necessitate a strategic response. First, the rapid evolution of digital technologies demands a significant recalibration of workforce skills to meet the changing requirements of the digital age. Second, organisations must undergo adaptive transformations to remain aligned with technological advancements. Lastly, the labour market is witnessing the rise of non-traditional employment models, such as outsourcing, job standardisation, and the expansion of digital platforms, which fundamentally alter traditional work arrangements (Goos et al., 2019).

On these lines, higher education institutions (HEIs) play a pivotal role in addressing these challenges by fostering digital literacy and competencies among the labour force. HEIs are uniquely positioned to bridge the gap between the current skill sets of the workforce and the demands of a digitalised economy (Trif et al., 2022). By integrating cutting-edge digital technologies into their curricula and emphasising practical, hands-on learning experiences, HEIs can equip graduates with the necessary skills to navigate and succeed in the digital landscape.

This research delves into universities' critical role in imparting digital skills to educators and learners, enabling them to effectively navigate the rapidly evolving digital learning age. To gain a more comprehensive understanding of the impact of digitalisation on HEIs and their corresponding approaches, we analyse the case of West University of Timisoara, a highly distinguished Romanian university that has made significant strides in the area of digitalisation.

2. HEIS RESPONSE TO DIGITALISATION

Digitalisation is transforming the skills demanded by Europe's workforce to succeed in a modern global economy. Therefore, HEIs represent 'an essential tool' for ensuring the quality of education by providing the digital skills required by the job market. In contrast, national education systems must adapt to the challenges posed by digitalisation to remain relevant and up-to-date (Haleem et al., 2022, p. 275).

Studies such as those by Banga and te Velde (2018) highlight the uneven development of the digital economy and its implications for employment and occupational structures. This research underscores the critical need for developing economies to navigate the changing skill landscape and bridge the digital divide with more developed nations. Other examinations of labour market trends, particularly in the realm of research and development (R&D), reveal a nuanced impact of digitalisation. The employment of R&D personnel within the business sector indicates the dual nature of digitalisation and labour market deregulation. While these forces can spur business growth and innovation, there is a pressing need for more in-depth research into how they affect the labour conditions and well-being of R&D workers, who are at the forefront of technological advancement. Degryse (2016) explores the potential that the digital revolution holds for transforming employee status, working conditions, and the nature of training and skill development. It also highlights the pivotal role that trade unions might play in navigating the digital economy, ensuring that the transition towards more digitised labour markets is equitable and inclusive. A specific case study from Romania, discussed by Noja and Pânzaru (2021), provides a concrete example of how digitalisation's effects are deeply intertwined with a country's socioeconomic fabric. The study explores how upskilling in the digital era is imperative for the working population, offering valuable insights that could apply to a broader European context and beyond.

To further grasp a comprehensive view of how the topic is being approached in relevant scientific literature, we performed a bibliometric analysis in VOSviewer based on a sample of articles available in Web of Science and Scopus (Fig. 15.1). Digitalisation, digital economy, artificial intelligence, digital transformation, digital skills, and digital technologies, particularly within the EU (and European countries), are key concepts at the core of main studies approaching similar issues. These terms are strongly related to other keywords like long-term youth employment, quality of life, economic development, and policymaking.

Education is more valuable than ever and is central to political, economic, and social debates on present and future challenges. For instance, the European Commission (2023) stresses the importance of higher education in enhancing individual potential and providing transferable skills, as well as the knowledge necessary for success in highly skilled occupations. However, curricula often fail to respond promptly to changing economic needs, leaving graduates struggling to find quality jobs aligned with their studies. Additionally, teaching and research staff have often failed to keep pace with the increasing number of students.

To ensure high-quality academic staff in Europe, better working conditions are crucial, such as transparent and fair recruitment methodology, lifelong professional development, and recognition and reward for excellence in teaching and research. For example, if we look closely at Romania, it currently lacks a comprehensive strategy for digitalising education. However, 'the National Strategy on Digital Agenda 2020' (Romanian Government, 2015) provides the framework for the digitalisation of education. To develop a national strategy for the

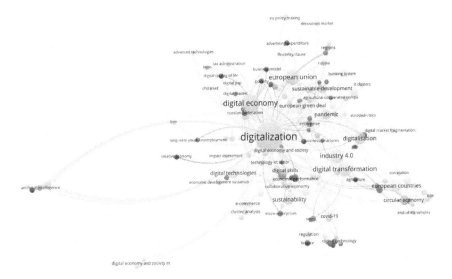

Fig. 15.1. Co-occurrence Map of Keywords/Concepts/Terms Related to the Broad Topic of Digitalisation. *Source*: Authors' contribution in VOSviewer based on data extracted from Web of Science- and Scopus-indexed articles.

digitalisation of education, the Ministry of Education and Research in Romania (2020) launched a public consultation process in October 2020 under the name SMART-Edu. This initiative is connected to 'The Digital Education Action Plan (2021–2027)' of the European Commission (2020). The SMART-Edu initiative is a bold and ambitious project committed to enriching digital competencies at all levels of education through specialised training and interdisciplinary activities. The goal is to provide unwavering support for both initial and ongoing digital training for educators and professors. Specialists in this field are determined to bridge connectivity gaps, offer technical assistance, and supply the necessary equipment to enhance digital infrastructure. The ultimate aim is to incentivise educational institutions to provide digital degrees and qualifications that cater to future professions. As a forward-thinking initiative, the focus is placed on constantly seeking new, innovative, interactive, and student-centred educational solutions to design digital tools and incorporate innovation, creating open-access and appealing educational resources, and establishing public–private partnerships with European and international institutions. Another first in this field relates to the exchange of best practices through local educational platforms, national e-learning platforms, and other global platforms such as SELFIE and e-Twinning, striving to encourage and support initiatives for online security, cybernetic and data protection, and information technology (IT) ethics. Finally, SMART-Edu plans to develop a strategic framework for a sustainable economy and adapt to future professions, being committed to revolutionising the education sector through an innovative and bold approach.

3. METHODOLOGY

The current study employed a thorough desk research methodology, scrutinising secondary data from public and private sources. Furthermore, in-depth qualitative interviews were carried out with ICT employers, HEI representatives, and policymakers to delve into the findings on addressing the region's emerging digital skill gaps. This research formed part of the ESCALATE Project, which was a rewarding Erasmus+ programme application (European Commission, 2019). The West University of Timisoara submitted the application to the Romanian National Agency under 'Key Action 2 – Cooperation for Innovation and the Exchange of Good Practices'. Six partners have developed the project, including the University of Exeter, Stirling University, Magdeburg University, Milano-Bicocca University, and Prospektiker.

The Escalator methodology developed by the University of Exeter was followed in this study by integrating qualitative and quantitative research. An 'Escalator' is a strategic initiative designed to facilitate upward mobility within a specific industry or sector. This framework aims to help individuals progressively elevate their skills and qualifications from generic, foundational levels to highly specialised, sector-specific competencies. The approach is intended to ensure that a region has a sufficient labour force skilled in areas critical to its economic success and make necessary training and skills development opportunities accessible at all levels locally. The ultimate goal is to drive economic success and inclusive growth by aligning workforce development with the region's specific economic needs and opportunities.

To develop the Escalator methodology, data were obtained through a rigorous five-step approach.

The first stage involved the focus area, considering several social, economic, and administrative specificities for Romania. Therefore, the analysis focused on the regional context at the county level. Despite low public investments in research, development, and innovation (RDI), the West region was initially selected for its skilled workforce and concerted efforts in digitalisation and innovation. The area boasts a thriving and diverse industrial infrastructure, encompassing sectors such as ICT, automotive, machine building, electronic parts, agro-food, textiles, wood processing, mining, and chemicals. Our study focused on Timis County (NUTS III), which is renowned for being a developed county in Romania and is of considerable size.

In *the second phase* of our research, we delved into datasets from the 'National Institute of Statistics' (NIS) and the 'National Trade Register Office' (NTRO) to zero in on the key sectors present in Timis County. Our approach used 'the number of employees within each sector' as a reference point. Both NIS and the NTRO provided statistical data about employees by the 'Nomenclature of Economic Activities (NACE)' level. In addition, we utilised data from an external source, www.topfirme.ro (Webber Ltd., 2023), to gain a more accurate and comprehensive understanding of specific economic sectors in Timis County.

In *the third stage* of the research, to identify the most required occupations in Timis County, we analysed 'the number of employees by occupation (ISCO 08)' and 'job vacancies' extracted from NIS. Furthermore, we gathered information from multiple reports, studies, and surveys to gain a deep insight into the current and future job market trends. We explored online job vacancies (OJV) using various digital platforms to identify the most critical (digital) skills in demand.

Based on the data collected and analysed in the second and third stages of the research, we pointed out, for Timis County, the representative and gap sectors where digital skills are less considered for future success. The identification of these sectors will help leaders and policymakers make informed decisions regarding the allocation of resources and the development of policies to encourage growth and development in these sectors.

In *the fourth stage*, we have identified the existing education providers and provisions in the analysed area. In Romania, the formal education system is divided into four levels: primary education (ISCED 1), which lasts for four years, followed by lower secondary education (ISCED 2), which also lasts for four years, then upper secondary education (ISCED 3), for four years, and, finally, higher education (ISCED 5–8), for three years or more. Additionally, the education system includes non-university tertiary education (ISCED 4) and adult education, namely training programmes organised either by the public or private providers. To understand the extent of educational resources available in the area, we have extracted the education providers and provisions from the websites of 'Timis County School Inspectorates' and the 'Ministry of Education' in Romania.

Following the interactions with stakeholders and local policymakers in the fifth stage of the research, our findings were further enriched. To assess the digital skills supply and demand in-depth, we held formal and informal discussions with HEIs, local employers' representatives, and local and regional public administration, namely interviews, to gain a comprehensive understanding of the current and future needs of the job market. The insights gained from these interactions would be helpful in designing and implementing policies aimed at bridging the gap between the current skills available and the future skills required for success in the identified sectors.

4. THE DIGITAL SKILLS PIPELINE

A notable aspect of literacy identified as digital literacy (Pangrazio et al., 2020), namely the ability to use digital technology, a vital competency that schools should provide.

In Romania, starting with the lower secondary level (ISCED 2), a subject in the field of ICT is mandatory, referred to as 'Informatics and ICT', to supply basic and moderate digital skills, according to the national curriculum. However, there is an optional subject at the primary level (ISCED 1) that teaches basic digital skills.

The curriculum for informatics and ICT is designed to provide students with a broad range of digital skills necessary for communication, problem-solving, and information management. The curriculum aims to promote the use of digital technology in innovative and creative methods. It provides a structured learning path for students to develop their digital literacy skills, starting from Grade 5 up to Grade 8.

At the *fifth-grade level*, students are taught the fundamental concepts of hardware and software components of a personal computer (PC), including operating systems and different types of devices. They also learn how to browse, search, and filter data, information, and digital content. Copyright and licences are also introduced, including knowledge of how to licence their digital production and find information on copyright and licence rules. Students learn how to protect their personal data and privacy, including taking appropriate measures to safeguard their privacy. They also learn how to create digital content in different forms using basic packages.

In *the sixth grade*, students learn how to modify digital content using edit functions, remixing different existing content into something new, and creating knowledge representations using digital media. They also learn how to communicate through digital technologies – using emails, writing a blog post, or editing information to communicate it through several means. Furthermore, they learn how to protect devices from digital threats, such as malware and viruses, and how to use algorithms and procedures, including stages, structures, and representations.

At *the seventh-grade level*, students are taught how to creatively use digital technologies to build meaningful knowledge and express themselves using a variety of media such as text, images, audio, and movies. They also learn how to develop digital content and edit it to enhance the final output. Students are introduced to programming digital devices and coding using software packages. They also learn how to collaborate through digital technologies using software packages and web-based collaborative services. In addition, they learn how to build and implement algorithms using source code.

At *the eighth-grade level*, students learn how to manage data, information, and digital content. They also learn how to create new content by mixing and matching old content, such as a web page. Furthermore, they learn how to evaluate data, information, and digital content from different sources and how to use spreadsheet calculation. Programming virtual robots, editing source codes, and implementing algorithms using source codes are also covered at this level.

In seventh and eighth grades, programming languages such as Python, C, C++, and Ruby are taught. Students are also introduced to programming virtual robots using Scratch, V-Rep (Coppelia Robotics), and MORSE (OpenRobots).

Romanian universities provide students with a curriculum organised based on a framework provided by ARACIS, which includes compulsory and optional disciplines. At the bachelor's level (ISCED 6), universities offer a wide range of digital skills in various areas. In programming, students are taught languages such as Python, C++, and Java, which are essential for developing software applications. They are also taught programming for mobile devices, which includes Android application development. In database management, students learn how to use SQL, Oracle, and SQLite, which are essential tools for managing and integrating data. In web design, students learn how to develop websites using HTML, CSS, ECMAScript, PHP, and MariaDB. They know how to create interactive and user-friendly websites that meet clients' needs. In the field of software engineering,

Skills Development and Smart Specialisation

students are taught an extensive range of topics, including data analysis, programming, cloud computing, artificial intelligence, and other critical digital skills. Similarly, network administration students learn about data structures, computer networks, security, and related areas that are essential in today's digital world.

Universities provide a comprehensive and diverse curriculum that equips students with the necessary digital competencies to succeed in the modern world. The two most prominent HEIs in Timis County, West University of Timisoara and Polytechnic University Timisoara, are the main providers of digital competencies, and they offer particular study programmes that cater to the individual needs of students (detailed examples are presented in Table 15.1).

Table 15.1. Examples of Master Programmes Providing Digital Skills (ISCED 7 Level).

Programme	Skills
Automotive embedded software	'Implementation of testing and diagnosis models and quality engineering principles to software applications implemented on embedded systems, development of hardware and software applications for automotive systems using up-to-date informatics technologies, innovative solving of core problems in inter-disciplinary co-operation and team-working'
Mechatronic and robotic/ ergo engineering in mechatronics	'Developing complex projects, identifying complex structures and solutions for special requirements, identifying appropriate modes, components, and knowledge of methods for the analysis of ergonomic systems dynamics, creative use of CDA methodology, using computer-assisted methods for analysing the quality systems, setting design and analysis software for assisted systems, structure optimisation'
Artificial intelligence and distributed computing	'Theoretical and practical knowledge useful in modelling, designing and implementing systems based on artificial intelligence methods and parallel and distributed approaches, performing cloud computing and high-performance computing; designing multi-agent systems; Configuring machine learning, deep learning models, configuring network security models and architectures, modelling and Verifying Algorithms in Coq'
Mechatronic and robotic/ artificially intelligent robotic systems	'Advanced knowledge of mathematics, CAD, and dynamic electromechanical systems, capabilities in construction, testing, and programming of advanced robotic systems'
Big data – data science, analytics, and technologies	'Skills in the design of efficient and robust models for statistical analysis of data, design implementation and using data mining algorithms, using technologies for big data processing and implementing scalable applications, Big Data Technologies, Data Warehouses, Cloud Computing, Data Mining, Machine Learning, Data Analysis and Programming in R, designing and implementing Probabilistic Models for Data Science, Predictive Models, and Analytics, Optimisation, Biostatistics'
Automated systems engineering	'Implementation and exploitation of complex control systems in condition of autonomy and professional independence, designing of control systems with different levels of intelligence for practical applications using current information technologies, application of testing and diagnosis methods at control systems, implication in the management of research projects in the field of control systems'

(Continued)

282   GRAŢIELA GEORGIANA NOJA ET. AL

Table 15.1.   (*Continued*)

Programme	Skills
Information technology and computer engineering	'Depth-level knowledge of the main issues and topics in the field of information technology, advanced knowledge in computer engineering, critical, innovative, and advanced digital capabilities'
Applied informatics systems in production and services	'Solving applied informatics problems by adequate data acquired methods and processing tools selection, processing and interpretation of relevant results, innovative problem solving based on interdisciplinary cooperation teamwork, automation structures design and implementation (hardware and software) including as embedded systems, using modern processing systems, developing automation application using modern computer technologies'
Information systems in healthcare/ bioinformatics	'Interdisciplinary capabilities, based on engineering and medical knowledge, from an informatics perspective of healthcare service applications, interdisciplinary cooperation in the engineering-medical domain, identifying and solving problems specific to healthcare information systems, design, implementation, testing, evaluation, deployment of information healthcare systems using different information technologies, advanced knowledge on biostatistics and programming in R, databases in bioinformatics, using software instruments for bioinformatics, designing computational models in biology'
Information systems for businesses	'Advanced knowledge of business intelligence, MS SQL Server Business Intelligence, Oracle Business Intelligence Tools and Technology, IBM – Cognos BI, advanced capabilities on SAP Enterprise applications, modelling business processes, advanced methods, and techniques for software engineering, web design, web programming, Enterprise reporting: SAP BEx, Crystal Reports, Web Intelligence, Design Studio, Lumira, Analysis for Office 2.2 report outputs in SAP BEx Query Designer, advanced methods and techniques to approach and investigate informatics systems (Agile, SCRUM, XP, DevOps, UP, MDA, MVC, ASAP), advanced use of supportive informatics applications to develop information systems (MS VISIO, MS WorkFlow, UI Path, Python, IBM INNOV8, IBM Websphere Business Modeller, ARIS, SAP Solution Manager), developing websites and online businesses, Web performance optimisation'
Software engineering	'Ability to understand and operate with fundamental concepts in computer science, ability to model, simulate, and solve problems in areas based on the use of a computational system, knowledge of current technologies and ability to apply them in project development, designing architectures for software systems, computer vision, applying methods and techniques based on XML, performing advanced logical and functional programming, designing software systems'
Cybernetic security	'Developing architectures and models of network security, ensuring the quality and reliability of software systems, developing robust applications, processing large amounts of data, developing multi-agent systems, data mining, applying methods and techniques based on XML, security, and share of public interest data'
Information technology	'Advanced technical knowledge essential to identify, design, and implement software applications, advanced capabilities in modelling, design, and programming, the ability to use information technology for design, implementation, testing, assessment, administration, and maintenance of complex information systems'

Source: Evidence base for a skills Escalator, Erasmus+ ESCALATE Project, https://escalate.projects. uvt.ro/ (European Commission, 2019).

Skills Development and Smart Specialisation 283

In summary, the universities in Timis County offer students a well-rounded and comprehensive education in digital skills, which prepares them to tackle the challenges of the digital world.

Both academic institutions periodically offer postgraduate courses to enhance digital competencies across various domains. Table 15.2 enumerates postgraduate courses that have been provided in the current academic year (2020–2021) as well as previous academic years.

At the ISCED 7 level, master and postgraduate programmes, many study programmes are aligned with the labour market demands. Some of these programmes are even developed in partnership with local or regional companies, to address skill gaps required by those companies.

At the ISCED 8 level, doctoral programmes, advanced digital skills by using specific software can be obtained from two doctoral schools at the West University of Timisoara and Polytechnic University. However, most PhD graduates do not aim for industry jobs, but rather for academic or research positions, including abroad.

Our analysis shows that apart from these study programmes and courses (ISCED 7–8) provided by HEIs in partnership with local and regional companies, there are no other customised policies and programmes at the county level to ensure the enhancement of digital skills.

Recent evaluations have shown that the digital skills training courses offered by the local 'Public Employment Services' (PES) may not be entirely sufficient for the needs of Timis County, Romania, beneficiaries. While these courses cover basic digital skills, they may not fully equip those seeking employment through

Table 15.2. Examples of Postgraduate Programmes Providing Digital Skills (ISCED 7 Level).

Course	Skills Trained
Blockchain entrepreneurship	'Advanced capabilities and knowledge of cryptocurrency programming and transactions, blockchain technology, programming applications on various blockchain platforms, blockchain entrepreneurship, and financial skills'
Applied web technologies	'Advanced analysis of software specifications, web technologies, and applications, Git, Github, JavaScript, React/Angular/Node.js, generating sequences, and diagrams, developing software prototypes, implementing the front-end design, using the software libraries'
Technologies and digital resources for online training	'Efficient use of resources and digital instruments, communication and collaboration based on digital technologies, problem-solving in terms of digital technology, G-suite for Education, Microsoft Teams for Education, (Learning Management System — LMS) Moodle'
Information and cybernetic systems security	'Effective use of advanced cryptographic techniques, computer network security, mobile and cloud apps security, embedded security and automotive, viruses and vulnerabilities of the information systems'
Digital skills in services	'Efficient use of computer systems, operating systems, and the Internet by employees from various organisations in the ICT sector, adequate use of office supplies and software products to solve specific problems'

Source: Evidence base for a skills Escalator, Erasmus+ ESCALATE Project, https://escalate.projects.uvt.ro/ (European Commission, 2019).

PES with the skills necessary to succeed. It's worth noting that the unemployment rate in Timis County is relatively low, below 1%, so PES has only seen a small number of applicants.

Furthermore, initiatives funded by the 'European Structural Funds (ESF)' that aim to provide digital skills training may also only offer basic instruction. Experts have pointed out that the skills taught may not always align with the curriculum and that there may be a gap between what is taught and what should be taught. For instance, teachers may decide on their own the level of complexity of the computer programmes they teach, and universities may not have close ties with employers. While the educational system is heavily centralised and the curriculum is relatively rigid, employers may develop training programmes to address these gaps.

5. RESULTANT SKILLS PRIORITIES AND RECOMMENDATIONS

The digital skills gap is widening at an alarming rate, making it increasingly difficult for recruiters to locate qualified candidates. Our team conducted research by interviewing employers from the ICT sector of Timis County to address this issue. Our primary focus was to identify gaps in advanced ICT skills such as developing software, applications, or programming, as well as computer syntax or statistical analysis packages. Timis County's ICT sector is a crucial component of its economic landscape, with over 500 companies and almost 10,000 employees (Webber Ltd., 2023). Timisoara is a flourishing technological environment, with a vast pool of potential candidates in the IT sector. Nonetheless, despite having around 1,000 ICT graduates each year, experts have reported difficulties in finding qualified IT professionals. Both interviews and OJV analysis found that the most challenging job to fill was that of a Java software developer, followed by a software tester. Nevertheless, all IT positions are challenging to fill due to the low unemployment rate in Timis County (below 1%). Furthermore, experts reported consistent ICT employee skills gaps, particularly in software development. Despite this, employers are more concerned about labour supply deficiencies, which is a quantitative issue that has forced them to hire candidates with any skill level. Employers are also willing to provide training and work-based learning to candidates lacking the necessary job skills. However, the experts believe the market will become more selective in the long run. Due to the economic contraction caused by the COVID-19 pandemic, the IT labour market shortages may relax, and companies that are still active in the local labour market may have a larger pool for recruitment. This is not necessarily a long-term solution since there is a possibility of an increase in the emigration rates of highly skilled graduates.

5.1. Higher-Level Smart Specialisation Sector Skills Gaps Need to Be Addressed

The smart specialisation policy is a crucial aspect of regional development in Romania and is closely linked to higher education and RDI policies at the national

Skills Development and Smart Specialisation 285

level. However, there are significant challenges when implementing regional strategies due to the limited capabilities of regional administrations regarding innovation policies. They often lack experience and expertise in this area, which can impede the successful implementation of the policy. While there are no formal regional innovation policies in Romania, the 'Research and innovation strategies for smart specialisation (RIS3)' strategies can enhance regional innovation policies and development.

One of the critical challenges in the higher education sector is that computer science degrees offered by universities are often not designed to meet the specific needs of employers. Furthermore, universities do not typically collaborate with employers closely to develop curricula that align with the job market requirements. The academic courses tend to provide broad specialisations, which may not equip graduates with the practical skills they need to succeed in the local labour market.

On the other hand, IT companies in Romania face significant challenges in hiring IT graduates, regardless of their skills. Many IT workers are employed while still students, often in their second academic year, even though they lack the necessary skills for their work. Companies prefer to hire early to secure their positions due to labour shortages and then invest in training to address the skills gap. Experts, including both employers and academics, have recognised this issue and called for a stronger collaboration between universities and employers to develop curricula that provide practical skills that match the needs of the labour market.

5.2. Recommendations to Tackle the Above Skills Gaps

The research reveals that software developers are the most in-demand ICT professionals in the local labour market. However, this field has a severe shortage of skilled professionals, resulting in many hard-to-fill positions. The digital skills gap is due to the lack of advanced ICT skills, such as software development, application development, and programming.

The study recommends several interventions to address this skills gap, including monitoring labour market dynamics to identify and analyse current skills gaps, anticipating future skills needs, and translating these findings into actions by better matching the supply and need for skills. This will help to bridge the skills gap and reduce the shortage of skilled labour.

HEIs have a significant role in reducing the digital skills gap and labour shortages. They can monitor skill gaps and shortages and inform policymakers, which will help them to make informed decisions. The study recommends two measures that HEIs can implement to tackle this issue. First, tracer studies can be conducted to monitor the insertion of graduates into the labour market. Second, employer skills surveys can be carried out to assess the skills needs of the industry.

The study proposes several recommendations to tackle the skills shortages and gaps that exist in the current education and employment landscape. One of the essential suggestions is to adopt a modified approach to curriculum reform that focuses on equipping graduates with the right skills and knowledge to thrive in the modern workforce. This could involve introducing new courses or enhancing existing ones to meet the changing needs of the job market. Another recommendation is to involve the private sector in developing postgraduate courses, enhancing internship schemes, implementing professional and lifelong learning schemes, and increasing local investment in education and training initiatives. By working with businesses, educational institutions can gain valuable insights into the specific skills and knowledge that are in demand and tailor their programmes accordingly. This can help to bridge the gap between education and employment and ensure that graduates are well prepared for the challenges of the 21st century.

In addition to these measures, businesses themselves can take specific actions to address digital skills gaps and labour shortages. One approach is to invest directly in skills and innovation, which can have positive spillover effects on financial performance (Pirtea et al., 2015). By encouraging a culture of continuous learning and development, businesses can ensure that their employees are equipped with the latest knowledge and tools to stay ahead of the curve. Another approach is to form partnerships with HEIs and recruit new staff from local startups to boost innovation. By collaborating with universities and research institutions, businesses can tap into a wealth of expertise and knowledge and develop new products and services that meet the market's needs. Finally, non-governmental organisations (NGOs) can play a crucial role in addressing the digital skills gap by organising multiplier events for digital upskilling, having debates with policymakers, and promoting policy initiatives on digital skills. These efforts can help raise awareness of the importance of digital skills and encourage more young people to pursue careers in Science, Technology, Engineering, and Math (STEM) fields. Overall, adopting a multipronged approach involving businesses, educational institutions, and NGOs can overcome the skills shortages and gaps in the current education and employment landscape.

5.3. HEIs and Digital Transformation in the New EU Member States

Overall, the digital transformation of HEIs in the new EU member states presents a multifaceted landscape shaped by opportunities and challenges, closely intertwined with addressing the skills gap in the labour market. As these countries transition towards knowledge-based economies, the demand for digitally skilled workers continues to grow. HEIs play a crucial role in bridging this gap by equipping students with the necessary digital competencies and fostering a culture of lifelong learning.

One key response of HEIs to the skills gap is integrating digital skills development into curricula across disciplines. By incorporating courses on coding, data analysis, digital marketing, and other relevant topics, HEIs ensure that graduates possess the technical skills required in today's digital workplaces. Furthermore, experiential learning opportunities, such as internships, projects, and collaborations with industry partners, enable students to apply their digital skills in real-world settings and gain practical experience.

Moreover, HEIs are investing in faculty development programmes to enhance teaching practices and promote digital literacy among educators. Training workshops, seminars, and online resources are provided to faculty members to familiarise them with emerging technologies and pedagogical approaches that facilitate digital learning. By empowering faculty with the necessary skills and knowledge, HEIs can deliver high-quality digital education and inspire students to become lifelong learners.

HEIs also foster innovation and entrepreneurship among students, thereby addressing the demand for digital skills in the labour market. Incubators, accelerators, and entrepreneurship centres within HEIs provide support and resources to students interested in launching startups or pursuing careers in technology-driven industries. By nurturing an entrepreneurial mindset and providing access to mentorship, funding, and networking opportunities, HEIs create a dynamic ecosystem of innovation and talent development.

However, despite these efforts, challenges remain in closing not only the skills gap in the labour market but also infrastructure limitations, digital skills gaps among staff and students, and data privacy concerns. Rapid technological advancements require continuous updating of curricula and training programmes to ensure their relevance and effectiveness. Additionally, there is a need for collaboration between HEIs, industry stakeholders, and government agencies to identify emerging skill needs and develop targeted interventions to address them.

Furthermore, HEIs must strive to promote diversity and inclusivity in digital education to ensure that all students have equal opportunities to acquire digital skills and participate in the digital economy. Efforts to increase access to education, particularly among marginalised groups, and to reduce gender disparities in STEM fields are essential for building a skilled and diverse workforce to drive innovation and economic growth in the new EU member states. Ensuring equitable access to technology and internet connectivity in rural areas remains a priority to prevent digital exclusion. Moreover, there is a need for comprehensive training programmes to empower faculty and staff with the necessary digital competencies to utilise technology in teaching and research effectively.

In conclusion, a more dynamic and responsive system can be created to meet the needs of both employers and employees and ensure that everyone has the skills and knowledge they need to succeed in the modern world. Overall, the study emphasises the importance of addressing the digital skills gap and labour shortages to satisfy the demands of the local labour market. HEIs, businesses, and NGOs can work together to overcome the skills gap and enable the local labour market to thrive. By fostering an ecosystem of innovation and collaboration, HEIs in the new EU member states can harness the power of digital technologies to drive academic excellence, research innovation, and socioeconomic development in the region.

REFERENCES

Banga, K., & te Velde, D. W. (2018). *Skill needs for the future* [Pathways for Prosperity Commission Background Paper Series 10]. Oxford. https://pathwayscommission.bsg.ox.ac.uk/sites/default/files/2019-09/skill_needs_for_the_future.pdf

Degryse, C. (2016). *Digitalisation of the economy and its impact on labour markets* [ETUI Research Paper-Working Paper 2016.02]. https://ssrn.com/abstract=2730550 or http://dx.doi.org/10.2139/ssrn.2730550

European Commission. (2020). *The digital education action plan (2021–2027)*. https://education. ec.europa.eu/focus-topics/digital-education/action-plan

European Commission. (2023a). *The digital economy and society index (DESI)*. https://digital-strategy. ec.europa.eu/en/policies/desi

European Commission. (2023b). *European year of skills 2023*. https://commission.europa.eu/strategy-and-policy/priorities-2019-2024/europe-fit-digital-age/european-year-skills-2023_en

Goos, M., Arntz, M., Zierahn, U., Gregory, T., Gomez, S. C., Vazquez, I. G., & Jonkers, K. (2019). *The impact of technological innovation on the future of work* (No. 2019/03). JRC Working Papers Series on Labour, Education and Technology, European Commission, Joint Research Centre (JRC), Seville. http://hdl.handle.net/10419/202320

Gordon, J., Halász, G., Krawczyk, M., Leney, T., Michel, A., Pepper, D., Putkiewicz, E., & Wiśniewski, J. (2009). *Key competences in Europe: Opening doors for lifelong learners across the school curriculum and teacher education*. CASE Network Reports 87, Center for Social and Economic Research (CASE), Warsaw. http://hdl.handle.net/10419/87621

Haleem, A., Javaid, M., Qadri, M. A., & Suman, R. (2022). Understanding the role of digital technologies in education: A review. *Sustainable Operations and Computers, 3*, 275–285. https://doi.org/10.1016/j.susoc.2022.05.004

Ilomäki, L., Kantosalo, A., & Lakkala, M. (2011). What is digital competence? In Linked portal. Brussels: European Schoolnet. http://linked.eun.org/web/guest/in-depth3

Ministry of Education and Research in Romania. (2020). *Strategy regarding the digitization of education in Romania 2021-2027 – SMART.Edu*. https://www.edu.ro/smartedu-strategia-privind-digitalizarea-educa%C8%9Biei-din-rom%C3%A2nia-2021-2027

Noja, G., & Pânzaru, C. (2021). Five possible impacts of digitalisation in Romania. *European Review of Applied Sociology, 14*(22), 1–10. https://doi.org/10.1515/eras-2021-0001

Pangrazio, L., Godhe, A. L., & Ledesma, A. G. L. (2020). What is digital literacy? A comparative review of publications across three language contexts. *E-learning and Digital Media, 17*(6), 442–459. https://doi.org/10.1177/2042753020946291

Pirtea, M., Nicolescu, C., Botoc, C., & Lobont, O. (2015). Board gender and firm value: an empirical analysis. *Economic Computation and Economic Cybernetics Studies and Research, 49*(4), 21–32.

Popelo, O., Kychko, I., Tulchynska, S., Zhygalkevych, Z., & Treitiak, O. (2021). The impact of digitalization on the forms change of employment and the labor market in the context of the information economy development. *IJCSNS International Journal of Computer Science and Network Security, 21*(5), 160–167. https://doi.org/10.22937/IJCSNS.2021.21.5.23

Romanian Government. (2015). *National Strategy on the digital agenda for Romania 2020*. https://www.gov.ro/en/government/cabinet-meeting/national-strategy-on-the-digital-agenda-for-romania-2020

Trif, S. M., Noja, G. G., Cristea, M., Enache, C., & Didraga, O. (2022). *Modelers of students' entrepreneurial intention during the COVID-19 pandemic and post-pandemic times: The role of entrepreneurial university environment. Frontiers in Psychology, 13*, 976675. https://doi.org/10.3389/fpsyg.2022.976675

Webber Ltd. (2023). *Top companies in Romania*. https://topfirme.ro/

World Economic Forum. (2018). *The future of jobs report 2018. Centre for the new economy and society*. https://www3.weforum.org/docs/WEF_Future_of_Jobs_2018.pdf

CHAPTER 16

CONCLUSIONS

Simon Grima[a,b], Inna Romānova[b], Graţiela Georgiana Noja[c] and Tomasz Dorożyński[d]

[a]University of Malta, Malta
[b]University of Latvia, Latvia
[c]West University of Timisoara, Romania
[d]University of Lodz, Poland

The book Economic Development and Resilience By EU Member States *analyses the development, experiences gained, and perspectives of 13 new member states of the European Union (EU): Bulgaria, Croatia, Cyprus, Czechia, Estonia, Hungary, Latvia, Lithuania, Malta, Poland, Romania, Slovakia, and Slovenia. Cyprus, Czechia, Estonia, Hungary, Latvia, Lithuania, Malta, Poland, Slovakia, and Slovenia became full-fledged members of the EU in 2004, Romania and Bulgaria joined the EU in 2007, and Croatia in 2013.*

Analysing the economic development, the main experiences, the lessons learned, and the challenges and perspectives ahead of the new member states of the EU, this book aims to identify the determinants of imbalances in the economic development of these countries. Besides, this book analyses the topical challenges in the countries related to the financial market, foreign direct investment, the development of the leading industries with export potential, and the necessity to achieve sustainability goals. The authors used a variety of qualitative and quantitative methods. The added value of the book is its interdisciplinary approach. We presented economic, legal, political, and even sociological perspectives.

Moreover, the COVID-19 pandemic and the recent economic and political turbulences exacerbate the issues related to the economic and political resilience of the countries. Concurrently, the war in Ukraine had significant geopolitical and economic consequences, with a particular impact on the new EU member states. Despite the challenges posed by the war, economic integration remains a key area of focus. The EU's success in creating a single market reflects its unwavering commitment to removing barriers to the free flow of goods, services, capital, and labour. The adoption of the euro and the accession of new member states have further propelled economic integration. The authors have analysed the implications of these initiatives and examined their impact on trade patterns, investment flows, and macroeconomic stability throughout the EU.

It is worth noting that while the integration of Europe and globalisation have driven economic growth in the new EU member states, they have also presented risks of economic instability and wage inequality. There are significant disparities in governance quality among the EU-13 member states, which is a crucial factor to consider when assessing a country's investment attractiveness, particularly in the context of foreign direct investment. Another critical challenge is the existence of regional disparities in the EU. However, positive developments are seen in the convergence in the Human Development Index, unemployment, quality of life, and medical access. Further efforts are vitally necessary to reduce regional disparities in gross domestic product (GDP) per capita, agricultural employment, and innovations to achieve better convergence and reduce regional disparities in these dimensions. Higher education institutions can help reduce the skills gap and labour shortage by providing lifelong education programmes. In this context, digitalisation, productivity improvement, reduction of regional disparities, sound educational policies, development of the labour market and human capital, and economic and social stratification need special attention from policymakers and businesses. Adequate solutions to these challenges are entailed by this book and will contribute to the enhancement of Europe's competitiveness.

The research shows that the new EU member states remain substantially behind in productivity compared to Western European countries. One of the main reasons for these disparities is the low total factor productivity and substantial differences in human and physical capital. Consequently, under quick technological advancements, digitisation and digital skills are vital for further economic development in the new EU member states, stimulating economic growth. The increase in productivity can ensure long-term sustainable growth. Additional support for digitalisation would help to reduce productivity differences between countries.

An essential advantage of European economic integration is the single market, which allows free international trade. Despite some substantial differences between the new EU member states, including infrastructure, a shortage of skilled labour, and a lack of transparency in certain areas, the single market has a substantial positive impact on economic growth in the EU.

Nowadays, countries' economic development is unimaginable without a well-developed, stable financial sector. The banking sector dominates the financial sector in all new EU member states. Despite the trend of decreasing the number of banks, the banking sector in these countries has become stronger during the last 20 years with policies focused on financial stability and sustainable development.

Conclusions 291

This book summarises the historical developments, existing trends and policies, and challenges of the new EU members during the last 20 years, making it unique and filling a gap in the literature. The chapters suggest policy measures to resolve these topical issues and ensure the full convergence of the countries. This book combines economic, political, and legal aspects, providing valuable insights to the policymakers in the EU, the EU candidate countries, and the developing countries. Joint efforts and coordinated policies will ensure further development of the new EU member states that contribute to the prosperity of the EU.

And finally, something more personal. First, most of this book's authors represent universities from the new member states. If it were not for our membership in the EU, this book would never have been written. European integration has intensified cooperation between researchers and made joint projects possible. Second, accession to the EU for the generation of today's 40- and 50-year-olds is the most tremendous success of their generation. The benefits of the freedoms of the single market, EU cohesion policy, investment incentives, and numerous other tools certainly outweigh the imperfections of bureaucracy, ineffective decision-making, inflexible procedures, or corruption. Realising how much is still to come, we must use the achievements of the European community wisely.

INDEX

Academic researchers, 233
Agenda-setting process, 69
Aggregate indicators, 32
Aggregate labour productivity in
    Latvia, 91
Aggregate measure, 181
Anglo-French model, 251
Anti-pattern, determination of, 185
Applied regression models, 211
ARACIS, 280
Artificial intelligence (AI), 234, 276
Association for Financial Markets in
    Europe, 131
Automation process, 223
Automotive industry, 147
Autonomous robots, 207

Bank profitability, 125
Banking industry, 137
Banking systems of new EU member
    states, 121–125
   banking assets as percentage of
    GDP in new EU member
    states, 122
   ROE and ROA in banking systems,
    125
   total capital adequacy in banking
    systems, 124
Banks in new EU member states
    before and after financial
    crisis, lending by, 125–130
Bibliometric analysis, 167
   of relevant scientific literature,
    12–16
Bibliometric network, 14
Bibliometric review of scientific
    literature, 167–174
Bibliometric visualization, 14–15
Brundtland Report, 202

C, 280
C++, 280
Capital flows, 24
Capital investment volumes, 125
Capital market development in new
    EU countries, 131–137
   financing of non-financial
    corporate, 133
   non-financial corporations funding
    structure 2017 and 2022,
    132
   progress of EU capital markets
    relative to key performance
    indicators, 133
Capital Market Union (CMU), 131
Case of Latvia, 90–93
Central and Eastern Europe (CEE),
    25, 29, 60
   countries, 106, 142, 145–146, 148,
    153–155, 258
   industrial development, 143
Central counterparty clearing houses
    (CCPs), 131
Central securities depositories (CSDs),
    131
'Central Statistical Offices' global
    approach, The, 180
Civic Coalition (KO), 266
Civic Democratic Party (ODS), 266
Climate Action Tracker (CAT),
    163–164
Climate change, 166–167
   risks, 161
Climate Law, 164
Climate risk, 161
Climate swaps, 160
Cloud computing, 207
Cohesion policy, 49, 62
Cohesion policymakers, 225

293

Comparative analysis, 85
Competitiveness
    literature review, 85–86
    main policies for fostering
            productivity growth, 93–95
    productivity dynamics in 13
            New EU-MS and factors
            contributing to productivity
            growth, 86–90
    structural changes and
            productivity, 90–93
Comprehensive analysis, 8
Comprehensive Economic and Trade
        Agreement (CETA), 13
Contingency table, 37
Convergence, 61
    of EU-13 countries, 56–57
    process in Central and Eastern
            Europe, 258–266
Correlation analysis, 224
Correlation matrix, 210
COVID-19 pandemic, 8, 30, 289
Credit growth, 261
CSS, 280
Cyprus, 96, 128, 145, 151, 154
Czech Republic, The, 127

Data analysis methods, 234
Degree of digitalization, 216
Demographic processes, 243
Demographic trends, 232
Destimulants, 183
Diagnostic variables, assigning weights
        to, 184
Digital business, 204
Digital constitutionalism, 70
Digital economy, 276
Digital Economy and Society Index
        (DESI), 275
    role in analysing impact of digital
            policies in EU, 71–72
Digital ecosystem, 70
Digital health innovation ecosystems,
        205
Digital infrastructures, 71
Digital innovativeness, 205

Digital literacy, 279
Digital Markets Act (DMA), 70
Digital platforms, 275
Digital policies, 74
    on economic growth, 68
    in EU, 69–71
    role of DESI in analysing impact
            of, 71–72
Digital public policies, 74
Digital Services Act (DSA), 70
Digital skills, 71, 276
    pipeline, 279–284
Digital sovereignty, 70
Digital technologies, 73, 275–276
    adoption, 204
Digital transformation, 71, 276
    of businesses, 71
    of enterprises, 206
    in new EU member states, 286–287
Digital world, 202
Digitalisation, 206, 244, 274, 276
    of businesses, 204
    economic growth through, 72–74
    European context and potential
            impact of, 68–69
    green and digital transition,
            202–206
    HEIs response to, 275–277
    of industry, 203
    interaction between manufacturing
            digitalisation and
            productivity, 220–224
    and labour productivity, 206–208
    of manufacturing, 216–219
    potential impact, 274–275
    productivity and differences
            between EU-14 and EU-13
            countries, 211–216
    of public services, 72
    research methodology and data,
            208–
    research variables and summary
            statistics, 210
Digitisation indicators, 210
Document analysis, 19
Domestic politics, 262–263

Index 295

Double-edged phenomenon, 9
Dynamic capabilities, 73
Dynamic digital governance, 70

E-commerce, 208, 219, 225
e-Twinning, 277
ECMAScript, 280
Economic activity support, 234
   practical research findings, 234–243
   theoretical findings, 233–234
Economic and Monetary Unions
   (EMUs), 103
Economic crisis (2008), 48
Economic development, 128
Economic disparities, 49–54
   GDP per capita adjusted by
      purchasing power in
      Euros, 51
Economic growth, 7, 10, 12, 15–16,
   19–20
   data and methodology, 74–76
   descriptive statistics, 77
   digital policies in EU, 69–71
   economic growth through
      digitalisation, 72–74
   empirical findings, 76–78
   European context and potential
      impact of digitalisation,
      68–69
   literature review, 69
   modelling impact of EU digital
      policies on, 74–78
   regression results, 78
   role of DESI in analysing impact
      of digital policies in EU,
      71–72
Economic inequality, 48
Economic integration, 8, 10–11,
   103–104
   in EU, 115
   process, 19
Economic intricacies, 2
Economic openness, 106
   degree of, 111, 115
Economic resilience, 2
Economic sustainability, 203

Economic theories, 58
Economic waters
   regional dynamics, 3–4
   social implications, 3
Education, 276
Educational institutions, 171
Environmental governance, 166, 171
   initiatives, 161
Erasmus+ programme, 278
ESCALATE Project, 278
Escalator methodology, 278
Euro, 250
European Bank Union (EBU), 123
European banks, 128
European Central Bank (ECB), 123,
   251–252
European Commission (EC), 84, 144,
   243
European context and potential
   impact of digitalisation,
   68–69
European digital policy, 70
European economic integration, 2,
   6–8, 290
European Green Deal, 166
European indicators, 180
European Innovation Council (EIC),
   68
European Innovation Scoreboard
   (EIS), 58, 93
European integration, 19, 21
European monetary union (EMU),
   250, 254
   architecture and crises, 255–258
European political unification process,
   250
European single market and new
   member states, 104–115
   exports from 2002 to 2022 for EU
      13 Countries, Billion Euro,
      107
   imports from 2002 to 2022 for EU
      13 Countries, Billion Euro,
      108
   trade openness from 2004 to 2022,
      110

European Single Supervisory
  Mechanism (SSM), 123
European Stability Mechanism
  (ESM), 19, 255
European Structural Funds (ESF),
  284
European Union (EU), 1, 6–7, 11, 15,
  84, 160, 250, 275
  accession, 25
  aerospace industry, 150
  boxplot for SIGQ, 37
  climate change risks, 161–165
  cohesion policy, 48–49
  contingency coefficients between
    six dimensions of
    governance and FDI inward
    stock, 40
  correlation matrix for groups of
    EU-13 MS, 40
  countries, 93, 188, 212–213
  dendrogram for EU-13 MS, 33
  DESI in analysing impact of digital
    policies in, 71–72
  digital policies, 69
  digital policies in, 69–71
  economic disparities, 49–54
  EU 27 member states, 173
  EU-10, 49, 51
  EU–13 MS, GQ and FDI inflow
    into, 32–40
  export potential, 142, 154
  FDI inflow to EU-13 MS, 29–31
  FDI inward stock in relation to
    GDP in EU-13, 36
  financing, 59
  framework programmes, 59
  global environmental governance,
    165–167
  globalisation, regional integration,
    and labour market
    inferences at level of, 16–18
  human development index, 55
  industrial strategy, 142
  industry, 142, 202
  integration process, 8, 11
  internal market, 105

intra-trade analysis, 114, 116
level of innovativeness, 58–59
level of internet access in
  households, 55
literature review, 161
mean value of SIGQ for EU-13
  MS, 34
membership, 145
modelling impact of EU digital
  policies on economic
  growth, 74–78
priorities of EU industrial policy
  and challenges confronted
  by new member states,
  144–146
productivity and differences
  between EU-13 countries
  and EU-14, 211–216
productivity and differences
  between EU-14 and EU-13
  countries, 211–216
ranking by SIGQ in EU-13 MS, 33
scatterplot for SIGQ and FDI
  inward stock, 36
self-reported unmet needs for
  medical examination, 56
single market, 104
social and health care disparities,
  54–58
Structural and Cohesion Funds, 19
sustainable development, 167
systematic and bibliometric review
  of scientific literature,
  167–174
European Union Emissions Trading
  Scheme (EU ETS), 164
European Union member states (EU-
  MS), 84, 137
European Union statistics on income
  and living conditions
  (EU-SILC), 57, 237
Eurostat
  data, 106
  labour market flow statistics, 17
Export growth, 101
Export orientation, 100

Index 297

Export potential of new EU countries, 146–154
Extensive legislative programme of single market, 105

Financial crisis (2008), 13, 48
    lending by banks in new EU member states before and after, 125–130
Financial globalization, 9
Financial markets, 121
Financial sector, 120
    banking systems of new EU member states, 121–125
    capital market development in new EU countries, 131–137
    lending by banks in new EU member states before and after financial crisis, 125–130
Financial stability, 267
Fiscal policy, 251
Fit for 55 package, 164
Food processing, 90
Foreign direct investment (FDI), 9, 24, 88
    FDI-driven export model, 146
    inflow into EU-13 MS, 29–31, 32–40
Foreign investors, 31
    FDI inflow to EU-13 MS, 29–31
    GQ and FDI inflow into EU-13 MS, 32–40
    literature review, 26–29
    quality of governance based on world wide governance indicators, 31–32
Free trade, 115
Free Trade Agreement, The, 102

Gauss–Markov theorem, 211
General data protection regulation (GDPR), 70
General equilibrium approach, 102
Generalised method of moment (GMM), 221

German model, 251
Global environmental governance, 165–167
Global financial crisis, 86, 88, 127
Global Innovation Index (GII), 93
Global Productivity Forum (GFP), 84
Global trade, 102
Global value chains (GVCs), 88, 146
Globalisation, 6–8, 11, 21
    at level of EU countries, 16–18
    phenomenon, 18
    systematic literature review on, 9–12
Good governance, 24–25, 27
Governance, 25–27
Governance quality (GQ), 25
    inflow into EU-13 MS, 32–40
Governments, 167, 171
Greenhouse gas (GHG), 161
Gross domestic product (GDP), 145, 161, 234, 253, 290
    per capita, 50

Health care disparities, 54–58
Hierarchical cluster analysis methodology, 32
High quality liquid assets (HQLA), 124
Higher education institutions (HEIs), 275
    digital skills pipeline, 279–284
    and digital transformation in new EU member states, 286–287
    methodology, 278–279
    potential impact of digitalisation, 274–275
    response to digitalisation, 275–277
    resultant skills priorities and recommendations, 284–287
Higher-level smart specialisation sector skills gaps, 284–285
Horizon, 59
Horizon Europe, 68
HTML, 280
Human Development Index (HDI), 49, 54, 290

Ideational processes, 69
Industrial competitiveness in new EU member states, need for new approach to, 154–155
Industrial landscape of new EU countries, 146–154
Industrial policy, 144–145
Industrial robots, 208, 219
Industrial sectors, 51, 213–214
Industrialisation of services, 52
Inequality, 48
Information and Communication Technologies (ICT), 56, 149, 206, 275
  capital, 206
  ICT-based information systems, 207
  revolution, 207
Information technology (IT), 205, 277
Innovation, 84, 91, 93–94
Innovativeness, level of, 58–59
Institutional dynamics, 69
Institutional quality, 26
Institutions, 26–27, 166
Integration process, 10–11
Intellectual Property Action Plan, 144
Intergovernmental Panel on Climate Change (IPCC), 166
Internal market, 104
International comparative analysis, 59
International competitiveness, 49
International economic integration, 102–103
International Monetary Fund (IMF), 86, 120, 144, 256
International trade, 100–102, 104, 109, 111, 115–116
  European single market and new member states, 104–115
  literature review, 101–104
  results of analysis of, 104–115
Internet of things (IoT), 207–208
Intra-EU trade, 104–115
Intra-trade analysis, 111
Investment, 87, 93, 102–103
  attractiveness, 25, 29

Java, 280
Job standardisation, 275
Just Transition Fund, 166

Kemp–Wan theorem, 102
Keynesian theory, 251
Knowledge-based economy, 58

Labour Force Survey (LFS), 234
Labour market
  flows, 19
  inferences at level of EU countries, 16–18
Labour productivity, 206–208
Labour supply deficiencies, 284
Law and Justice Party (PiS), 266
Leading industries in new EU member states
  Cyprus and Malta's strengths and weaknesses of industrial potential, 148
  exports of goods and services, 147
  industrial landscape and export potential of new EU countries, 146–154
  literature review, 143–144
  need for new approach to industrial competitiveness in new EU member states, 154–155
  priorities of EU industrial policy and challenges confronted by new member states, 144–146
Lending by banks in new EU member states before and after financial crisis, 125–130
Liquefied natural gas (LNG), 163
Liquidity coverage ratio (LCR), 124
Long-term care (LTC), 233

Maastricht convergence criteria, 252–255
Maastricht parameters, 252
Maastricht Treaty, 251

Index 299

Macro-level approach, 92
Macroeconomic approach, 85
Macroeconomic imbalances, 88
Malta, 145, 151, 153–154, 197
Manufacturing
digitalisation of, 216–219
industry, 203, 208, 223
MariaDB, 280
Market capitalisation to GDP, 134
Market economy, 145
Medical access, 290
Member states (MS), 25
Methodological framework, 69
Monetarist counterrevolution, 251
Monetary policy, 252
Monetary sovereignty, 265
Monte Carlo method, 184
MORSE, 280
Multicriteria methods, 181, 196
Multicriteria/multidimensional
analysis method, 181
Multidimensional approach, 19
Multinational enterprises
(MNEs), 29
Mundell's theory, 111

National Energy and Climate Plans
(NECPs), 165
National health-care expenditures, 243
National Institute of Statistics (NIS),
278
National Productivity Boards (NPBs),
84
National Strategy on Digital Agenda
2020, 276–277
National Trade Register Office
(NTRO), 278
Nationally Determined Contributions
(NDC), 163
Net-Zero Industry Act, 165
New EU countries
capital market development in,
131–137
industrial landscape and export
potential of, 146–154
New EU industrial strategy, 154

New EU member states
before and after financial crisis,
lending by banks in,
125–130
banking systems of, 121–125
need for new approach to industrial
competitiveness in, 154–155
New Legislative Framework, 105
New member states
European single market and,
104–115
priorities of EU industrial policy
and challenges confronted
by, 144–146
Next-generation EU (NGEU), 255
Nomenclature of Economic Activities
(NACE), 278
Non-financial corporations, 131
Non-governmental organisations
(NGOs), 32, 286
Normalisation of variables, 184

Objects, 186
classification of, 186
Online job vacancies (OJV), 279
Open trade, 100
Open-access Gretl program, 220
Optimum currency area (OCA), 111
Oracle, 280
Ordinary least squares (OLS)
regression models, 211
Organisation for Economic
Co-operation and
Development (OECD), 11,
84, 137, 146, 223
Organisations, 166
Outright Monetary Transactions
(OMT) programme,
255–256
Outsourcing, 275

Pandemic, 204
Panel econometric models, 75
Panel-corrected standard errors
(PCSE), 75, 77
Paris Agreement, 161

Pattern, determination of, 185
Personal computer (PC), 280
PHP, 280
Physical climate risk, 162
Physical risks, 162
Pigouvian theory, 162
'Place-sensitive distributed
    development policy', 62
Policies, 20
Polish banking system, 122
Portugal, Italy, Greece, and Spain
    countries (PIGS countries),
    50
Pragmatic policy measures, 2
Productivity
  councils, 84
  digitalisation and labour
    productivity, 206–208
  digitalisation of manufacturing,
    216–219
  dynamics in 13 New EU-MS and
    factors contributing to
    productivity growth, 86–90
  green and digital transition,
    202–206
  growth, 88
  interaction between manufacturing
    digitalisation and, 220–224
  interaction between manufacturing
    digitalisation and
    productivity, 220–224
  issue, 84
  literature review, 85–86
  main policies for fostering
    productivity growth, 93–95
  paradox, 73
  productivity and differences
    between EU-14 and EU-13
    countries, 211–216
  productivity-enhancing policies, 86
  research methodology and data,
    208
  research variables and summary
    statistics, 210
  structural changes and, 90–93
Public Employment Services (PES), 283

Public finance, 253, 265
Purchasing power standard (PPS), 49
Python, 280

Qualitative analysis, 85
Quality of governance, 26
  based on world wide governance
    indicators, 31–32
  definitions of GQ indicators in
    WGI, 31–32
Quality of life, 290
  assigning weights to diagnostic
    variables, 184
  classification of objects, 186
  concept, 178
  construction of synthetic measure,
    185–186
  description of VMCM, 183–186
  determination of pattern and
    anti-pattern, 185
  diagnostic variables character, 183
  in European Union, 182
  materials and methods, 182–183
  normalisation of variables, 184
  research results, 186
  research study, 186–196
  selection of variables and
    elimination of variables,
    183–184
Quantitative analysis, 85
Quantitative easing (QE), 256
Quasi-transit, 115

Regional economic integration,
    systematic literature
    review on globalisation
    and, 9–12
Regional integration, 11
  in EU, 104
  at level of EU countries, 16–18
Regression analysis, 224
Regression parameter, 57
Renewable energy, 151
RePowerEU plan, 164
Research, development, and
    innovation (RDI), 278

Index 301

Research and development (R&D), 93, 208, 263, 276
Research and innovation systems (R&I systems), 94
Research institutes, 171
Research methods, 234
Robotics, 223
Robotisation, 224
Robust regression with Huber iteration (RRHI), 75, 77
Ruby, 280

Samuelson's analysis, 102
Science, technology, engineering, and mathematics (STEM), 59, 155, 286
Scopus, 276
Scratch, 280
SELFIE, 277
Servitisation, 52
Shift-share analysis, 85, 92
σ-convergence, 49
Silver economy, 233, 241, 243
Single European Act (1987), 104
Single market, 104
Single Market Act, 105
Single Market Act I, 105
Single Market Act II, 105
Single Market Programme, 104
Single Resolution Mechanism (SRM), 123
Small-and medium-sized enterprises (SMEs), 8, 70
Smart connected products, 73
Smart specialization, 284–285
SMART-Edu initiative, 277
Social disparities, 54–58
Social economy, 233
Social justice theories, 48
Solidarity economy, 233
Sovereign debt crisis, 255
SQL, 280
SQLite, 280
Stability and Growth Pact (SGP), 257
Standardisation, 184

Static effects, 102
Stimulants, 183
Subject-matter literature, 28
Sustainability, 160–161, 168, 171
Sustainable development, 167, 202
  indicators, 203
Sustainable European Investment Plan, 166
Sustainable manufacturing
  concept, 202
  practices, 203
Synthetic index of governance quality (SIGQ), 32, 34
Synthetic measure, construction of, 185–186
Systematic literature review on globalisation and regional economic integration, 9–12
Systematic review of scientific literature, 167–174

Technological sectors, 51
Tertiary education, 279
Tertiary sector employment, 52
Three-dimensional (3D) printing, 207
Timis County, 278–279, 283–284
Total factor productivity (TFP), 206
Trade balance, 114–116
Trade in Value-Added database (TiVA database), 146
Trade unions, 276
Trading, 100
Transatlantic Trade and Investment Partnership (TTIP), 13
Transition climate risk, 161–162
Transition risks, 161
Transportation solutions, 233
Treaty of Rome, The, 104
Two-panel regression models, 77

Unconditional basic income (UBI), 234
Unconventional measures, 257
Unemployment, 290
  rate, 50, 52

302 INDEX

Unit labour costs (ULCs), 88
United Nations Environment
Programme (UNEP), 165
Unsatisfactory institutional
quality, 29

V-Rep (Coppelia Robotics), 280
Value added per employee (VAemp),
220
Variables, normalisation of, 184
Vector measure construction method
(VMCM), 181–186
Visegrád Group, 3
Visualisation, 16
VOSviewer analysis tool, 12, 14

'Wait-and-see' approach, 265
Ward's method, 32
Web of Science, 276
Wood processing, 90
World Bank (WB), 24, 27, 86
World Health Organization (WHO),
The, 180
World Stock Exchange Federation, 136
World Trade Organisation (WTO),
10, 146
World wide governance indicators,
quality of governance based
on, 31–32
Worldwide Governance Index
(WGI), 27

www.ingramcontent.com/pod-product-compliance
Lightning Source LLC
LaVergne TN
LVHW011720070225
803225LV00004B/293